STEM Education Approaches and Challenges in the MENA Region

Fatimah Alhashem
Gulf University for Science and Technology, Kuwait

Heather Pacheco-Guffrey
Bridgewater State University, USA

Jacquelynne Anne Boivin
Bridgewater State University, USA

A volume in the Advances in Educational Technologies and Instructional Design (AETID) Book Series

Published in the United States of America by
IGI Global
Information Science Reference (an imprint of IGI Global)
701 E. Chocolate Avenue
Hershey PA, USA 17033
Tel: 717-533-8845
Fax: 717-533-8661
E-mail: cust@igi-global.com
Web site: http://www.igi-global.com

Copyright © 2023 by IGI Global. All rights reserved. No part of this publication may be reproduced, stored or distributed in any form or by any means, electronic or mechanical, including photocopying, without written permission from the publisher.
Product or company names used in this set are for identification purposes only. Inclusion of the names of the products or companies does not indicate a claim of ownership by IGI Global of the trademark or registered trademark.

Library of Congress Cataloging-in-Publication Data

Names: Alhashem, Fatimah, 1980- editor. | Pacheco-Guffrey, Heather, 1975- editor. | Boivin, Jacquelynne Anne, editor.
Title: STEM education approaches and challenges in the MENA region / edited by Fatimah Alhashem, Heather Anne Pacheco-Guffrey, Jacquelynne Anne Boivin.
Description: Hershey : Information Science Reference, 2023. | Includes bibliographical references and index. | Summary: "STEM Education Approaches and Challenges in the MENA Region contributes to the existing STEM literature by exploring factors that influence student participation in STEM in MENA countries. The book also identifies the gaps in STEM education research in MENA countries and presents the current practices and challenges. Covering key topics such as gender equity, school administration, and education systems, this premier reference work is ideal for administrators, policymakers, researchers, scholars, academicians, practitioners, instructors, and students"-- Provided by publisher.
Identifiers: LCCN 2022061132 (print) | LCCN 2022061133 (ebook) | ISBN 9781668468838 (hardcover) | ISBN 9781668468876 (paperback) | ISBN 9781668468845 (ebook)
Subjects: LCSH: Science--Study and teaching--Middle East. | Technology--Study and teaching--Middle East. | Mathematics--Study and teaching--Middle East. | Science--Study and teaching--Africa, North. | Technology--Study and teaching--Africa, North.
Classification: LCC Q183.4.N36 S74 2023 (print) | LCC Q183.4.N36 (ebook) | DDC 507.1/056--dc23/eng20230331
LC record available at https://lccn.loc.gov/2022061132
LC ebook record available at https://lccn.loc.gov/2022061133

This book is published in the IGI Global book series Advances in Educational Technologies and Instructional Design (AETID) (ISSN: 2326-8905; eISSN: 2326-8913)

British Cataloguing in Publication Data
A Cataloguing in Publication record for this book is available from the British Library.
All work contributed to this book is new, previously-unpublished material.
The views expressed in this book are those of the authors, but not necessarily of the publisher.
For electronic access to this publication, please contact: eresources@igi-global.com.

Advances in Educational Technologies and Instructional Design (AETID) Book Series

ISSN:2326-8905
EISSN:2326-8913

Editor-in-Chief: Lawrence A. Tomei, Robert Morris University, USA

MISSION

Education has undergone, and continues to undergo, immense changes in the way it is enacted and distributed to both child and adult learners. In modern education, the traditional classroom learning experience has evolved to include technological resources and to provide online classroom opportunities to students of all ages regardless of their geographical locations. From distance education, Massive-Open-Online-Courses (MOOCs), and electronic tablets in the classroom, technology is now an integral part of learning and is also affecting the way educators communicate information to students.

The **Advances in Educational Technologies & Instructional Design (AETID) Book Series** explores new research and theories for facilitating learning and improving educational performance utilizing technological processes and resources. The series examines technologies that can be integrated into K-12 classrooms to improve skills and learning abilities in all subjects including STEM education and language learning. Additionally, it studies the emergence of fully online classrooms for young and adult learners alike, and the communication and accountability challenges that can arise. Trending topics that are covered include adaptive learning, game-based learning, virtual school environments, and social media effects. School administrators, educators, academicians, researchers, and students will find this series to be an excellent resource for the effective design and implementation of learning technologies in their classes.

COVERAGE

- Bring-Your-Own-Device
- Adaptive Learning
- Educational Telecommunications
- Game-Based Learning
- Classroom Response Systems
- Collaboration Tools
- Curriculum development
- Instructional Design Models
- Virtual School Environments
- Digital Divide in Education

IGI Global is currently accepting manuscripts for publication within this series. To submit a proposal for a volume in this series, please contact our Acquisition Editors at Acquisitions@igi-global.com or visit: http://www.igi-global.com/publish/.

The Advances in Educational Technologies and Instructional Design (AETID) Book Series (ISSN 2326-8905) is published by IGI Global, 701 E. Chocolate Avenue, Hershey, PA 17033-1240, USA, www.igi-global.com. This series is composed of titles available for purchase individually; each title is edited to be contextually exclusive from any other title within the series. For pricing and ordering information please visit http://www.igi-global.com/book-series/advances-educational-technologies-instructional-design/73678. Postmaster: Send all address changes to above address. Copyright © 2023 IGI Global. All rights, including translation in other languages reserved by the publisher. No part of this series may be reproduced or used in any form or by any means – graphics, electronic, or mechanical, including photocopying, recording, taping, or information and retrieval systems – without written permission from the publisher, except for non commercial, educational use, including classroom teaching purposes. The views expressed in this series are those of the authors, but not necessarily of IGI Global.

Titles in this Series

For a list of additional titles in this series, please visit:
http://www.igi-global.com/book-series/advances-educational-technologies-instructional-design/73678

Empowering Students Through Multilingual and Content Discourse
Stacie Lynn Finley (Missouri State University, USA) Pamela Correll (Missouri State University, USA) Cathy Pearman (Missouri State University, USA) and Stephanie Huffman (Missouri State University, USA)
Information Science Reference • © 2023 • 340pp • H/C (ISBN: 9798369305430) • US $215.00

Perspectives on Indigenous Pedagogy in Education Learning From One Another
Sheila Cote-Meek (York University, Canada) and Taima Moeke-Pickering (Laurentian University, Canada)
Information Science Reference • © 2023 • 279pp • H/C (ISBN: 9781668434253) • US $215.00

Implementing Rapid E-Learning Through Interactive Materials Development
Mohammad Issack Santally (University of Mauritius, Mauritius) Yousra Rajabalee (Mauritius Institute of Education, Mauritius) and Ravi Rajputh (University of Mauritius, Mauritius)
Information Science Reference • © 2023 • 232pp • H/C (ISBN: 9781668449400) • US $215.00

Perspectives on Enhancing Learning Experience Through Digital Strategy in Higher Education
Afzal Sayed Munna (University of Sunderland in London, UK) Vipin Nadda (University of Sunderland in London, UK) Theo Ammari Allahyari (University of Sunderland in London, UK) Giuseppe Cantafio (University of Sunderland in London, UK) and Sahidi Bilan (University of Sunderland in London, UK)
Information Science Reference • © 2023 • 325pp • H/C (ISBN: 9781668482827) • US $215.00

For an entire list of titles in this series, please visit:
http://www.igi-global.com/book-series/advances-educational-technologies-instructional-design/73678

701 East Chocolate Avenue, Hershey, PA 17033, USA
Tel: 717-533-8845 x100 • Fax: 717-533-8661
E-Mail: cust@igi-global.com • www.igi-global.com

Table of Contents

Preface xiv

Acknowledgement xxvi

Chapter 1
Exploring Challenges of Online STEM Education Pedagogy and Practice in
the MENA Region: Literature Review 1
    Meryem Ouelfatmi, Sidi Mohamed Ben Abdellah, Morocco

Chapter 2
STEM in Turkey: Initiatives, Implementations, and Failures 28
    Ahmet Baytak, Independent Researcher, Turkey

Chapter 3
The Development of STEM Education in the Sultanate of Oman 56
    Mohamed A. Shahat, Sultan Qaboos University, Oman & Aswan
        University, Egypt
    Sulaiman M. Al-Balushi, Sultan Qaboos University, Oman

Chapter 4
Saudi Arabia's Vision 2030 and Its Impact on STEM Education 74
    Holly Nicole Babineau, Northcentral University, USA

Chapter 5
STEM Education in Iraq 2004-2022: Strategies, Challenges, and Outcomes 91
    Jabbar A. Al-Obaidi, Bridgewater State University, USA
    Tahir Albakaa, Bridgewater State University, USA

Chapter 6
Opportunities and Challenges of Introducing Digital Health Training in
Medical and Health Sciences Education in Palestine 128
    Mohammad J. Ghosheh, Ghosheh Medical and Surgical Complex,
       Palestine
    Ghadeer O. Ghosheh, Ghosheh Medical and Surgical Complex,
       Palestine

Chapter 7
Analyzing the Role of Popular Scientific Journalism in STEM and Turkey's
Science Communication Model 168
    Hasan Gürkan, Girona University, Spain & Istinye University, Turkey
    Carmen Soler Echazarreta, Girona University, Spain

Chapter 8
STEAM Education in an Online Modality: Teaching and Learning Tradeoff –
A Case Study..189
    Mohamed El Nagdi, American University in Cairo, Egypt
    Heba EL-Deghaidy, American University in Cairo, Egypt
    Gihan Osman, American University in Cairo, Egypt

Chapter 9
Teachers' Perceptions Towards the Implementation of STEM Education in
the State of Kuwait...209
    Abrar Almoosa, Kuwait Foundation for Advancement of Sciences,
       Kuwait

Chapter 10
Reimagining Curriculum: Responding to Qatari Culture Through
Mathematics..222
    Summer Bateiha, Virginia Commonwealth University School of the Arts
       in Qatar, Qatar
    Sadia Mir, Virginia Commonwealth University School of the Arts in
       Qatar, Qatar

Compilation of References 244

Related References 275

About the Contributors 297

Index 303

Detailed Table of Contents

Preface xiv

Acknowledgement xxvi

Chapter 1
Exploring Challenges of Online STEM Education Pedagogy and Practice in
the MENA Region: Literature Review 1
    Meryem Ouelfatmi, Sidi Mohamed Ben Abdellah, Morocco

With the increased need for technology implementation, educational systems across the world have made various efforts to utilize technology to optimize learning efficacy. With regard to the MENA region, many reforms have been administered in order to effectively digitize education. Pedagogical aspects remain in great need of further investigation. Thus, through a conceptual review of applied pedagogical strategies, this chapter aims to explore issues related to such implementation in the MENA region. As pedagogy varies according to age, teaching environment, and subject, the author aims to explore the theory and practice of Mathematics teaching in online environments. The educational policy also diverges from one country to another, especially in terms of STEM education. The present study is based on a focus on the MENA region context which allows for a better understanding and development of STEM education. Moreover, this review provides issues and challenges to consider for future research and proposes pedagogical modifications to suit the online teaching environments.

Chapter 2
STEM in Turkey: Initiatives, Implementations, and Failures 28
    Ahmet Baytak, Independent Researcher, Turkey

The concept of STEM has gained extensive usage in Turkey after gaining popularity worldwide. The need for improvement in mathematics performance, as indicated by low PISA results, prompted the implementation of math-integrated education models within the Turkish Education System. This chapter aims to outline the system's impact on the implementation of STEM. Notably, the FATIH project has played a crucial role by equipping schools with modern technologies and distributing tablets to students. The contribution of the science centers is discussed. Science centers serve as a promising starting point for fostering STEM studies. However, significant obstacles to the implementation of the STEM model in Turkey lie in the high school entrance and university placement exam systems. These obstacles will be explained in detail within this chapter. Additionally, this section will explore the failures of the STEM approach and provide suggestions for its successful implementation. Moreover, the authors propose exploring the applicability of an Augmented STEM system to further enhance STEM education.

Chapter 3
The Development of STEM Education in the Sultanate of Oman........................56
Mohamed A. Shahat, Sultan Qaboos University, Oman & Aswan University, Egypt
Sulaiman M. Al-Balushi, Sultan Qaboos University, Oman

This overview includes the impact of STEM programs in Oman, significant improvements in delivery, and plans for the future. The chapter outlines the research efforts underway in Oman regarding STEM and describes a nationally-funded strategic project by His Majesty Trust Fund Strategic Grants to enhance teachers' capabilities in STEM-based competencies and students' interest in STEM-related specialties. The chapter sheds light on the different scholarship opportunities offered by on the Oman Ministry of Higher Education, Research, and Innovation for students to pursue further education in specific disciplines of study in higher education institutions (HEIs) in Oman and abroad. The chapter also clarifies the stages of implementing the STEM Oman program in schools. The chapter includes a detailed description of training programs designed to prepare science teachers for the STEM Oman program. Next, the authors discuss the future development and plans for STEM Oman.

Chapter 4
Saudi Arabia's Vision 2030 and Its Impact on STEM Education........................74
Holly Nicole Babineau, Northcentral University, USA

The Kingdom of Saudi Arabia (KSA) released a plan in 2016 to achieve goals set for the country by the year 2030. Included in this plan, 'Vision 2030,' is a plan for transforming the education system into one that will better suit the Kingdom's needs, increasing the amount of science, technology, engineering, and math (STEM) studies and trainings in the nation. It is with this vision that Saudi Arabia has fully taken on the task of training educators across the Kingdom in different programs that teach all aspects of STEM. To see the impact of these programs, and to ensure they are working, there are studies being conducted that follow participants in the programs and receive feedback throughout all stages. These studies allow challenges to be uncovered early in the process and therefore make it possible to establish solutions. The purpose of this chapter is to examine the Saudi Vision 2030's impact on STEM education.

Chapter 5
STEM Education in Iraq 2004-2022: Strategies, Challenges, and Outcomes 91
    Jabbar A. Al-Obaidi, Bridgewater State University, USA
    Tahir Albakaa, Bridgewater State University, USA

This chapter explores STEM in Iraq from 2004 through 2022. It investigates the educational strategies and policies of the Ministry of Education (MOE) and the Ministry of Higher Education and Scientific Research (MOHEASR). MOE oversees curriculum, pedagogies, annual assessments, learning outcomes, and quality assurance for kindergarten, elementary (primary), middle, and high schools, while MOHEASR supervises educational and academic affairs for colleges and universities. A survey was distributed to random teachers and faculty members in various Iraqi schools, colleges, and universities throughout the 18 Iraqi governorates. Written questions were sent to superintendents, principals of schools, and deans of colleges. The theoretical framework for this study is informed by the primary educational learning of social and cognitive theories as learning and teaching are based on external environmental, internal conditions, and social factors and the process of knowledge. Challenges and strategies are discussed. Finally, the chapter proposes recommendations and directions for future research.

Chapter 6
Opportunities and Challenges of Introducing Digital Health Training in
Medical and Health Sciences Education in Palestine 128
    Mohammad J. Ghosheh, Ghosheh Medical and Surgical Complex,
        Palestine
    Ghadeer O. Ghosheh, Ghosheh Medical and Surgical Complex,
        Palestine

Over the past decade, there has been an increase in the spread of digital health tools in the Middle East and North Africa (MENA), including Palestine. This spread is changing the role of medical and health sciences students, which necessitates educational training to prepare a new generation of professionals. This chapter reviews the programs in Palestine in terms of offering classes in the three main areas in Digital Medicine, Artificial Intelligence and Robotics, and Genomics. Each of the areas is discussed in terms of state-of-the-art applications, opportunities and challenges that could be faced regarding its inclusion in Palestinian education programs. While many Palestinian universities offered classes that target computer skills, most programs lacked a focus on new applications that are projected to change the future of healthcare. The chapter concludes by discussing the promise of developing competencies in digital health on job opportunities and improving the Palestinian education indicators for medicine and health sciences on the local and international levels.

Chapter 7
Analyzing the Role of Popular Scientific Journalism in STEM and Turkey's
Science Communication Model 168
 Hasan Gürkan, Girona University, Spain & Istinye University, Turkey
 Carmen Soler Echazarreta, Girona University, Spain

This study examines the contributions of popular science magazines in Turkey to STEM as a field and discusses science journalism's support of the STEM world. The study explores the rules and perspective of science journalism and discusses the contributions of this field to STEM and STEM literacy. In its discussion of the impact of popular science magazines on STEM literacy, the study encompasses magazines in Turkey that publish science journalism and popularize science, making it easier for the public to understand. The study's interviews reveal that popular science magazines deliberately construct gendered language to increase popular knowledge and awareness of this field. Finally, the study summarizes the goals for scientific publications and science journalism in Turkey seeking to promote STEM literacy: (i) preparing content that will strengthen the public's relationship with science, (ii) promoting the number and quality of scientific studies in Turkey, (iii) challenging political power to realize the role of science, and (iv) reducing fake news.

Chapter 8
STEAM Education in an Online Modality: Teaching and Learning Tradeoff –
A Case Study 189
 Mohamed El Nagdi, American University in Cairo, Egypt
 Heba EL-Deghaidy, American University in Cairo, Egypt
 Gihan Osman, American University in Cairo, Egypt

This chapter investigates the status of one of the online programs at a not-for-profit university in Egypt offering professional development diplomas to school teachers and leaders. The program focuses on a STEAM online modality track. To explore the program, both graduates and instructors teaching in the online modality program were part of this research. Two main instruments were designed and administered: one was a focus group discussion with instructors in addition to individual interviews with 9 graduates. The research utilized a case study approach and data were analyzed using thematic analysis. Findings show areas of strength in the program design and delivery. Learners were clearly impacted by the online modality, although for some it started as a shock then gradually improved as they too started to replicate instructors' scaffolding and interdisciplinary design with their students. Recommendations were provided related to the start of the program to include more guidance and the final practicum course where it turned out to be an opportunity for innovative thinking.

Chapter 9
Teachers' Perceptions Towards the Implementation of STEM Education in
the State of Kuwait..209
    *Abrar Almoosa, Kuwait Foundation for Advancement of Sciences,
        Kuwait*

Recent long-term policy plans in the MENA region stress the growing importance of transitioning to 21st-century skills and pursuing sustainable development objectives through the preparation of highly skilled nationals holding credentials in STEM fields that align with current and future labor market demands. Despite multiple educational reforms, national and international indicators of student performance still demonstrate insignificant improvement in MENA students' achievement. This study explored the current status of STEM education in Kuwait from the teachers' perceptions. A qualitative research design was used, with semi-structured interviews as the main data collection method. The results showed that teachers had generally positive perceptions of STEM education and believed that it is important for the learners and their future careers. However, several challenges were identified including the curriculum and instructional strategies. The findings suggest that adopting new curriculums and teachers training are important towards successful implementation of STEM education.

Chapter 10
Reimagining Curriculum: Responding to Qatari Culture Through
Mathematics...222
    *Summer Bateiha, Virginia Commonwealth University School of the Arts
        in Qatar, Qatar*
    *Sadia Mir, Virginia Commonwealth University School of the Arts in
        Qatar, Qatar*

The authors of this chapter propose that the decolonization of Western course content and teaching practice is one of the necessary next steps to build a more equitable and inclusive mathematics curriculum in Qatar. Decolonization of curriculum and pedagogy involves a multilayered process including recognition of constraints placed upon curriculum and pedagogy, a disruption of these constraints, and a creation of alternatives. In this chapter, the authors outline three areas of concern: non-Eurocentric representation, single ways of learning, and elitism in mathematics; and offers pedagogical strategies as a roadmap forward towards decolonization of mathematics curriculum. This is followed by a description of a series of workshops designed for and held with teachers in the community. Finally, the authors present data about teacher perceptions of adopting culturally relevant storytelling as a tool for math education when combined with best practices in mathematics pedagogy.

Compilation of References 244

Related References 275

About the Contributors 297

Index 303

Preface

WHAT IS STEM EDUCATION?

STEM is a curriculum founded on the idea of educating students in four precise disciplines — science, technology, engineering and mathematics — in an interdisciplinary and applied approach (Bybee, 2013). STEM integrates the four disciplines rather than teaching them separately. In addition to that STEM brings the four disciplines into an interconnected learning model based on real-world applications (Bybee, 2013).

What differentiates STEM education from the regular traditional method of teaching science and math is the joint learning settings and the ability to demonstrate the scientific method in a form where it could be applied to student's everyday life (Fairweather, 2008). STEM enforces students' computational thinking and focuses on the real world applications of problem solving which prepares them for the actual job market and future careers (Fairweather, 2008). STEM education should introduce engineering during pre-college education because it is directly involved in problem solving and innovation (Bybee, 2013). Even if students do not choose STEM careers in the future, it is critical that our communities have people trained in systematic and logical thinking processes for understanding and solving problems. STEM training provides this while also affording learners foundational knowledge about the sciences and technology (Bybee, 2013). Regardless of the profession students choose to follow, they will benefit from having developed systematic problem solving skills (Bybee, 2013; Fairweather, 2008). For those who do pursue STEM careers, STEM K-12 training provides a strong base for their futures enabling them to engage in systems-thinking and problem solving, which is the core purpose of STEM education (Bybee, 2013). Therefore, a well-designed STEM curriculum will increase students' understanding of how the natural and designed world work and improve their use of technologies in everyday life (Fairweather, 2008; Bybee, 2013).

Educators also must have the ability to teach STEM through conceptual and experiential methods to ensure every student gains the precise benefits of integrating the four disciples; this requires educators to be knowledgeable and well-trained in

Preface

best practices for STEM education in order to deliver the best teaching (Rockland et al., 2007). In well-designed systems, STEM education can work toward bridging ethnic and gender gaps often found in math and science fields. Female students, for instance, are significantly less likely to enroll in college major or apply career STEM related fields (UNESCO, 2017). Male students are also more likely to join engineering and technology fields, while female students prefer science fields, like biology, or chemistry (UNESCO, 2017). Though the challenges are not new, the gaps persists. Different initiatives and schools have been established to increase the roles of women and minorities in STEM-related fields. STEM education breaks the traditional gender roles. In order to compete in a global economy, STEM education and careers, therefore, are considered nowadays a national priority among different nations (UNESCO, 2017).

WHY IS STEM EDUCATION IMPORTANT FOR YOUTHS IN MENA?

Quality education is a global priority for UNESCO. The United Nations Sustainable Development Goals (UNSDGs) promote the right to education and support the academic achievement for all (UN, n.d.). Through the Education 2030 Framework for Action (UN, 2015), SDG 4 aims to 'Ensure inclusive and equitable quality education and promote lifelong learning opportunities for all.' UNESCO's *Right to Education* initiative distinguishes education quality as a required approach that 'ensures that girls and boys, women and men not only gain access to and complete education cycles, but are empowered equally in and through education (UNESCO, 2017).

MENA is an acronym for the Middle East and North Africa (MENA) region. The region is typically considered to include approximately 21 countries (World Bank, 2022) and accounts for approximately 6% of the world's population. It is important for the MENA region to improve all aspects of its educational system. Thirteen million children in the region are unable to attend school because of conflict in their native countries, according to the World Bank report (2022). The MENA area has the highest percentage of youth unemployment in the world at 30.5% in North Africa and 28.2% in the Middle East (World Bank, 2022).

UNESCO states that there are multiple gaps still exist in terms of accessing, learning achievement and continuation in education in many settings (World Bank, 2022). Despite progress the MENA region still faces challenges in terms of some children never set foot in a classroom (World Bank, 2022). Many MENA region children face numerous encounters that limit their education opportunities. One area of longstanding concern is the low rate of children able to participate in STEM education and, consequently, STEM careers. This is a major concern, as STEM careers are often called 'jobs of the future,' driving social and personal well-being, inclusive growth and sustainable development, through innovation and creativity.

By enacting significant reforms in their educational policies and launching projects to raise the standard of education in their nations, MENA states have made significant investments in their educational systems. However, because these reforms did not achieve the intended results, the educational system in the region has not benefited from them. International tests like PISA, TIMSS, and PIRLS show low scores for students in the MENA region (Boudihaj & Sahli, 2022), which is reflected in how poorly they learn. There is an urgent need for structural educational reforms to promote civic engagement and citizenship. For the MENA region to become economically viable and consistently democratic, strong market-oriented skills and vocational training programs, critical thinking skills-based curriculum, and well-run educational systems are required.

STEM education is considered to be a support to narrow the gap when it comes to ethnic and gender underrepresentation in STEM fields (UNESCO, 2017). By implementing STEM education in schools, students of all genders and backgrounds have the opportunity to discover a passion for a subject they might not have before. Nevertheless, UNESCO reported that gender differences in STEM education participation are more visible at higher levels of education. Girls' interest in participation in advanced studies at secondary-level decreases; female enrollment is lowest in engineering, mathematics and ICT fields representing only about 35% of females enrolled college programs (UNESCO, 2017). While gender differences in science and mathematics achievement seem to have declined in current years in many countries, female are still significantly under-represented in STEM careers in many MENA countries.

In the Middle East region, specifically the Arab States, advancement in science and technology fields is a critical goal because it is considered crucial for economic and social development. Attaining this goal rests considerably on establishing educational policies that value increasing scientific knowledge and promoting pedagogical practices that support engagement in science (World Bank, 2016). One of the policies that needs more attention is STEM education. MENA children and youths face many barriers to an equitable and high-quality education; however, these obstacles are being addressed in the strategic plans of the MENA countries as well as support from country-based initiatives (Ostrosky, 2015). The major categories of obstacles to education are social settings, lack of use of resources, and the structure of educational systems. Children enrollment in public schools has been increasing across the Middle East for the past two decades; however, the education that they take is not always one that enhances their knowledge and skills and prepares them to work (Ostrosky, 2015).

Preface

HOW IS STEM EDUCATION IMPLEMENTED?

The success of any STEM program rests in how much the nation supports it. The call in the United States came from the President Obama in the third annual White House science fair in 2013:

"One of the things that I've been focused on as President is how we create an all-hands-on-deck approach to science, technology, engineering, and math… We need to make this a priority to train an army of new teachers in these subject areas, and to make sure that all of us as a country are lifting up these subjects for the respect that they deserve." (Handelsman & Smith, 2016).

After that speech policies and budgets focused on maximizing Federal investment to increase student access and engagement in active, rigorous STEM-learning experiences; and meaningful efforts to inspire and recognize young inventors, discoverers, and makers (Williams, 2011).

In the U.S., public education is available for children ranging from age five (Kindergarten) through approximately age 18 (Grade 12), creating "K12" education. Some regions also include Pre-Kindergarten for four-year olds (PK-12). This public education is funded by tax money and is generally guided by individual state interests and priorities. In Fall 2021, 49.5 million students were enrolled in PK-12 education in America (IES, 2023). Approximately 90% of PK-12 students attend public school in America (CAPE, 2023).

In 2013, the first multi-state K-12 science education standards initiative "Next Generation Science Standards" (NGSS, 2013) in the U.S. became the primary influencing document for STEM education in the nation. While the U.S. does not use a national curriculum model, these standards have been widely adopted by states in various forms. In order to fully adopt the NGSS, states needed to commit to including all aspects of the framework with the option of including additional content; this latter requirement was designed to satisfy regional differences in priorities for the many states in the country. Forty-four of the fifty states as well as several U.S. territories have adopted NGSS fully (20) or developed standards based on NGSS (24) (NSTA, 2014a). NGSS came in the wake of the Common Core Standards (National Governors Association Center for Best Practices, Council of Chief State School Officers, 2010), an earlier U.S. multi-state initiative with wide adoption by states. Common Core provides standards for mathematics and English language arts. Though interest in the Common Core is now waning, the initiative paved the way for establishing more uniform curriculum and assessment in the states.

Four features distinguish the NGSS (2013) from earlier state-based science frameworks. First, NGSS was designed for adoption across the nation, rather than solely for a single state, so priorities for content were less bound to regional interest. Second, the multi-state commitment with federal oversight meant greater resources went into the creation of these standards, compared to traditional state-based standards. This enabled the developers to bring broader expertise to the designing table. The U.S. National Research Council (NRC) launched the development of the NGSS Frameworks by creating a committee of experts to advise the process including those from science education and research, cognitive science, science education policy, as well as practicing scientists. Once the Frameworks were in place, Achieve, Inc managed the development of the actual Standards. This is where individual U.S. states were involved, alongside representation from industry, higher education, and the science and science education communities. Public drafts were released throughout the process for comment.

The third feature that distinguishes NGSS from previous state-based standards reflects a new and innovative approach to standards including "three dimensions of learning": disciplinary core ideas (DCI), science and engineering practices, and crosscutting concepts (CCC). This approach includes traditional standards-like benchmarks as performance expectations for the DCIs (NSTA, 2014b) organized into four domains: physical science, life science, Earth and space science, and engineering. More on the novel inclusion of engineering below. The codes for each performance expectation are used in all states that adopted NGSS as well as states that adopted components of NGSS. Keep in mind that the U.S. does not have a national curriculum, therefore individual states and, in many cases, town-or city-based districts, are responsible for their own curricular choices. Having the consistent codes for standards across the U.S. enables educators to share and find learning activities and resources online with far greater ease than in the past. NGSS also brings unprecedented attention to the practices of scientists and engineers (SEP). There are eight SEPs provided in NGSS and the expectation is that students in grades K-12 will be able to engage in all eight at developmentally appropriate ways (NSTA, 2014c). The SEPs are transformative and clear in their message that students must be engaged in science learning through social constructivist (Vygotsky, 1978) practices. Finally, the CCCs are the big ideas relevant across the science and engineering fields. They serve to unify concepts and provide overarching sensemaking to the many topics in the standards; the expectation is that students will engage with CCCs at all K-12 levels so they are presented in a developmentally appropriate sequence (NSTA, 2014d).

Fourth, NGSS also includes standards for engineering and technology, domains that received little to no formal attention in earlier state-based K-12 standards documents. They are organized by grade band (e.g. K-2, 3-5, 6-8, 9-12) rather than grade level, leaving wide room for interpretation and implementation. In addition to the explicit integration of engineering and technology, NGSS includes standards with a quantitative focus across the K-12 span as well as one SEP dedicated entirely to math, "mathematics and quantitative thinking", thereby building mathematics into the science standards. Therefore, NGSS provides robust and thoughtful guidance for STEM education in the U.S.

STEM education training for teachers has also been impacted by NGSS. In the U.S.,teacher training initiatives are available to classroom teachers and teacher educators at a range of levels including school district (town- / city-based), regional, and also from professional societies, such as National Science Teachers Association (NSTA), as well as state and federal government science agencies, such as National Oceanic and Atmospheric Administration (NOAA), National Aeronautics and Space Administration (NASA) and many others. In addition, universities and colleges provide teacher training through formal licensure programs that prepare teachers for careers in teaching; some institutions of higher education also provide ongoing professional development for educators already working in the field. Some programs require pay by educators or districts for professional development, while others are grant funded. For most states, NGSS has either been adopted or serves as the basis for state-crafted standards. Therefore these many professional development providers are able to offer teacher trainings that are relevant to a wide audience of educators in America because the U.S. has, for the first time, most of its states targeting the same STEM content.

A tremendous area of growth in STEM for American educators has been in the engineering design process. Part of the beauty and the challenge of NGSS is that it works best when students are engaged in science and engineering practices at each grade-level; the alternative is skipping over engineering and assuming that teachers in later grades will address it. Engineering design requires a different kind of thinking. In engineering, creative and divergent thinking is encouraged; it situates learners are creators, a role they rarely get to play. Districts approach engineering in different ways including the purchase of engineering kits that teachers can use to teach engineering units and the purchase of curricular resources that claim to integrate engineering. When teachers are trained in the engineering design process, they can reduce their reliance upon kits and provide engineering challenges for their learners with household resources or laboratory resources they are already using for science classes. Organizations around the nation are offering professional development and training for educators in engineering. Each year, since NGSS, engineering has become more normalized and common across public K-12 education in the U.S.

Other nations carried on the message differently based on availability of resources and programs. Some countries were able to shift their curriculum to STEM education while others needed help from different in-country entities such as Non-Governmental Organizations (NGOs). An international report (The role and impact of NGOs in capacity development: From replacing the state to strengthening education by UNESCO states that as development actors, NGOs have become the main service providers in countries the government is unable to fulfill its traditional/ basic role in some areas as education (UNESCO, 2017 A). In the education sector, many NGOs have moved beyond the "gap-filling initiatives" (UNESCO, 2017 B). to step into innovation and capacity building. For example, companies and organizations that offer summer internships provide a chance to learn more about different possibilities in the STEM fields, training teachers, or providing resources for the education system to build itself while the reform takes place.

IN THIS BOOK

STEM education has been applied differently across the globe; therefore, in this book we shed light on some of the practices in the MENA region. An overview of the practices of this region will allow us to present relevant solutions and provide pathways for addressing challenges to enable STEM education to be accessible to all. This book's contents have important lessons for educators worldwide about how STEM education can be applied differently based on the cultural, country's policies and systems.

Each chapter of this book looks at a different country and its STEM education features.

Chapter 1: Exploring Challenges of Online STEM Education Pedagogy and Practice in the MENA Region: Literature Review

Chapter 1 offers a well-researched examination of the constraints and affordances associated with implementing high quality online instruction in STEM, with a focus on mathematics. Though the context is Morocco, the challenges identified are relevant across MENA and the world. The author provides an excellent review of the literature and policies that have informed STEM in MENA. Issues such as the legacy of inequitable access to resources and the impacts of such long-standing disparities are addressed. Readers are presented with an intricately woven argument for the importance of keeping both research-based pedagogies rooted in theory as well as the needs of learners at the forefront of technology-rich STEM education that pushes the boundaries of traditional approaches in education.

Chapter 2: STEM in Turkey: Initiatives, Implementations, and Failures

In chapter 2, authors trace the history, policies, and trends that have paved the road for modern-day STEM education in Turkey. The detailed chronology enables readers to track the progress of this "ever-evolving field" and gain insights about the foundations of this learning area, so integral to 21st century education. Equitable access to STEM education and opportunities is a clear priority in Turkey; it is built

Preface

into many STEM education initiatives currently running. Authors discuss a wide array of topics related to STEM in Turkey, including teacher professional development, STEM centers, challenges related to the allocation of STEM education resources. Each is addressed succinctly with explicit ties to research. Despite the obstacles identified, much exciting work is underway in Turkish STEM education communities.

Chapter 3: The Development of STEM Education in the Sultanate of Oman

In the study on STEM education in Oman, the authors focused on the importance of STEM disciplines for Omani students and their role in positioning the country as a regional and global leader. The authors highlighted the need for equipping youth with problem-solving, evidence evaluation, and information sense-making skills through STEM subjects. Recommendations were provided to improve STEM education in Oman, including creating a community-wide vision for STEM-based teaching, incorporating play and exploration activities, implementing project-based learning, integrating global challenges into learning, and building flexible learning spaces. The findings emphasized the importance of implementing these strategies to improve STEM education in Oman and to align with the goals of the Omani curriculum.

Chapter 4: Saudi Arabia's Vision 2030 and Its Impact on STEM Education

This chapter outlines 'Vision 2030', which is the Kingdom of Saudi Arabia's goals for the future in terms of advancing STEM education throughout the country. Low international testing has been a call-to-action for the Kingdom to may sweeping educational changes in their approach to STEM education. In this review of the literature, the focus on teacher training is highlighted as means to improve STEM teaching and learning, with great emphasis on participant feedback, to guide next steps to guide "Vision 2030" into the realm of success and innovation the Kingdom seeks.

Chapter 5: STEM Education In Iraq 2004-2022: Strategies, Challenges and Outcomes

This chapter provides a critical overview of Iraq's education system historically, presently, and with a gaze of aspiration toward the future. The need for STEM education to have a greatest presence in Iraq is emphasized, with ideas of how this could happen with the support of the Ministry of Education and the Ministry of Higher Education and Scientific Research. A call-to-action to have STEM courses available to those even not on "pure science" tracks is underscored to enhance students' educational experiences and to improve Iraq's global standing.

Chapter 6: Opportunities and Challenges of Introducing Digital Health Training in Medical and Health Sciences Education in Palestine

The central objective of this chapter is to closely explore the modern medical education curricula in Palestine. This deep dive leads to an analysis of the obstacles and opportunities that exist when integrating digital health training Palestinian medical curricula. The challenges to bring more technology to Palenstine is shared amongst other MENA countries. The focus of this chapter serves as a powerful reminder that true ongoing growth in STEM cannot take place without the "T" for technology. For medical training and education to not be able to progress means a lack of progress could cost lives, a sobering reality that should spark a sense of urgency to push for digital health training in Palestine, as well as other MENA countries.

Chapter 7: Analyzing the Role of Popular Scientific Journalism in STEM and Turkey's Science Communication Model

In the context of Turkey, popular scientific journalism played a crucial role in promoting STEM education, scientific literacy, and public engagement with scientific topics. The media focused on STEM-oriented publishing and language to increase knowledge and awareness in this field, including the use of specifically gender-oriented language. The study emphasized the importance of a structural equation model for scientific publications and science journalism in Turkey to enhance STEM literacy and popularize science in a more understandable manner. The overall aim was to align STEM with society's approach to science, ensuring that STEM education and research are relevant, responsive, and aligned with the needs and interests of the public. This alignment called for an understanding of public perspectives, values, and concerns about science, and incorporating them into scientific endeavors for the betterment of society.

Chapter 8: STEAM Education in an Online Modality: Teaching and Learning Tradeoff. A Case Study

The worldwide COVID-19 pandemic accelerated the timeline for a non-profit University's Professional Educator Diploma (PED) program in Egypt to move to fully asynchronous online delivery. Prior to the pandemic, the program was being intentionally designed to target the same learning outcomes as the face-to-face version of the program and provide the same high-quality instruction and rigor in a web-based modality. This chapter reports on findings from the STEAM component of this PED program. Themes of access and equity are prevalent and the students identify assets that result from the unique virtual learning experience. Authors share concrete takeaways and lessons learned that are relevant for the wide range of instructional contexts.

Chapter 9: Teachers' Perception Towards the Implementation of STEM Education in the State of Kuwait

The chapter aimed to address the gap in the existing literature on STEM education in Kuwait by conducting qualitative research and exploring the perceptions of teachers in the field of education. The research provided valuable insights into the educational landscape in Kuwait, highlighting the challenges and gaps that exist. The chapter suggested the need for adopting new curriculums and providing training for teachers to successfully implement STEM education.

Chapter 10: Reimagining Curriculum: Responding to Qatari Culture Through Mathematics

This study explored the need for visibility and inclusivity in mathematics education, in the context of the Qatari curriculum. It emphasized the importance of challenging Eurocentrism and Western-focused contexts and shifting the perception of mathematics as an elite discipline rooted in procedural rules. The research highlighted the potential of a culturally-responsive curriculum that incorporates indigenous and culturally diverse themes, promoting deep learning and connecting students to their own cultural mathematical ideas and contributions. The study suggested that implementing such educational change requires a collaborative approach involving researchers, educators, and the local community. Overall, this study contributes to the understanding of the Qatari curriculum and highlights the significance of a culturally-responsive approach in mathematics education.

Fatimah Alhashem
Gulf University for Science and Technology, Kuwait

Heather Pacheco-Guffrey
Bridgewater State University, USA

Jacquelynne Anne Boivin
Bridgewater State University, USA

REFERENCES

Boudihaj, A., & Sahli, M. (2022). Education in the Mena Region. Wolhuter, C.C. and Wiseman, A.W. (Ed.) World Education Patterns in the Global South: The Ebb of Global Forces and the Flow of Contextual Imperatives (International Perspectives on Education and Society, Vol. 43B). Emerald Publishing Limited, Bingley. doi:10.1108/S1479-36792022000043B002

Bybee, R. W. (2013). *The case for STEM education: Challenges and opportunities.* National Science Teachers Association.

Council for American Private Education (CAPE). (2023). *Private School Statistics at a Glance.* CAPE. https://capenetwork.org/private-school-statistics-at-a-glance/#:~:text=There%20are%2034%2C576%20private%20schools,of%20all%20PK%2D12%20students

Fairweather, J. (2008). *Linking evidence and promising practices in science, technology, engineering, and mathematics (STEM) undergraduate education.* Board of Science Education, National Research Council, The National Academies.

Handelsman, J., & Smith, M. (Feb 11, 2016). *STEM for all.* The White House President Barack Obama Archives. https://obamawhitehouse.archives.gov/blog/2016/02/11/stem-all

Institute of Education Sciences (IES). (2023). *Fast Facts: Back to School Statistics.* National Center for Education Statistics. https://nces.ed.gov/fastfacts/display.asp?id=372

National Governors Association Center for Best Practices, Council of Chief State School Officers. (2010). *Common core state standards.* NGACB. http://corestandards.org/

National Science Teachers Association (NSTA). (2014a). *About the Next Generation Science Standards.* NGSS@NSTA. https://ngss.nsta.org/About.aspx

National Science Teachers Association (NSTA). (2014b). *Disciplinary Core Ideas.* NGSS@NSTA. https://ngss.nsta.org/DisciplinaryCoreIdeasTop.aspx

National Science Teachers Association (NSTA). (2014c). *Science and Engineering Practices.* NGSS@NSTA. https://ngss.nsta.org/PracticesFull.aspx

National Science Teachers Association (NSTA). (2014d). *Crosscutting Concepts.* NGSS@NSTA. https://ngss.nsta.org/CrosscuttingConceptsFull.aspx

NGSS Lead States. (2013). *Next Generation Science Standards: For States, By States.* Washington, DC: The National Academies Press. https://www.nextgenscience.org/

Ostrosky, C. M. (2015). *Women's access to education in the Middle East.* Whatbrug College Undergraduate Research Project. http://public.wartburg.edu/mpsurc/images/ostrosky.pdf

Rockland, R., Bloom, D. S., Carpinelli, J., Burr-Alexander, L., Hirsch, L. S., & Kimmel, H. (2010). Advancing the "E" in K-12 STEM Education. *The Journal of Technology Studies, 36*(1), 53–64. https://www.learntechlib.org/p/55436/. doi:10.21061/jots.v36i1.a.7

United Nations. (2015). *Transforming our world: The 2030 agenda for sustainable development.* Department of Economic and Social Affairs. https://sdgs.un.org/2030agenda

United Nations. (n.d). *The 17 goals.* Department of Economic and Social Affairs. https://sdgs.un.org/goals

United Nations Educational, Scientific and Cultural Organization. (2017). A. *Cracking the code: Girls' and women's education in science, technology, engineering and mathematics (STEM).* UN. http://go.nature.com/2hlzccm

United Nations Educational, Scientific and Cultural Organization. (2017) B. *UNESCO Global education monitoring report gender review: Right to education.* UN. https://www.right-to-education.org/resource/unesco-global-education-monitoring-report-gender-review

Vygotsky, L. S. (1978). *Mind in society: The development of higher psychological processes Cambridge.* Harvard University Press.

Williams, P. J. (2011). STEM education: Proceed with caution. *Design and Technology Education: an International Journal, 16,* 26–35.

world

World Bank. (2016). *The Arab world.* World Bank. https://data.worldbank.org/region/arab-

World Bank. (2022). *Population - Total Middle East and North Africa.* World Bank. https://data.worldbank.org/indicator/SP.POP.TOTL?locations=ZQ&view=map

Acknowledgement

This remarkable project was undertaken with the constant support and expertise of the book's Editorial Advisory Board (EAB). Board members worked tirelessly to consult with editors, review chapters, and provide constructive, actionable feedback to authors for their work in the MENA region. Their efforts were critical to the success of this exceptional endeavor.

Editorial Advisory Board

Saouma Boujaoude, *American University of Beirut, Beirut, Lebanon*
Jonah Firestone, *Washington State University, USA*
Shawn O'Neill, *Bridgewater State University, Bridgewater, USA*
Irasema Ortega, *Chadron State College, Chadron, USA*
Cynthia Villanueva, *Spanish Legal & Scientific Translator, Framingham, USA*
Alexander Wiseman, *Texas Tech University, Lubbock, USA*

Chapter 1
Exploring Challenges of Online STEM Education Pedagogy and Practice in the MENA Region:
Literature Review

Meryem Ouelfatmi
https://orcid.org/0000-0002-1180-9652
Sidi Mohamed Ben Abdellah, Morocco

ABSTRACT

With the increased need for technology implementation, educational systems across the world have made various efforts to utilize technology to optimize learning efficacy. With regard to the MENA region, many reforms have been administered in order to effectively digitize education. Pedagogical aspects remain in great need of further investigation. Thus, through a conceptual review of applied pedagogical strategies, this chapter aims to explore issues related to such implementation in the MENA region. As pedagogy varies according to age, teaching environment, and subject, the author aims to explore the theory and practice of Mathematics teaching in online environments. The educational policy also diverges from one country to another, especially in terms of STEM education. The present study is based on a focus on the MENA region context which allows for a better understanding and development of STEM education. Moreover, this review provides issues and challenges to consider for future research and proposes pedagogical modifications to suit the online teaching environments.

DOI: 10.4018/978-1-6684-6883-8.ch001

INTRODUCTION

E-learning is a term that has become widely used. It can be defined as "the use of information and communication technologies to teach students from another location" (El-Khayma, 2021, p. 140). Technological advancement in the field of education has expanded the limits of traditional learning. With many platforms and open sources, students are no longer confined to the walls of the classroom, and can instead attend class, contact professors, and self-learn from the comforts of their homes.

This chapter aims to open a discussion concerning pedagogical issues related to teaching Mathematics online. Through examining the literature on this account, the author aims to propose modifications to allow for effective e-pedagogies. The conceptual nature of this research strives to create a conceptual and theoretical framework for e-pedagogies, taking as a focal point of concern the Moroccan context. The lack of literature on this topic can be considered a limitation and an addition to this research. Although technology acceptance and use in education research have become a scientific trend in Morocco, there remains a great need for theoretical propositions that have pragmatic potential. Providing a theoretical framework for e-pedagogy development not only adds to the theoretical literature but also sets the ground for testing such strategies.

Main Focus of The Chapter

This chapter aims to provide insights into challenges concerning online STEM education in the MENA region, specifically in the Moroccan context, and aims to add to the representations in this book. Additionally, such discussions will entice researchers and practitioners in the field of education to consider constructing e-pedagogies that can increase the efficacy of e-learning technologies. On a more specific level, it will help Moroccan Mathematics teachers to consider modifying the implemented methods in order to suit online environments. Thus, the following objectives are set:

1. To provide a conceptual analysis of e-learning, andragogy, and pedagogy.
2. To explore the impact of e-learning on andragogy in terms of math teaching.

Issues, Controversies, Problems

Educational policy refers to "a rationale, a set of goals, and a vision for how education systems might [work] with the introduction of ICT and how students, teachers, parents, and the general population might benefit from its use in schools" (Kozma, 2008, p. 1084). With the rise of technology use across various fields, most developed countries have administered somewhat of a smooth transition to the virtual. Developing countries, on the other hand, lag behind due to various issues, especially those struggling with political conflict.

Middle East

Education is an integral constituent of the development of countries. With the ever-growing technology, education struggles to keep up with the various advancements, especially in developing countries. In recent years, countries around the world have shifted their focus to modernizing education, through various reforms, including countries in the MENA region. Examining these different reforms and their outcomes will provide insights into the efficacy of ICT implementation in education.

In Saudi Arabia, the Tatweer project was administered in 2007 to globalize and modernize education. To realistically and effectively reform education on these terms, this project follows five principles: excellence, commitment, accountability, professionalism, and transparency (Alyami, 2014). These principles entail values that should be believed and practiced by students as well as the educational staff. Students and teachers are expected to be committed to their educational skills. According to the authors, teachers must proceed with a high level of professionalism and are responsible for their students' learning and progress. This allows for equal opportunities for excellence, educationally for students and professionally for teachers. These schools are considered autonomous in terms of decision-making and evaluation. Although these schools are perceived to be of great efficacy, they remain to be numbered. The excessive budget needed for a successful implementation of this model across the country constitutes a great challenge (Ablugami & Vian, 2015). In this context, regardless of ICT implementation "Implementation at the school level is through pedagogy that relies predominantly on textbook use" (Alayyar et al., 2018, p.9). Similar to other Islamic countries, the Kingdom of Saudi Arabia employs Islamic values across various fields, including education. The social and cultural aspects are of significant impact on educational policy. Based on gender segregation values in Islam, formal education was only allowed for men. Recent changes on this account allowed for gendered schools which allowed women access to formal education. Although middle eastern countries have many socio-cultural aspects in common, they each have a unique cultural identity. Thus, having an overview of educational policies provides great insights into the effect of culture and religion on education.

Similarly, Jourdan recognizes the importance of ICT implementation not only in education but also in business. The most recent effort made in this context is REACH 2025. This action plan sets a vision for ICT accessibility and affordability across health, education, and business private and public sectors. This is to "Boost economic development in key knowledge sectors" (Gedeon & Al-Qasem, 2019, p. 13). Efforts of this kind have been underway for several years, namely in 2012, when the Jordanian Education Initiative (JEI) was introduced. This project focused on equipping schools with educational technologies such as smart boards, internet-based curricula, and computers. In this respect, Menchaca & Khwaldeh, (2014) state that "there is discrepancy between urban and rural areas, including the use of ICT" (p.1). These major differences existing in Amman, the capital, and throughout the country are a great challenge for the development of the country. The authors specify that these challenges are both of social and economic nature. This creates a large gap in terms of implementation which leads to an uneven distribution of knowledge, accessibility to technology, and learning.

As previously mentioned, the sociocultural and political aspects of a country influence various fields and their adopted policies. For the past decade, Syria has been an area of conflict that heavily impacted the state of education in the country. What started as peaceful protests against the president, Bachar Al Assad, developed into an armed conflict that continues to affect the lives of millions of people. The conflict in this country has been unstable during the past few years. Qaddour & Husain (2022) acknowledge that "Despite a decline in active armed conflict in recent years, approximately 6.9 million Syrians have been internally displaced as of early 2022" (p. 7). In this respect, many citizens struggle with accessing basic necessities such as food, water, and shelter, let alone having a formal education. Since the country remains politically divided, there is a lack of consensus in terms of educational policy which lead to the use of different curricula as well as formal and non-formal modes of education. In an attempt to resolve this crisis, efforts to incorporate technology for communication and educational purposes have been initiated. However, due to the state's economy, cost, and accessibility of such technologies, these efforts remain heavily challenged (Alfarah & Bosco, 2016).

Similar to Syria, Iraq has witnessed armed conflict for decades. This has made ICT implementation significantly challenging, making the country one of the last to implement technology in education (Matar et al., 2010). Technology and its role in creating a wide reach for education have long been acknowledged, especially in areas of conflict. Thair & Marini (2012) address efforts made in this respect, namely in the Babylon province. Their study highlights the lack of infrastructure and accessibility to educational technologies. Foreign organizations have also been involved in an attempt to aid the state of education. The Economic and Social Commission for Western Asia (ESCW) collaborated with the country's Ministry of Education to ensure effective implementation of technology, especially in terms of education. However, this process took longer than the intended five-year vision. This is due to economic challenges on one hand and political barriers on the other

(Makki & Hanna, 2011). To this day, Iraq still struggles to ensure and maintain the accessibility of telecommunication networks, especially to rural areas, as well as the affordability of e-learning technologies.

North Africa

As a part of North Africa, Libya is characterized by its vast Saharian areas. The country has a high literacy rate in comparison with Arab countries and even its neighboring countries (Almgadmi, 2018). It is also a country faced with political and religious conflict which impeded technology incorporation. Although Libya generates great revenue from oil, with several militias and Islamic groups attempting to take control of the country, the country's economy struggles immensely from this conflict. As seen in the Middle-Eastern countries of socio-political unrest, development whether economic, educational, or technological becomes slow and, in most cases, ineffective. Official efforts to incorporate ICTs in education have been ongoing since 2005 with hopes of developing and modernizing education, expanding scientific research, and attracting funding (Hamdy, 2007). Despite these efforts, Kenan et al. (2012) "the country is still facing a lack of usage of ICT tools and techniques, promising infrastructure, access to ICT resources, national ICT policy to cover all the different domains, and research activities are lacking behind" (as cited in Alshref et al., 2021, p. 10). These challenges alongside the ongoing political crisis hinder the initial introduction of technology as an educational tool, let alone the successful transition from traditional pedagogies to e-pedagogies.

Similar to other North African countries, Algeria began acknowledging and advocating the use of technology in education. In an effort to do so, the country's Ministry of Education worked alongside the World Bank back in 2002. However, the progress of this process remains ongoing, putting Algeria in the 131st according to the World Economic Forum (WEF) report in 2013, as cited in Gherbi (2015). Nevertheless, Algerian universities are more equipped with computers and provide internet access to staff members as well as students, with many governmental collaborations with UNESCO and foreign governments (Hamdy, 2007). Learning management systems, namely MOODLE, have been adopted in Algerian universities, allowing students to access course material, download and submit assignments, as well as undergo assessment. However, training and technical support still lack which does not necessarily promote the use of such systems. These issues have been a focal point of scientific research in the country. At the academic conference held by the National Institute of Telecommunications and ICT of Oran in 2013, a few key challenges were highlighted as stated in (Gherbi, 2015, p.7):

- The mismatch between the available equipment and the training of the technical staff trained in ICT.
- The weak flow which often leads to dysfunctions of the microphone and the synchronization between the picture and the sound.
- The absence of motivation of teachers for E-learning.

Such issues, alongside affordability and accessibility, hinder the effectiveness of modernization, and digitalization of education and render change and technology use rather difficult to implement across the country.

E-Learning in Morocco

The incorporation of e-learning technology in education has witnessed fast-paced growth all across the world. Prior to Co-vid, the Moroccan government made many efforts to incorporate technology into the educational system. Projects such as CATT (Computer-Assisted Teacher Training, 1999), MARWAN (Moroccan Academic Wide Area Network, 1998), and CVM (Moroccan Virtual Campus, 2002) were implemented with the purpose of facilitating administrative functions (Hajji, 2018, p.99-101). MARWAN, for example, aimed to create a network that allows for communication and collaboration between universities. A notable project which sought to incorporate technology for educational purposes is GENIE (2005). The latter was an attempt to make the use of technology mainstream by building media rooms accessible in schools across the country.

Although these efforts made a significant impact, e-learning technologies are still not used to their full potential. However, the pandemic of Co-vid called for a lockdown, which created a sudden need for an online switch. E-learning efforts started with WhatsApp and Facebook groups to ensure constant communication between students, parents, and teachers. This developed to the use of other platforms such as Zoom and Google Meets which was also supported by lesson broadcasts on TV (high school). Concerning higher education learning management systems were also implemented. However, the use of technologies such as MOODLE or MOOC is limited due to many limitations, basic of which is weak infrastructure (Jouicha et al, 2020). Similarly, Ouajdouni et al. (2021) highlight the lack of use of online learning platforms and the crucial impact of learner satisfaction and social influence on such use. These issues seem to be shared among developing countries, especially in the North African region, holding back such integration. On another hand, El Hammoumi et al. (2022) emphasizes the potential of using interactive 3D animation as an educational tool to teach Biology in higher education.

The adoption of "traditional" teaching strategies within the online context has rendered this implementation rather difficult. Among the abundant issues concerned with technology acceptance and use, matters of pedagogy are rarely prioritized. However, recent efforts led to the founding of Pedagogical Innovation Centers (PIC) throughout Moroccan universities with the aim of improving teaching practices through research (Machwate et al, 2023).

An Overview of Pedagogy

From an etymological perspective, pedagogy is a term that stems all the way back to Ancient Greece, as its origin, *Paidagogos,* translates to a teacher of children (Shah, 2021). The author adopts a general view of pedagogy, as he defines it as "the discipline of study related to the field of education and teaching methods" (p. 357). Along similar lines, "education" stems from the Latin term *Educare*, meaning to bring up or raise. In this sense, education is separate from pedagogy in that it can be lifelong as well as formal or informal, by teachers or parents. It is a difficult matter to arrive at a consensus in terms of defining pedagogy, as authors attribute it to various constructs. As Shah (2021) discusses in his article, pedagogy can be viewed in relation to culture (Stairs, 1995), dynamicity (Pollard, 2002), and theory and practice (Alexander, 2008). A pedagogue can be a transmitter of cultural beliefs and norms, as cultural identity, values, and history are unescapable in any community. In his talk at the International Association for Cognitive Education and Psychology (IACEP) 10th International Conference held in 2005, Alexander (2008) proposes that:

Pedagogy is not a mere matter of teaching technique. It is a purposive cultural intervention in individual human development which is deeply saturated with the values and history of the society and community in which it is located. Pedagogy is best defined, then, as the act of teaching together with the ideas, values and collective histories which inform, shape and explain that act. (p. 2)

The author also considers theory and practice in his understanding of pedagogy. The theoretical framework of pedagogy may be somewhat unified, it is through the application of such theories that one teacher differs from another. This highlights the dynamic nature of pedagogy. As discussed by Pollard (2002) and Shah (2021), this dynamicity is in terms of both theory and practice. With continuous scientific research in the educational field, new modifications and models are constantly proposed, thus, making the pedagogue a long-life learner. To any experienced teacher, the classroom is an unpredictable environment, requiring the teacher to constantly make decisions, implement appropriate pedagogies, and, in some cases, modify them as they see fit.

Pedagogy has been used as a broad term that refers to the teaching of students of all ages. The previously mentioned definitions exclude age, which is a crucial aspect of pedagogy. On this account, Knowles (1980) separates pedagogy from andragogy stating that the latter refers to "the art and science of helping adults learn" (p. 43). The main concern, in this case, is one of agency, as it is assumed that adults tend to be more intrinsically motivated while children are extrinsically influenced (Cziesielski, 2020). Thus, in this case, pedagogy can be viewed as teacher-centered whereas, andragogy is more student-centered (Schmidt et al., 2010). Pedagogy and andragogy are considered to vary in terms of educational focus:

In Pedagogy, the educational focus is on transmitting, in a very teacher-controlled environment, the content subject matter. In Andragogy, the educational focus is on facilitating the acquisition of and critical thinking about the content and its application in real-life practical settings (Pew, 2007, p. 17-18)

However, holding such a view may be deterministic, as not all adult students are intrinsically motivated. Motivation and learner styles are varying factors that can from one student to another, and even during different stages of an individual's life. To exemplify this, the case of higher education can be taken. An individual may voluntarily choose a particular major in which they are interested, however, there may be required modules that, if given the choice, the individual may opt out of (Rachal, 2002). This is one of many issues relating to andragogy as a concept and theory, which renders it the center of many debates (Merriam & Caffarella, 1991).

Didactics is another term used interchangeably in this context. Although pedagogy, andragogy, and didactics all relate to the theory and practice of education, didactics are regarded as subset theoretical components of education (Disterveg, 1956, as cited in Riskulova & Yuldashova, 2020). In this respect, the authors highlight the scientific foundational nature of didactics pertaining to the structure of teaching. It can be argued that this field of study is more teacher-centered, as its focus lies on the managerial aspects of teaching, considering educational goals. Content is another crucial element of didactics, which can be separated into an independent field of study (Kansanen & Meri, 1999). On this account, the authors differentiate between general didactics and subject didactics. The latter entails a focus on the implemented curricula, which can vary according to the social and political contexts. This further demonstrates the dynamic nature of this field. Subject didactics consists of contextualizing learning goals in terms of learning goals and institutionalized curricula. On this account, Schneuwly (2011) state that "subject didactics are thus born as practices and theories of practice, in the realm of disciplinary school system, above all by its main actor, the teacher profession" (p.279). This field can be of great significance to the online context. Considering the rapid implementation of e-learning technologies, little to no attention was given to the design of a curriculum that is based on theory, practice, and subject. Considering the minor conceptual gap between pedagogy and andragogy as terms and fields of study, the term pedagogy, in this chapter, is used to refer to strategies pertaining to the practice of teaching adults.

As previously discussed, age is not the only factor to consider when it comes to teaching methods. Subject and context are also influential elements. Mathematics teaching strategies diverge from that of language learning. Similarly, formal and non-formal contexts also have a significant influence on methods. Thus, it is only fair to assume that an online and offline environment have a similar effect.

Traditional Pedagogy and E-Pedagogy

With the rise of technology, its use across various fields has also been constantly increasing. As previously discussed in section one, some developing countries are still lagging behind due to economic, social and political issues. However, even among those which managed a better technology incorporation, especially in regards to education, still struggle with its effectiveness. Although implementing technology in teaching and learning has been the center of discussion and debate for many decades, questions relating to implemented pedagogy remain unanswered (Serdyukov, 2015). The author outlines various issues hindering the effectiveness of online education, including the negative effect of online environments on attention span and memory, as well as the lack of the use of writing. The latter has been advocated as a significant tool of retention and memorization by many scholars (Ibn Khaldun, 1377; Sousa, 2014;...). Other discussed issues revolve around student-centeredness, where it is, in some cases, misconceived as the absence of the teacher. However, this approach only serves to empower students and allow them to become active agents responsible for their own learning with the teacher's guidance and support. This perspective has gained attention at the turn of the 20th century and became known as constructivist theory. Piaget (1936) founded this theory arguing that children have their own mode of thinking which must be considered when teaching. The author adopts a cognitive approach, as he presumes that the construction of knowledge is an internal cognitive process. In other words, this view posits that individuals use reality to structure and form their knowledge, as opposed to the traditional view which assumes that the external world is the provider of knowledge (Bodner, 1986). Along similar lines, Vygotsky (1978), a household name in constructivist literature, stresses the importance of the social world in the acquisition of knowledge. This scholar stands in the middle ground as he argues that society impacts the way an individual forms knowledge, and consequently it can shape knowledge itself (Morin, 2012). Contextualizing this view in terms of pedagogy would entail a focus on social interaction as a teaching strategy, rather than the "lecture" method, which is among the current pedagogical trends. This collaborative approach falls along the lines of Dewey's (1916) work, which advocates active learning. The latter entails that in order to achieve effective learning, students must engage in problem-solving situations where they interact, share and infer knowledge. This can also be referred to as collaborative learning, also discussed by Vygotsky (1978), which helps learners develop their team-work skills all while learning. Problem-solving is not the only approach included in active learning, the author also mentioned the use of inquiry. Through providing a curiosity-stimulating situation, a teacher can prompt students to ask questions, brainstorm solutions and deduce answers (Feldman & Mcphee, 2008). Active learning methods can be utilized separately as well as simultaneously. For instance, teachers can provide problem-solving activities for students to work on as groups. This would allow for peer conversations as well as teacher-student dialogue, which is another method of active learning. As often misconceived, this does not entail a passive role for the teacher. The latter's presence and instructional guidance are crucial elements for effective learning. According to Shah (2021), this can be observed in the cognitive apprenticeship approach, which regards the teacher's role as a mentor. With the use of theory, practice, and previous experience, the teacher can entice curiosity and inquiry as well as guide the student with his/ her learning. As Shah (2021) states: "Cognitive Apprenticeship inside the classroom focuses on cognitive skills and can be applied to teaching reading comprehension, writing, and mathematical problem solving" (p. 377). Although some of these approaches can be viewed as practical or pragmatic and, thus, can only be employed in applied subjects, they can also be useful in terms of more theory-driven fields such as mathematics, philosophy, and even in language teaching.

Contrastingly, traditional pedagogy is characterized by its focus on the teacher as the only source of knowledge. On this account, Rashty (1999) highlights Teacher Talking Time (TTT) as an element of the traditional approach. The teacher, in this context, adopts a lecturer role and provides information rather than prompt students to deduce it. Although this approach is deemed most popular in the higher education context (Wilson & Sipe, 2014), it is also employed with younger students. The latter is through, for instance, providing a grammatical rule and practicing it using exercises. It can also include memorization and repetition as a core pedagogical tool, after which students are evaluated through written or oral tests (Sultanov, 2022). Additionally, the teacher is a power figure who is in control of setting learning objectives, choosing course material, and evaluating learning effectiveness (Khalaf & Zin, 2018). This gives little to no consideration to individual learners' needs, learning styles, and knowledge acquisition. The traditional approach is criticized for exclusive students as it considers teaching, as opposed to constructivist active learning strategies which focus on students and their learning (Greenberg, 1987; Dewey, 1993; Mitra, 2007; Russell & Greenberg, 2008, as cited in Khalaf & Zin, 2018). Such criticism, among many others, called for more creative and inclusive strategies to allow for more student engagement and thus effective learning. With the rise of technology incorporation, what is currently regarded as traditional pedagogy is the practice of teaching without the use of Information and Communication Technologies (ICTs).

It is argued that learning is dependent on attention, motivation, emotions, and experience (Bransford et al. 2000, as cited in Mödritscher, 2006). As previously discussed, adult learners tend to be more intrinsically motivated and can take charge of their learning, and, thus, can be more attentive in an online learning environment. However, young learners, namely children, can struggle in this respect. As opposed to traditional learning environments, it can be argued that teachers have less control. This is due to being physically isolated and consequently fracturing the sense of community, which, as previously discussed, is an important element of learning (Vygotsky, 1978). Withal, pedagogy remains a critical issue, as "instead of designing new pedagogy or, at least, transforming the conventional pedagogy to integrate the educational capabilities of new technologies, a common trend in higher education institutions has been to merely adapt technology to traditional teaching ways" (Serdyukov, 2015, p. 62). Thus, it is important to investigate the gap existing between what can be referred to as "traditional" and online pedagogy. Pedagogy can be viewed as a science that serves to form strategies that optimize learning and increase educational quality. On this account, Shah (2021) highlights what he referred to as "constituted" and "non-constituted", where the first is based on a significant body of literature. Whereas, the second refers to "new sciences [that] are usually formed through increased findings about a particular topic or problem and their subsequent separation from traditional pedagogical sciences" (p.365). Thus, "non-constituted" pedagogy can entail the recent developments of the pedagogical theory which are yet to be tested and proven effective by research. This is one of the crucial challenges impeding successful online education, as e-pedagogy literature is limited and consists of mere suggestions rather than strategies tested for effectiveness. In this respect, Mehanna (2004) incorporated previously tested pedagogies provided by Marzano (2001), which were retested in terms of online learning environments. The study's findings highlight the significant correlation between seven of these pedagogies and students' performance. It is important to note that this study sampled higher education students and regarded performance in terms of test scores. The author highlights the effectiveness of summarizing and note-taking, homework and practice, as well as generating and testing hypotheses. These elements are not practiced by the teacher themselves, but they are for students to implement with the prompt and guidance of the teacher. Additionally, the use of non-linguistic presentations which consist of images, graphs, and diagrams proved to be effective and can be utilized by both teachers and students. In terms of strategies that can be implemented by teachers, results demonstrate the importance of feedback and recognition, as well as goal setting. These pedagogies stem a concrete theoretical and empirical background emanating from constructivist, behaviorist and cognitive theories and which can be applicable to various subjects (Mehanna, 2004). Similarly, Simuth & Schuller (2012) underline few principles to consider when online teaching, which include constant teacher-student contact facilitating feedback. The authors also state the role of collaborative learning alongside forming positive learning environments that recognize individuals' talents and learning styles. It is crucial to consider large numbers of students, as it is the case of most higher education classrooms. The authors do not specify whether they refer to online classes or project-based activities which can be conducted on online platforms. Finally, providing technical support is also deemed of great importance as having access to training facilitates the use of online learning platforms and decreases anxiety that may be felt when using an unfamiliar system. With the switch to online platforms, many educators maintained the focus on textbook material and lecturing approach which in turn can hinder the effectiveness of e-learning, affecting students' attention and retention (Arvan, 1998, as cited in Simuth & Schuller, 2012).

As previously discussed, student-to-teacher and student-to-student interaction is a key element of effective learning, which, in most cases can lack in an online environment. This constitutes a great challenge for e-learning (Muilenburg & Berge, 2005). Although the authors did not explicitly focus on pedagogy as a subject of study, exploring such issues can allow insights into how pedagogy can be modified to fit the online context. Alongside social interaction, which is the dominant issue in this study, the findings demonstrate other significant challenges. Administrative and instructor-related issues entail a lack or delay of feedback and the lack of administrative support. Additionally, availability and support for online classes was also found to be of significant effect, as peer and the overall social attitudes tend to affect the user's own attitudes and use of online education (Beck & Treiman, 1996; Venkatesh et al, 2003...). Lastly, motivation was discussed in this case in relation to student's ability to avoid distraction and procrastination. In this case, it is worth mentioning that interaction and active learning can also be determining and influential motivational factors.

The lack of empirical studies outlining and designing a pedagogical model for online education is perceived as a downside. However, this opens up ground for future research opportunities (Rebolj, 2009). As the works discussed in this section entail, pedagogy is often viewed as a term which encompasses various fields, subject and ages. However, as the author discloses, pedagogical strategies must be tailored to the context in which they are implemented. In this case, Rebolj (2009) demonstrates this issue with the example of the online teaching of biology. In this case, the use of microscope proved challenging even with the use of an e-simulation program. This raises further concerns in terms of applying traditional practices online which remain dependent of the current level of technological advancement in this respect. Thus, this calls for two options. The first, as suggested by the author, consists of the use of blended learning. the latter consists of dealing with the theoretical aspects in an online environment while using in-person classes for the practical aspect. The second option in this case requires developing appropriate platforms which allow students to practice such activities. On this account, the author argues against the focus on theoretical aspects as pedagogy highly depends on practice, stating that "[n]evertheless, the theory cannot offer solutions to all the problems and cannot answer all the questions that arise in practice" (Rebolj, 2009, p.12). However, a set background of theory allows for strengthening and developing practice. On another hand, practice can be used as a background to infer theory, which later on can be tested and modified. Serdyukov (2015) stresses the importance of theory in this respect, asserting that "Online educators need a comprehensive, re-search-based, and consistent theory of online education offering a holistic and insightful view of the field without which there will be no quality teaching and learning" (p. 70). As the previous sections demonstrate, the field of education remains dynamic and all-inclusive of new strategies, curricula and technologies. This opens many grounds and further research in hopes of optimizing the effectiveness of learning, especially in relation to the implemented method and the online context.

To define the effectiveness of a method, Luscinski (2018) states that it is "a technique or methodology that has been shown by experience and/or research to lead to a desired result" (p.22). This may be an issue in regard to online pedagogy as there is little research on this account. This calls for more focus on a contextualized theoretical and conceptual framework that is applicable to real-life online learning environments.

Mathematics Teaching in Context

It is well established that Mathematics is a significant element of education, whether it being primary, secondary or higher. Not only that, but it also plays a crucial role in various fields such as health, technology, and economy which aid the development of countries, as well as the overall human knowledge and civilization. The Mathematics teaching and learning process remains faced with divergent challenges (Kusmaryono, 2014), of which the move to the online environment is a crucial area of concern. To better understand the latter, it is important to contextualize the theory and practice of online and offline mathematics teaching, specifically in the MENA region.

Mathematics Pedagogy Policy in Higher Education Through the MENA Region

As previously mentioned, Saudi Arabia has made many efforts to implement e-learning technologies, which remain heavily challenged. A main issue in this respect is deemed to be lack of preparation (Al-Wakeel, 2001). On this account Yamani (2014) conducted an experiment that consists of creating and implementing an e-learning platform specific to teaching mathematics in primary education. The website used for this study implemented active learning methods, including educational games, which address the issue of attention and concentration. The findings demonstrate the effectiveness of e-learning platforms in mathematics teaching when design and active learning strategies are considered. This study also highlights the learner's ability to learn at their pace, an aspect lacking in traditional education. However, it is important to note that primary level mathematics consists of simple concepts and constructs that can easily be translated to and applied online. This raises the question, does this also apply to higher education level teaching and learning of Mathematics? Although existing literature on this topic does not explicitly pose the question of pedagogy, the issues and challenges discussed provide great insights into existing pedagogical gaps. On this account, Alsmadi et al. (2021) underline the lack of interaction as an impeding factor of the effectiveness of learning management systems. Another issue in this context is that of e-assessment, which is the focal interest of Azmi, & Khoshaim's (2021) study. The latter utilized Web-Assign, a platform previously used by students and teachers for homework and assignment. This platform, after the outbreak of Co-vid, has been implemented as a tool for tests and assessment. The findings highlight the variance between auto-correction and manual correction, which entails that e-assessment is another aspect that needs to be developed, at least in the case of Saudi Arabia.

Similarly, the pandemic influenced the generalization of e-learning platforms for cautionary measures. During this period, Jourdan implemented distance learning using TV broadcasts of lessons and platforms such as Darsak. In terms of Mathematics online teaching, Alqiam (2021) explored the challenges facing primary students. Similar to Azmi, & Khoshaim' (2021), this study demonstrates the lack of reliability when concerned with e-assessment. Assessment is a crucial element of the educational system, thus having unreliable testing and assessment systems obscures educational objectives and students' progress. The authors also call attention to learners' individual educational needs, which, in the case of primary e-learning of mathematics, were unmet. This is mainly due to the lack of student-teacher contact, which results in a lack of feedback. This was also observed in the case of tenth-grade students using an online based platform for mathematics learning. Alomari (2009) reported that participants struggled with the lack and in some cases absence of teacher feedback, which is deemed to be a major contributing factor to the decrease in student motivation. In relation to pedagogy, students noted a lack of collaboration and active learning. This is mainly due to, according to this study, the teacher assuming the "lecturer" role and transmitting knowledge rather than collaboratively help built it. Contrastively, university students learning mathematics through the use of MOODLE (learning management system) and Zoom platform demonstrate higher mastery of mathematics skills (Alzubi, 2022). Although the authors did not explain this variance, the latter can be due to the accessibility of course material and lectures, which allows the students to go back and review the course any time without teacher guidance. However, it must be noted the participants of this study also preferred to have more teacher feedback and technical support.

As mentioned in the first section, the field of education is most affected in times of political conflict and civil unrest, as is the case in Syria. As infrastructure is also impacted, e-learning tends to be less prioritized. In this case, technical issues become the most significant impeding factor. In such circumstances, the only constant education Syrian students have access to is foreign. The population displacement has led many to seek refuge in neighboring countries. This creates a major barrier in terms of language, adaptation, and policy (Kaya & Ok, 2021). The authors highlight middle school mathematics and science teachers' struggles, out of which behavioral issues were most significant. More efforts were made in terms of higher education, as the country adopted SVU (Syrian Virtual University), which proved to significantly and positively impact learners' satisfaction (Al Azmeh, 2019). However, the author noted that technical issues, especially pertaining to e-service, remain a critical issue. These issues can also be observed in the case of Iraq, as both countries witness an ongoing political unrest. Providing an inclusive accessibility to e-learning technologies, whether it being for primary, secondary, or higher education, continues to be held back by the lack of infrastructure (Serin, 2022; Dhurgham, et al., 2011). It is important to note that, with safety being a priority, pedagogical issues are rarely a focal point of concern whether in terms of research or practice.

Another country facing infrastructure difficulties is Libya. As mentioned in section one, Libya has also witnessed civil unrest, leading to the displacement of civilians and the lack of accessibility to internet service. However, the Libyan government continues to make efforts to reform and enhance the quality and effectiveness of education. These efforts include implementing technology, especially in terms of higher education, and considering curricula to fit e-learning standards and needs (Andersson & Grönlund, 2009). As this process is still in its early stages, the body of research available on this topic rarely considers pedagogical strategies when concerned with the teaching of mathematics and science online. On this account, Bukhatowa et al. (2010) note the availability of free software allowing for the assistance of lessons and practice of mathematical concepts and theories. The country continues to have support from both internal (Ministry of education) and external (UNICEF) organizations to initiate technology adoption and accessibility. Similarly, Algeria has also witnessed the shift to online learning due to the pandemic, however, this implementation was not all-inclusive as many students did not have access to mobile learning technologies and internet. This is a common but crucial impeding factor which slows the technology incorporation and consequently hinders the development of scientific research, particularly pertaining to theory and practice of mathematics teaching.

As the previously discussed countries, Morocco continues to exert and explore technology implementation opportunities. The Moroccan government incorporated the E-TAKWINE platform which allows access to learning management systems such as MOODLE and provides distance learning to high-school and higher-education students. This was in collaboration with USAID, an international development agency based in the US. Despite such efforts, mathematics teachers struggle with a lack of tech support, IT training, and relevant resources (Brahim et al., 2014). In terms of higher education, it has been acknowledged that technology can aid not only as an e-learning tool but also pedagogically. El Jaoussi & Al Achhab (2013) highlight the importance of 3D technology use in the conceptualization, representation, and application of mathematical concepts. The authors also examine the implemented curricula and call attention to the need for its modification and/or design to fit the online context. Currently, the MathICs project, in partnership with Erasmus program, aims to provide sufficient infrastructure, training for teachers and staff, as well as pedagogies suitable for the teaching of Mathematics online (Kerello, 2021).

As discussed in this section, technology implementation in the MENA region is still at its beginning. This opens a wide range of educational research opportunities which, considering the fast pace of technology incorporation is highly needed. As the body of literature on this topic is limited when it comes to providing pedagogical models that serve the effectiveness of online mathematics teaching and learning.

SOLUTIONS AND RECOMMENDATIONS

The examination of the body of literature and research pertaining to the online teaching of mathematics provided insights into the challenges facing this incorporation. Based on the investigation of works on this topic in the MENA region, common factors impeding the effectiveness of online learning can be highlighted. The latter can be organized into two categories: institutional and pedagogical.

The institutional factors consist of governmental and organizational efforts which can include support, as well as accessibility of resources. A common issue encountered in this respect, whether in countries under political unrest or not, is that of digital inequality. Having access to mobile learning technologies and high-speed internet is basic but fundamental to the acceptance and use of technology. This calls for more funding as well as the creation of support program that help provide such technologies to students in need. This step is particularly detrimental in countries struggling with technological infrastructure due to conflict, which directly impacts education both as a field and practice. Along the same line, the lack of resources in terms of the professional development of teachers. As previously discussed the field of education is dynamic, thus educators must be up to date with new pedagogical research and theories. This deficit and, in some cases, absence limit teachers' ability to enhance their competence and practice, thus affecting the effectiveness of learning. Finally, a common challenge in this respect is that of tech support and training. Most universities in the MENA region have insufficient institutional support that allows for the training of teachers and students in terms of the platforms used for e-learning. This can impede students' motivation and the optimization of learning efficacy. These institutional elements must be first considered and fulfilled to allow for a successful digitalization of education.

Pedagogical factors entail challenges concerned with the practice of teaching mathematics online. In this respect, two major issues can be highlighted. With the recent fast-paced used of distance learning, many teachers maintained the role of a lecturer. This is important to consider as: "physical and logico-mathematical knowledge cannot be transferred intact from the mind of the teacher to the mind of learner" (Bodner, 1986, p.10). The latter is specific but not limited to teaching mathematics, as active learning methods have been proven to facilitate learning. additionally, mathematical constructs require a representation and application in order to be fully understood and mastered. This stems from Chevallard's didactic approach (1992), which: "considers mathematical objects, not as existing in itself, but as entities that emerge from practices in systems and institutions" (El Jaoussi & Al Achhab, 2013, p. 639). According to the examined literature, there remains a lack of available software and platforms that are able to properly do so. This calls for more efforts pertaining to IT and tech design not only in the context of the MENA region but worldwide.

Taking these issues into consideration, the following conceptual pedagogical model (Figure 1) is proposed. This model consists of a compilation of the most significant pedagogies and challenges pertaining to the online teaching of Mathematics in the MENA region. Active learning is at the core of the model due to its importance concerning achieving effective learning. An examination of literature on active learning demonstrates the abundance of its strategies. However, considering the MENA region and higher education, the lack of implementing goal setting, problem solving, as well as interaction and collaborative learning is an issue that needs addressing (Mehanna, 2004; Simuth &Schuller, 2012; Muilenburg & Berge, 2015). Thus, these elements are included as subset constituents of active learning in the model below. Moreover, teacher and student feedback are crucial elements of the learning process. As the model shows, establishing feedback and semiotic representation is especially crucial in the context of Mathematics e-learning. Without these elements, it would be challenging to efficiently practice active learning methods. It is important to note that instant feedback is of particular impact, as it increases students' motivation (Muilenburg & Berge, 2015). Specific to Mathematics context, the ability to achieve and practice semiotic representations and apply them to context allows for a better understanding of mathematical constructs and theories. However, as previously discussed, current technologies are still lagging behind in this respect. This calls for more efforts on the part of teachers and most importantly IT development agencies, whether governmental or private.

Figure 1. Pedagogical model for teaching mathematics online

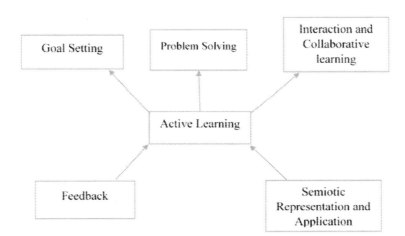

CONCLUSION

This chapter investigates the conceptual and practices of online implementation of pedagogy to teach mathematics in the MENA region. Through an examination of the progress level and challenges facing technology implementation and its ramifications on applied pedagogies. This work summarizes important issues to consider into two categories: institutional factors (digital inequality, availability of resources, and tech support/training) and pedagogical factors (representational application of mathematical constructs and active learning). Based on this a conceptual pedagogical model was proposed in hopes of encompassing pedagogies to be implemented for the effective teaching and learning of mathematics. This study may be limited due to its focus on the theoretical aspect and the lack of extensive empirical studies in this respect. However, this work hopes to entice further scientific questions on the matter as well as open ground for further empirical research.

REFERENCES

Ajzen, I., & Madden, T. J. (1986). Prediction of goal-directed behavior: Attitudes, intentions, and perceived behavioral control. *Journal of Experimental Social Psychology, 22*(5), 453–474. doi:10.1016/0022-1031(86)90045-4

Al Azmeh, S. (2019). The relationship between e-learning service and student satisfaction a case study at the Syrian virtual university (SVU). *Business. Management in Education, 17*(0), 49–71. doi:10.3846/bme.2019.7451

Al-Wakeel, S. (2001). Innovation in computer education. Curriculum for the computerization of Saudi Arabia: A model for developing countries. In *Proceedings from Frontiers in Education Conference (vol.3,* pp. 2–7).

Alayyar, G. M., Aljeeran, R. K., & Almodaires, A. A. (2018). Information and Communication Technology and Educational Policies in Primary and Secondary Education in the Middle East and North African (MENA) Region. *Springer International Handbooks of Education, 1–21.* Springer. doi:. doi:10.1007/978-3-319-53803-7_91

Albugamis, S., & Vian, A. (2015). Success factors for ICT implementation in Saudi Secondary schools: From the perspective of ICT directors head teachers, teachers and students [IJEDICT]. *International Journal of Education and Development Using Information and Communication Technology, 11*(1), 36–54.

Alexander, R. (2005). Culture, dialogue and learning: Notes on an emerging pedagogy (Keynote Address). *10th International Conference: Education, Culture and Cognition: intervening for growth, International Association for Cognitive Education and Psychology (IACEP).* University of Durham, United Kingdom.

Alexander, R. (2008). In Education for all, the quality imperative and the problem of pedagogy. Consortium for Research on Educational Access. Transitions and Equity.

Alfarah, M. & Bosco, A. (2016). The role of icts in rebuilding education in areas of armed conflicts: the syrian case. *Edulearn.* . doi:10.21125/edulearn.2016.0359

Almgadmi, N. Y. (2018). *Use of ICT in Secondary Schools in Libya: A Teachers' Perspective.* [Master's thesis, Eastern Mediterranean University (EMU)-Doğu Akdeniz Üniversitesi (DAÜ)].

Alomari, A. M. (2009). Investigating online learning environments in a web-based math course in Jordan. [IJEDICT]. *International Journal of Education and Development Using Information and Communication Technology, 5*(3), 19–36.

Alqiam, H. A. A. (2021). The challenges facing primary school students in Jordan in learning math online during the Coronavirus Crisis. *Journal of Arts, Literature. Humanities and Social Sciences, 64.* doi:10.33193/JALHSS.64.2021.421

Alshref, M. H., Abas, H., & Abu Bakar, N. A. (2021). The adoption of ICT in Libyan Higher Education Institutions (lheis): Theoretical models and challenges. *Journal of Physics: Conference Series, 1897*(1), 012003. doi:10.1088/1742-6596/1897/1/012003

Alsmadi, K. M., Al-Marashdeh, B., Alzaqebah, M., Jaradat, G., Alghamdi, F. A., Rami, M., Alshabanah, M., Alrajhi, D., Alkhaldi, H., Aldhafferi, N., Alqahtani, A., Badawi, U. A., & Tayfour, M. (2021). Digitalization of learning in Saudi Arabia during the COVID-19 outbreak: A survey. *Informatics in Medicine Unlocked, 25,* 100632. doi:10.1016/j.imu.2021.100632 PMID:34150983

Alyami, R. (2014). Educational Reform in the Kingdom of Saudi Arabia: Tatweer Schools as a Unit of Development. *Literacy Information and Computer Education Journal, 5*(2), 1515–1524. doi:10.20533/licej.2040.2589.2014.0202

Alzubi, K. A. (2022). The effect of teaching mathematics supported by e-learning platforms on the students' mathematical skills in a college course in Jordan. [IJET]. *International Journal of Emerging Technologies in Learning, 17*(12), 269–275. doi:10.3991/ijet.v17i12.30049

Anandarajan, M., Igbaria, M., & Anakwe, U. P. (2002). IT acceptance in a less-developed country: A motivational factor perspective. *International Journal of Information Management, 22*(1), 47–65. doi:10.1016/S0268-4012(01)00040-8

Andersson, A., & Gronlund, A. (2009). A Conceptual Framework for E-Learning in Developing Countries: A Critical Review of Research Challenges. *The Electronic Journal on Information Systems in Developing Countries, 38*(1), 1–16. doi:10.1002/j.1681-4835.2009.tb00271.x

Arvan, L. (1998). The SCALE efficiency projects. *Journal of Asynchronous Learning Networks, 2,* 2.

Azmi, F. M., & Khoshaim, H. B. (2021). The COVID-19 pandemic and the challenges of E-assessment of calculus courses in higher education: A case study in Saudi Arabia. *International Journal of Learning. Teaching and Educational Research, 20*(3), 265–281. doi:10.26803/ijlter.20.3.16

Bahri, H., El Mlili, N., Akande, O. N., Abdel-ilah, K., & Madrane, M. (2021). Dataset of Moroccan nursing students' intention to use and accept information and communication technologies and social media platforms for learning. *Data in Brief, 37*, 107230. doi:10.1016/j.dib.2021.107230 PMID:34179321

Beck, K. H., & Treiman, K. A. (1996). The relationship of social context of drinking, perceived social norms, and parental influence to various drinking patterns of adolescents. *Addictive Behaviors, 21*(5), 633–644. doi:10.1016/0306-4603(95)00087-9 PMID:8876762

Bodner, G. (1986). Constructivism: A Theory of Knowledge. *Journal of Chemical Education, 63*(10), 873. doi:10.1021/ed063p873

Brahim, N., Mohamed, B., Abdelwahed, N., Ahmed, L., Radouane, K., Khalid, S., & Mohammed, T. (2014). The use of the internet in Moroccan high schools mathematics teaching: State and Perspectives. *Procedia: Social and Behavioral Sciences, 116*, 5175–5179. doi:10.1016/j.sbspro.2014.01.1095

Bransford, J. D., Brown, A. L., & Cocking, R. R. (2000). *How People Learn: Brain, Mind, Experience, and School*. National Academy Press.

Bukhatowa, B. Porter, A. & Nelson, M. I. (2010). *Emulating the Best Technology in Teaching and Learning Mathematics: Challenges Facing Libyan Higher Education* (Working Paper). https://ro.uow.edu.au/cssmwp/97

Chevallard, Y. (1992). Fundamentals of didactics: Perspectives made by an anthropological approach. *Research in Mathematics Education, 12*(1), 73–112.

Cziesielski, M. J. (2020). Andragogy: The Art of Effectively Teaching Adults. *Limnology and Oceanography Bulletin, 29*(1), 29–30. doi:10.1002/lob.10358

Dewey, J. (1916). *Democracy and Education: An Introduction to the Philosophy of Education*. Free Press.

Dewey, J. (1993). *How We Think: A Restatement of the Relation of Reflective Thinking to the Educative Process*. D. C. Heath.

Dhurgham, A., Kadhim, T. A., Qasim, R. M., & Abid, A. (2011). E-learning in Iraq: Challenges and Opportunities. *International Conference on Teaching and Learning Education*. Research Gate.

Disterveg, A. (1956). *Rukovodstvo k obrazovaniyu nemeskix uchiteley. Izbranniye pedagogicheskiye sochineniye* [A guide to the education of German teachers. Selected pedagogical essays]. Uchpegdiz.

El Hammoumi, S., Zerhane, R., & Janati Idrissi, R. (2022). The impact of using interactive animation in biology education at Moroccan universities and students' attitudes towards animation and ICT in general. *Social Sciences & Humanities Open*, 6(1), 100293. doi:10.1016/j.ssaho.2022.100293

El Jaoussi, Z., & Al Achhab, S. (2013). *The mathematics in Moroccan universities. 1st Annual International Interdisciplinary Conference*, Azores, Portugal.

Elkhayma, R. (2021). Distant Learning in Morocco: Examining students' attitudes and motivation at the tertiary level. *International Journal of English Literature and Social Sciences, 6*(3), 001–009. . doi:10.22161/ijels.63.1

Fahim, J., Brammer, D., & Elass, R. (2017, April 20). *Experiences of creating e-learning programs in the Middle East*. Middle East Institute. https://www.mei.edu/publications/experiences-creating-e-learning-programs-middle-east

Feldman, J., & Mcphee, D. (2008). *The science of learning and the art of teaching* (1st ed.). Thomson Delmar Cengage Learning.

Gedeon, S. & Al-Qasem, L. (2019). *Jordan's ICT Sector Analysis* and *Strategy* for *Sectoral Improvement*: GIZ *Jordan*. Employment-oriented MSME Promotion Project (MSME).

Gherbi, M. (2015). ICT and the reality in Algeria. *International Academic Conference on Education, Teaching and E-learning*, (IAC-ETeL 2015), Prague, Volume: ISBN 978-80-88085-01-0

Greenberg, D. (1987). Teaching Justice through Experience. *Journal of Experiential Education, 10*(1), 46–47. doi:10.1177/105382598701000112

Hajji, A. K. (2018). ICT in Education System: Comparing Morocco and Korea. *Sun Moon Islam Center.*, 7, 2018.

Hamdy, A. (2007). *ICT in Education in Libya. Survey of ICT and education in Africa: Libya Country Report*. Libya Government.

Ho, H. C. Y., Poon, K.-T., Chan, K. K., Cheung, S. K., Datu, J. A., & Tse, C. Y. (2023). Promoting preservice teachers' psychological and pedagogical competencies for online learning and teaching: The T.E.A.C.H. program. *Computers &amp. Computers & Education, 195*, 104725. doi:10.1016/j.compedu.2023.104725

Jouicha, A. I., Berrada, K., Bendaoud, R., Machwate, S, Miraoui, A. & Burgos, D. (2020). Starting MOOCs in African University: The Experience of Cadi Ayyad University, Process, Review, Recommendations, and Prospects. *IEEE Access*. IEEE. . doi:10.1109/ACCESS.2020.2966762

Kansanen, P., & Meri, M. (1999). The didactic relation in the teaching-studying-learning process. *TNTEE Publications.*, *2*, 107–116.

Kaya, D., & Ok, G. (2021). Problems encountered by mathematics and science teachers in classrooms where Syrian students under temporary protection status are educated and suggestions for solution. *International Journal of Contemporary Educational Research*, *8*(1), 111–127. doi:10.33200/ijcer.774094

Kenan, T., Pislaru, C., Elzawi, A., & Restoum, M. (2013). Improving the effectiveness of collaborative learning processes in Libyan Higher Education. *8th International Conference for Internet Technology and Secured Transactions* (ICITST-2013) (pp. 411- 416). IEEE.

Kerello, C. (2021). *Mathics - strengthening mathematics education by the use of icts in Morocco*. Centrale Nantes. https://www.ec-nantes.fr/erasmus/key-action-2-cooperation-for-innovation-and-the-exchange-of-good-practices/mathics-strengthening-mathematics-education-by-the-use-of-icts-in-morocco

Khalaf, B., & Zin, M. Z. (2018). Traditional and Inquiry-Based Learning Pedagogy: A Systematic Critical Review. *International Journal of Instruction*, *11*(4), 545–564. doi:10.12973/iji.2018.11434a

Knowles, M. S. (1980). *The modern practice of adult education: From pedagogy to andragogy*. Association Press.

Kozma, R. B. (2008). Comparative analysis of policies for ICT in education. In J. Voogt & G. Knezek (Eds.), *International handbook of information technology in primary and secondary education* (pp. 1083–1096). Springer. doi:10.1007/978-0-387-73315-9_68

Kusmaryono, I. (2014). The importance of mathematical power in mathematics learning. *International Conference on Mathematics, Science, and Education*.

Luscinski, A. (2018). Best practices in adult online learning. *Dissertation Abstracts International. A, The Humanities and Social Sciences*.

Machwate, S., Echajari, L., Bendaoud, R., Berrada, K., & Daadaoui, L. (2023). *Pedagogical Innovation Centres*. Precursor for Research in Educational Sciences Promotion in Moroccan Higher Education. doi:10.2991/978-2-38476-036-7_4

Makki, S. & Hanna, K.Y. (2011). Iraq ICT Situation and its effect on Iraq Rebuilding: Study, Analysis, and Suggestion. *Journal of Madenat Alelem college, 3*(2), 57-70.

Marzano, R. (2001) Analyzing two assumptions underlying the scoring of classroom assessments. SuDoc (ED 1.310/2:447169).

Matar, N., Hunaiti, Z., Halling, S., & Matar, Š. (2010). E-learning acceptance and challenges in the Arab Region. In S. Abdallah & F. Albadri (Eds.), *ICT acceptance, investment and organization: Cultural practices and values in the arab world* (pp. 184–200). Information Science Reference. doi:10.4018/978-1-60960-048-8.ch013

Mehanna, W. (2004). E-pedagogy: The pedagogies of e-learning. *Research in Learning Technology, 12*(3). Advance online publication. doi:10.3402/rlt.v12i3.11259

Menchaca, M., & Khwaldeh, N. (2014). Barriers to utilizing ICT in education in Jordan. *International Journal on E-Learning, 13*, 127–155.

Merriam, S. B., & Caffarella, R. S. (1991). *Learning in adulthood: a comprehensive guide*. Jossey-Bass Publishers.

Miles, R., Al-Ali, S., Charles, T., Hill, C., & Bligh, B. (2021). Technology enhanced learning in the MENA region: Introduction to the special issue. *Issue 1.2 Technology Enhanced Learning in the MENA Region, 1*(2). doi:10.21428/8c225f6e.df527b9d

Mitra, S. (2007). *Sugata Mitra: Kids Can Teach Themselves* [Video File]. TED. https://www.ted.com/talks/sugata_mitra_shows_how_kids_teach_themselves

Mödritscher, F. (2006). E-Learning Theories in Practice: A Comparison of three Methods. *Journal of Universal Science and Technology of Learning, 0*(0), 3–18.

Morin, A. (2012). Encyclopedia of Human Behavior. Inner Speech. 436–443. doi:10.1016/B978-0-12-375000-6.00206-8

Muilenburg, L. Y., & Berge, Z. L. (2005). Student barriers to online learning: A factor analytic study. *Distance Education, 26*(1), 29–48. doi:10.1080/01587910500081269

Ouajdouni, A., Chafik, K., & Boubker, O. (2021). Measuring e-learning systems success: Data from students of higher education institutions in Morocco. *Data in Brief, 35*, 106807. doi:10.1016/j.dib.2021.106807 PMID:33604428

Pew, S. (2007). Andragogy and Pedagogy as Foundational Theory for Student Motivation in Higher Education. *InSight: A Journal of Scholarly Teaching, 2*. . doi:10.46504/02200701pe

Pollard, A. (2002). Readings for Reflective Teaching. (2ndEd.). London, UK: Continuum International Publishing Group.

Qaddour, K., & Husain, S. (2022). *Syria's education crisis: a sustainable approach after 11 years of conflict.* Middle East Institute.

Rachal, J. R. (2002). Andragogy's detectives: A critique of the present and proposal for the future. *Adult Education Quarterly, 52*(3), 210–227. doi:10.1177/0741713602052003004

Raddad, B. & Etlib, A. & Nuseir, N. (2018). *Implementing e-learning in the Libyan Open University.* Research Gate.

Rashty, D. (1999). *Traditional learning vs. eLearning.* Dostopno na.

Rebolj, V. (2009). E-education between pedagogical and didactic theory and practice. *Organizacija, 42*(1), 10–16. doi:10.2478/v10051-008-0027-1

Riskulova, K., & Yuldashova, U. (2020). The role of didactics in teaching process. *Theoretical & Applied Science., 85*(5), 786–792. doi:10.15863/TAS.2020.05.85.146

Russell, A. L., & Greenberg, D. A. (2008). *Turning learning right side up: Putting education back on track.* Wharton School Pub.

Schmidt, S., Dickerson, J. & Kisling, E. (2010). From Pedagogy to Andragogy: Transitioning Teaching and Learning in the Information Technology Classroom. *Integrating Adult Learning and Technologies for Effective Education: Strategic Approaches.* 63-81. . doi:10.4018/978-1-61520-694-0.ch004

Schneuwly, B. (2011). *Subject Didactics: An Academic Field Related to the Teacher Profession and Teacher Education.* JSTOR. . doi:10.2307/j.ctvhktksh.20

Serdyukov, P. (2015). Does Online Education Need a Special Pedagogy? *CIT. Journal of Computing and Information Technology, 23*(1), 61–74. doi:10.2498/cit.1002511

Serin, H. (2022). Challenges and opportunities of e-learning in secondary school in Iraq. *International Journal of Social Sciences &Educational Studies.*

Shah, R. (2021). Revisiting Concept Definition and Forms of Pedagogy. *IJARIIE-ISSN(O)*-2395-4396.

Simuth, J., & Schuller, S. I. (2012). Principles for e-pedagogy. *Procedia: Social and Behavioral Sciences, 46*, 4454–4456. doi:10.1016/j.sbspro.2012.06.274

Sousa, D. (2014). *How the Brain Learns Mathematics.* Korwin.

Stairs, A. (1995). Learning processes and teaching roles in Native education: Cultural base and cultural brokerage. In M. Battiste & J. Barman (Eds.), *First Nations education in Canada: The circle unfolds.* University of British Columbia Press.

Sulaiman, T. T. (2023). A systematic review on factors influencing learning management system usage in Arab Gulf countries. *Education and Information Technologies*. Advance online publication. doi:10.100710639-023-11936-w PMID:37361806

Sultanov, T. M. (2022). Traditional and Progressive Pedagogical Approaches in Primary Education. *International Journal of Innovative Research in Science, Engineering and Technology, 11*, 2343–2346. doi:10.15680/IJIRSET.2022.1102052

Thair, K., & Marini, O. (2012). *A development of an ICT transformation framework for Iraqi schools (ICTIS). Proceedings National Graduate Conference 2012 (NatGrad2012)*. Universiti Tenaga Nasional, Putrajaya Campus.

Thowfeek, M. H., & Jaafar, A. (2011). Pedagogical approach to design an e-learning courseware. *2011 International Conference on Pattern Analysis and Intelligence Robotics*. IEEE. 10.1109/ICPAIR.2011.5976927

Venkatesh, V., Morris, M. G., Davis, G. B., & Davis, F. D. (2003). User acceptance of information technology: Toward a unified view. *Management Information Systems Quarterly, 27*(3), 425–478. doi:10.2307/30036540

Vygotsky, L. (1978). Interaction between learning and development. *Readings on the development of children, 23*(3), 34-41.

Weber, A. S., & Hamlaoui, S. (2018). *E-learning in the Middle East and North Africa (MENA) region*. Springer International Publishing. doi:10.1007/978-3-319-68999-9

Wilson, L., & Sipe, St. (2014). A Comparison of Active Learning and Traditional Pedagogical Styles in a Business Law Classroom. *Journal of Legal Studies Education, 31*(1), 89–105. Advance online publication. doi:10.1111/jlse.12010

Yamani, H. (2014). E-learning in Saudi Arabia. *Journal of Information Technology and Application in Education, 3*(4), 169. doi:10.14355/jitae.2014.0304.10

Zoric, V. (2019). *History of Education as a Scientific Pedagogical Discipline and a Teaching Subject – Past*. Present and Perspectives.

KEY TERMS AND DEFINITIONS

Active Learning: This refers to the learning process in which the learner has agency. In other words, the learner has more control and is more engaged in his/her learning journey.

Behavioral Intention: Constitutes of the factors relating to the intent of performing a particular behavior. The measurement of this variable allows for the prediction of the likelihood of the behavior in question occurring.

Didactics: A field of study that focuses on the knowledge and skill of teaching. It provides the theoretical background pertaining to teaching a particular subject. Didactics focuses more on teachers' skill and knowledge rather than students' learning strategies and approaches.

E-Learning: This entails any formal or informal learning conducted on an online platform.

Pedagogy: This refers to the theory and practice of teaching. It combines learning theories, teaching approaches and strategies.

Semiotic Representation: This is, in the context of Mathematics, the representation of abstract concept into symbols.

STEM Education: It is commonly known that STEM stands for science, technology, engineering and math. However, STEM education is not only learning such subject separately, but it can also be viewed as an approach of building and applying knowledge.

Chapter 2
STEM in Turkey:
Initiatives, Implementations, and Failures

Ahmet Baytak
Independent Researcher, Turkey

ABSTRACT

The concept of STEM has gained extensive usage in Turkey after gaining popularity worldwide. The need for improvement in mathematics performance, as indicated by low PISA results, prompted the implementation of math-integrated education models within the Turkish Education System. This chapter aims to outline the system's impact on the implementation of STEM. Notably, the FATIH project has played a crucial role by equipping schools with modern technologies and distributing tablets to students. The contribution of the science centers is discussed. Science centers serve as a promising starting point for fostering STEM studies. However, significant obstacles to the implementation of the STEM model in Turkey lie in the high school entrance and university placement exam systems. These obstacles will be explained in detail within this chapter. Additionally, this section will explore the failures of the STEM approach and provide suggestions for its successful implementation. Moreover, the authors propose exploring the applicability of an Augmented STEM system to further enhance STEM education.

DOI: 10.4018/978-1-6684-6883-8.ch002

1 BACKGROUND AND OVERVIEW OF STEM EDUCATION IN TURKEY

1.1 Demographics of Turkey

It is a multifaceted situation for countries or societies to utilize different education models or technologies. The economic situation, cultural landscape, and political structure of a country are important factors in the selection and implementation of a system and technology within the education systems. This situation becomes even more significant for countries with multicultural and rich historical backgrounds, such as Turkey. Thus, before delving into the details of STEM usage in Turkey[1], it is necessary to briefly explain the economic situation, political structure, cultural dynamics, and educational status of the country.

1.1.1 Cultural Structure

Although the Republic of Turkey was founded in 1923, its lands have hosted various states and empires throughout history. After the Turks migrated to Anatolia from the Central Asian region in 1071 and embraced Islam, they established powerful states such as the Seljuk and Ottoman Empires. Through these conquests, Turkish society coexisted with communities in Anatolia, Arabia, and Africa, resulting in the reshaping of Turkish culture under the influence of Islamic civilization. The Ottoman conquests in European lands, starting in the 14th century, further expanded Turkish cultural structures. Following the establishment of the modern Turkish state, the main ethnic groups residing within its borders were Turks, Kurds, Arabs, Armenians, Greeks, and other minorities. While some minority communities have experienced a decline in the use of their languages and preservation of their cultures, others continue to thrive. Additionally, in the wake of rapid Westernization movements and the modernizing world, Turkish society has aspired to become culturally aligned with Europe (Mutlu, 1995).

In terms of religious belief, the majority of the population identifies as Muslims. Islamic customs have become an integral part of the culture for most of society. Historically, the rural population constituted the majority but, especially after 1980, economic and social reasons prompted a significant migration of people from rural areas to mega cities, particularly Istanbul and Izmir. This migration movement has given rise to a new sociological and cultural mass in Turkey over the past quarter-century (Baytak, 2014). The emerging cultural structure within this mass can also influence the society's perspective on education and technology.

1.1.2 Politics and Economic Situations

The Ottoman Empire was ruled by sultans from the Ottoman family. However, with the establishment of the Republic, administrative elements such as the 'sultan' and the 'caliph' were abolished, and a new form of government based on elections came to the forefront. While the early stages of the republic witnessed a one-party system, it later transitioned to a multi-party system. In the 2018 elections, the parliamentary system was abolished, and a presidential system was introduced. Under this presidential system, the office of the president comprises members of parliament, and the government consists of party deputies. The presidency is responsible for enacting all laws, amendments, and appointments related to education and science.

1.1.3 Turkish Education System

The Turkish education system has undergone numerous changes throughout history due to historical and political transformations. The madrasah system, which provided combined religious and science education, was abolished with the establishment of the Republic in 1923. During this period, the use of Latin letters replaced Arabic letters through the alphabet revolution. These changes significantly affected the philosophical, sociological, and pedagogical aspects of the country's educational structure. While it made it challenging for children to benefit from older books, it also posed difficulties for the older generation to adapt to new resources. However, the transition to the Latin alphabet marked a crucial step towards the 'Westernization' pursued during the republican period (Maralli, 2019).

While there haven't been radical changes in the later years of the Republic, different governments have implemented varying education policies. Over the past 20 years, the education system in Turkey has undergone significant changes, even with the change of the Minister of Education. The current Turkish education system, addressed in this book chapter, consists of three stages: 12-year compulsory education, which includes kindergarten and university education. It is organized into four-year primary school, four-year secondary school, and four-year high school.

Primary school, the initial level of education, is compulsory for all students. Secondary school, although compulsory, offers a choice between regular secondary schools and İmam-Hatip secondary schools, which focus on religious education. High school education encompasses different fields. Alongside general education high schools, known as Anatolian high schools, there are İmam-Hatip high schools, Fen Lisesi which is based on science and math, Sosyal Bilgiler Lisesi which is based on social sciences, and Spor and Sanat Lisesi which are based on sports and art. Admission to these schools is based on examinations. Students who cannot be placed in their preferred schools are assigned to Anatolian high schools based on their address. Moreover, vocational high schools and technology schools offer vocational education, where students receive technical courses in addition to basic subjects, according to their program.

Since the late period of the Ottoman Empire, private schools established by foreign countries have gained prevalence in Turkey. Today, private schools are in high demand, particularly after elementary school, as students seek admission to prestigious high schools. Private high schools, also known as collages, are popular alternatives to public education. They are categorized as either Anatolian High Schools or Science High Schools. Similarly, post-secondary students must take a general exam to gain admission to reputable universities.

Apart from private schools, families often enroll their children in private education centers to supplement their lessons, excel in high school entrance exams, or secure admission to esteemed universities. These informal education institutions are typically located within neighborhoods and consist of several classrooms. Their number has increased in recent years.

Completion of high school education in Turkey is not obligatory. Students have two options to continue their education: vocational school or university. To gain admission to these institutions, students must pass two separate exams held simultaneously nationwide. Placement is based on exam performance and students' university preferences. Vocational schools offer two-year programs across various fields such as health, technical, social, and agriculture. In addition to education, these schools aim to provide qualified personnel in respective industries through short-term internships. University education is divided into different departments, as is common worldwide. Medical faculties require six years of study, while veterinary, pharmacy, and dentistry programs take five years. Other fields typically have duration of four years. However, some universities offer one year of compulsory or optional foreign language education, primarily English (but Arabic for divinity faculties).

In Turkey, both the public and private education systems are overseen by the Ministry of National Education (MNE). Its structure and functions may vary under different governments. Similarly, the Higher Education Institution (HEI or YÖK), is responsible for organizing university education in Turkey, has faced constant criticism from university students since its establishment. This institution oversees the appointment of university staff and manages universities. Some applications and rector appointments mandated by the institution have been subjects of debate in different periods (Baytak, 2009).

1.1.4 The Examination System and the Role of Teachers

The Turkish education system differs from the education systems of Western countries due to the country's economic structure and level of development. In countries like the USA or Germany, students have a wide range of job opportunities in various professions. However, in Turkey, especially in recent years, there is a trend where students predominantly focus on fields like medicine, as they provide more assured employment prospects. Consequently, there is higher demand than expected in fields such as medicine. To ensure fair distribution of opportunities amidst this demand, the country implemented an exam system where all students take the same test simultaneously. Although the names of these exams have changed over the years, they generally serve the same purpose. A similar situation occurs in high school entrance exams. Since 'science high schools' that perform well in university entrance exams are highly sought after, a nationwide simultaneous exam is conducted in the final year of secondary school to fairly allocate students to these schools. Through this exam, students can secure a place in these limited-capacity schools in each province. Additionally, apart from the central examination, another criterion is considered for students to be placed in reputable high schools or their desired university programs (such as skill tests in areas like music, painting, and sports).

The existence of the central examination system in Turkey brings challenges in terms of selection and evaluation. To ensure a fair selection and evaluation in the university entrance exam, which approximately three million students take each year, the results must be evaluated quickly (within approximately three weeks). Considering that these exams take place in June, towards the end of the academic year, and students make their university choices and placements based on their scores, it is necessary for the exam to be assessed promptly. Hence, the central exams in Turkey are conducted only as multiple-choice tests. Although some politicians made promises to include questions with short answers and analytical components, these promises were never implemented.

In contrast, countries like the USA consider factors beyond standardized exams (such as the SAT) when placing students into universities or specific departments. A student's previous projects, high school activities, or community service involvements are also considered for university admission. Since the only criterion to enter a university is the state-wide exam, the students in Turkey may see STEM or other similar social and extracurricular activities unnecessary.

The education system in Turkey revolves around the examination system as an educational practice and the assumption that good job opportunities are only available in certain fields (Tarman, 2016). This is especially evident in the 8th grade, where the high school entrance exam is held, and in the 12th grade, where the university entrance exam takes place. Students primarily focus their studies on preparing for these exams, leading to a de facto curriculum that is heavily exam-oriented. Although the national education curriculum includes STEM and other diverse courses, the actual course structures and content are often limited to what is relevant for the exams, driven by the demands of students and parents (Durmuşoğlu & Yıldız Taşdemir,

2022). The content of the exams varies depending on the fields that students aim to enter. For instance, students aspiring to pursue Medicine need to answer questions focused on Science and Mathematics, while those interested in the field of law must tackle questions related to Turkish and Mathematics.

Significant changes have been made to the question structure of these exams in recent years. Since Turkey has achieved low scores in international assessments such as the PISA (Program for International Student Assessment) and TIMSS exams (Trends in International Mathematics and Science Study), a new question type called 'next generation questions' has been gradually introduced in central exams across the country since 2017. These 'next generation questions' tend to be more complex than previous exam questions, often involving long reading texts or info graphics that require students to understand and analyze the information provided. As these question types were not common in primary school education, students may feel anxious during exams (Karabulut et al., 2022). From an educational perspective, it is desirable that these questions focus on interpretation rather than memorization. To solve these new question types, students need to engage in processes such as assimilation and reasoning. Introducing these question types in the exam system has partially aligned the questions with STEM-based content. For example, a Turkish language question may involve analyzing the process of an experiment, or a mathematics question may require detailed calculations for a project. It is believed that students with applied STEM education find it easier to understand and solve these types of questions. Further academic studies are needed to support this argument.

PISA scores indicate that student success in Turkey varies across different years. While Turkey's average score increased in some years, it subsequently decreased in others. In the latest PISA 2018 test, approximately 600,000 students from 79 countries, representing 32 million students in the age group of 15, participated. The average PISA score in Science is 489. According to the results of this exam, Turkey scored below the average. A similar pattern emerged in the fields of mathematics and reading. When examining the results of international exams that measure knowledge in STEM disciplines, Turkey consistently obtains lower scores compared to countries with a strong STEM policy (Ay & Seferoğlu, 2021).

Turkey's 2015 TIMSS report shows that students had improvement in mathematics and science but still remained below the TIMSS average (Mullis et al., 2016). There may be many reasons for this development, as well as the effect of reorganizing the 'science' course as a 'science and technology' course in recent years. It may reflect the effect of STEM activities in these courses on the success of students in TIMSS and PISA tests.

The need in the field of education has emerged in parallel with the concerns about raising the qualified workforce of the future (Badmus & Jita, 2022). However, the fact that Turkey is ranked lower than other countries in the PISA and TIMMS exams, which are international assessment studies, has created the need for innovation in the field of education in the context of our country's development and existence in international competition. As a result of the developments, the MNE published a roadmap for the integration of STEM education in 2016 (Yıldırım & Gelmez, 2020).

1.2 Stem in Turkey

1.2.1 Early Stages of Stem in Turkey

With the collapse of the Ottoman Empire and the later established Republic in Turkey, several social revolutions took place. As a result of the effects of these revolutions and a society that emerged from the war, there was a serious shortage of teachers in the country. At the request of Atatürk, the American educational philosopher John Dewey was invited to Turkey and he was asked to prepare reports on the Turkish Education System. Due to the majority of the rural population in this period, Dewey proposed an education reform that would make rural schools the center of community life. Within the scope of this education reform, the first 'village institute' was opened in 1940 to train primary school teachers. Teachers trained in these schools were expected to be both school teachers and community educators. In these institutions, the training of teachers started with helping in the construction of buildings, hoeing fields or pruning trees, etc. In this way, teacher candidates began to learn by living (Kaya, 2022). An individual who graduated from the village institute was learning the subjects of agriculture, health, masonry, blacksmithing, tailoring, fishing, beekeeping, viticulture and carpentry in addition to being a teacher. These educational institutions, which were successful in the early stages of education, can be considered as the first institutions where STEM education was implemented in Turkey. The fact that all of these institutes had their own agricultural lands and workshops provided the most basic condition for the applied education required for STEM. However, these institutions got closed within the scope of the economic development plans made to get rid of the economic stalemate between 1946 and 1948 (Akgündüz & Ertepınar, 2015).

The chronology of implications related to STEM education in Turkey is not straight forward. However, to provide an overview of the timeline, the following timeline can be a guideline to understand the keystones of STEM in Turkey (Çavaş et al, 2020).

Figure 1. Timeline of some key changes about STEM and STEM education in Turkey

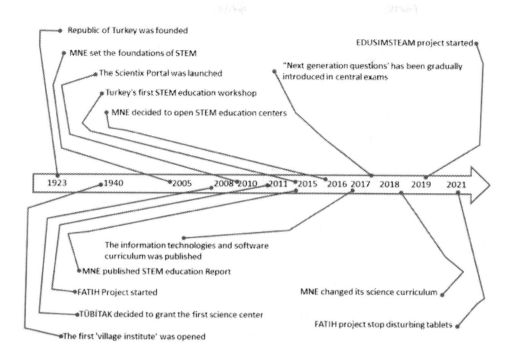

1.2.2 STEM Policies

With the renewal of the curriculum in 2005 by the MNE, the foundations of STEM, which is an interdisciplinary approach, were laid in the Science and Technology course curriculum. In order to change the negative perceptions developed for mathematics and science courses in schools and professions related to these fields, STEM understanding has entered the Turkish education literature (Arslan & Arastaman, 2021). In the STEM Education Report prepared by the MNE in Turkey in 2016, the steps to be taken for STEM education were included and the establishment of STEM Education centers, conducting STEM education research in cooperation with universities in these centers, training teachers to adopt the STEM education approach, and curricula to include STEM education. Plans have been prepared to update the curriculum, to create teaching environments for STEM education in schools and to provide course materials (Gökçe Tekin, 2022; MEB, 2016).

According to the information technologies and software curriculum published in January 2017; It has been planned and programmed to be able to teach the lesson with the initiative of the teacher during the free activity times between the 1st and 4th grades, as compulsory two course hours per week in the 5th and 6th grades, and two course hours per week as optional in the 7th and 8th grades (Olgun, 2021). Based on the international need analyzes for STEM education, preparations have been made in Turkey by universities and institutions such as TUBITAK and MEB to make STEM popular in the country (Olgun, 2021).

1.2.3 How is 'STEM' perceived in Turkey?

STEM is a hot topic that has been used a lot in recent years. It is frequently used and promoted by a wide range of people, from education to business and policy makers (Bybee, 2013). In Turkey, which is in the category of developing countries, this concept is overused. Although the definition of this concept is simply Science and Technology Engineering and Math, its usage or meaning can sometimes be different. In the following, after giving the perspectives on which the concept of STEM is examined in the field of education, depending on the literature, it explains how this concept is perceived in the reports written in Turkey.

Looking at the definitions made about STEM in Turkey, different interpretations have been made. According to the report published by the MNE, which is the most important institution in the implementation of STEM, STEM education has been accepted as an interdisciplinary approach that covers the entire education process from pre-school education to higher education (MEB, 2016). However, in the report prepared by PwC Turkey and the Turkish Industry and Business Association (TUSIAD), which is the most important non-governmental organization report on STEM studies in Turkey, STEM fields were emphasized and job opportunities and graduate status in these fields were examined at length. According to this report, STEM education is very important in terms of enabling the transformation of theoretical knowledge into practice, product and new inventions. STEM education provides the development of behaviors such as trial and error, learning by doing, questioning, research and invention, which are necessary strategies to increase the quality of workforce in the world. This will serve for production, R&D, innovation, technical infrastructure and process development and closing the qualified workforce gap in the labor market (TUSIAD, 2014). However, in the interpretation made about this STEM, the application of STEM in the country was interpreted by looking at the number of graduates in the fields of Science, Technology, Engineering and Mathematic in general. Contrary to the existing literature, the statistics of graduating or starting a job separately from these fields have been interpreted as STEM success statistics.

In another definition, Yıldırım and Altun (2015) interpreted STEM as the integration of courses. Akgündüz and Ertenpınar (2015), on the other hand, based on the definition made by Bybee (2010), evaluated STEM as a phenomenon that enables the integration of lessons with each other by collaborating interdisciplinary, instead of using four disciplines separately. According to these researchers, a real STEM education is an education that enables individuals to understand how tools, equipment and mechanisms work, and increases individuals' use of technology.

1.2.4 How STEM Became Important in Turkey

With the developing technology and the globalizing world, the expectations of the societies from education have changed. Especially in the last quarter century, the goal of raising citizens with 21st century skills has been expressed by many countries. Likewise, employees are expected to have these skills (Ay & Seferoğlu, 2021). Although 21st century skills may vary in different sources, basically the following skills are listed; critical thinking, communication skills, creativity, problem solving, perseverance, collaboration, information literacy and technology skills. When an effective STEM education is carried out, it is expected that these desired skills will be gained by the students. In this context, STEM education has gained importance in Turkey recently.

In the curriculum that started to be implemented in Turkey in the 2013-2014 academic year, the evaluation of student achievement based on instant performance was abandoned and a process-oriented evaluation integrated with the learning process was preferred (MEB, 2016). One of the most important factors for the Ministry to set such a target is the failure of Turkey to achieve the expected results in exams such as TIMSS and PISA. Thus, the MNE included the objectives of strengthening STEM in its 2015-2019 Strategic Plan (MEB, 2019).

2 THE FATIH PROJECT AND ITS CONTRIBUTIONS TO STEM EDUCATION IN TURKEY

2.1 STEM Implementations

Bringing the concept of STEM to education in international literature and putting this concept into practice in Turkey have been different. Especially with the development of internet technologies, the name of the '*Science*' course in Turkey was changed to '*Science and Technology*' in 2005 by the MNE and the content of this course was rearranged (MEB, 2006). After the increasing need and interest in STEM education in Turkey, STEM centers have started to be established by different universities, the first of which was in 2009 (Ergül, 2020).

In 2015, Turkey's first STEM education workshop was held and the '*STEM education Turkey Report*' was published. In the report, the activities carried out in Turkey in the field of STEM education were included and it was stated that in the exams held by the Measurement, Selection and Placement Center (ÖSYM) between 2000 and 2014, there was a decrease in the placement rate of the first thousand students who were placed in universities in numerical fields. At the end of the report, Turkey's need for STEM education was emphasized and a 16-item proposal package was presented for STEM education (Akgündüz & Ertepınar, 2015). In the STEM education report prepared by the MNE in 2016, a model proposal was made for the transition to STEM education in Turkey, issues such as the establishment of STEM education centers, conducting STEM education research, training teachers for STEM education approach, updating the curriculum according to STEM education were emphasized (Ergül, 2020; MEB, 2016). An update was made in the Science Curriculum by the MNE in 2017, and the '*Science and Engineering Applications*' unit was added for STEM education from the 4th to the 8th grades. '*Engineering and Design Skills*' has been added to the skill learning area of the program. The FTTC (Science-Technology-Society-Environment) learning area of the program was updated as FMTTÇ (Science-Engineering Technology-Society-Environment) by adding Engineering (Ergül, 2020). In 2018, the '*Science and Engineering Applications*' unit removed from the education program and replaced with '*Science, Engineering and Entrepreneurship Applications*' (Ergül, 2020).

2.2 STEM Activities Conducted by MNE

Although there is no direct action plan prepared by the MNE for STEM education in Turkey, there are aims to strengthen STEM in the 2015-2019 Strategic Plans. It is found that the aims of STEM overlap to a certain extent with the objectives of the *Technology and Design* course. It can be interpreted that the classes carried out at the 7th and 8th grade levels within the scope of Technology and Design course are for STEM.

Although it is not explicitly included in the curriculum prepared by the MNE, studies and applications in the field of STEM education are increasing. In this sense, the STEM Education Report was published by the MNE (2016) and an action plan was prepared for the dissemination of STEM education. The STEM Education Action Plan proposed to be implemented by the Ministry should be composed of the following steps (Bircan et al, 2019);

- Establishment of STEM Education centers,
- Conducting STEM education research in cooperation with universities in these centers,
- Educating teachers to adopt the STEM education approach,
- Updating curricula to include STEM education,

- Creating teaching environments and providing course materials for STEM education in schools.

STEM centers operating under the MNE have begun to be established, albeit in limited numbers. Although the fields of activity of these centers are not clear, it has been observed that they provide project-based technology design-oriented trainings. The absence of a legal basis for the establishment of STEM centers causes difficulties in the assignment of teachers to work in these centers. Some national education directorates have found a solution to this problem by assigning teachers to the R&D unit and then gathering them within the STEM center. However, they could not find any solution to the financial losses of the teachers working in these centers. Establishment of STEM centers in Turkey should have a legal basis like Science and Art Centers. Thus, the working procedures and principles of the teachers who will work in these centers can be clarified. The absence of teachers from all school levels can be considered as a weakness of the centers (Bircan et al, 2019).

The task of developing educational materials and technologies within the MNE was given to the General Directorate of Innovation and Educational Technologies. Different STEM projects are carried out within this unit. Projects such as FATIH and Scientix Project made by the MNE and their effects on STEM education and practices will be examined below.

2.3 FATIH Project

FATIH[2] (Movement to Increase Opportunities and Improve Technology) is an educational movement prepared for the use of technology in education. This project had the initiative to ensure that every student gets the best education, access to the highest quality educational content, and equal opportunities in education. The amount spent within the scope of the FATIH Project, which started in 2011, is 4 Billion 768 Million TL ($257 Million) as of the end of 2021. Within the scope of the project, 503,241 interactive boards have been installed in schools so far. In-school network infrastructure was established in 16,500 schools and over one million data points were installed. Internet connection is provided to schools that do not have internet infrastructure by using cable, satellite and mobile access technologies (MEB, 2023).

Providing internet to schools and putting smart boards in classrooms can be seen as an important step for STEM studies. In cases where it is not possible to supply insufficient laboratories and materials in schools, appropriate STEM activities can be developed by using internet technologies. Although it was expected that tablet distribution would facilitate access to information and students would develop design-oriented development, this project did not meet the expectations in STEM because of the lack of adequate education, lack of support for technical difficulties and the lack of determination of course strategies to be made with the use of these devices. After the rapid development of tablet technology, the tablets distributed at the beginning of the project are out of date. Many of these devices have become unusable. Although the programs to be installed on these tablets are limited, it has been observed that some students only use it as a gaming device (Baytak et al, 2013). In their study, Ekici and Yılmaz (2013) concluded that FATIH Project was not designed according to the project development logic and cannot be integrated with the education system in this form.

In addition to FATIH project, there are some small scaled projects that focused specifically on STEM applications. The Scientix Project, started by the MNE in partnership with the European Union, is a project open to teachers, academics, administrators, families and all people interested in Science and Mathematics education, aiming to disseminate inquiry-based education in STEM teaching through the Scientix Portal. The Scientix Portal was launched in May 2010. In this online portal, inquiry-based STEM education projects and materials are shared that all teachers can use in their classes, aiming to develop students' inquiry, scientific thinking, research, invention and production skills. Within the scope of this project, with the contribution of many teachers and educators, a STEM Education Practices Book in Different Disciplines from Pre-School to Secondary Education was prepared.

SOSACT (STEM and Coding Education Standardization) aimed to determine the quality standards of STEM and Coding Trainings conducted in Turkey and to provide teachers with the STEM and Coding information needed. Coordinated by the MNE-General Directorate of Innovation and Educational Technologies, the partners of the project include Gazi University, European Schoolnet, University of Poland and University of Barcelona. Within the scope of the project, trainings and field visits were carried out at stakeholder institutions.

EDUSIMSTEAM aims to use information and communication technologies in innovative learning environments, to transfer developing and changing applications to multi-disciplinary fields, and to deliver scenarios based on real life problems to all education stakeholders online. The Innovative Online Platform, which will be supported by simulations, is of great importance for the sustainability of the project (EDUSIMSTEAM, 2022).

3 THE ROLE OF SCIENCE CENTERS IN STEM EDUCATION

Science centers are at the forefront of the most important investments made in Turkey for the development of STEM and Technology. Science centers aim to make science and technology understandable and accessible to the society and to increase the importance of science and technology in the eyes of society by bringing individuals from different age groups and with different backgrounds together with science; including experimental and hands-on activities, encouraging its visitors to try and discover; These are centers that take care of the public interest, are not established for the purpose of making profit, and are financed by public or private sector resources. Science Centers, which were established with the support of the Scientific and Technological Research Council of Turkey (TÜBİTAK), have started to become widespread in Turkey in recent years. In this part of the book chapter, the science centers opened by different institutions and organizations and the STEM studies carried out in them will be examined.

3.1 TÜBİTAK-Supported Science Centers

TÜBİTAK's 2011-2016 Science and Technology Development Plan includes some activities that support STEM education of students. According to this strategy, it is desired to support science education with science fairs at primary and secondary school level, and activities to be held in the fields of space sciences, mathematics, science and technology for young people. TÜBİTAK conducts project studies and organizes competitions in order to reveal successful students and teachers in STEM education. In addition, science centers have started to be opened in various provinces by TÜBİTAK regarding STEM education in Turkey (Baran et al, 2015). Science centers aim to eliminate prejudices against science in society by making students love science and scientists. In the science centers established for this purpose, STEM activities are held with students during extracurricular times.

Based on the foresight that science centers will play a critical role in disseminating the science culture in our society, TÜBİTAK aims to establish these centers in Turkey and increase their number over the years, within the framework of the decision taken at the 23rd meeting of the Science and Technology High Council. Within the scope of this support, the projects of establishing science centers by provincial municipalities or, where deemed appropriate by the President of TÜBİTAK, of public institutions such as governorships and universities in the provinces are also supported. The science centers completed, ongoing and planned by this project are listed below.

- Completed science centers; Konya Science Center, Kocaeli Science Center, Kayseri Science Center, Bursa Science Center, Elazığ Science Center
- Ongoing science centers; Gaziantep Science Center, Antalya (Kepez) Science Center, Şanlıurfa Science Center, Üsküdar Science Center, Düzce Science Center, Denizli Science Center, Trabzon Science Center, Yozgat Science Center,
- Science centers in the planning process; Afyonkarahisar Science Center, Karaman Science Center, Tokat Science Center

Different activities are held in these science centers. For example, Konya Science Center offered a STEM camp for students during the mid-term break of 2022 (https://www.konyabilimmerkezi.com/). However, the projects carried out in these science centers are limited to what the employees do. Since the projects to be done are not controlled or recommended by a central institution, the studies may remain at the local level. In addition, STEM studies may not be at the desired level due to the fact that the trainers and employees assigned here do not undergo certain training in the field of specialization.

In addition to science centers, there are Science Fairs projects numbered *4006* supported by TÜBİTAK. These fairs allow students to showcase different science and STEM projects. This project support is made every year and takes place in every province if requested. Although the content of the projects done here is based on simple academic studies, it plays an important role in directing children to STEM studies. In addition, some STEM projects with small participation in Turkey are listed below.

- STEM: Engineers of the future: learning the teaching methods of the countries that are partners in STEM projects
- Sting: Integrating gender into life through teachers' professional development activities
- Little science heroes meet: Introducing children aged 6-10 to STEM activities, raising awareness in the field of coding
- CodeWeek: Making coding and digital literacy fun and interesting (Hişmi, 2022).

3.2 Joint Science Centers with Private Institutions and Municipalities

Since families in Turkey are more directed to private education institutions for higher quality education, there have been attempts by different institutions and organizations to open science centers apart from the official science or education centers of the MNE. For example, it is seen that municipalities have opened science centers for children and young people to benefit from different scientific activities in line with the demands received in their region. Since these science centers are not connected to a central place and are not named with a single name, the exact number is not known. For example, some of these centers are called with different names such as astronomy center (Karaköprü) in some places, science center in some places (Bilim Üsküdar) and STEM center in some places. Below is a list of some of these science centers along with the locations.

- METU Society and Science Center-Ankara,
- Urfa STEM-Şanliurfa,
- Polatlı Municipality Science Center and Uluğ Bey Gökevi-Ankara
- Diyarbakır STEM Center-Diyarbakir
- ITU Science Center-İstanbul
- Bağcılar Municipality Science Center-İstanbul
- Bayrampaşa Municipality Science Center-İstanbul
- Sancaktepe Science Center-İstanbul
- Istanbul Yesilkoy Air Force Museum-İstanbul
- Science Fatih -İstanbul
- Science Beyoğlu -İstanbul
- Science Şehitkamil -Gaziantep
- Science Şahinbey-Gaziantep
- Bornova Municipality Mevlana Society and Science Center-İzmir
- Konya Science Center and Space House-Konya
- Science Experiment Center and Sabancı Space House-Eskişehir
- Bursa Science and Technology Center-Bursa
- Gaziantep Metropolitan Municipality Turkcell Planetarium and Science Center-Gaziantep
- Kocaeli Seka Park Science Center-Kocaeli
- Science Erzurum - Erzurum
- Elazığ Science Center SOBİLDEM-Elazığ
- ITAP Science and Society Center-Muğla

The most common activities announced on the website of these centers are 'STEM'. There are doubts about whether these activities are fully STEM activities. In an academic study on this subject, it has been determined that the STEM centers examined differ in administrative and structural terms and are structured within the framework of public services and education. In addition, it has been understood that there is no framework legislation that determines the working procedures and principles of STEM education centers (Bircan et al, 2019).

3.3 University Science Centers and STEM

As summarized above, universities in Turkey work under the state-owned HEI. In a recent study, academic studies and practices related to STEM in all private and state universities in Turkey are listed below (Gökcül, 2022).

- Only 10 education faculties have a defined STEM policy (There are 208 universities in Turkey (129 of them are public and others are private).

- Only 16 education faculties have courses in the field of STEM education at the undergraduate.
- None of them has a master's or doctoral program in STEM.
- Only 13 education faculties have STEM laboratories.
- Only 13 education faculties have faculty members with doctorate degrees in STEM.
- Only 6 education faculties have books written in the field of STEM.
- Only 8 education faculties have EU projects in the field of STEM.
- Only 3 education faculties have a web portal on STEM.
- Only 5 education faculties have STEM research institute or STEM centers.
- Only 30 education faculties provide STEM education courses (Gökcü, 2022)

Although private universities are dependent on HEI in terms of supervision and formality, they are independent in their expenditures or activities since their budgets are covered by themselves. In this context, private universities can take action faster, especially in innovations such as STEM. For example, the STEM Education Turkey report published by Istanbul Aydın University in 2015 is one of the first academic studies that underline the introduction and implementation of a qualified STEM education into the K-12 curriculum (Akgündüz and Ertepınar, 2015). In addition, some universities have opened centers with different names and structures for STEM studies in recent years. Some of these centers are listed below.

- Bahçeşehir University, STEM Center
- Hacettepe University, Science, Technology, Engineering and Mathematics Education and Applications Laboratory (Hacettepe STEM & Maker Lab)
- Muğla Sıtkı Koçman University, Science Education Application and Research Center
- Mus Alparslan University, STEM Education Application and Research Center
- Özyeğin University, STEM Academy
- Middle East Technical University (METU), Science, Technology, Engineering and Mathematics Center (BİLTEMM)

4 OBSTACLES AND CHALLENGES TO IMPLEMENTING STEM EDUCATION IN TURKEY

4.1 Gender Inequality and Social Equality

In the report submitted by the MNE, the schooling rate of girls in secondary education was 39 percent in the 2000s, and reached 95 percent by 2022. According to these new statistics, the schooling rate of girls for the first time exceeded that of boys (MEB, 2022). However, it is found that the average STEM field placement rate for boys is 81.39% and for girls is 18.61% among the numerical department students who are among the top 1000 students in the central examination for university placement in Turkey (Akgündüz & Ertepınar, 2015). In addition, the schooling rate of girls may differ due to regional development, cultural and population density differences. Particularly in the eastern provinces, the enrollment rate of these boys and girls is lower than the national average.

Although there are no direct STEM projects for female students or underdeveloped regions, different STEM studies are carried out with the efforts of some entrepreneurial teachers and educators. For example, within the scope of the 'STEM for Disadvantaged Students especially Girls' project carried out by Istanbul Aydın University, it was aimed to train both teachers and students in STEM fields and to create programs accordingly (STEM School, 2015). In addition, some projects related to STEM by different institutions or schools are listed below;

- My Madame Curie: Increasing female student participation in STEM fields
- STEM for disadvantaged students especially girls
- Honey bees become engineers: girls meet engineering in 81 science high schools in 81 provinces
- Aziz Sancar: STEM camps for girls: Introducing girls to science at an early age, integrating Syrian refugee students into society (Hişmi, 2022)

In the global pandemic, Turkish educational institutions have switched to their own distance education systems according to their means. Classes were given every day by the MNE via state television. In addition, live lessons and course materials were offered through the online system called EBA. However, disadvantaged groups had problems accessing these courses due to the students' lack of computers or tablets. In the same way, there were many students who could not attend these classes because the internet was not provided to the families who did not have internet. In addition to these social differences, although some students had the opportunity to complete their education with private lessons, some were deprived of this due to financial opportunities. In this pandemic period, it has become difficult to make STEM applications as students have limited access to normal courses. Especially in the activities carried out with primary school students through distance education, accidents that cause economic damage such as accidentally spilling water on the computer occurred without the help of parents.

4.2 Teachers and STEM

Education in Turkey is carried out through private schools and public schools. Although private schools are inspected by the MNE, their personnel and expenses are covered by those who enroll in the school. Public schools, on the other hand, are run by the state budget, free of charge to the student. Providing professional and personal development of teachers working in public schools, adaptation to developments, increasing their productivity, training them in areas needed individually or institutionally and preparing them for high-level duties are provided by in-service training courses. The authorized unit to organize these courses, which can be organized as face-to-face and distance education, is the Professional Development Support and Monitoring Department, established under the General Directorate of Teacher Training and Development (Erbilgin & Şahin, 2021; MEB, 2019). Although there is no action plan prepared by the MNE on STEM education, three different levels of in-service training courses have been designed as of 2017 for Science and Technology, Mathematics, Biology, Physics, Chemistry, Classroom, Preschool, Technology-Design and Information Technologies teachers (Gökcül, 2022; MEB, 2019):

- Basic STEM Course: The activity, which is planned as 30 lesson hours, aims to inform the participating teachers about STEM education. It has been prepared to develop basic knowledge and skills. It is aimed that each teacher who successfully completes this activity will achieve general information about STEM (Gökcül, 2022).
- Advanced STEM Course: The activity, which is planned as 40 lesson hours, has been prepared in order to improve the knowledge and skills gained in the basic level course on STEM education and to enable them to use them practically. A 'Course Certificate' (e-certificate) is given to the trainees who successfully complete the course (MEB, 2019). It is aimed that each teacher who successfully completes this activity will understand coding in STEM Education (Gökcül, 2022).
- STEM Trainer Training Course: The activity planned as 40 lesson hours; it has been prepared to train teachers who have successfully completed STEM basic and advanced courses as STEM trainers. A 'Course Certificate' (e-certificate) is given to the trainees who successfully complete the course. It is aimed that each teacher who successfully completes this activity will make project-based course designs in STEM education (Gökcül, 2022).

In Kayseri province, which was selected as a pilot region in the 2013-2014 academic years regarding the field of STEM education model, STEM education model training was given to teachers in some schools. Shortly after, the STEM education model started to be implemented in all schools in the city. In addition, Kayseri MNE was invited to the 2014 STEM Conference in the USA and the paper was featured in ELA (Education Leadership Action) magazine (Doğan, 2019). In their study, Eroğlu and Bektaş (2016) asked the teachers involved in the project in Kayseri for their thoughts on the activities. Teachers stated that STEM education model activities are compatible with science lessons and teachers approach these activities positively, but there are deficiencies in materials (Durucu, 2022).

In a field study planned by the MNE in 2017, 66% of mathematics, physics, chemistry, biology and technology teachers in Science and Social Sciences high schools reported that they did not have knowledge about STEM (Karadaş, 2021). However, it was aimed to examine the awareness, attitudes and self-efficacy perceptions of teachers towards STEM education recently, and according to the results obtained in the study conducted in Turkey with 609 teachers; teachers' awareness levels for STEM education, the scale; It is high in the sub-dimensions of 'Student Impact' and 'Teacher Impact'. Awareness levels of teachers for STEM education, scale; It is in the 'Course Effect' sub-dimension and at medium level. Teachers' attitudes towards STEM education are positive. Teachers' in-class practice self-efficacy perceptions for STEM education are positive both in general and in sub-dimensions (Yaman & Aşılıoğlu, 2022). In a qualitative study conducted with science teachers, it was revealed that these teachers had a positive attitude towards STEM education, but they had problems in STEM education arising from themselves, students, school management and parents.

4.3 Critics

With the popularity of STEM studies around the world, awareness of academics and educators in Turkey has increased. However, it is understood that STEM studies carried out in Turkey are insufficient and what is done is not at the desired level. In a meta-analysis study conducted by Yılmaz et al in 2018, it was stated that there was academic study intensity in the field of STEM between 2012 and 2017. The common feature of these studies was integrating stem with science course but no other areas. Indeed, these studies are generally carried out with primary school or university students, but studies with high school students are few. Moreover, while most of the studies in this field focused on student opinions, studies on material development were very limited (Yılmaz et al, 2018). These findings also show that the stem phenomenon is limited only to the science course. Thus, in this part of the chapter, deficiencies and failures about STEM studies applied in Turkey is listed.

- The limited number of computer teachers who are most active in STEM practices. The information technology course in schools was included in the elective courses with the new program in 2006. Until 2010, two hours a week, from 4th grade to 8th grade. The elective courses were removed from the 4th and 5th grades. Thus, the number of computer teachers in schools has decreased.
- Lack of appropriate laboratories in schools for STEM studies
- The absence of a central STEM policy
- Deficiencies in infrastructure (Keteci, 2021)
- Inadequate teacher training, which plays a leading role in the implementation of STEM applications
- There is no direct undergraduate or graduate study in the STEM field.
- Lack of sufficient practice time for students (Akgündüz & Ertepınar, 2015)
- There are high school transition and university placement exams and the questions asked in these exams are limited to multiple choice questions.
- Teachers being trained for a single discipline, having difficulties in keeping up with technology, and lack of in-service training. The field of STEM is only added to the last unit of the Science course and limited to a maximum of 12 hours under the name of Science and Engineering.

5 RECOMMENDATIONS AND CONCLUSION

5.1 Recommendations

Since the STEM subject covers many areas in terms of content and structure, it may not be easy to create an ideal STEM structure (Chong & Quek, 2022). Indeed, it is difficult to find a common solution because the perspectives on this field differ according to the teachers. However, it is hoped that STEM courses and practices in the world and in Turkey will be more efficient when some of the recommendations listed below are implemented.

- Informing in detail what the STEM phenomenon means and what is expected from teachers and students across the country
- Establishing STEM laboratories in educational institutions and supplying materials that students will need for all kinds of design and development in this laboratory
- Arrangement of course content in accordance with STEM course structure
- Reminding students of the contribution of STEM applications to permanent learning and the benefits of their applications in their lives

- Providing STEM education especially to teachers working at primary school level
- Recruiting enough experts for Science centers established under the leadership of municipalities and private institutions
- Arranging teachers' lesson hours accordingly
- Adding STEM courses apart from the courses that students are responsible for in the central exams, asking questions in the central exams for this purpose
- Raising awareness of parents and getting support from parents for the supply of materials in schools that have budget problems
- Raising awareness of the businesses and non-governmental organizations on this issue and setting joint projects
- Increasing the hours of the material development course given in teacher training institutions and processing it as applications
- Bringing a recycling perspective and developing environmentally friendly materials by using waste materials in the STEM training given
- Expecting a product, especially from young children, by following the developmental stages and taking into account their hand skills and mental skills
- Evaluating students' academic progress based on these products
- Explaining occupational health and safety in studies and informing both teachers and students about this issue
- Receiving support from craftsmen for the development of some products, visiting workshops
- Providing an ideal grouping or cooperative learning environment for sharing skills and experiences
- Providing the products produced to different audiences and receiving feedback from different users
- Processing the subjects and scopes that are not included in the curricula
- Arranging materials and tools to be used for age level
- Reporting the different abilities of students in different fields due to the presence of different fields for the studies in STEM applications
- Providing art knowledge to students so that the artistic side of the products to be developed within the scope of STEM is not missing (STEAM) (Okwara & Henrik Pretorius, 2023; Shatunova et al, 2019)
- Providing additional points to award successful students to be placed in a good high school or university so that there could be an increase of participation and interest in project competitions held by Tübitak for secondary and high school students

- Integrating social science fields at the last stage of the developed products for students in order to improve their skills in such areas as marketing, business management, and expense calculation (STEAMS)

In addition, some of the following questions will remain unclear and need answers worldwide.

- Will STEM be an extracurricular activity or part of formal education?
- Will the materials be supplied from schools or from parents?
- Who will be responsible for occupational health and safety?
- According to which field criteria will the course outputs and products be arranged? For example, in terms of engineering? Will it be evaluated in terms of the subject?
- Which lesson will be taught first?
- What will be the weight of the main lesson?
- To what extent will other branch teachers be involved in subject matter other than themselves?
- What will be done in case the project goes out of scope?

5.2 A New Approach to STEM: A-STEM

STEM is an ever-evolving field and there are many different views on it as it is used in most education systems in the world. Over time, different concepts such as STEAM are used and developed. However, the problems experienced in accessing materials and equipment, especially in the engineering applications part in school environments, make the implementation of STEM difficult (Tsakeni, 2022). These STEM studies are disrupted when some studies are dangerous for students or when it is impossible to apply them in a laboratory setting. With the developing Augmented Reality technology, 3D reality applications facilitate many experiments and designs. Augmented Reality applications, which have been used in education recently, can also be applied in studies in the field of STEM (A-STEM). It is possible with A-STEM to test how a STEM work that students will do in 3D environment is perceived with this system. It will be also possible to use the digital materials used again and again. It is easy to send the designed virtual products to other subject experts in different fields and get tested and evaluated instantly. Overall, there is a rapid change in technology and thus, the field of STEM also needs to be reshaped to take advantages of these developments. Augmented Reality is an opportunity to this field to fully integrate related subject areas. In addition, the A-STEM may cost less and this may help developing countries such as Turkey to implement STEM easily.

As discussed above, the historical developments have shown that Turkey is open to developments and changes due to its geo-political position. There are companies that have made significant progress in the field of science and technology industry in the last century. However, education and technology of this country is also affected by the changing political structures. In this context, it is difficult to predict what STEM will look like in the future in Turkey. In addition to technological developments, the resources that the current political power in Turkey or the new powers in case of change will transfer to the STEM field, the policies they will issue in this regard and the future visions will also guide STEM education. As the author, my most important suggestion is that for the advancement of STEM or a similar education model in Turkey, educational institutions should be made by independent organizations that are only supervised by the state, examination systems should be changed and education curricula should be constantly updated. In addition, in order to implement this technological change, school administrators and parents, especially teachers, should be constantly informed and trained.

REFERENCES

Akgündüz, D., & Ertepınar, H. (2015). *Stem Eğitimi Türkiye Raporu, Günün Modası mı Yoksa Gereksinim mi?* Scala.

Arslan, S. Y., & Arastaman, G. (2021). Dünyada Stem Politikaları: Türkiye İçin Çıkarımlar ve Öneriler. *Nevşehir Hacı Bektaş Veli Üniversitesi SBE Dergisi, 11*(2), 894–910. doi:10.30783/nevsosbilen.903115

Ay, K., & Seferoğlu, S. S. (2021). Farklı ülkelerin STEM eğitimi politikalarının incelenmesi ve Türkiye için çıkarımlar. *Erzincan Üniversitesi Eğitim Fakültesi Dergisi, 23*(1), 82–105. doi:10.17556/erziefd.669988

Badmus, O., & Jita, L. (2022). What is Next for Africa's Youthful and Useful Population? STREAM Education for Global Inclusivity. *Journal of Culture and Values in Education, 5*(2), 32–46. doi:10.46303/jcve.2022.18

Baran, E., Canbazoğlu-Bilici, S., Mesutoğlu, C., & Ocak, C. (2016). Moving STEM Beyond Schools: Students' Perceptions About an Out-of-School STEM Education Program. *International Journal of Education in Mathematics. Science and Technology, 4*(1), 9–19. doi:10.18404/ijemst.71338 PMID:27453919

Baytak, A. (2009). *Reforms for Technology Integration into education.* Bilisim Teknojileri Işığında Eğitim Kongresi.

Baytak, A. (2014). Metropolitan Law: A Sociological Perspective. Daily Sabah. https://www.dailysabah.com/opinion/2014/05/13/metropolitan-law-a-sociological-perspective

Baytak, A. Tarman, B., & Duman, H. (2013). Does Fatih Project Ensure Social Justice In Education: Looking In Depth *II. Uluslararası Sosyal Bilgiler Eğitimi Sempozyumu (USBES II)* 26-28 April 2013 Aksaray.

Bircan, M. A., Köksal, Ç., & Cımbız, A. T. (2019). Examining The Stem Centres in Turkey and Stem Centre Model Proposal. *Kastamonu Education Journal, 27*(3), 1033–1045. doi:10.24106/kefdergi.2537

Bybee, R. W. (2010). What is STEM education? *Science, 329*(5995), 996–997. doi:10.1126cience.1194998 PMID:20798284

Çavaş, P., Ayar, A., & Gürcan, G. (2020). Türkiye'de STEM eğitimi üzerine yapılan araştırmaların durumu üzerine bir çalışma. *Van Yüzüncü Yıl Üniversitesi Eğitim Fakültesi Dergisi, 17*(1), 823–854. doi:10.33711/yyuefd.751853

Chong, Y. S., & Quek, A. H. (2022). Navigating the Contemporary Rites of Passage: A Typology of STEM Professional Identity Transition. *Research in Social Sciences and Technology, 7*(3), 86–100. doi:10.46303/ressat.2022.19

Doğan, İ. (2019). *STEM etkinliklerinin 7. sınıf öğrencilerinin bilimsel süreç becerilerine, fen ve STEM tutumlarına ve elektrik enerjisi ünitesindeki başarılarına etkisi.*[Doctoral thesis, Balıkesir University], tez.yok.gov.tr/

Durmuşoğlu, M. C., & Yıldız Taşdemir, C. (2022). Determining the parent education preferences and needs of parents with children in preschool education institutions in Turkey. *Theory and Practice in Child Development, 2*(1), 1–21. doi:10.46303/tpicd.2022.7

Durucu, A. S. (2022). *Öğretmenlerin Stem+S İçin Sorgulamaya Dayali Öğretim Öz-Yeterlilikleri İle 21.Yy. Becerileri Öğretimi Arasındaki İlişkinin İncelenmesi.* [Master Thesis, Gaziantep University], tez.yok.gov.tr/

EDUSIMSTEAM. (2022). *Fostering STEAM Education in Schools*. Edusimsteam. https://edusimsteam.eba.gov.tr/en/home/

Ekici, S., & Yılmaz, B. (2013). FATİH Projesi Üzerine Bir Değerlendirme. *Türk Kütüphaneciliği,27*(2), 317-339. https://dergipark.org.tr/en/pub/tk/issue/48832/622078

Erbilgin, E., & Şahin, B. (2021). The Effects of a Professional Development Program for Technology Integrated Algebra Teaching. *Research in Educational Policy and Management, 3*(2), 1–21. doi:10.46303/repam.2021.4

Ergül, A. (2020). 2012-2018 yılları arasında Türkiye'de gerçekleştirilen STEM eğitimi konulu lisansüstü tezlerin incelenmesi. *Mediterranean Journal of Educational Research, 14*(31), 393–421. doi:10.29329/mjer.2020.234.19

Eroğlu, S., & Bektaş, O. (2016). STEM eğitimi almış fen bilimleri öğretmenlerinin STEM temelli ders etkinlikleri hakkındaki görüşleri. *Eğitimde Nitel Araştırmalar Dergisi, 4*(3), 43–67.

Gökçe Tekin, Ö. (2022). *Ortaokul Ve Lise Öğrencilerinin Stem Öz-Yeterlik Algıları Ve Kariyer İlgileri İle Problem Çözme Becerileri.* [Doctoral Thesis, İnönü Üniversitesi].

Gökcül, M. (2022). *Türkiye'de Stem Eğitimine Yönelik Öğretmen Yetiştirme Uygulamalarinin Değerlendirilmesi.* [Doctoral Thesis, Gazi University]. tez.yok.gov.tr/

Hişmi, E. (2022). *Stem Etkinliklerinin İlkokul Öğrencilerindeki Stem'e İlişkin Tutumlar, Akademik Başarı, Problem Çözme ve Sosyal Beceri Geliştirme Süreci Açısından İncelenmesi.* [Doctoral Thesis, Çukurova University]. tez.yok.gov.tr/

Karabulut, H., Tosunbayraktar, G., & Kariper, A. (2022). Ortaokul Öğrencilerinin Beceri Temelli (Yeni Nesil) Fen Bilimleri Sorularına Yönelik Görüşlerinin İncelenmesi. *Akdeniz Üniversitesi Eğitim Fakültesi Dergisi, 1*(2), 301-320. https://dergipark.org.tr/en/pub/akuned/issue/73080/1190147

Karadaş, Ö. F. (2021). *Fen Bilimleri Öğretmenleri Ve Stem Uygulamaları: Tercih Gerekçeleri, Sorunlar ve Çözüm Önerileri.* [Master Thesis, Kırşehir Ahi Evran University]. tez.yok.gov.tr/

Kaya, M. (2022). The First Life Studies Curriculum in the History of the Turkish Republic and the Influence of John Dewey. *Journal Of Curriculum Studies Research, 4*(2), 59–88. doi:10.46303/jcsr.2022.13

Keteci, H. E. (2021). *Çevrim İçi Stem Uygulamalarının (E-Stem) Öğrencilerin Kavram Öğrenmeleri Ve Bilimsel Süreç Becerilerine Etkisi.* [Master Thesis, Marmara University]. tez.yok.gov.tr/

Maralli, S. (2019). Harf inkilâbi'nin uygulanmasi ve birtakim etkileri. *Eskişehir Osmangazi Üniversitesi Tarih Dergisi, 2*(1), 112-131. https://dergipark.org.tr/en/pub/esogutd/issue/46078/546953

MEB. (2019). *Kazanim Merkezli Stem Uygulamalari*. T.C. MEB Özel Öğretim Kurumları Genel Müdürlüğü.

MEB. (2022). *Kız Çocuklarının Okullaşma Oranları Rekor Seviyeye Ulaştı*. MEB. https://www.meb.gov.tr/kiz-cocuklarinin-okullasma-oranlari-rekor-seviyeye-ulasti/haber/27958/tr

MEB. (2023). *Fatih Projesi*. MEB. http://fatihprojesi.meb.gov.tr/

Mullis, I. V. S., Martin, M. O., Foy, P., & Hooper, M. (2016). *TIMSS 2015 International Results in Mathematics*. Boston College, TIMSS & PIRLS International Study Center. http://timssandpirls.bc.edu/timss2015/international-results/

Mutlu, S. (1995). Population of Turkey by ethnic groups and provinces. *New Perspectives on Turkey*, *12*, 33–60. doi:10.1017/S0896634600001138 PMID:12290933

Okwara, V., & Henrik Pretorius, J. P. (2023). The STEAM vs STEM Educational Approach: The Significance of the Application of the Arts in Science Teaching for Learners' Attitudes Change. *Journal of Culture and Values in Education*, *6*(2), 18–33. doi:10.46303/jcve.2023.6

Olgun, Ş. (2021). *Fetemm Kapsamında Yaygın Eğitimde Robotik Kodlama Dersi Alan Fen Bilgisi Öğretmenliği Öğrencilerinin Görüşlerine İlişkin Durum Çalışması*. [Master Thesis, Necmettin Erbakan University]. tez.yok.gov.tr/

Shatunova, O., Anisimova, T., Sabirova, F., & Kalimullina, O. (2019). Steam as an innovative educational technology. *Journal of Social Studies Education Research*, *10*(2), 131–144.

STEM School. (2015). *İstanbul Aydın Üniversitesi Stem Okulu*. STEM. http://stemokulu.com/

Tarman, B. (2016). Innovation and Education. *Research in Social Sciences and Technology*, *1*(1). doi:10.46303/ressat.01.01.4

Toker Gökçe, A. & Yıldırım, D. (2019). Öğretmenlerin STEM eğitiminde yaşadığı sorunlar ve çözümleri. *14. Uluslararası Eğitim Yönetimi Kongresi Tam Metin Bildiri Kitabı*, 45-50.

Tsakeni, M. (2022). STEM Education Practical Work in Remote Classrooms: Prospects and Future Directions in the Post-Pandemic Era. *Journal of Culture and Values in Education*, *5*(1), 144–167. doi:10.46303/jcve.2022.11

TÜSİAD. (2017). *2023'e doğru Türkiye'de STEM gereksinimleri.* Tusaid. https://www.tusiadstem.org/images/raporlar/2017/STEM-Raporu-V7.pdf

Yaman, F., & Aşılıoğlu, B. (2022). Öğretmenlerin Stem Eğitimine Yönelik Farkındalık, Tutum Ve Sınıf İçi Uygulama Özyeterlik Algılarının İncelenmesi. *Milli Eğitim Dergisi, 51*(234), 1395–1416. doi:10.37669/milliegitim.845546

Yıldırım, B., & Altun, Y. (2015). STEM Eğitim ve Mühendislik Uygulamalarının Fen Bilgisi Laboratuar Dersindeki Etkilerinin İncelenmesi. *El-Cezerî Fen ve Mühendislik Dergisi, 2*(2), 28–40.

Yıldırım, H., & Gelmez-Burakgazi, S. (2020). Türkiye'de STEM eğitimi konusunda yapılan çalışmalar üzerine bir araştırma: Meta-sentez çalışması. *Pamukkale Üniversitesi Eğitim Fakültesi Dergisi, 50,* 291–314. doi:10.9779/pauefd.590319

Yılmaz, A., Gülgün, C., Çetinkaya, M., & Doğanay, K. (2018). Initiatives and new trends towards stem education in Turkey. *Journal of Education and Training Studies, 6*(11a), 1–10. doi:10.11114/jets.v6i11a.3795

ENDNOTES

[1] The Turkish government officially requested from the United Nations in 2022 to be referred to as 'Türkiye' instead of 'Turkey'. Although some new articles and documents have begun using 'Türkiye', this chapter will continue using 'Turkey' to avoid any confusion.

[2] The term 'fatih' means conqueror in Turkish. The selection of this term itself also holds a very political goal of the project.

Chapter 3
The Development of STEM Education in the Sultanate of Oman

Mohamed A. Shahat
https://orcid.org/0000-0002-9637-8192
Sultan Qaboos University, Oman & Aswan University, Egypt

Sulaiman M. Al-Balushi
Sultan Qaboos University, Oman

ABSTRACT

This overview includes the impact of STEM programs in Oman, significant improvements in delivery, and plans for the future. The chapter outlines the research efforts underway in Oman regarding STEM and describes a nationally-funded strategic project by His Majesty Trust Fund Strategic Grants to enhance teachers' capabilities in STEM-based competencies and students' interest in STEM-related specialties. The chapter sheds light on the different scholarship opportunities offered by on the Oman Ministry of Higher Education, Research, and Innovation for students to pursue further education in specific disciplines of study in higher education institutions (HEIs) in Oman and abroad. The chapter also clarifies the stages of implementing the STEM Oman program in schools. The chapter includes a detailed description of training programs designed to prepare science teachers for the STEM Oman program. Next, the authors discuss the future development and plans for STEM Oman.

DOI: 10.4018/978-1-6684-6883-8.ch003

Copyright © 2023, IGI Global. Copying or distributing in print or electronic forms without written permission of IGI Global is prohibited.

The Development of STEM Education in the Sultanate of Oman

INTRODUCTION

In recent years the Oman Ministry of Education has begun to play a significant role in promoting Science, Technology, Engineering and Mathematics (STEM) education in school and higher education settings. Using a retrospective approach to the earlier and current practices of STEM education in Oman, this chapter gives an overview of the initiatives related to STEM education by both the Ministry of Higher Education, Research, and Innovation, and by the Ministry of Education. This overview includes the impact of STEM programs, significant improvements in delivery, and plans for the future. The chapter also outlines the research efforts underway in Oman regarding STEM and describes a nationally-funded strategic project by His Majesty Trust Fund Strategic Grants to enhance teachers' capabilities in STEM-based competencies and students' interest in STEM-related specialties. The chapter sheds light on the different scholarship opportunities offered by on the Oman Ministry of Higher Education, Research, and Innovation for students to pursue further education in specific disciplines of study in Higher Education Institutions (HEIs) in Oman and abroad. The chapter also clarifies the stages of implementing the STEM Oman program in schools and illustrates this through the use of an example. Additionally, the chapter includes a detailed description of training programs designed to prepare science teachers for the STEM Oman program. Next, we discuss the future development and plans for STEM Oman, which includes a nationally funded project by His Majesty Trust Fund Strategic Grants to enhance teachers' capabilities in STEM-based competencies and increase students' interest in and engagement with STEM-related specialties. The authors of this chapter are the PI and Co-PI of this strategic project, which aims to positively impact Oman by improving STEM teaching and developing a sustainable and successful STEM program for school students in the future. Different studies have tackled the topic of STEM education. The chapter concludes by summarizing and critically analyzing research efforts into STEM in education in Oman, the engineering design approach to STEM and on the implementation of the STEM Oman program.

The Role of the Oman Government in STEM Education

The strategic aims of *Oman Vision 2040* include the provision of inclusive education, lifelong learning, and scientific research that can lead to a knowledge society and capable teachers who can improve the quality of education in Oman (Omani Education Council 2040, 2018). The STEM Oman program is one way Oman is striving to build national capabilities. The government is playing a significant role in promoting STEM Education in both school and higher education settings. Although government intervention has only begun in recent years, their initiatives are well intentioned and important for new generations in Oman. The following section highlighting Oman STEM Education is divided into two main parts: the STEM Scholarships program, and the STEM Oman program in Omani schools. In what follows, we provide a detailed overview of the scholarships available, the training programs implemented by STEM Oman, Omani research on STEM in schools and HEIs, the national STEM training program funded by His Majesty Trust Fund Strategic Grants (HMTF), the Barriers to STEM education in Oman, and finally the future of STEM education in Oman.

STEM Scholarships program

The Oman Ministry of Higher Education, Research, and Innovation (MoHERI) provides different higher education scholarship opportunities for students at home and abroad, with the aim that these scholarships will contribute in a significant way to the Sultanate's economic growth. A principal aim of the Oman Government is to ensure that students pursue educational programs in areas relevant to the country's labor needs. The aim is to produce graduates at different degree levels with technical competence; knowledge in core disciplines; and soft skills sought by employers such as critical thinking, problem-solving, teamwork, and communication skills (MoHERI, 2021).

Regarding education students in particular, the MoHERI provides scholarships for students preparing to become teachers in STEM and other disciplines (MoHERI, 2020-2021). According to MoHERI (2020-2021), the scholarships are divided into two groups: scholarships in Science, Technology, Engineering, and (applied) Mathematics (STEM); and scholarships in Education, Social sciences, Arts and Management (ESAM). These scholarships support STEM or ESAM careers, and the scholarship eligibility criteria are flexible, with some courses having further requirements. Students receiving STEM scholarships are usually focused on (pure) mathematics and science. In contrast, ESAM students favor arts or social sciences that involve math to a certain extent – e.g., economics.

The STEM scholarship program started in 2016-2017 and at the time of writing (academic year 2022-2023) was still available. The STEM scholarship program was created with the following aims:

- Provide all sectors in the Sultanate of Oman with competent graduates from a variety of scientific disciplines.
- Enable students to choose the country of study and science specialization based on interest.
- Enroll students in the highest-quality universities possible (MoHERI, 2022).

The Development of STEM Education in the Sultanate of Oman

From the academic year 2016 to 2021, a total of 128 students studied abroad in countries such as Australia, Canada, Holland, Malaysia, New Zealand, the United Kingdom (UK), and the United States of America (USA). The following table summarizes the country distribution of Oman STEM scholarships:

Table 1. Oman STEM scholarship program awards distribution*

Country	no. of scholarships	\multicolumn{6}{c} Scholarship Distribution by Academic Year					
		2016	2017	2018	2019	2020	2021
Australia	1				1		
United Kingdom	81	12	12	10	12	14	21
United States of America	40	6	2	8	9	10	5
Canada	3				2		1
Malaysia	1						1
New Zealand	1						
Holland	1						1
Total	128						

* The authors requested the above data directly from MoHERI.

In an interview, Rahma Al Mahrooqi, Minister for HERI, was asked about the pandemic impacting the number of local students entering STEM studies and related career paths. She confirmed that MoHERI "has taken specific steps to ensure the availability of a wide range of STEM programs at both the undergraduate and postgraduate levels". Al Mahrooqi also stated that MoHERI has encouraged students to conduct research studies in STEM subjects, and energy and disaster sciences to develop expertise in these areas and promote high levels of practical preparedness. (Oxford Business Group, 2021).

The STEM Oman Program in Omani Schools

The aims of the STEM Oman program are: a) to create a generation capable of effectively participating in the sustainable development of Omani society, and of helping to create a knowledge-based economy based on the disciplines of science, mathematics, engineering, and technology; b) use current education theory to innovatively integrate the four STEM disciplines in order to create practical lessons that focus on linking education to everyday life and develop creativity and critical thinking skills (Oman Observer, 2019b). In the academic year 2017-2018, the

STEM Oman program was established by the Ministry of Education in collaboration with the British Rolls Royce Foundation and the Public Authority for Privatization and Partnership. The Ministry of Education supervised this program through the Department of Innovation and Scientific Olympiad.

Program Stages

According to the Ministry of Education (2021), the STEM Oman program was implemented in three main stages:

First Stage in the Academic Year 2017-2018

This stage included the selection of six schools in educational governorates close to the Ministry's general office to facilitate the follow-up and feedback process (four schools were in the Muscat Governorate, and one was in the Governorate of Al Batinah South and one in Ad Dākhilīyah). The program was implemented during the second semester of the academic year, with one lesson per week for a period of 13 weeks (Ministry of Education, 2021). At this stage, the program targeted 420 secondary school students (Grade 10) and 14 science teachers and supervisors (Oman Observer, 2018).

Second Stage in the Academic Year 2018-2019

In this stage, the program was expanded to include 12 other schools for boys and girls, totaling 18 schools that implemented the STEM program. During this stage, the teachers of the program participated in providing workshops and presentations for the program's activities during the National Week for STEM subjects during the period 10-14 March 2019.

Third Stage in the Academic Year 2019-2020

The process of expanding the implementation of the STEM Oman program continued during the academic year 2019/2020 to include 12 other schools selected from various educational directorates, bringing the total number to 30 schools from all governorates in Oman (see Table 2.) Participation in the trial meant the school's teachers received training in science education so they could implement the STEM Oman program. Also at this stage a group of expert Omani STEM teachers provided workshops and presentations as part of the STEM Oman program in the Oman Science Festival 2019, which was held at the Oman Convention and Exhibition

Center from 4-8 November 2019. These experts presented a paper on the Omani experience of the STEM program trial in schools during a symposium the festival.

Table 2. Number of Omani Schools that implemented the STEM OMAN program

Governorate	Number of Schools by Academic years			Total School Number
	2017-2018	2018-2019	2019-2020	
Muscat	4			4
Al Batinah South	1	1	1	3
Al Batinah North		2	2	4
Ad Dākhilīyah	1	1	2	4
Ash Sharqiyah North		2	1	3
Ash Sharqiyah South		1	1	2
Dhofar		1	1	2
Musandam		1	1	2
Ad Dhahirah		1	1	2
Al Wusta		1	1	2
Al Buraymi		1	1	2
Total School Number	6	12	12	30

Training Programs Implemented by STEM Oman

According to the Ministry of Education (2021), a set of training programs has been implemented to prepare science teachers for the STEM Oman program, these programs can be summarized as follows:

The Initial Training Program of the STEM Oman Program

The first training program was held from November 19-23, 2017, in cooperation with the British Rolls Royce Foundation, to train Omani teachers nominated for the STEM Oman program implementation. It targeted 12 male and female teachers from the schools assigned to implement the program. Th training was conducted jointly by six experts, educational supervisors, specialists from the Department of Innovation and Scientific Olympiad in the ministry, and other members of the Innovation and Scientific Olympiad departments in the eleven Omani governorates. This program aimed to provide participants with skills and experiences that would qualify them to start implementing the STEM Oman program during the second semester of the academic year 2017-2018. This initial program was carried out over five days under the supervision of British expert Mark Langley, a specialist in STEM programs from the STEM Center at York University in the United Kingdom. The location of the training program was the headquarters of the Public Authority for Privatization and Partnership (formerly Knowledge Oasis Muscat) (Ministry of Education, 2021).

Overseas Professional STEM Oman Training Program

The second STEM education training took place at the STEM Center at York University in the UK from April 30 to May 4, 2018. The Ministry of Education sent 14 male and female science teachers from the various governorates in Oman to be trained on the scientific and practical aspects of implementing the STEM Oman program in Omani schools. In the future, these teachers will utilize their newly acquired expert knowledge of the STEM Oman program to train others, and facilitate the expansion of the program to the rest of the Omani schools. This step resulted from a memorandum of understanding signed between the Ministry of Education and the Public Authority for Privatization and Partnership. This understanding also helped cement the Rolls Royce Foundation's commitment to supporting teachers, technicians and others involved in implanting the STEM Oman Education in schools (Ministry of Education, 2021).

Phrase 1: STEM Oman Program Training at the National Level

This training program was supervised by the British expert Mark Langley from the STEM Center at York University in the UK (Ministry of Education, 2021). The program was arranged under the auspices of the Innovation Department and the Scientific Olympiad at the Ministry of Education. The actual training was carried out by trainers who had undergone the STEM Oman External Program for Training of Trainers at York University, UK. The training period lasted for five days, from August 26 to August 30, 2018, and took place at the Specialist Institute for Professional Training of Teachers in Muscat. At the training were 22 male and female science teachers selected from different educational directorates that applied to the program. The aim was to provide participants with the skills and knowledge needed to start implementing the STEM Oman program in the twelve new schools. The content of the STEM Oman program included 13 teaching lessons for Grade 10 on topics such as movement, power, and weights.

Phrase 2: STEM Oman Program Training at the National Level

To prepare for the third stage of the STEM Oman program, the Ministry of Education organized a training workshop targeting 20 female science teachers. It took place between 18 - 22 of August 2019 at the Specialist Institute for Professional Training of Teachers in Muscat. This training program was delivered by Omani science supervisors and teachers who studied in the UK. It aimed to provide science teachers with the skills and experiences to start implementing the STEM Oman program in the twelve new schools in the third phase of the rollout. It was implemented under the supervision of the Innovation Department and the Scientific Olympiad in cooperation with the British STEM education expert Mark Langley (Ministry of Education, 2021).

Establishment of the STEM Oman Education Website

From the onset of the STEM Oman program, the Ministry of Education's goal was for the program to be a nationally accessible national education initiative organized and supervised by the ministry. Therefore, a website for the STEM Oman program was created by the British Rolls Royce Foundation. The website was completed in cooperation with the General Directorate of Information Technology and hosted on the ministry's educational portal.

The site contains a forum specific to the program through which opinions and experiences are exchanged between teachers associated with the program. In addition, the site has illustrative case studies whereby teachers share their experiences with various activities that form part of the STEM Oman program. Students can also benefit from the site and its contents through the link (https://stemOman.moe.gov.om/) (Ministry of Education, 2021).

Other Forms of STEM Oman Program Training

To further support the STEM Oman aims, the ministry has devised other training opportunities, such as the National Week for STEM Sciences and the Oman Science Festival. These additional training opportunities were adopted to raise awareness regarding sustainable development, science disciplines, and new technology.

The specific objectives of the National Week for STEM sciences are to:

1- Increase awareness of science and technology.
2- Encourage positive attitudes among students towards science.
3- Keep up with global trends related to the dissemination of information about science and technology.

4- Make science more accessible and spread a culture of scientific thinking among all segments of society.
5- Consolidate a scientific approach to problem solving among students.
6- Establish a link between students and science professionals to enable the discussion of scientific topics.
7- Change society's view of science by linking learning with entertainment and spreading a culture of fun education.
8- Encourage and motivate all members of society to think scientifically by arousing their passion for science.
9- Foster positive attitudes related to keeping up with future changes and developments in science. (Ministry of Education, Oman Educational Portal).

In 2019, the STEM Oman program training initiative morphed into a festival with a more holistic focus on the role of STEM in promoting teaching and learning science education. According to the Oman Observer (2019a), the following papers were presented at the Oman Science Festival:

Table 3. Papers presented at the Oman Science festival related to the STEM Oman program

Paper title
1. Supporting STEM Education: How Rolls-Royce and the STEM Ambassador network effectively engage primary and secondary education with STEM industries, leading to a wide benefit to society.
2. STEM Oman: Omani experience of STEM Program.
3. An Introduction to Makers Oman.
4. In Search for the Perfect STEM.
5. The Potential of 5G to transform STEM skill development.
6. Science and innovation in a changing world.
7. Brain Science: The Key to Successful in the 4th Industrial Revaluation.
8. The National Strategy for Research and Development 2040.

These intensive workshops based on published papers were conducted at the festival to help raise awareness of the benefits and ways of implementing the STEM Oman program. The festival was chosen as a place where students, teachers, and broad audiences could come to enjoy hands-on experiences and a wonderful atmosphere for learning about science and science education. The Oman Science Festival, 2019 is considered by Mohammed Al-Toobi as a new educational platform, which he contends is in line with the latest trends of using technology to provide educational learning processes within an interactive environment on a large scale for students, teachers, and society in general (Oman Observer, 2019a)

In 2021, the National Science Week STEM took place between 21-25 March 2021 as an online event due to the COVID-19 pandemic. The central theme for this series of events was "Our Sustainable Environment" and morning and evening sessions were held every day for five consecutive days (Oman Observer, March 22, 2021). Examples of topics covered in the National Science Week STEM are listed in the following table:

Table 4. Examples of topics covered in the National Science Week STEM (Oman Observer, March 22, 2021, & Oman Observer, March 27, 2021).

First Day	Second Day	Last day
• Smart Shopping • Farming without Soil • Renewable Energy is the Best Choice for Environmental Sustainability. • Plastic Waste Disposal • Methods for using Lab Equipment to Detect Food Safety. • Falaj Alassarni Drought Turned into Tourist Environment. • Green School initiative • Smart City Design • Food Security System • AI for Environmental Protection • Marine Pollution Control • Precision Instruments in Oil and Gas Fields, and their impact on preserving the environment. • The Green House • GLOBE Program's Environmental Impact.	• Alternative Energy • Palm Waste Recycling • Weather Changes • Implementation for the Aquaculture System. • The Scientific Café • Malpractice towards the Environment. • Using Moth to Conserve the Environment. • Satellite Environmental Application. • Biodiversity	• Ras Al Jinz Turtle Reserve: An integrated ecosystem. • Air pollution. • How do I make products from environmental waste? • Environmental photography skills. • Environmental compensation project for OQ8 Company. • Simple ways to recycle waste are to use it in our homes, school, and community. • Sustainability for waste resources. • How can we transfer knowledge of the sustainable environment to the market? • Peaceful nuclear techniques in the fields of environment and agriculture. • Eco 3D Environment. • How do we reduce our carbon footprint? • Use of augmented reality technology to promote and teach environmental sustainability. • Our sustainable environment and solar energy.

Omani Research on STEM

Several studies covering the implementation of STEM in Oman have been carried out to date. For instance, in 2015 Al-Shuhaimi conducted a study aimed at investigating the impact of STEM on the development of creative thinking and science achievement among 3rd grade students enrolled in basic education (grades 1-8) in the Muscat governorate. Results revealed that there were statistically significant differences between the experimental the control groups in creative thinking and science achievement in favor of the experimental group. The study showed that the higher growth in the experimental group was in three dimensions - knowledge, application and reasoning. Another study, by Ambusaidi et al. (2015), investigated Omani science teachers' beliefs towards STEM and their impact. The results of the study showed that, in general, teachers have firm beliefs toward the STEM approach. The results also showed no statistically significant differences in science teachers' beliefs about STEM for gender and teaching experience.

Elayyan and Al-Shizawi (2019) investigated teachers' perceptions of integrating STEM in Oman Schools. Their research findings showed that science teachers had positive perceptions towards integrating STEM in teaching science, believing it helps students acquire the critical skills and competencies needed to help them to keep pace with modern scientific developments and compete in the labor market. Ealyyan and Al-Mazzroi (2020) also researched obstacles that limit the implementation of STEM in Omani science education from the teachers' point of view. The findings showed high to medium barriers. Obstacles related to content ranked first (high barrier) followed by obstacles related to the learning environment (medium barrier), and finally obstacles related to the teacher (medium barrier). The researchers found no statistical significances due to teacher gender.

Alkharusi (2020) carried out a study aimed at identifying the perceptions of science teachers and students about the STEM Oman program. The result showed that science teachers and their students had significantly positive perceptions regarding of the design, implementation, and impact of the STEM Oman program. The results also revealed that the participants perceived moderate difficulties in implementing the program, most notably the weakness of the school internet and the insufficient time allocated to implement the activities. The results also indicated no statistically significant differences in teachers' perceptions of the STEM program due to gender, years of teaching experience, and years of supervision. However, there were statistically significant gender differences in students' perceptions about the "design and implementation of the program" (females were more positive) as well as in the "difficulties in implementing the program" (males perceived more difficulties). A recent study by Shahat et al. (2022) revealed that student science teachers believed themselves to be highly successful in teaching science using the engineering design process as an approach to STEM education. A more recent study by Shahat et al. (2023) showed low and moderate levels of proficiency related to the stages of engineering design among preservice science teachers in Oman. Differences between males and females in terms of performance on tasks related to the stages of engineering design were found, with females scoring higher overall on the assessment. Biology preservice teachers scored higher than teachers from physics and chemistry majors in the following of engineering design stages: problem identification, solution investigation, planning, production, testing, communication, production, and improvement. There were also differences between teachers studying in the Bachelor of Science (BSc) program and the Teacher Qualification Diploma (TQD) program. In the BSc program, student teachers study for four years, and the subjects include pedagogy and science. While in the TQD program, BSc graduates majoring in physics, chemistry, and biology can enroll in the two semester program that covers pedagogy only (Shahat et al., 2022b).

A STEM related study was carried by Al-Hinai et al. (2020) to examine how learning engineering design impacts the engineering approaches of eighth-grade students. The students were challenged to solve real-world problems using the engineering design process. The findings showed significant improvement in the student's ability to identify problems, optimize and develop solutions, and utilize systems thinking. However, there was no statistically significant difference in their ability to visualize, demonstrate creativity in problem-solving, and adapt to changing circumstances.

A recent study implemented in Oman by Al-Shukaili et al. (2023) aimed to determine the level of inclusion of the fields of Science, Technology, Engineering, Art, and Mathematics (STEAM) in the Omani science curricula content for Grades 5-8. The results showed a total percentage of 37.83% (medium inclusion level) and considerable variation in the level of inclusion of these fields. The results also showed differences in the inclusion of STEAM fields across the different grades. These differences were between 41.87% for the fifth and 36.18% for the eighth grade.

There is a healthy interest by postgraduate researchers in Omani universities to study different aspects of STEM education. For instance, the postgraduate programs at Sultan Qaboos University (SQU) encourage doctoral and master's level students to explore aspects of STEM education using different qualitative and quantitative research methods. One topic that has garnered particular attention is the exploration of the effectiveness of innovative STEM-related teaching methods such as engineering design, gamification, virtual reality, augmented reality, 3D printing, and mobile education. Some educational technologies have resulted from these postgraduate projects, such as a mobile application called Dr. Science and an immersive science lab (Al-Hosni et al., 2022); both of these research projects received regional awards. There is also a doctoral project to train science teachers on using Next Generation Science Standards (NGSS), which share different elements with STEM education, such as the use of engineering design and science and engineering practices.

The National STEM Training Program Funded by His Majesty Trust Fund Strategic Grants (HMTF)

A training program for science teachers was launched in 2022 in light of the STEM education model that emanated from the strategic project "Developing a National Training Framework for Science, Technology, Engineering, and Mathematics (STEM) based competencies in Oman". An important aspect of this initiative is the measurement of its impact on science teachers' content knowledge and teaching practices, and the assessment of the influence on their students' engineering task performance related to STEM. The program trains science teachers over four teaching modules on integrating STEM education according to a specific novel STEM teaching model. The training program lasted two weeks. It included a presentation of the general theoretical framework for the STEM approach and its importance; as well as a presentation on the concept of engineering design and its applications in STEM teaching, which is one of this project's most important training goals. The authors of this chapter developed this training to enable science teachers to integrate the STEM approach into their teaching of scientific topics covered by the science curricula of the Sultanate of Oman. The focus was on the core principles and previous studies on which the approach is based and the provision of general guidance to teachers to enable them to offer effective STEM lessons. Emphasis was also placed on the need to clarify the concepts of technology, engineering, and engineering design and the relationship between them. Additionally, teachers received support in the form of plans for engaging activities that can be utilized in the classroom. Following this, the participants were trained on modules from the STEM education model, which included preparatory activities aimed at clarifying technological and engineering concepts related to the scientific topic of the different modules. Participants were also given practical tasks based on scientific challenges – in this stage groups had to find practical solutions to problems by following engineering design steps. The program included an in-depth examination of four modules targeted at fifth and sixth-grade students. To facilitate this, participants worked in groups to prepare lessons related to the modules using the STEM learning model; these plans were then presented, discussed, and suggestions given for improvement. The impact of this training program will be evaluated during the second semester of the 2023 academic year.

The Barriers to STEM Education in Oman

Research has showed that most Omani teachers believed they are hampered by the poor quality of their school internet and the insufficient time allocated to implement the STEM activities (Alkharusi, 2020). The MoE needs to set standards consistent with the needs of STEM education in schools; however, STEM education in Omani schools is not considered by the MoE as a formal part of education but as an enriching activity that is only provided to grade 10 students. As a result, there are no official ongoing STEM preparation programs or schools explicitly prepared for STEM education, and there are no teachers officially trained to effectively teach integrated STEM - only science and mathematics separately (Shahat et al., 2022). Issues with content, the learning environment, and teachers are limiting the implementation of the STEM approach in Oman science education. Teachers thought that the curriculum content was not presented as fully integrated subjects, that the learning environment makes implementing the activities very challenging, and that teachers were not adequately prepared regarding STEM education requirements. Hence, STEM education has material, training, and logistical shortcomings that Oman should seek to remedy (Ealyyan & Al-Mazzroi, 2020).

In general, there is a gap between school requirements and the actual teaching in STEM programs. One reason for this, according to the MOE, is that teacher education programs and the courses they offer to prepare prospective teachers to teach the national school curriculum may be lacking. They state, in particular, that teacher training programs lack cohesion between scientific and educational content. Specialized STEM subject courses such as biology and physics are studied in isolation from each other, and they are not integrated with pedagogy courses. There seems to be little integration across STEM subjects, and evaluation guidelines from bodies such as the National Science Teachers Association (NSTA) are very much based on individual topics (Shahat & Al-Amri, 2023). Additionally, due to limited resources, a limited number of schools were incorporated into the STEM Oman program, and thus other schools are still waiting for inclusion. HEIs that train science teachers do not explicitly offer STEM-based programs and initiatives, thus impacting teacher classroom performance related to STEM topics.

Future of STEM Education in Oman

Sakil Malik, the Senior Global Practice Lead for Education at Development Alternatives, Inc. (DAI), an international development company, argues that STEM disciplines are vitally important for today's Omani students. He addressed many issues at the 2019 International Conference of the Fourth Industrial Revolution organized by the Omani Ministry of Education's General Directorate of Education in the Governorate of North Al Batina, Oman. STEM has become a necessity if the country wishes to be a regional and global leader. He asserts, "It is crucial for youth to be equipped with the knowledge and skills to solve tough problems, gather and evaluate evidence, and make sense of information. These are skills that students learn by studying the subjects collectively known as STEM." (DAI, 2019). To improve STEM education in Oman, Malik recommends the following (cf. DAI, 2019):

- Creating a community-wide vision for STEM-based teaching supported by businesses, libraries, museums, community organizations, and schools.
- Making "play" an intentional aspect of teaching because children are attracted to games -including video games - that intrigue them and provide rewards and recognition.
- Including exploration and discovery activities in nature.
- Using project-based learning that children can pursue in teams and accomplish within a set timeframe.
- Incorporating large scale global challenges - food, housing, transportation, climate change, security, and other areas in children's learning - so today's students are better prepared to address real-world challenges in coming decades.
- Building flexible learning spaces that integrate tools, games, immersive media, and augmented and virtual reality, as well as accommodating children of varying abilities, including the disabled (DAI, 2019)

Current development related to implementing STEM Oman education is a partnership project between DAI's Sustainable Business Group (SBG) and Oman Children's Museum. This project started in 2019-2022, and it was designed and implemented by the SBG to provide services to a sizeable segment of the Omani population. As indicated on the DAI website, the project will provide services to children across Oman. The STEMAzone Initiative will inspire young Omanis to enter STEAM fields and set them on the STEMA pathway from an early age, which studies show is critical to building a skilled workforce. The STEMAzone will be national in scope and implemented in partnership with the Oman Children's Museum. Under this partnership, Oman's Children's Museum will serve as the anchor location in Muscat for the initiative, hosting visitors from the public and schools interested in engaging in STEAM-related activities, including coding, robotics, and 3D printing. Due to the COVID-19 pandemic, the project pivoted to a hybrid model combining in-person and virtual activities. The Virtual STEMAzone featured online webinars and courses on a range of topics, and it will be accessible for free to students across Oman. The goals of the STEMAzone activities are to (1) Spark interest in and passion for STEAM fields in Omani youth, (2) Equip Omani youth with the skills they need to engage in and benefit from the modern economy, and (3) Support the next generation of STEAM innovators and leaders in Oman (DAI, 2019-2022). Considering the results of Al-Shukaili et al. (2023) study, it is recommended that the level of inclusion of STEAM subjects in the Omani science curricula content for grades 5-8 be increased.

To improve STEM education in Oman, diverse strategies must be implemented at various educational levels - from primary and secondary schools to HEIs. A larger number of schools should be incorporated into the STEM Oman program, while schools that are still not included should be urged to introduce STEM education using their own resources, rather than waiting for inclusion in the national program. HEIs ought to offer additional STEM-based programs and initiatives, as well as collaborate with schools to support their STEM education endeavors. Teacher training and professional development for both pre-service and in-service teachers must feature more STEM-related topics. Additionally, teacher preparation programs should consider courses such as communication, technology and curriculum design, the engineering design process in math and science education, transdisciplinary learning approaches, and the implementation of STEM in the classroom. Also, teacher training programs must help teachers integrate STEM subjects more effectively through reflection on student teaching, field-based experiences, and, more specifically, teaching during microteaching. Furthermore, there is a need to reduce the number of isolated science and pedagogy courses and offer a more integrated range of subjects. There is also a need to focus more on the practical rather than the theoretical aspects of science teaching. Providing more activities that incorporate problem solving and engineering design are therefore essential, and these could be improved by making prototype lessons available, allowing students to solve realistic problems, and fostering creativity in classes (Shahat & Al-Amri, 2023).

REFERENCES

Al-Hinai, M., Al-Balushi, S.M. & Ambusaidi, A. (2020). The effectiveness of engineering design in developing engineering habits of mind among eight grade students in Sultanate of Oman. *Journal of Education & Psychological Studies (Oman), 14*(2), 362-380. doi:10.24200/jeps.vol14iss2pp362-380

Al-Hosni, A., Al-Balushi, S. M., Ambusaidi, A., & Alkharusi, H. (2022). ((accepted). The effectiveness of teaching using a phone application based on the gamification approach in developing the motivation for achievement among fourth-grade students in light of the Corona pandemic (Covid-19). [University of Jordan]. *Studies: Educational Sciences.*

Al-Shukaili, A., Shahat, M.A., & Said, S. I. (2023). *Level of including the fields of Science, Technology, Engineering, Art, and Mathematics (STEAM) in the Omani Science Curricula content for Grades 5–8.* [Submitted for publication]

Alkharusi, A. (2020). *Perceptions of teachers and students participating in the STEM OMAN program*. [Unpublished Master's Thesis, Sultan Qaboos University. Muscat, Sultanate of Oman].

Ambusaidi, A., Al-Harthi, A., & Al-Shuhaimi, A. (2015). *Science teachers' beliefs in the Sultanate of Oman towards science and technology and engineering and mathematics (STEM) and their relationship to some variables*. The 1st Excellent Conference in Teaching & Learning in Science and Mathematics. King Saud University, Riyadh, Saudi Arabia.

DAI. (2019). *DAI's Sakil Malik presents recommendations for improving STEM education in Oman*. DAI. https://www.dai.com/news/dais-sakil-malik-presents-recommendations-for-improving-stem-education-in-oman#:~:text=To%20improve%20STEM%20education%20in,organizations%20as%20well%20as%20schools

DAI. (2022). *Oman—Corporate Social Investment Science, Technology, Engineering, and Mathematics (CSI STEM) Program*. DAI. https://www.dai.com/our-work/projects/oman-corporate-social-investment-science-technology-engineering-and-mathematics-csi-stem-program

Elayyan, S., & Al-Mazroi, Y. (2020). Obstacles that limit the implementation of STEM approach in science education from teachers' point view. *Journal of Educational and Psychological Sciences*, *4*(2), 57–74.

Elayyan, S., & Al-Shizawi, F. (2019). Teachers' perceptions of integrating STEM in Omani schools. *International Journal of Education*, *8*(1), 16–21. doi:10.34293/education.v8i1.1136

Ministry of Education. (2021). *STEM Oman Overview of external undergraduate scholarships.* . Ministry of Education Ministry of Higher Education, Research and Innovation (2020-2021). https://heac.gov.om/media/doc/DE001_2021.pdf

Ministry of Higher Education, Research and Innovation. (2022). *Information and data about STEM program at the Ministry of Higher Education, Research and Innovation*. [Unpublished requested report]. Muscat, Sultanate of Oman. Ministry of Higher Education, Research and Innovation. https://www.moheri.gov.om/InnerPage.aspx?id=612cd2b4-f14c-4f48-9dc0-1fa809efe308&culture=en

Oman Educational Portal. (2018). *The national strategy for education 2040*. Oman. https://www.educouncil.gov.om/downloads/Ts775SPNmXDQ.pdf

Oman Educational Portal. (2020). *Objectives of national week for STEM sciences.* MOE. https://home.moe.gov.om/region/stem2021/page-prog

Oman Observer. (2018). First phase of STEM Oman' launched in six public schools. *Oman Observer.* https://www.Omanobserver.om/article/61954/Local/first-phase-of-stem-Oman-launched-in-six-public-schools

Oman Observer. (2019). 915 Students sign for STEM. *Oman Observer.* https://www.Omanobserver.om/article/38014/Local/915-students-sign-up-for-stem

Oman Observer. (2019a). Ministry of Education launches new educational platform. *Oman Observer.* https://www.Omanobserver.om/article/21617/Main/ministry-of-education-launches-new-educational-platform

Oman Observer. (2021). National science week STEM begins with online events. *Oman Observer.* https://www.Omanobserver.om/article/1784/Local/national-science-week-stem-begins-with-online-events

Oman Observer. (2021). Science week observed with focus on environment. *Oman Observer.* https://www.Omanobserver.om/article/1558/Local/science-week-observed-with-focus-on-environment

Oxford Business Group. (2021). *Interview with: Rahma bint Ibrahim Al Mahrooqi, Minister for Higher Education, Research and Innovation (MoHERI).* OBG. https://oxfordbusinessgroup.com/views/rahma-bint-ibrahim-al-mahrooqi-minister-higher-education-research-and-innovation-moheri

Shahat, M. A., & Al-Amri, M. (2023). Science teacher preparation in Oman: Strengths and shortcomings related to STEM education. In S. Al-Balushi, L. Martin, & Y. Song (Eds.), *Reforming science teacher education programs in the STEM Era: International practices.* Springer. doi:10.1007/978-3-031-27334-6_10

Shahat, M. A., Al-Balushi, S. M., & Al-Amri, M. (2022). Investigating pre-Service science teachers' self-efficacy beliefs for teaching science through engineering design processes. *Interdisciplinary Journal of Environmental and Science Education, 18*(4), e2291. doi:10.21601/ijese/12121

Shahat, M. A., Al-Balushi, S. M., & Al-Amri, M. (2023). Measuring preservice science teachers' performance on engineering design process tasks: Implications for fostering STEM education. *Arab Gulf Journal of Scientific Research.* doi:10.1108/AGJSR-12-2022-0277

Chapter 4
Saudi Arabia's Vision 2030 and Its Impact on STEM Education

Holly Nicole Babineau
Northcentral University, USA

ABSTRACT

The Kingdom of Saudi Arabia (KSA) released a plan in 2016 to achieve goals set for the country by the year 2030. Included in this plan, 'Vision 2030,' is a plan for transforming the education system into one that will better suit the Kingdom's needs, increasing the amount of science, technology, engineering, and math (STEM) studies and trainings in the nation. It is with this vision that Saudi Arabia has fully taken on the task of training educators across the Kingdom in different programs that teach all aspects of STEM. To see the impact of these programs, and to ensure they are working, there are studies being conducted that follow participants in the programs and receive feedback throughout all stages. These studies allow challenges to be uncovered early in the process and therefore make it possible to establish solutions. The purpose of this chapter is to examine the Saudi Vision 2030's impact on STEM education.

DOI: 10.4018/978-1-6684-6883-8.ch004

Copyright © 2023, IGI Global. Copying or distributing in print or electronic forms without written permission of IGI Global is prohibited.

VISION 2030'S GOALS FOR STEM IN EDUCATION

With Saudi Arabia's Vision 2030 having several objectives, a common theme among them succeeding is the need for a world-class education system. Having goals such as a strong economy, effective government, improved healthcare system, and so much more, the demand for students with a strong STEM background is apparent (Kingdom of Saudi Arabia, 2022). It is with this Vision that students will be given the skills they need to take on this task and play a part in accomplishing these goals. Unfortunately, implementing STEM practices in the classroom is not such an easy task. With the knowledge of what STEM is being a question amongst some teachers in Saudi Arabia, proper training and professional development are needed. However, it is something the Kingdom anticipated in the Vision and thus has implemented programs to train and educate teachers on the basics of STEM (Pearson, 2016). Partnering with companies and universities such as Pearson Education, DigiPen Institute of Technology, Monash University, and so many more, a lot has gone into designing and implementing these trainings and information sessions (Smith et al., 2019).

LITERATURE REVIEW OF PROGRAMS IN PLACE

Given the apparent need for solid STEM practices and skills to be brought into the classroom, the Kingdom of Saudi Arabia needs to prepare its teachers and all others involved in this endeavor. To do this, the Kingdom has established many programs to assist teachers in making these changes and introducing these ideas. With STEM ideas being relatively new to the Kingdom, all involved must understand this concept before taking on the task of teaching it. The KSA has worked with many organizations and universities to do what is needed to give its teachers the best chance possible at completing this mission.

Immersion Programs

Having plans to train as many as 25,000 teachers across the Kingdom of Saudi Arabia, the KSA Ministry of Education partnered with international universities and education-based companies to implement different programs involving STEM (Smith et al., 2019). One of these programs, working in collaboration with Pearson Education, is a Math and Science Professional Development Program. In this program, 500 'master trainers' will receive the skills and practice they need to go out then and train other teachers throughout the Kingdom (Pearson, 2016). In addition, in another program taking place, the KSA partnered with Monash University to initiate a 44-

week program in which participants learned the ins and outs of STEM education and how to implement it in the classroom (Smith et al., 2019). Included in this program is the opportunity to observe the actual implementation of STEM practices for 17 weeks in the classroom, hosted by Australian schools. This opportunity provides program participants with the tools they need and the chance to see everything they are learning in action. With this, program participants can fully understand the concept of STEM and what it is and how it can be brought into the classroom in simple ways.

More recently, the KSA Ministry of Education and Saudi Arabia Culture Mission partnered with other international universities to provide teachers with STEM immersion programs in different countries. From 2019 to 2020, over 1,000 teachers and their families were sponsored by this partnership and able to participate in a one-year abroad experience in locations such as Britain, Canada, Australia, and Finland (Kewalramani et al., 2022). Throughout this experience, the teachers in this program that have been located in Australia participated in a study, giving the insight needed to determine what methods are most successful. This information provided by these 45 teachers from the program help significantly in preparing Saudi Arabia's educators to implement STEM practices in their classrooms. The goal of this professional learning program is to not only produce teachers confident in applying the learned skills to their instruction but also able to take what they learned through the immersion and educate other teachers in the Kingdom. While in this learning community, teachers can develop a deep understanding of STEM practices and all their benefits and establish implementation practices they can apply in their classrooms. Each of these practices and skills held by participants are evaluated through the completion of a capstone project in which they create lessons and practices that they will take to their own classrooms and share with coworkers and collogues.

These skills and practices are just some of the things participants in this program are gaining from this experience. In addition to leaving the program with a deeper understanding, teachers who participated also left with many resources. These resources include networks created to help these teachers stay in contact and continue to share ideas and struggles. It is through these networks that educators will be able to continue to evolve their practices and ideas, as well as see what might be working elsewhere. This opportunity to connect via networks opens a whole other door of possibilities. It allows for the connection of educators and experts, as well as new teachers and seasoned. It is this communication by all and sharing of ideas and concepts that teachers all over the Kingdom will be able to continue to grow and reform their ideas and practices.

While many of the immersion programs and other opportunities offered for teachers in developing their STEM practices can benefit educators of all grade levels, as understanding continues to flourish, it is primitive that this is broken down further. Looking at what needs to be done in each grade level or grouping will allow teachers to establish their roles better and determine what is going to help their students the most.

Programs and Practices by Education Level Groupings

Many of the STEM skills that need to be taught can be broken down and allocated to where they are deemed most appropriate, identifying which material is best fit for each educational level groupings. For example, the STEM concepts that should be taught to middle schoolers will be much different from those taught in preschool. However, both are vital to the success of the students. By establishing the roles of teachers in each grade level and what the most beneficial STEM concepts to teach are, students will have the best opportunity possible to build their STEM knowledge while having the proper foundation. With this, while establishing this practice is vital to the students' learning, as is the reflection on what has been decided. Thus, each of the determinations per age grouping needs to be continuously evaluated to ensure it is still appropriate and deemed the best fit. This is crucial as we continue to learn more about STEM practices globally, and what might have been thought to be best at one point may not still be true. It is because of this that consistent evaluation needs to happen, with reformation where needed.

Early Childhood and Kindergarten

The early childhood stage is one in which concepts and ideas can be introduced in a fun, creative way. It is the most crucial time for a play-based environment in which students can be exposed to multisensory ways of learning while having the freedom to explore and develop their own ideas. Given this time of exploration, it is imperative that STEM practices be introduced. At this stage, STEM practices incorporate art, and are often referred to as STEAM (Science, Technology, Engineering, Arts, and Mathematics). It is through these STEAM practices that students can learn how to ask questions and think of, search for, or invent solutions to real-world problems from a young age (Alghamdi, A.A, 2022). With this integration of STEAM, students of young ages are building their creativity and ability to problem solve, both necessary skills to have when continuing to build STEM practices.

Through building this foundation of curiosity, question-asking, and problem-solving from a young age, students are given the chance to thrive in a STEM world before the age of 6. Without even realizing it, through play and creativity, students are increasing their innovation skills in playful ways, while building the foundation they'll need as they continue their educational journeys in STEM. This is not to be said that all of this is done just through play. In fact, as stated in an article from the Early Childhood Education Journal (Alghamdi, A.A, 2022), after working with the National Association of the Education of Young Children, the Kingdom of Saudi Arabia's Ministry of Education released Saudi Early Learning Standards, or SELS. It is with these SELS that the Kingdom has set standards for the learning of children ages 3 to 6, with the purpose of providing information on best practices to educators, parents, and care providers. Each of these standards included the vital skills needed to succeed when continuing STEM practices, including inquiry, logical thinking, creativity, and familiarity with technology. To help make this possible, the KSA has worked to introduce technology and training into the classroom and schools across the Kingdom through a few different innovations.

These innovations, also mentioned in Alghamdi's Early Childhood Education Journal article (2022), were not done by one organization alone. One of the innovations, for example, that was introduced to the KSA was made possible by a partnership between the Ministry of Education and the Ministry of Communication and Information Technology. Together, the two launched the 'Future Trucks' initiative, where trucks that contained fourth industrial revolution (4IR) tools and scientific materials can provide a STEAM approach to learning for children and public-school students (Alghamdi, A.A, 2022). Using these trucks, not only are students able to create and develop STEM skills but can also be used to help educate their parents and guardians. These trucks are giving young students the hands-on learning experiences they need to have fun while establishing the foundation they need to thrive in STEM education.

While in early childhood education the incorporation of STEM largely involves playful tactics and exploration, in kindergarten the need for technology to be introduced is imperative. The introduction of technology can be as simple as using it to teach lessons across the curriculum, as with students that are still in this young stage the most important aspect is exposure. This use of technology can be a large asset to the presentation of concepts being taught, from interest levels to understanding, as many of the technological materials being used can be extremely helpful in supporting learning. In addition to this, the integration of technology in the classroom at a young age has been found to enhance the cognitive and social development of children, as well as facilitate collaboration and encourage children to cooperate when attempting to problem solve (Alghamdi, J. et al., 2022). This integration also enhances the development of academic skills such as reading, writing, and mathematics. Given this knowledge, the existence of a link between tech and the teaching of content areas is crucial for students' continued development before entering elementary school.

Primary

To best support primary (elementary) school students in their journey of STEM education, 21st-century skills need to be present in the classroom. Included in these skills are critical thinking, creativity, collaboration, communication, several types of literacy (information, media, technology, digital), flexibility, leadership, initiative, productivity, social skills, and local and global connections (Alotaibi & Alghamdi, 2022). Knowing this, the Kingdom of Saudi Arabia's Education and Training Evaluation Commission (ETEC) took a monumental step in submitting a proposal to include 21st-century skills in KSA public education curriculum. It is with this proposal that the linking of different domains across the curriculum is suggested, allowing for the deepest understanding of concepts by students. One intention of this proposal is to help educate people about the skills and qualifications that are currently in high demand, as well as create a general framework to help include the future teaching of these skills.

One of the most beneficial ways to accomplish the goal of this cross-curriculum framework, and establish the skills needed, is by rigorous reading materials being introduced and used throughout instruction. An example of these rigorous reading materials includes scientific texts, which foster deeper thinking by students. It is through the reading of scientific texts that students are able to learn and develop critical thinking, analysis, and communication skills, as the understanding of the text requires them to do so. Not only are these texts presenting students with the challenge of establishing comprehension of the concept they are reading but are also helping them to build an in-depth understanding of scientific concepts and principles (Alotaibi & Alghamdi, 2022). It is through the habit of reading these challenging texts that students will be able to have early exposure to 21st-century skills.

Through the addition of scientific, and other rigorous content, based texts at the elementary school age, students can develop a stronger appreciation for these subjects, leading to further curiosity and discovery. By getting into the habit of reading scientific texts from a young age, not only are students exposed to advanced concepts and vocabulary but are also able to uncover the prevalence of science in everyday life. It is with this realization that students can connect deeper with what they are learning and embed it into the foundational skills for STEM they are creating, as well as help them to become self-motivated learners (Alotaibi & Alghamdi, 2022). It is these skills specifically that the Kingdom needs in its citizens to achieve the goals set, and by beginning to establish them from an elementary age these students will be most prepared to continue their journey in STEM education.

Secondary

As students continue into the secondary education portion of their lives (middle school and high school), it is the hope that they have established the skills and habits needed to continue to embark on the rigorous journey that is STEM education. With these skills and habits, students are well prepared to take on the next challenges presented to them in their education, as well as in their daily lives. As the Kingdom of Saudi Arabia is continuing to increase the introduction of science curricula into classrooms and education standards, it is crucial for students to be exposed to and explore prevalent topics. One extensive example of this is COVID-19. Experiencing global happenings in which STEM subjects and practices are at the center, it is imperative for students to be educated on such topics. In a world in which citizens have just been forced to see the importance of science-based knowledge and critical thinking, not to mention the goals of the Kingdom's Vision 2030, it is vital that students are equipped with the understanding needed to prevail in light of a pandemic or other medical-based emergencies. This being said, students in secondary education (middle school and high school), need to be exposed to medical terminology and vocabulary to be successful in the ever-evolving STEM world.

In an article produced by the Journal of Science Education and Technology (Alghamdi, A.K.H., et al., 2022), it is argued that the teaching of science-based knowledge, such as pandemics, medical terminology, and epidemiology of diseases, can be helpful to students at a middle school age. It is stated that this teaching can be beneficial to students' long-term memory, as well as help them to create successful habits and lifestyles necessary in a STEM world. With the knowledge that history tends to repeat itself, and the knowledge gained on pandemics, and everything involved in them, it is a necessity to teach this to the youth, as we have seen the effect of pandemics on all of humanity. It is with this argument that the article states the importance of updating the secondary education curriculum to include updated scientific knowledge to best prepare the youth to approach challenges with the most relevant and timely health knowledge.

The learning of this knowledge not only helps students build the foundational skills they need in terms of the information they have but also their ability to think critically and overcome challenges in innovative ways. By preparing students from a young age, they can be best equipped to confidently handle all future challenges with the most up-to-date information, as well as the strongest skills. This will allow students to continue to approach STEM subjects and topics with ease, as well as work independently and collaboratively on projects and tasks, as they will have a strong foundation built with the skills and knowledge they need.

Teacher Prep and Professional Development

To give students every opportunity possible to thrive in STEM education, it is imperative that teachers receive the proper training they need to implement these practices. It is with this that teacher prep programs, as well as continued education for teachers in practice (professional development), need to be extremely effective for all participants. With the changing curriculum and the requirement for so many new practices, teachers need to be given the time and leniency to learn and understand what is being asked of them. This can be made possible through successful teacher preparation programs, as well as professional development and professional learning community opportunities for teachers working in the field.

As STEM practices become more and more apparent in the field of education and throughout the curriculum, the need for teachers to be prepared is extremely obvious. While professional development will help the educators in the field continue to learn and establish these practices, it is vital that the teachers in prep programs are being held to the highest of standards. These programs need to demand full understanding and preparedness of STEM skills and practices, as well as their implementation of them before teachers are in classrooms of their own. To do this, education prep programs need to look at what is working in different programs and apply those factors to their own. An example of this may include the completion of capstone projects as seen in some of the immersion programs, where participants are required to take everything they have learned throughout the program and apply it to a project they need to fulfill before program completion. This can include the creation of lessons and practices they plan to implement in their own classrooms, or innovations they may find beneficial to student learning. By creating these practices ahead of time, teachers will feel more confident when implementing, and thus the lessons will reach a higher level of success.

The requirement of a capstone or other similar projects prior to teacher prep program completion fosters educators that are ready to enter the field with solid ideas and the confidence needed to establish them in a classroom of their own. As teachers come out of these rigorous programs, they will be able to take on the task of not only implementing STEM practices in their own classrooms but also sharing the ideas and practices they have learned with others in the school. It is through this collaborative community that all educators will be able to reach a level of success in their implementation, and only grow from there. As these teachers continue to grow through participation in professional development, they also need to be given the chance to discuss and collaborate. This can be done through the establishment of Professional Learning Communities (PLCs). Professional learning communities are an opportunity for educators, and all involved in schools, to get together and discuss and collaborate on practices and lessons. These can be used to help teachers better understand STEM and all that goes into it, as well as give struggling teachers the boost they need to achieve success in their own classrooms. It is through these PLCs and professional development opportunities that teachers will be able to continue to gain the knowledge and confidence they need to teach the youth these vital STEM skills.

The need for professional development is not only held by teachers. In fact, for Saudi Arabia to be most successful in their implementation of STEM practices, everyone involved should be fully educated continuously (Maashi et al., 2022). This includes teachers, leaders, supervisors, administration, and anyone else that is involved in this execution of STEM practices. Having everyone work together as a team, and everyone participating in professional development opportunities, each can understand what is expected of them, as well as what others will need from them. Just as teachers cannot be expected to take on this entire implementation of STEM on their own, all others involved need support as well. This means the collaboration of policymakers, administrators, educators, and so many more to ensure every basis of what is needed can be achieved.

In a study done through Research in Science & Technological Education (2022), the effectiveness of science teachers' professional development programs, held both online and face-to-face was evaluated. Through this study, it was found that professional development programs held online were just as successful, if not more, than the programs held in person, face-to-face. This was looked at in terms of conceptual understanding, showing that the teachers participating in the online setting gathered a similar (or deeper) understanding of concepts. In addition to this, the study also found that participants in the online professional development had a more positive overall satisfaction with the program. This study has shown not only that online professional development options are available but just as effective, if not more, than those held in person. This realization creates several more opportunities for STEM professional development through online settings. With the online model being easy to deliver, training can be offered to anyone from anywhere in the Kingdom, making it possible for teachers to continue to expand their knowledge, on any given subject.

This online format that can be used for professional development not only makes it possible for teachers to learn more about any content area but also provides the opportunity to connect with other educators in various locations. This allows for not only the sharing of current ideas but can also help to foster the development of new ones. Connecting with other teachers, as well as experts, administrators, and anyone else that may be present for the program creates an environment in which questions can be asked and answered, as well as a creative space where inspiration can soar. It is through these connections, collaborations, and conversations that STEM practices continue to evolve and develop, showing the importance of making them possible for all.

EVALUATING PROGRAMS IN PLACE

Currently, there are several programs in place to train and educate teachers on STEM education. To find out if these programs are achieving what they are hoping to, studies have been conducted in which participants complete surveys throughout the course of the program. These responses make it possible to evaluate whether the program is succeeding or if there are issues to be worked out.

In the case of many of the mentioned STEM programs, when looking at the answers from the first survey it is clear there is a misunderstanding of what STEM is for many participants. For example, after being asked to describe what they believe STEM education means, many answers were unclear or stated, "Honestly do not know but I have heard before that it involves the programming of robots" (Smith et al., 2019). This response shows a clear disconnect in the understanding of what is hoped to be achieved through the implementation of STEM education, as well as what it is. To reach the goals the Kingdom has set, it is crucial that teachers have a solid understanding of KSA's plans, what is needed from them, and the basics of what STEM actually is. It is not until there is a firm understanding of these concepts that teachers will be able to even start thinking of implementing STEM practices in their classrooms.

This disconnect in the understanding of what STEM means was seen in teachers not only across the Kingdom but across all grade levels. It is with this that the need for understanding is obvious, as is the need for further looking into other possible misunderstandings. Similarly to how the needs of students can be broken down by grade level groups, as can the needs of the teachers. With something different being required of each of them, it is imperative that every single person involved feels comfortable and confident in their role.

Looking at the requirements and happenings in Saudi Arabia's early education and kindergarten programs, it seems as though what is needed is set in place and well on its way to being achieved. However, despite the release of the SELs standards previously mentioned for early childhood learners, there still seems to be some disconnect when it comes to what STEM is. A large reason behind this could be the fact that even in the release of SELs standards, not once was "STEM" mentioned by name (Alghamdi, A.A., 2022). Despite all the practices and skills required in these standards having a direct correlation to STEM and what it is, it is not once classified by name. With the large need for STEM and all of its practices in the Kingdom, it should be mentioned in any context possible, allowing everyone to become more familiar with it. Through the naming of what these practices and skills are, the Kingdom has a great opportunity to make the connection between STEM and what is right there in their standards. With this minor change in wording, so much more can be achieved and accomplished simply due to the understanding it could foster.

CHALLENGES IN IMPLEMENTING STEM EDUCATION STRATEGIES

With the fact that several teachers in the Kingdom of Saudi Arabia struggle to identify the concept and meaning of STEM, there are many challenges found in the attempt of implementation. Despite the fact there were many program participants that did understand what STEM is and what it contains, there were still other challenges found when said teachers tried to execute the practices they learned in their own classroom (Madani, 2020). Having a strong set curriculum that teachers need to follow, many reported they found it difficult to include STEM in their classroom. However, this challenge alone again rises the issue that teachers in KSA are still not fully understanding what STEM is, and the everyday use that it has (Smith et al., 2019). Many teachers are struggling to see the amount of uses and implementations possible throughout the day, from use of problem-solving skills to simply asking a question in a different way, both fostering students' deeper understanding. It is these small changes that allow students to use higher order thinking and problem solve, both crucial pieces of STEM education.

In addition to the misunderstandings of what STEM is and what it means for the classroom, there is also a large call for the increased use of technologies in the classroom. The KSA has made the need for this use clear, as well as the expectations of technology being used to support instruction across curriculums. However, while this implementation of technology in younger grades seems easy enough, the newness of these materials cannot be forgotten. With many teachers across the Kingdom having limited knowledge of technology and all its uses, the integration of STEM practices and materials can be a challenge for these educators. While there are some teachers entering the field that have been exposed to these technologies and the ideas of using them in the classroom, not all are as comfortable and confident with them. In addition to this, the number of materials needed is a lot higher than the limited amount that is had. Without having access to the quantity of computers or technologies needed to make this integration possible, not all areas of the Kingdom are able to achieve this (Alghamdi, J. et al., 2022). This shows regardless of the grade level or youngness of the students, all teachers need to be prepared to put these practices into action. It is not until all educators achieve that level of comfort and confidence that the implementation of STEM integration will be successful.

Along with teachers' feelings of not being prepared to incorporate the use of technology in the classroom, many teachers are also struggling with understanding the STEM content itself. For example, while many teachers in the Kingdom know and understand that students need to be able to read scientific texts, they are still hesitant to use them in their instruction. Instead, it is commonly seen that teachers are only providing them as reference materials, if at all (Alotaibi & Alghamdi, 2022).

This may be due to the teachers' lack of comprehension of the materials themselves, thus making it difficult for them to teach. This hesitation shows the extreme need for educator learning opportunities in which they can continue their own educations to better fit the needs of their students. It is through opportunities such as these that teachers will be able to develop the skills they need. In addition to presenting these opportunities for current teachers, the Kingdom needs to ensure instances such as this are prevented through the reflection of teacher preparation programs and the questioning of why this is happening in the first place.

While teachers' understanding of the content they are using is crucial, as is the effectiveness of the materials being used. In a study completed by *Education Sciences* (Alotaibi & Alghamdi, 2022), the science materials being used in the KSA intermediate-level classes were found to have little to no presence of 21st-century skills. Based on having previously been deemed important to include in the KSA science curricula, these 21st-century skills should be included in the texts and resources being used in the Kingdom's education system to give students the best chance at adapting these skills themselves. Also mentioned in the study, when the biology books were evaluated, they were found to have similar results. This goes to show the direct need for updated materials that match the needs of the Kingdom and their goals.

MOVING FORWARD

Overall, while there are many seemingly good programs in place for the future of STEM education in the Kingdom of Saudi Arabia, the question of whether it will be successful is still at play. When looking at recent data from the Trends in International Mathematics and Science Study (TIMSS), KSA ranked lowest across the board compared to other Gulf Cooperation Council Countries, in both grade four and eight mathematics and science tests (Kayan-Fadlelmula et al., 2022). With this expansive international assessment giving a lot of information on students' success in these STEM subjects, and how they are doing compared to other countries surrounding them, Saudi Arabia still has a lot to do with their STEM education implementation. Given the programs in place, as well as the data and studies that go with them, there is hope for the KSA to evaluate what needs to be done further to reach the goals set in the Saudi Vision 2030.

Moving forward there are growths to be achieved on everyone's part. From policymakers to administration and teachers, all people involved in the increasing of STEM practices need to reflect on their roles and determine what is needed from them to help the Kingdom succeed. In terms of policymakers, that might be playing a larger role in the implementation of standards being created. When establishing these standards, it may be beneficial to also look at the curriculum in place, as well as the resources being used, and make changes where necessary. This can help to make it easier for teachers to incorporate STEM lessons in a more significant way. Whether this means evaluating the content currently required to teach and making modifications to include more STEM subjects or updating and expanding the resources given to be used in the classrooms, more changes need to be made by those with the power to do so.

For administration, changes may look like participating in trainings to better understand STEM practices and all it entails, to best help their teachers and answer any questions they have throughout the implementation process. In addition to this, the administration of schools should ensure to make time in the schedules to allow teacher collaboration and planning timing, as well as professional learning communities. With this, to make these communities successful, the administration needs to listen to the needs of teachers and their misunderstandings around this concept to best help and prepare them. Through the listening of teachers and what they need and the understanding of STEM by the administration, opportunities can be made to help teachers explore these concepts and develop their own understandings. It is not without the support of each other, as well as their higher-ups, that teachers will have the confidence they need to make the changes being asked. Finally, teachers need to take the time to understand and appreciate the bigger picture of STEM and all the opportunities it offers, not only for the students but for the Kingdom of Saudi Arabia as a whole. Without the appreciation and understanding of the doors that can be opened through STEM, teachers may not be as motivated to implement these practices in their classrooms, which is needed to achieve the goals set by the Kingdom. With necessary changes made and the full understanding of STEM by all, the teachers in the Kingdom have a much better chance at successful and meaningful implementation.

However, changes and revisions are not only needed by those in the schools. Given what can be learned through the trials of implementation, it is crucial that the Kingdom takes these findings and applies the proper training to the teacher preparation programs. Strengthening the courses and programs teachers in the Kingdom need to complete before teaching will allow upcoming educators to learn the necessary skills and knowledge needed, setting them up for success. Working through a rigorous program in which teacher candidates are given opportunities to test STEM theories and practices will give them the hands-on experience they need to gain confidence in their skills. By making these changes teachers will be much better prepared and ready to apply these practices to their own classrooms, as well as share their knowledge with coworkers.

It is through this sharing of information that the deepest level of STEM understanding may be able to be achieved, and thus implementation can thrive.

Through the collaboration between teachers, lessons can be shared and better understood, and practices that are working or struggling can be discussed and evaluated. Having educators in this collaboration that have gone through a rigorous prep program prior to teaching will allow the sharing of different ideas and concepts that may not have been applied yet. This background knowledge combined with what teachers should be learning in Professional Development and Professional Learning opportunities makes for a well-rounded informed community in which ideas can be shared and developed together. These communities are crucial for teachers to feel most comfortable in the work they are doing, as well as to feel confident with it. The environment in which teachers are able to communicate different ideas, problem solve, and connect with each other is one that is extremely important to successful implementations in the classroom.

It is not only the people involved in the incorporation of STEM to the Kingdom's education system that need to reflection and reform, but also the materials. The need for updated materials that include current information such as the 2020 pandemic and the COVID-19 virus is imperative in preparing youth for future challenges and obstacles (Alghamdi, A.K.H., et al., 2022). Knowing that history repeats itself, and the possibility for there to be several other medical emergencies or pandemics, not to mention the constant need for more medical personal anyway, it is crucial for students to have the most accurate and up to date information possible. Students should be given the best chance possible to succeed, which means being given the proper resources. To not update and revise materials to ensure they are of upmost quality, students and educators alike are being cheated of higher opportunities and the chance to delve so much deeper into the world of STEM. To give all in the Kingdom the best chance of achieving what they have set out to accomplish, students need proper learning materials, just as teachers need proper teaching materials. While this is a change that may seem simple, it is one that is capable of a large impact.

In a globalized world filled with innovation and progression, Saudi Arabia is not the only country working towards growth and development and will not be the only country continuing to do so. Knowing this, it is of most importance for the Kingdom to investigate what other nations are doing, and what is working for them, and to make connections in which they can share ideas and practices. It is with the increase of STEM practices being a global initiative, that the KSA should use every resource available to them to continue gaining knowledge and ideas they can use to further their own practices. It should be a mission of theirs to continue to work with organizations around the globe to develop new ideas and concepts they can implement in the Kingdom. Having already partnered with many other organizations around the world, it is more than possible for the KSA to continue to do so and achieve great things.

In addition to the organizations they have already worked with, the Kingdom of Saudi Arabia has many other resources they can look to for guidance on how to implement STEM practices into their classrooms. As referenced in the previously mentioned article from *Education and Information Technologies* (Alghamdi, J., 2022), some of these organizations include the National Association for the Education of Young Children, Fred Rogers Center for Early Learning and Children's media, the International Society for Technology in Education, just to name a few. In addition to these resources that can be used to help include technology use in the classroom, the *Early Childhood Education Journal* (Alghamdi, A.A., 2022) also mentioned the success of the Next Generation Science Standards, and the helpfulness it had in the creation of KSA's early childhood STEAM practices. Having other countries that are looking to achieve similar goals is extremely useful in the adaptation of practices, as there are examples to reference. These few resources mentioned have played a large role in the development of STEM implications in Saudi Arabia and can continue to do so.

Through the support of everyone involved in this process, along with the continued reflection and research on what is being done currently, the Kingdom of Saudi Arabia is well on its way to reaching its 2030 goals. The importance of STEM to the Kingdom is apparent through the implementation of new development plans that strive to reach each of the goals they have set (Khan & Khan 2020). With the continued reflection and reformation of programs, initiatives, and standards in place, the KSA's education system has the chance to be great. It is with this that teachers can feel more prepared and ready to implement STEM practices in the classroom, students can reap the benefits, and the Kingdom can accomplish the goals they have set.

REFERENCES

Alghamdi, A. A. (2022). Exploring early childhood teachers' beliefs about STEAM education in Saudi Arabia. *Early Childhood Education Journal*. doi:10.100710643-021-01303-0

Alghamdi, A. K. H., Al Ghamdi, K. S., & Kim, S. Y. (2022). Epidemiology in middle school science curricula: A COVID-19 pre–post intervention. *Journal of Science Education and Technology*, *31*(5), 583–593. doi:10.100710956-022-09975-y PMID:35730014

Alghamdi, J., Mostafa, F., & Abubshait, A. (2022). Exploring technology readiness and practices of kindergarten student-teachers in Saudi Arabia: A mixed-methods study. *Education and Information Technologies*, *27*(6), 7851–7868. doi:10.100710639-022-10920-0 PMID:35233174

Alotaibi, W. H., & Alghamdi, A. K. H. (2022). Teaching 21st century skills in Saudi Arabia with attention to elementary science reading habits. *Education Sciences*, *12*(6), 392. doi:10.3390/educsci12060392

Binmohsen, S. A., & Abrahams, I. (2022). Science teachers' continuing professional development: Online vs face-to-face. *Research in Science & Technological Education*, *40*(3), 291–319. doi:10.1080/02635143.2020.1785857

Kayan-Fadlelmula, F., Sellami, A., Abdelkader, N., & Umer, S. (2022). A systematic review of STEM Education research in the GCC countries: Trends, gaps and barriers. *International Journal of STEM Education*, *9*(1), 2. doi:10.118640594-021-00319-7

Kewalramani, S., Adams, M., & Cooper, R. (2022). STEM professional learning: Supports and tensions with the Kingdom of Saudi Arabian teachers' immersion experiences in Australian schools. *Teachers and Teaching*, *28*(4), 398–419. doi:10.1080/13540602.2022.2062736

Khan, M. B., & Khan, M. K. (2020). Research, innovation and entrepreneurship in Saudi Arabia [Routledge.]. *Vision (Basel)*..

Kingdom of Saudi Arabia. (2022). *Vision 2030 Overview*. Vision 2030. https://www.vision2030.gov.sa/

Maashi, K. M., Kewalramani, S., & Alabdulkareem, S. A. (2022). Sustainable professional development for STEM teachers in Saudi Arabia. *Eurasia Journal of Mathematics, Science and Technology Education*, *18*(12), em2189. doi:10.29333/ejmste/12597

Madani, R. A. (2020). Teaching Challenges and Perceptions on STEM Implementation for Schools in Saudi Arabia. *European Journal of STEM Education*, *5*(1), 03. https://doi.org/ doi:10.20897/ejsteme/8468

Pearson. (2016). *Building STEM capability in Saudi Arabia [web log]*. Pearson. https://middleeast.pearson.com/Blogsocialmedia/blog/2016/11/building-stem-capability-in-saudi-arabia.html

Smith, K., Lancaster, G., & Johnson, L. (2019). *Exploring Saudi Arabian teachers' changing understandings of STEM education.* pp. 377-389. Paper presented at Asian Conference on Education 2019, Tokyo, Japan. https://papers.iafor.org/proceedings/conference-proceedings-ace2019/

Chapter 5
STEM Education in Iraq 2004–2022:
Strategies, Challenges, and Outcomes

Jabbar A. Al-Obaidi
https://orcid.org/0009-0008-9588-7535
Bridgewater State University, USA

Tahir Albakaa
Bridgewater State University, USA

ABSTRACT

This chapter explores STEM in Iraq from 2004 through 2022. It investigates the educational strategies and policies of the Ministry of Education (MOE) and the Ministry of Higher Education and Scientific Research (MOHEASR). MOE oversees curriculum, pedagogies, annual assessments, learning outcomes, and quality assurance for kindergarten, elementary (primary), middle, and high schools, while MOHEASR supervises educational and academic affairs for colleges and universities. A survey was distributed to random teachers and faculty members in various Iraqi schools, colleges, and universities throughout the 18 Iraqi governorates. Written questions were sent to superintendents, principals of schools, and deans of colleges. The theoretical framework for this study is informed by the primary educational learning of social and cognitive theories as learning and teaching are based on external environmental, internal conditions, and social factors and the process of knowledge. Challenges and strategies are discussed. Finally, the chapter proposes recommendations and directions for future research.

DOI: 10.4018/978-1-6684-6883-8.ch005

INTRODUCTION

This section introduces education in Iraq as both a right and a privilege and explains who administers and manages educational affairs in the country. The Iraqi Constitution of 2005 recognizes education as a force to induce social and economic development. The constitution states "Education is a fundamental factor for the progress of society and is a right guaranteed by the state. Primary education is mandatory, and the state guarantees that it shall combat illiteracy." (Article 34, First).

Education is managed and supervised by the Ministries of Education (MOE) both the Federal Government of Iraq and the Kurdistan regional government. According to the UNICEF 2014 Summary Iraq Country Report, education has witnessed striking development since 2004 under the supervision of the Ministries of Education. However, the risk of dropping out of school or "school exclusion" ((UNICEF, 2014, p. 1) is still a threat to educational development in the country. The report adopted the methodology developed by the Global Out-of-School Children Initiative (OOSCI), which consists of Five Dimensions of School Exclusion:

"Dimension 1: Pre-primary age children not in pre-primary or primary school, Dimension 2: Primary age children not in primary or secondary school, Dimension 3: Lower secondary school age children not in primary or secondary school, Dimension 4: Primary school children at risk of dropping out (exclusion), and Dimension 5: Lower secondary school children at risk of dropping out (exclusion)" (UNICEF, 2014, pp.1-2). This is a serious threat to the development of Iraqi children, especially girls who are at high risk of dropping out of school before reaching the sixth grade of primary (elementary) school. Naturally, limitations in local information management and tracking systems for Iraqi education represent a challenge for researchers as it reduces the availability of data analysis which leads to some findings and recommendations for future growth. According to UNESCO, "the Arab world has a very low-level gross expenditure on research" (Kjerfve, 2014, para 11). Lack of information gathering "reduces the availability of baseline data up-to-date information" (ODI, 11/05,2020).

CHAPTER'S RANGE

The scope of this chapter covers the seventeenth years of the status of STEM in Iraq from 2004 through 2022. In 2004 Iraq witnessed the formation of the first Iraqi government after the departure of Lewis Paul Bremer III who led the Coalition Provisional Authority in Iraq in 2003. Eight Iraqi governments were formed in the count as of 2022. The last national democratic election was held in October 2022.

Interestingly, all previous and current governments kept the two federal ministries, MOE and MOHEASR.

MOE administers and oversees the educational affairs, including curriculum, pedagogies, annual assessments, learning outcomes, and quality assurance for kindergarten, primary (elementary), middle (intermediate), and high (secondary) schools. MOHEASR, however, administers and supervises the general policies, and regulations, and draws strategies for colleges and universities in the country. Occasionally, MOE and MOHEASR work on collaborative educational projects about sciences, technology, engineering, and mathematics (STEM).

Examining available strategies and plans for MOE over the period of this study exhibited serious challenges that contributed to the waning of attention to provide and maintain a level of STEM programs that benefit Iraqi children, girls, and boys, the lack of deliberate effort to promote teaching critical skills, and to introduce modern schooling programs. STEM programs and instructions appeared to be optional or nonexistent. There are no intentional plans for providing appropriate training for teachers who are willing to learn new teaching skills, which would enable them to better serve their students and include STEM classes for primary, middle, and high schools. Therefore, this chapter is designed to offer a comprehensive and descriptive analysis of strategies and available educational plans concerning education in general and especially the status of STEM education. It also aims to highlight the educational challenges that teachers, school principals, students, and families are dealing with daily. The purpose is to propose pragmatic solutions that are designed to overcome some of these challenges including weak policies, lack of qualified teachers, cultural misunderstanding of the importance of STEM, inadequate curriculum, and crumbling infrastructure.

SIGNIFICANCE OF RESEARCH

The significance of this chapter comes from the need for developing STEM education in developing countries like Iraq. The study highlights the critical need for initiating practical strategies for promoting STEM programs. For example, "The United States subsequently introduced several educational reform movements and initiatives in STEM, including "Nation at Risk", "Rise Against Gathering Storm", and "Educate to Innovate" (Kulakoglu & Kondakci, 2023, p. 68; Gardner,1983; Augustine,2008; Office of the Press Secretary, 2009). STEM education is a key to economic growth and a knowledge-based economy.

Since 2002 STEM education has become popular and attracted the attention of policymakers and educational thinkers and leaders. Students in various countries began to learn how to work with computers, make programs, collect data, design robots, and engaged in experiential learning. The latter involves hands-on activities and training. Cultural and societal changes and exchanging economic open market conditions are also affirming the need and raising the level of interest in STEM education at the level of K-12 to higher education. This observation conforms with the statement of the World Bank as noted by Bjorn Kjerfve "The key to prosperity is a well-educated, technically skilled workforce producing high-value-added, knowledge-intensive goods and services" (Kjerfve, 2014, para 5, World Bank, 2019; Islam, 2019).

The Positive Peace Index (PPI) and the Institute of Economics and Peace (IEP) have identified eight pillars of peace, which are considered a new contextual framework for understanding and understanding, and describing the factors that create peaceful societies. The pillars are: (a) a well-functioning government, (b) a sound business environment (c) the equitable distribution of resources, (d), acceptance of the rights of others, (e) good relations with neighbors, (f) Free flow of information, (g) a high level of human capital, and (h) low levels of corruption. According to the Institute, peace can be viewed through the lens of both negative and positive peace. Negative peace is the absence of violence or fear of violence, while positive peace can be defined as the attitudes, institutions, and structures that when strengthened can lead to a more peaceful society. Citizens who have access to education and information tend to be more productive and settled. (PPI, para 1 and 2).

Iraqi authorities and businesspeople have realized the need for cultivating social peace among the citizens of Iraq and widening the opportunities for learning from K-12 to college education. However, this realization lacked two important components, a comprehensive vision, and a clear strategy. Meanwhile, Iraqi businesspeople with some provincial investors clutched this opportunity and rushed to open many college-university private institutions, and private K-12 schools. Proponents argue that non-governmental colleges, universities, and schools (primary, middle, and high schools) are offering an alternative to overpopulated and underfunded governmental institutions including K-12. Regardless of the level of quality, private colleges and schools are self-managed in funding, admission, staff appointment, and administration. It is also an economic enterprise. Both MOE and MOHEASR took notice and created the "Council of Private Colleges and Universities." MOHEASR's Supervision and Evaluation Department examined the requirements that must be met for the establishment of a college or university, including the presence of established academics who are not affiliated with a non-governmental university, and academic quality assurance. Other requirements include infrastructure (e.g., buildings, laborites, equipment, computers, parking lots, cafeterias, libraries, Internet services, etc." as well as sufficient teaching staff in each department, and a high-standard academic curriculum for majors, tracks, and specializations (concentrations).

It is worth noting that Albakaa, the coauthor of this chapter served as president of one of the governmental universities in Baghdad and he also served as the minister of MOHEASR in Iraq. In this capacity, he recommended in 2004 that for qualitative purposes and academic integrity, the ministry should administer and publish an annual evaluation report, showing scores for academic performance, curriculum, learning outcomes, and graduation rates for private colleges and universities. Albakaa also recommended more collaboration between MOHEASR and MOE to ensure students were academically prepared and ready to join higher education institutions. All of this must be put in place to help these colleges and universities to succeed in providing the best possible learning opportunities to thousands of Iraqi students. There is no justification to impose unnecessary guardianship on private colleges, universities, and schools. Thus, the ministries of MOHEASR and MOE ought to exercise their legitimate role of monitoring and evaluative bodies, which may be extended to all Iraqi public universities and schools as well.

PURPOSE AND OBJECTIVES

The purpose of this chapter is to provide historical data and information background to targeted readers such as educators and decision-makers and the public as well. The main objectives are to view administrators' and teachers' attitudes to science, technology, engineering, and mathematics as an important set of components in STEM teaching proficiency; examine historical and current challenges for the Iraqi educational system, and propose practical strategies. While teachers' attitudes toward STEM may not be directly translated to their instructional skills and content competency in STEM, it is suggested that "such general dispositions operating in daily life may contribute to the gradual development of creative convergence competency that teachers exhibit open, flexible, and curious minds" toward teaching and learning (So, et al, 2018. P. 50). It should be noted that "Gaining knowledge about all technical knowledge, terms, and tools required in STEM education, however, is a daunting task for many teachers ((So, et al, 2018. P. 51). However, the authors of this chapter posit that providing professional training for teachers and students is indispensable. Finally, this chapter is designed to address an educational area that has been lacking attention. To develop a knowledge economy Iraq must establish a solid foundation in science, technology, engineering, and mathematics (STEM). Nurturing a strong foundation in STEM also requires including both girls and boys right from the start at elementary, middle, and high schools and through all levels of higher education.

METHODOLOGY

Two interrelated research methodologies were applied to serve the aims and purpose of this chapter. The authors conducted limited written and virtual interviews with school managers, executive directors, deans, faculty, school principals, and teachers who volunteered to participate in this study. In addition, the authors designed a survey of 19 close-open questionaries focusing on STEM education. The survey was distributed virtually by selected contact persons in Iraq. The contact persons were able to distribute 300 surveys in Iraq. The number of respondents reached 211, which represents 18 (100%) Iraqi governorates. This methodological approach was complemented by examining various educational plans and strategies as introduced and executed by MOE and MOHEASR. In addition to the survey, the authors had personal communication and received written responses provided by teachers, faculty, deans, and administrators. The following sections are designed to provide answers to these two questions: 1. What specific challenges have contributed to the lack of attention to STEM programs in Iraqi schools? 2. Are there any current efforts to address issues regarding the attitude of the population and sociocultural barriers hounding STEM education in schools, colleges, and universities in Iraq?

Based on the responses and analysis, a set of strategies and recommendations is provided for improving STEM education in Iraq.

HISTORICAL BACKGROUND

Iraqi education witnessed significant expansion in the period from 1968-2003 (Albakaa, 2018, para 6). For instance, in 1970 the dissolved Iraqi constitution stipulated that the state guarantees the right and freedom of education and learning, at all levels of study … and to all Iraqis regardless of their ethnic, religious, or sectarian affiliation and it also made primary education compulsory (Albakaa, 2018, para 7). However, from 1968 to 1980, education in Iraq at all levels reached its highest level of development due to comprehensive strategic planning, sustainable funding from the government, quality of learning materials and textbooks, and well-trained teaching staff from kindergarten through grade 12 (K-12), to two-year institutions, colleges, and universities. In the 1980s Iraqi educational system was considered as the best system in the Arab world (UNOHCI, 2003; relifweb. int). Iraq received two awards from UNESCO for eradicating illiteracy and establishing national primary education in the country (UNESCO, 1981).

According to the UN Office of the Humanitarian Coordinator, "Gross Enrollment Rate for primary schooling was around 100%. Higher education, especially the scientific and technological institutions were of international standard, staffed by high-quality personnel" (UNOHCI, 2003; relifweb.int). However, the signals for the deterioration of the Iraqi educational system began in 1980-1988 due to the Iran-Iraq war, which lasted for eight years, and intensified in the 1990s because of the Iraqi invasion of Kuwait on August 2, 1990, followed by severe economic sanctions and the embargo authorized by the General Council of the United Nations in 1990-2003. UNOHC reported that the primary enrollment dipped to 85% in 1988 (UNOHCI, 2003; relifweb.int). Furthermore, in 2002 "the literacy rate among females in the 15-45-year group reached 45% and for males 71%" (UNOHCI, 2003; relifweb.int). For instance, the dropout rate was risen to "40-50% for children in primary school between grades 1 and 6, while for intermediate school (grades 7 and 9) the percentage of dropping out reached 30%-40%. The number of buildings dedicated to primary schools has decreased from 9,092 in 1989/90 to 7,572 in 1997-1998" (UNOHCI, 2003; relifweb.int). The Iraqi education system collapsed after the U.S. and Coalition invaded the country in 2003.

The introduction and imposition of the so-called educational amendments led to a fundamental change in the contents of Iraqi curricula for sectarian reasons (Khalil, 2018). Nearly 80% of the Iraqi schools throughout the country (15,000 schools) need to be renovated between 2018 and 2019. Still, schools suffer serious shortages in scientific laboratories, lack of libraries, shortage of funds, and human recourses. Iraqi "institutions are fiefdoms of conflicting parties competing for power, resources, and status" (Al-Qarawee, April 23, 2014, para 3).

THE ORDEAL OF EDUCATION AFTER 2003

This section discusses the background of education and its development in Iraq. The education sector in Iraq has suffered a serious decline after the invasion of Iraq in 2003 due to several factors of which the most important are:

1- The de-Beatification Order (Coalition Provisional Authority (CPA) Order Number 1 of 16 May 2003) issued by the American Civil Administrator Paul Bremer on that is, 37 days after the occupation of Baghdad on April 9, 2003. The order uprooted tens of thousands of teachers and university professors with competence and scientific and administrative experience and gradually replaced them with less efficient and experienced people. This order stipulated that senior party members would be banned from serving in the government. Consequently, teachers, professors, and experienced employees were removed even if they were not senior members of the dissolved Baath Party. Bremer regrated this order a few years later because "This decision effectively eliminated the leadership and top technical capacity for universities, hospitals, transportation, electricity, and communications. For example, in the Health Ministry, a third of the staff were forced out, and eight of the top twelve officers in the organization were excluded' (Ferguson, 2007, p.155". Bremer disbanded and rendered unemployment over 400,000 Iraq Army men in a matter of a moment (CPA Order Number 2 on 23 May 2003; Pfiffner, 2010).

2- The implementation of partisan and sectarian quotas. A method was adopted and adhered to by the sectarian parties that took control of Iraq with the support of the previous American administration. The governing parties adopted quotas, which became a norm, contrary to what was stipulated in the 2005 constitution.

3- The Islamic State of Iraq and Syria (ISIS) or (Da'esh) took control of several Iraqi cities in the north of Iraq and the war to liberate those cities led to the displacement of millions of people to live in camps that lack the simplest means of living conditions and no schools for children, resulting in having a generation of illiterate children and youth. It is believed that ISIS was one of the main reasons "behind the high illiteracy rate in the country, in addition to a shortage of educational institutions, lack of financial allocations and educational staff"(Saadoun, December 5, 2018, para 16).

4- Decreased financial allocations for the MOE, which reflected negatively on the maintenance of existing school buildings, halting the construction of new schools, and decreasing support for providing textbooks, learning materials, and educational supplies.

5- Although the law is compulsory and guarantees a free-of-charge education in primary school at all educational levels, successive governments did not necessarily abide by this law after 2003, which led to the non-enrolment of many children in primary school, which led to the emergence of alphabetic illiteracy among thousands of children, especially in rural and poor areas.

6- The severe shortage of school buildings led to two or three schools sharing one building, which led to a reduction in daily working hours. This was reflected in the reduction of weekly lessons for all subjects, including mathematics and science, the cancellation of other programs such as sports and drawing, and the absence of extra-curricular activities. In addition, the severe shortage in school buildings forced the school administrations to double the number of students in a small classroom. Hence, under these circumstances, a small classroom with a capacity of 20 students was jammed with additional 15 or 20 students. A small classroom with 35-40 students became the norm in Iraq. Schools in the big cities are overcrowded and school administrations are forced to put 70 students in a tiny classroom. In addition, classrooms lacked many of the required conditions such as having enough seats and adequate heating and cooling system. In a classroom like this, the teacher cannot control the students, and the scientific material cannot be explained so that it is understood by all students.

LITERATURE REVIEW

As a developing country, Iraq enjoys a wealth of natural resources like petroleum, natural gas, the rivers of Tigris and Euphrates, the body water of al-Ahwar (Iraqi Marshlands) of Southern Iraq, agriculture, and untapped minerals. Most importantly, Iraq has strong human resources, and its youth represents 19.6% of the more than 42 million population in Iraq, and the median age is 21.0 years (Worldometer). Hence, the development of STEM education and 21st-century skills are essential for creating and enhancing a knowledge-based and participatory economy in the country. The 21st-century skills refer to the knowledge, life skills, career skills, habits, and traits that are critically essential to individual success, particularly for K-12 students as they move on to college, the workforce, and adult life (panaramaed.com, para. 5).

In the era of consistently increasing technological development and "the integration of new technology throughout society, individuals must be trained for fluency in new information technologies and for proficiency in science, mathematics, and industrial engineering" (Yamada, 2021, p.45). Since its inception in the U.S. in the early 2000s STEM education expanded in the U.S., member countries of the European Union, China, Japan, and South Korea. Gradually, other countries around the world decided to advance their education policies to introduce and enhance their STEM education in primary, secondary, and higher education. This includes Organization for Economic Cooperation and Development (OECD) countries such as the United States (PCAST, 2012), Australia (Office of the Chief Scientist, 2014), and the United Kingdom (House of Lords, 2012). Recent studies demonstrated that interdisciplinary and multidisciplinary programs and collaboration between STEM and the humanities, social sciences, and arts are critical tools for education in general and higher education in particular for honing the "next generation competencies": (Yamada, 2021, p.45). Clearly "STEM fields have become a top priority worldwide for nations to secure and enhance their competitiveness in an increasingly globalized and knowledge-based economy" (Yamada, 2021; Benek & Akçay, 2022; Islam, 2019). For instance, Benek & Akçay (2022) and Bybee, (2010) and other researchers pointed out that "The USA needed a comprehensive and coordinated education approach and developed STEM education to raise STEM-literate individuals who have technical knowledge and skills" (Benek & Akçay, p.26; Bybee, 2010).

Consequently, STEM schools were established and equipped with programs and facilities in many states (Akgunduz et al., 2015). Subsequently, the implementation of STEM education and engineering activities in the classroom has expanded around the world (Cavas & Cavas, 2018). The K-12 teachers, superintendents, executive managers" and general directorates of education (as it refers to in Iraq) as well as deans, chairpersons, and faculty at the level of colleges and universities, need to deeply understand and model the skills that students need to acquire including STEM, critical thinking, communication, creativity, and collaboration and be life readiness (panoramaed.com). Elaborating on the idea of "life readiness" the American Association of School Administrators (AASA) argued: "Being life ready means students leave high school with the grit and perseverance to tackle and achieve their goals by demonstrating personal actualization skills of self-awareness, self-management, social-awareness, responsible decision-making, and relationship skills. Students who are life ready possess the growth mindset that empowers them to approach their future with confidence, to dream big, and to achieve big" (https://www.panoramaed.com/blog/comprehensive-guide-21st-century-skills, para 8).

In addition, Shari Camhi, 2022-2023, president of the American Association of School Administrators (AASA), also known as the School Superintendents Association stated:

The world is a different place than it was in 1965, 1985, and 2005. It is incumbent upon us as school district leaders to reinvent the experiences our students take in daily and create experiences that are amicable to the jobs they will have in the future" (Karen, 2022, para 4)

Bushra Sadoon Mohammed Alnooria (2018) cited (p. 266) Allen and Peach (2007) argument that "a concern is that: "One of the biggest dangers one faces is preparing teachers who know theory and know nothing about practice" (p. 23). This big danger still looms as a threat to the quality of educational preparations in the colleges of education in Iraq. In their study Hence Sadoon and Alnoori (2018) recommended to the concerning leaders and educators "undertake comparative studies in the evaluation of college of education programs in public and private universities, and to develop exchange student-teacher training placement schemes" (p. 277).

Evaluation of academic programs and teachers', administrators', and students' attitude toward teaching STEM or other subjects is important and applicable to this study. Dickson et al (2019) emphasized: "Key to the uptake of technology in education is the attitudes, perceptions, and self-efficacies of teachers, faculty, and administration" (Abstract, p.1.) Another study about what constitutes Korean pre-service teachers' competency in STEAM Education defines "the attitude toward science as one's affective interest, preference, and curiosity about science. To measure this construct, So et al (2018) adopted the instrument developed by Kim and Myeong (2009), which was designed to determine students' attitudes toward science in a nationwide study in Korea (So et al. 2018, p. 53). Other studies illustrated in their research that students' motivational beliefs (e.g., competence beliefs, attitudes, values, interests) about math learning are more critical determinants of future educational and career choices (Maltese and Tai, 2010, 2011; Wang, 2015). Furthermore, So et al (2018) identified multi-functional factors that may affect teachers' competency in teaching STEM or STEAM (science, technology, engineering, arts, and mathematics), "namely art appreciation, attitude toward science, technology acceptance, and creative convergence competency" (p. 48). So et al. 2018 stated:

In Korea, the rise of interest in STEM education has been driven by the alarming result of international comparison studies such as PISA and TIMSS, which found that Korean students generally lack self-confidence and interest in learning science and mathematics, whereas their academic achievement in these subjects was among the highest in the world. That is, Korean students perform well in science and mathematics, but they do not like or are not even interested in learning these subjects (So et al. 2018, p. 48).

The Korean government acknowledged this dilemma. Hence, the government introduced two rounds of policy plans for STEM education (Jo et al., 2012). The first plan from 2006 to 2010 aimed to support STEM education in gifted programs and universities. The second plan from 2011 to 2015 expanded the implementation of STEM education in elementary and secondary schools (So et al. 2018, p. 48). The MOE in Iraq can benefit from the Korean policy for improving STEM education in the country. In Iraq, teaching competency in STEM education is still weak. According to Sami Al-Muzaffar, member of the Iraqi Council, Minister of Education 2004-2005, and Minister of Higher Education 2005-2006, perpetual changes and instability of the curriculum impacted the quality of teaching and learning in Iraq including STEM education (S. Al-Muzaffar, personal communication, January 5, 2021). Similarly, Iraqi educators are encouraging policymakers to adopt policies that allow for the development of school curricula, applying modern educational methods and means, and moving away from the indoctrination method adopted by our schools until now (A. Al-Humairi, personal communication, January 5, 2021).

Enhancing diversity, equity, and inclusion in science, technology, engineering, and mathematics (STEM) disciplines in Iraqi colleges and universities has been a lingering project for decades. However, in the U.S. and other countries, educational initiatives are required and welcomed. For example, recently there is a strong interest in studying how such initiatives create sustainable institutional-wide change in education (Reeves, Bobrownicki, Bauer, & Graham, 2020). Cobian et al., (2022) and McCreath et al. 2017 argued that "internal and external evaluators must shift approaches to conduct assessments that monitor program goals, modify approaches, and provide external feedback (McCreath et al., 2017) in ways that address the complexity of organizational change" (p.29). Geographically closer to Iraq, Dickson, et al. discussed the ever-growing need for a highly-skilled, gender-inclusive STEM workforce, children's perceptions of science, and scientists and their work in the Arab Gulf states (Dickson et al., 2023).

The literature review substantiated with evidence that the growth of the knowledge economy calls on countries and governments to have a strong foundation in science, technology, engineering, and mathematics (STEM). Iraq is not an exception case. It should be noted that "Iraqi and Yemeni women face severe obstacles in attaining education, with girls from socioeconomic classes having 76% and 94%, chances, respectively, of never entering any form of education throughout their lives" (Wang, et al.,2020, p. 5). Overcoming this issue is a gargantuan task for Iraqi authorities.

DISCUSSION

This section discusses education from primary to high school and from high school to the level of college and university.

From Primary to High School

This part connects previous sections with the status of Iraqi education. The Iraqi constitution recognizes that education is a key factor in the progress of Iraqi society, and it is free for all Iraqis. It also confirms that the state shall care for people with disabilities and special needs, ensure their basic rights are provided and their human needs met, and safeguard their rehabilitation to reintegrate them into society. However, this very right is not necessary, equally accessible, or within reach for every child because of economic hardships and sociocultural obstacles. Therefore, the educational path for children in Iraq encounters structural barriers and technical complications. In addition, school attendance is low, completion rates, especially among girls, are declining, dropping out from school is rising, and reading and writing skills are deteriorating. According to the Iraqi Ministry of Planning, the illiteracy rate increased to 8.3% among Iraqi youth. The Iraqi Commission of Human Rights (IHCHR) estimated the rate to have risen to 9% (Saadoun, 2018). The youth population in Iraq represents 10.5% of the total population of Iraq (Saadoun, 2018).

Table 1 shows the results of 82 Iraqi teachers of primary, middle, and high schools who were surveyed randomly in September 2022. In the open-ended question regarding the importance of teaching STEM in schools, teachers emphasized a significant need for providing more teaching and learning opportunities for STEM education in the country. As for the evaluation of the status of STEM education, only 1.1% of the surveyed teachers evaluated the status of STEM education in Iraq as "Excellent," while 13.7% marked it as "Very Good," 36.1% rated it as "Good," followed by 27.3% "Acceptable" and 14.1% "Poor" and 7.7 "Very Poor."

Personal communication with Iraqi educators and administrators held in the

Table 1. Status of STEM Education as Rated by 82 Iraqi Teachers

Excellent	1.1%
Very Good	13.7%
Good	36.1%
Acceptable	27.3
Poor	14.1%
Very Poor	7.7%

fall of 2021 indicated that teachers and principals are calling for making a change in the means and ways of communication between teachers, principals of schools, families, and the executive administrators and managers at the MOE (R. Dhouib; W. Al-Samarrai; & A. Al-Asadi, personal communication, October 16, 2021). The hierarchy of management is based on rigid centrality and top-down communication. Students and families are at the bottom of the communication pyramid which becomes a source of concern among students and their families and a cause for dropping from school. Chart 1 shows that the hierarchy structures start at the authoritative and legislative ministerial rank, the executive general director of directorate education level, and down to the principal and students and their families. They are the recipients of whatever decisions are made by the authoritative and legislative ministerial rank with no or little feedback, if any, from principals, teachers, students, or their families.

Figure 1. Hierarchy of Educational Management

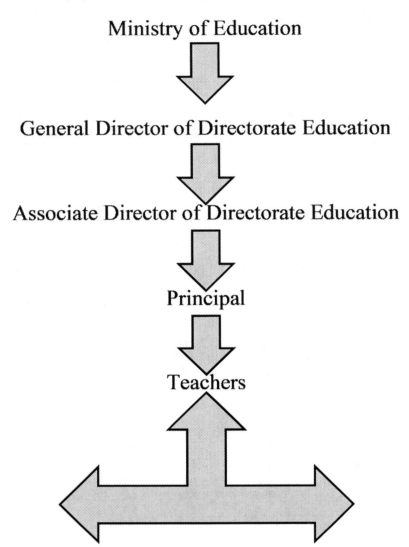

The Right for Education V. Child Labour and Displacement

The right to education is denied for thousands of individuals because of wars, interior conflicts, and the like. According to the Iraqi Ministry of Planning and Development in collaboration with the United Nations Development Program (UNDP), there was about 5% of Iraqis (approximately 1.35 million people) have been forced to displace their residences. Almost 4.2% of children under the age of eighteen are orphans of one or both parents. However, in April 2021 the Iraqi government announced its National Plan to End Displacement under the patronages of the Ministry of Migration and Displacement and the Ministry of Planning. (OCHA Iraq Humanitarian Bulletin, 2021, para 2). The plan offers displaced people and families the return to their areas of origin or chooses to stay and integrate with their families. Most importantly, this plan secures the safety of everyone and returns children to school. The OCHA's report stated: "Child labor has been on the rise in Iraq in recent years due to a combination of factors including armed conflict, displacement, and economic challenges, which have been further compounded by COVID-19, forcing a growing number of children into the workforce. The campaign aims to inform communities about the negative consequences of child labor and ultimately change the behavior of society and institutions alike" (OCHA Iraq Humanitarian Bulletin, 2021, p.4). Families were forced to leave their homes and jobs behind due to interior conflicts. Consequently, the economic hardship, harsh living conditions, and the absence of a schooling system in the refugee camps, families permitted their children to work. Under these conditions, work to make a living became the priority for everyone including children while education retreated to the bottommost if at all. STEM education was not on the family menu. Most developing countries including Iraq, encounter challenges and issues like poverty, lack of equitable access to clean food and water, increase illiteracy, inadequate school buildings, and shortage of qualified teachers. Wang et al (2020) and Hajjar et al (2015) warned "Addressing these issues is technologically demanding, requiring a robust foundation in science, technology, engineering, and mathematics" (Wang, et al., 2020, p. 1); Hajjar DP. et al, 2015).

General Framework of the Curricula

In updating all curricula, including science and mathematics curricula from primary grade 1 to grade-9 high school, the Ministry of Education (MOE) relies on the general framework of the curricula prepared by the Ministry in 2012 with technical support from UNESCO (UNESCO Institute for Curriculum Specialists, and UNESCO's International Bureau of Education (IBE, 2012).

The general framework of the curricula is a unified document that presents the vision of the curriculum and education regarding what, why, and how, i.e., updating a curriculum based on the competencies that the learner should acquire (knowledge, skills, and attitudes) as well as content quality standards. The visionary framework identified the main directions for developing Iraqi curricula for all educational courses, including mathematics and science.

According to Majeed Al-Allaq, Director General of Curriculum at the Ministry of Education (MOE), the curriculum framework emphasizes the following objectives (M. Al-Allaq, personal communication, October 16, 2021):

1. Providing high-quality education for all people is a basic human right.
2. Developing an integrated, balanced, flexible, and advanced curriculum that deepens skills, and positive attitudes, and promotes respect for human rights, gender equality, cross-cultural understanding, and sustainable development.
3. Considering both the learner's needs and the requirements of national development plans, including the current and future needs of the labor market.
4. Taking into consideration new scientific changes and developments at the local and international levels, through updated and culturally appropriate educational programs.
5. Educating Iraqi citizens on the principles and best practices of democracy, freedom, and social justice.
6. Promoting creativity, critical thinking, problem-solving skills, and encouraging participation, and becoming proactive and embracing lifelong learning experiences.

Educational Vision and Framework

The visionary framework has resulted in publishing three books for each class from Grade 1 to Grade 6, namely the student's book, the activity book (exercises), and the teacher's guide. These three books were built based on the 5E Model of Instructions introduced by Rodger Bybee, Chair of the Science Forum, and Science Expert Group. Bybee explained this "Model of Instruction includes five phases: Engage, Explore, Explain, Elaborate, and Evaluate. It provides a carefully planned sequence of instruction that places students at the center of learning. It encourages all students to explore, construct an understanding of scientific concepts, and relate those understanding phenomena or engineering problems" (BSCS and Bybee, para 1) The 5E educational model assists students to understand, comprehend, and participate in science, technology, engineering, and mathematics. MOE has adopted the 5E cycles educational model to build modern curriculum and curricula for mathematics and science. MOE also prepared plans to educate and train administrative leaders, managers, principals, and teachers.

However, teachers and principals complained that none of these plans were executed. An interview with Mea'd Hasan Al-Bakaa, a mathematics teacher at Al-Shakerin Secondary School for Boys, in Baghdad, outlined among many issues the lack of professional development and the nonexistence of teachers' training for E5 educational model or science teaching pedagogy (M. Al-Bakaa, personal communication, January 8, 2021). Rodger Bybee wrote, "I do use [the 5E model] in my classroom and can say it is wonderful in getting students to become independent thinkers, risk takers, and great inquirers" (Bybee, para 2).

Table 2. 5E-Model-of-Instruction

Phases	Student Task	Teacher Role	Supervision
Engage	Mentally focus on a phenomenon, object, problem, situation, or event	Ask questions, discussion, and making connections	Principals and General Director of Education Curriculum
Explore	Individually and as a team explore ideas and concepts	Facilitate discussion and clarify and answers	Principals and teachers
Explain	Share their initial projects and explanations from experiences in the Engage and Explore phases.	Provide resources and information to support student learning and explains scientific and technological concepts	Teachers
Elaborate	Relate their understanding of concepts and skills to other situations	Use new vocabulary, definitions, and explanations learnt from engagement and exploration	Teachers
Evaluate	Participate in summative evaluation and feedback	Asks open-ended questions	MOE, General Director of Education Curriculum, Principal, and Teachers

Source: adapted from BSCS and Rodger Bybee and San Diego County Office of Education https://ngss.sdcoe.net/

These three books are annually reviewed for updating (revision) in light of field visits by curriculum specialists to schools, reports of educational and specialist supervision, analysis of general exam results (baccalaureate), opinions of academics and parents of students, and this is what is called feedback. Majeed Al-Allaq, the Director General of Curriculum explained that there are not enough qualified teachers to teach science subjects: physics, chemistry, biology, computer, and mathematics, especially in government schools. As for their professional qualifications, most of the teachers are graduates of basic education colleges for primary school teachers, and graduates of colleges of education for secondary school teachers, and some of them are from supporting colleges such as Colleges of Sciences (M. Al-Allaq, October 16, 2021).

Most of the teachers held an educational bachelor's degree, and 10% of them obtained higher degrees such as a master's or doctoral. As for qualifications, they are qualified, but they need to have additional training and professional development. Factors like lack of financial issues, inaccurate infrastructure, and the unavailability of professional leaders or experts who could design and lead training. In addition, there is a serious lack of data and criteria, which usually helps with identifying the areas where training is needed.

Furthermore, what makes things even more complicated is the issue of the reluctance of most Iraqi teachers to participate in this training and professional development because they are being held either in spring or summer breaks (M. Al-Baka, personal communication, January 8, 2021). Nevertheless, teachers are committed to making it work for their students and themselves.

As acknowledged by the teachers who participated in the survey, the scientific topics and devoted time for each topic is equal throughout the week. Table 3 illustrates the time devoted to teaching sciences and mathematics.

Table 3. Topics and number of hours

Science	Technology	Minutes Per Week	Engineering	Minutes Per Week	Mathematics	Minutes Per Week
Physics	Force and motion axis	120	Engineering hub	120	Focus of Preparation and Operations	120
Chemistry		120	Measurement axis	120	Measurement axis	120
Biology		120	Data axis	120	Algebra	120
Environment		120	Force and motion axis	120	Data axis	120
Characteristics of living organisms		120	Trigonometric functions	120	Trigonometric Functions	120

As for the content of mathematics and science textbooks for all stages of schooling, it would be according to the range and sequence matrix defined by the general framework of the curricula, and the scientific content of the textbooks for the primary stage will be according following blocks:

1. Mathematics Block: The focus is on preparations and operations. It describes as an engineering hub, measurement block, and data block.

These blocks are expanded in the intermediate stage to include other algebraic topics such as polynomials, arithmetic sequences, and triangles, and expand again, in the preparatory stage to include topics of trigonometric functions and differentiation and integration.

2. Science Block: The focus is on energy and its transformations, force and motion, and scientific classification and diversity.

3. Characteristics of living organisms Block: The focus is on the human body, health sciences, and the environment.

Likewise, these blocks are extended to the intermediate and preparatory stages. The science textbook is organized and divided into sections that deem appropriate for the third intermediate grade to introduce physics, chemistry, and biology. It should be noted that each block includes many topics that are integrated horizontally and vertically into the curriculum and presented per the age of students and their mental abilities to understand the content of each topic. Personal communication (2021) with Al-Allaq and Al-Bakaa, this effort has encountered many challenges as prioritized below:
1. Double and triple-doubles in the same school building.
-2. A large number of students are in the classroom.
3. Fewer hours in the school day due to many official holidays and religious events.
4. No temporary substitution the well-deserved maternity and childbirth leaves.
4. Unfilled vacancies, especially in schools on the outskirts of cities and in rural areas.
5. Poor distribution of qualified teachers among schools.
6. Lack of use of technology for learning and teaching.
7. Declining in the number of graduates from colleges of education.
8. Lack of training courses and professional development for teachers.

STEM FROM PRIMARY TO HIGH SCHOOL

Children at the age of 6 years are entitled to join primary schools, which involve 1-6 grades. Students in the 6th grade are required to pass a national examination of Primary School to earn the Primary certificate (PC). The PC enables them to join the Middle School (Intermediate School). It is worth noting that compulsory education lasts 6 years from age 6 to age 11. The academic year begins in September and ends in June. There are approximately 34 weeks of classes per academic year.

The Middle School consists of 7th, 8th, and 9th grades. Students in the 9th grade are required to pass the Baccalaureate National Examination of Middle School. Passing this national exam qualifies them to join a high or vocational school. High School consists of 10th, 11th, and 12th grades. The 10th grade is designed to serve as the preparatory or general grade. Upon passing the 10th grade, students choose to join Literature Branch (humanities and social sciences and art) or Scientific Branch (mathematics, medicine, biology, physics, chemistry, computer, and other sciences. Usually, students who score high grades in classes like biology, chemistry, mathematics, and physics, could join the Scientific Branch.

For example, in the Middle School, students attend 34 classes per week. Classes include Arabic and Kurdish languages, English, Science (biology, chemistry, and physics), mathematics, social sciences, history, geography, national education (patriotism), sociology, economics, fine arts education, and household education (for girls only). Additionally, there are vocational schools, which include Agricultural, Applied Arts, Commercial, and Industrial. Students in the 12th grade, whether Scientific or Literary, are required to pass the Baccalaureate National Examination of High School, which enables them to pursue their undergraduate education and apply to governmental or private colleges and universities in the country.

During the academic year, students in the 7th and 8th grades of Middle School (Intermediate School) take 4 classes of biology, chemistry, and physics per week. The length of each class is 40 minutes. However, students in the 9th grade of Middle School are required to complete a combination of 2 classes: biology, chemistry, and physics because science is separated into physics, chemistry, and biology for this grade.

It should be noted that there are 4 branches of high school (or secondary school) and 4 vocational branches; industrial, commercial, agriculture, and applied arts in Iraq. However, the most popular branches are science and literature. Each high school branch consists of three years: high school 4th grade, high school 5th grade, and high school 6th grade. The fourth-grade high school students who chose the literary branch are required to take 3 classes, biology, chemistry, and physics, 40 minutes each period, three times per week (12 minutes per topic) during the academic year. However, the fifth grade of high school takes 3 classes in biology, chemistry, and physics, and 5 classes in the sixth grade of high school for biology, chemistry, and physics. The study of science appears to take priority at the level of middle and high schools.

Table 4. STEM classes

Grade	Number of Math Classes	Number of Science Classes
Primary	6	4
Middle School	5	4
High School, Literary Branch	4	3
High School, Scientific Branch	4	5

An interview with Mrs. Miad Hasan Al-Bakaa, a mathematics teacher at Al-Shakerin Secondary School for Boys, in Baghdad indicated that mathematics is taught in the same curriculum in public and private schools. It's identical to what

Turkish and British schools are offering. Miad Hasan Al-Bakaa also confirmed that the curriculum is considered solid, but it contains a lot of information to be addressed in a very short time. This makes students strive to pass by memorizing the information without necessarily achieving a deeper scientific knowledge or building student understanding of a concept (M. Al-Bakaa, personal; communication, January 8, 2021). It's alarming to note that "Across the Arab region the gross enrollment in secondary education was 74.2%, well below that of East Asia and the Pacific 84.5%, Central and Eastern Europe 93%, and Central Asia 98.6%" (UNPD, 2014, Wang, et el., 2020, p.3).

Table 5. School-age population by education level

Pre-primary	2,180,383
Primary	6,042,916
Secondary	5,192,775
Tertiary	3,815,494

The literacy rate among the population aged 15 years and older, males was 91.2% in 2017, 79.9% among females, and the total is 85.6%.

Colleges and Universities

A survey of 19 questions was sent out to 300 deans and faculty members throughout the country in October 2022. As demonstrated in Table 6, the number of respondents reached 211, which represented 18 of 18 (100%) Iraqi Governorates. Deans' responses were at 7.7%, while the responses received from faculty at the ranks of professor, associate professor, assistant professor, and lecturer amounted to 30.6%, 7.3%, 38.1%, and 16.3% respectively.

Table 6. Colleges and universities and respondents

Governorates	100%				
Colleges and Universities	Governmental		Private		
	99.5%		0.5%		
Type of Colleges and Universities	Males and Females	Females Only		Males Only	
	88.5%	11.5%		0%	
Participants	Males		Females		
	71.3%		28.7%		
Positions	Dean	Professor	Associate Professor	Assistant Professor	Lecturer
	7.7%	30.6%	7.3%	38.1%	16.3%

The MOHEASR runs higher education in Iraq and appears to pay more attention to STEAM education. The focus of the survey was whether the academic programs include teaching science, technology, engineering, and mathematics, not just significantly within the colleges of so-called "pure sciences" (e.g., Colleges of Engineering, College of Medicine, College Sciences, College of Pharmacy, and the like) but also for the colleges of humanities and social sciences, business administration and management, and the arts. Colleges and universities apply a credit hours system along with required core and elective courses. Tables 6 and 7 display the maximum and minimum hours that a student is required to register for each semester, the number of years, and the minimum of credits/hours for the academic year 2019-2020 (cope.uobaghdad.edu.iq).

Table 7. Maximum and minimum required hours per semester

Semester	Maximum Credits/Hours	Minimum Credits/Hours
First	21	12
Second	21	12
Third (Summer)	12	6

Table 8. Number of years and totals of credits/hours

Number of Years	Minimum of Total Credits/Hours
4	132
5	180
6	205

The minimum of total credits (132, 180, or 205) is designed to (Nouri, 2019):

A) Satisfy university requirements (institutional), which are compulsory and elective courses. They aim at expanding student's knowledge in the area of scientific, social, and professional skills. One of the scientific courses that a student can enroll in any semester is computer science but not to exceed 1 hour per week.
B) Meet college requirements, which comprise compulsory and elective courses. The college requirements provide a foundational base for a student's specialty (major), like English language and mathematics. Both are essential for the major but don't take priority over the required courses for specialty or track.
C) Concentration (specialization) requirements aimed at enhancing students' knowledge, experience, and competencies in the concentration (e.g., economics, human resources, business administration, management).

Examining items, A, B, and C in Table 8 revealed that the concept of STEM education is embedded, though not as equally, in the academic curriculums for sciences, humanities, and social sciences. Simply by design, students whose majors are "pure sciences" received more STEM education than their counterparts at the colleges of humanities and social sciences. This strategic issue is critical and awaiting for both MOE and MOHEASR to address it.

Given the challenges and the harsh circumstances that the country went through along with other crises that negatively affected the entire educational process like the economic hardship, social and security changes in the lives of students and teachers, the quality and standard of teaching science and mathematics in the country is below the level of ambition or satisfaction (M. Al-Allaq, personal communication, October 16, 2021).

CHALLENGES

Colleges and Universities

As displayed in Table 9, the challenges for colleges and universities in Iraq as reported by surveyed deans and professors in the fall of 2022. The challenges listed as they were prioritized by survey participants. The following data and discussion provided an answer to the question regarding specific challenges that have contributed to the lack of attention to STEM programs in Iraqi schools.

Table 9. Challenges as identified by 211 deans and faculty members

Priority	Types of Challenges
1	A. Technical and Professional Challenges
	Need advanced trained staff
2	Lack of infrastructure, teaching space and laboratories
3	Shortage in availability of electronic devices (e.g., computer, iPad, and the like)
4	The lack of interest among teaching staff or his inclusion in training courses
5	Lack of professional development whether annual or quarterly, which keeps the teaching away from modern pedagogy
6	Students do not exert the required effort to study and prepare themselves for participation
7	Lack of supporting materials for teaching and learning science and technology
8	Lack of knowledge of how to use technological means in teaching and learning
7	Financial difficulties
	B. Financial challenges
1	Lack of fundings
2	Unequal financial distributions
	C. Vision and Strategy
1	Absence of vision and strategy
2	Lack of concept of modernity and development

Primary to High Schools

Similarly, table 10 illustrates the challenges for administrators and teachers as outlined by 82 surveyed teachers in the fall of 2022. The challenges appeared as prioritized by them and shared by the Director General of Curriculum in the MOE (M. Al-Allaq, personal communication, December 10, 2022).

Tables 10. Challenges identified by administrators and teachers

Priority	Type of Challenges
1	Double and triple doubles in the same school building
2	The large number of students in the classroom
3	Less hours in the school day
4	Official holidays and many religious events
5	Maternity and childbirth leaves that happen to be vacant
6	The large number of vacancies, especially in schools on the outskirts of cities and in rural areas
7	Poor distribution of qualified teachers in schools
8	Lack of use of technology in education
9	Weak numbers of teachers and teachers in educational colleges
10	Lack of training courses

Tables 11 and 12 show specific concerns and the sense of urgency to attend to these concerns as identified by surveyed teachers.

Table 11. Specific concerns as outlined by 82 teachers

Issue	Yes %	No %
Availability of computers	98.9	1.1
Laboratories for STEM teaching and learning	95.6	4.1
Internet Services	73.2	26.8
Availability for Resources for STEM teaching and learning	82	18
Curriculums include STEM education	68	32
Teaching Sciences for all college and university students	84.2	15.8
Teaching Technology	74.9	25.1
Offering Computer science courses	48.1	59.9
Teaching Mathematics	71	29
STEM Teaching embedded into the curriculum	52.5	47.5

Table 12. The struggle for need and urgency

Question	No Urgent	Urgent	Moderately Urgent	Somewhat Urgent	Tremendously Urgent
Need for updated Technology	8%	16%	32%	24%	20%
Lack of Resources	2.2%	7.1%	13.1%	40.4%	37.2%

STRATEGIES

Referring to the importance of STEM education, Dickson et al wrote: "STEM (science, technology, engineering, and mathematics) subjects are at the top of most countries' national agendas in terms of planning for future economies, investment in knowledge and development, industries, commerce, and innovative growth" (Dickson et al, para,1, p. vii). The following section emanated from this meaningful statement. Hence this section outlines three strategies:

Strategy 1. Data and Information Collection

Studies conducted about STEM education in Iraq and the Arab world showed that while the gender gap is not as large as the one observed in some Western countries, it exists nonetheless, with males presenting a higher level of interest in subjects such as physics and females exhibiting a higher level of interest in subjects such as biology (Mozahem, 2021, p.143; Baram-Tsabari and Kaadni, 2009). Other studies conducted in universities in Arabic countries have revealed a gender gap in enrollment in engineering majors, always preferring male students (Mozahem, 2021, Alaraje and Elaraj, 2018; Al-Sanad and Koushki, 2001; Imran et al., 2014). For example, Mozahem's study (2021) indicated that the gross tertiary enrollment and the ratio of female rate to male rate in Iraq was 0.59 (p.143). This result was also found in the UNDP report issued in 2009. However, the Share of graduates from STEM programs in tertiary education who are female was not reported in the UNDP, 2019. This has occurred because of the lack of data and information regarding STEM education in Iraq. The need for gathering data and information is an essential tool to build a strong foundation for STEM education in Iraq.

Strategy 2. A National Action Plan

The discussion and findings of this chapter indicate an urgent need for the Ministry of Education (MOE) and the Ministry of Higher Education and Scientific Research (MOHEASR) to draw a national action plan for the country and to create a map road for STEM education from kindergarten and to higher education. To put this strategy in perspective, below is what the National Science Foundation (NSF) wrote concerning STEM education in the U.S.:

"A National Action Plan for Addressing the Critical Needs for U.S. Science, Technology, Engineering, and Mathematics Education System, *"In the 21st century, scientific and technological innovations have become increasingly important as we face the benefits and challenges of both globalization and a knowledge-based economy. To succeed in this new information-based and highly technological society, students need to develop their capabilities in STEM to levels much beyond what was considered acceptable in the past."* (NSF 2007).

Strategy 3. Shared Vision

MOE and MOHEASR, school boards, school administrators, principals, superintendents, local leaders, and councils of parents, business leaders, policymakers, and other stakeholders should identify a shared vision and goals, and pathways for developing STEM education. A shared vision "includes embracing new approaches to STEM teaching, creating new definitions of learning success, and considering new ideas about the physical structure of the educational environment so that it is more inclusive and conducive to exploration, discovery, and design iteration" (The National Science Teaching Association (NSTA) para 12).

FINDINGS

As discussed in the previous sections and illustrated in the tables, the findings section is divided into several headings as follows:

Students' Learning and Skills

Results of this chapter showed "Students lack both the fundamental skills, as a result of poor educational quality, to pursue STEM, and are further swayed away by poor exposure to the benefits of a STEM education" (Wang et al, 2020, p.3). Nevertheless, teaching and learning continue in Iraq despite the infrastructural and financial challenges and the lack of specialized teachers and faculty to teach STEM. The main obstacles to the implementation of STEM education in Iraq include theoretical and logistical issues, ineffective policies, and negative attitudes toward STEM. In addition, cultural and social misunderstanding increases the gaps between male and female enrolment in science, technology, engineering, and mathematics. The reduction of school days during the official academic year is a serious problem in the country due to having too many national and religious holidays, commemorations, and celebrations (M. Al-Allaq, personal communication, October 16, 2021).

Educational Policies

The analysis illustrated a disconnect between policies issued by MOE and MOHEASR and the inadequate conditions under which teachers, professionals, and students live and operate (i.e., financial concerns, and knowledge and skill gaps). Public schooling in Iraq is indeed almost free at all levels, however, it is only mandatory for children between the ages of 6 and 12. Policies and regulations are unclear regarding required programs and curriculum reviews. Hence, doubts cloud the perception of the quality of education in public institutions at all levels in the Middle East and North Africa (MENA) including Iraq (Wang et al., 2020; Assad R &Krafft C, 2016).

The Internet and Technology

Schools in general and particularly schools in suburban and remote areas suffer from a lack of science laboratories, computers, Internet services, and instructional technologies. Wafaa Naji Al-Samarrai, Principal of the Dar Al-Salam Primary School in Baghdad, recommended introducing teachers to training courses to develop their skills in keeping up with developments in technology and access to the Internet. filling major shortages of computers, equipment, and laboratory materials stand imposes serious challenges for schools in Iraq (W. Al-Samarrai, personal communication, September 15, 2022).

Rote-Learning Methods vs. Student-Centered

Traditionally, Iraqi teachers are trained to rely on memorization in their teaching rather than engaging students in critical thinking and problem-solving. The whole learning operation is based on the concept of teacher-centered as opposed to student-centered and individualized approaches. Majeed Al-Allaq the Director General of Curriculum Explained why teaching STEM is still unsatisfactory. There are not enough qualified teachers in general, and teachers to teach science subjects (physics, chemistry, biology, and computer) in particular. Iraq is far alone in having this issue. In its 2014 report, the United Nations Educational, Scientific, and Cultural Organization (UNESCO) noted the reliance on teacher-centered pedagogical approaches in many Arab countries. A rote-learning teaching methodologies overlook critical thinking, problem-solving, inquiry, and investigative skills ((UNDP, 2014; Qureshi S et al, 2016; Dagher ZR & BouJaoude S, 2011). Teachers identified the severe shortage of educational materials and textbooks. Schools' buildings in rural and fringe areas are decayed and in need of renovation. There are not enough seats for students in classrooms. The absence of professional development and training workshops for teachers is highlighted by teachers, staff, and college and university faculty.

Teachers and Staff Economic Hardship

The lower salaries and inadequate conditions under which teachers, professionals, staff, and students live and operate hamper the quality of teaching and learning. Insufficient salaries force teachers to seek another job to generate additional income to support themselves and their families (M. Al-Allaq, personal communication, October 16, 2021). Teachers are in dire need to improve their health insurance and living standards. Both MOF and MOFHEASR have been criticized for the lack of accountability, equity, and the deficiency in providing financial incentives to teachers to boost their morals. There is an urgent need to conduct a comprehensive assessment of the academic programs and curriculums of colleges of education and primary, middle, and high schools as well (M. Al-Allaq, personal communication, October 16, 2021).

Ineffective Chains of Communication

The gap in communication between the chains of command is wide. Hence, developing effective communication channels between administrations, teachers, students, and their families is considered one of the most effective strategies for building collaborative educational models in the country (A. Al-Douri, Principal of Baghdad Central High School, personal communication, August 3, 2022).

CONCLUSION

In Iraq, the general enrolment in secondary school is below the level in other neighboring countries such as Qatar, United Arab Emirates, Saudi Arabia, and Turkey. Though evidence suggests that Iraq is far from alone in this case "Across the Arab region, the gross enrolment in secondary education was 74.2%, well below that of East Asia and the Pacific 84.5%, Central and Eastern Europe 93%, and Central Asia 98.6% (UNDP, 2014). The same gap exists in higher education, with a gross rate of 26% in 2012 for the Arab region; in comparison, the global average was 32%.

Despite many scholars dedicating themselves to studying STEM education in the Middle East and North Africa region, the extant literature is limited in several ways. Hence, exposing the readers to the analysis and findings of this chapter should contribute to the previous research. This study adopted two interrelated methodologies to discuss and analyze the data and information collected from previous studies, interviews, and a survey questionnaire of 19 close-open questions focused on science, technology, engineering, and mathematics. Valuable views were obtained via personal communication with school executive managers, former ministers of education, directors, deans, faculty, school principals, and teachers. The survey was made available to 300 randomly selected persons in Iraq. The number of respondents reached 211, which represents 18 (100%) Iraqi governorates.

As discussed in this chapter, the Ministry of Education (MOE) nor the Ministry of Higher Education and Scientific Research (MOHEASR) developed an explicit strategy regarding STEM education in Iraq over the long period of 2004-2022 (S. Al-Muzaffar, personal communication, January 5, 2021). January 5, 2021). But what is known, however, STEM subjects are included in the school curriculums, which are science subjects, humanities, and social sciences. For instance, at the high school level, students who enroll in the "Science Branch" or "Division" would have many STEM classes. Meanwhile, their colleagues who enrolled in the "Literature Branch" or "Division" will have fewer STEM subjects. This choice will also determine the kind of colleges graduates would be allowed to apply to their higher education. In another way, graduates from the "Scientific Branch" or "Division" are eligible to apply to colleges of sciences (mathematics and science, medicine, engineering, and the like. Graduates from the "Literature Branch" or "Division" can only join humanities and social sciences or art colleges to pursue higher education. Regarding question (2) there are no notable efforts aimed at addressing issues regarding the attitude of the population, parents, and sociocultural obstacles toward STEM education in schools, colleges, and universities in Iraq. Melissa McMinn (2023 proposed that "A critical evaluation of the image of science in schools might be one way to overcome gender-image-driven barriers of both female and students to career aspirations of both female and male students"(p.16).

Because of the social challenges, economic hardship, insufficient funds, and lack of accountability, the quality of teaching science, technology, engineering, and mathematics in the country suffers and went below the satisfactory level. Majeed Al-Allaq, Director General of Curriculum at the Ministry of Education, said that teaching science and mathematics is weak especially in state schools because of the shortage of qualified teachers who could teach, for example, physics, chemistry, biology, computers, and mathematics (M. Allaq, Personal Communication, October 16, 2021).

In the words of Wang et al (2020) "Solutions are urgently needed, among which ought to include science diplomacy and international institutional partnerships" (p.2). Expanding on this point, the MOE and MOHEASR in Iraq are required to utilize technology and diplomacy to enrich their interconnectedness with the advanced world and to maintain strong collaboration with regional and international to "move from the STEM educational "periphery" to its "core," and successfully lay the foundation for a strong future" (Wang et al, 2020, p.2).

RECOMMENDATIONS

1. Colleges and universities in collaboration with Senior Teaching Supervisors at Baghdad Provincial Directorate of Education, which is under the Iraqi government's MOF provide regular in-person and online training and workshops to STEM teachers in Iraq to improve their skills and teaching capacity and the development of course curriculum.
2. Public universities in Iraq should take advantage of Federal grant opportunities provided by the U.S. Embassy in Baghdad and the U.S. General Consulate in Erbil in the region of Kurdistan, to submit proposals in coordination with their U.S. partners. It's estimated that there are more than 25 Memorandum of Understanding (MOU) between U.S. and Iraqi universities (Al-Mayahi, 2023).
3. Holding a national conference to develop a comprehensive national educational strategy, and to distance educational institutions from partisan and political quotas.
4. Upgrading the level of teachers and professors of science, technology, engineering, mathematics (STEM), and other subjects by offering advanced courses to improve their qualifications, scientifically and professionally, and enable them to follow up and be exposed to the huge scientific progress globally in these subjects, and contemporary teaching methodologies.
5. Ensuring that teachers at all levels stay up to current with teaching pedagogies and have access to the latest relevant research in STEM and other subjects, rapidly changing educational technologies, and research in using modern and disruptive methodologies and game-based to enhance transversal skills.
6. Both MOE and MOHEASR are in urgent need to reexamine their approaches to developing and sustaining international academic and educational collaborations at all levels. For example, there are currently 13 U.S.-Iraq Higher Education Partnerships Program (HEPP),(www.irex.org). HEPP partnerships between Iraqi and U.S. institutions strengthen curricula and enhance research and teaching methods. It also targets the development of STEM, digital learning, and information systems among other needs.

FUTURE RESEARCH

The contribution of this chapter lies in its comprehensive historical data and educational background in Iraq. It provided a solid foundation for understanding the importance of STEM education to the future of Iraq. However, future comprehensive survey research is needed to offer more targeted solutions to specific educational issues in STEM education and the educational system and policies in Iraq. In addition, further research to examine women's role in STEM education in Iraq is indispensable.

REFERENCES

AASA. (n.d.). *Presenting Educational Leadership*. AASA. https://www.aasa.org/

Abulibdeh, E. S., & Hassan, S. S. S. (2011). E-learning interactions, information technology self efficacy and student achievement at the University of Sharjah, UAE. *Australasian Journal of Educational Technology*, *27*(6). doi:10.14742/ajet.926

ADDITIONAL READING

Akgunduz, D., Aydeniz, M., Cakmakci, G., Cavas, B., Corlu, M. S., Oner, T., & Ozdemir, S. (2015). STEM egitimi Türkiye raporu: Günün modasi mi yoksa gereksinim mi? (*A report on STEM Education in Turkey: A provisional agenda or a necessity?*) Istanbul: Aydin University Publication. https://files.eric.ed.gov/fulltext/EJ1317828.pdf

Al-Awidi, H. M., & Alghazo, I. M. (2012). The effect of student teaching experience on preservice elementary teachers' self-efficacy beliefs for technology integration in the UAE. *Educational Technology Research and Development*, *60*(5), 923–941. doi:10.100711423-012-9239-4

Al-Awidi, H. M., & Ismail, S. A. (2014). Teachers' perceptions of the use of computer-assisted language learning to develop children's reading skills in English as a second language in the United Arab Emirates. *Early Childhood Education Journal*, *42*(1), 29–37. doi:10.100710643-012-0552-7

Al-Qarawee, H. (2014). *Iraq's Sectarian Crisis: A Legacy of Exclusion*. Carnegie Endowment for International Peace. https://carnegieendowment.org/sada/55372

Albakaa, T. (2018). *Unpublished Notes*.

Allen, J. M., & Peach, D. (2007). Exploring pre-service teachers' training program. *Asia Pacific Journal of Cooperative Education*, 8(1), 23–36.

Alwan, A. S. (2004). *Education In Iraq: Current Situation And New Perspectives*. Baghdad, IRQ: Ministry of Education Ministry of Education of Iraq.

Augustine, N. (2008). *Rising above the gathering storm: Energizing and employing America for a brighter economic future*. National Academy Press.

Benek, I. and Akçay, B. (2022). The effects of socio-scientific STEM activities on 21st-century skills of middle school students. *Participatory Educational Research*, 9 (2), 25-52. http://dx.doi.org/ doi:10.17275/per.22.27.9.2

Bybee, R. (n.d.). Implications of Education. *Rodger Bybee Blog*. https://rodgerbybee.weebly.com/implications.html

Bybee, R. W. (2010). Advancing STEM education: A 2020 vision. *Technology and Engineering Teacher*, 70(1), 30–35.

Cavas, P., & Cavas, B. (2018). STEM egitiminde mühendislik uygulamalari (Engineering applications in STEM education). In D. Akyüz (Ed.), *Okul öncesinden üniversiteye kuram ve uygulamada STEM egitimi, STEM education in theory and practice from preschool to university* (pp. 113–131). Ani Publishing.

Cobian, K. P., White-Lewis, D. K., Hurtado, S., & Ramos, H. V. (2022). Implementing case study design to evaluate diverse institutions and stem education contexts: Lessons and key areas for systematic study. *New Directions for Evaluation*, 2022(174), 21–31. doi:10.1002/ev.20507 PMID:37333467

Corlu, M. S., Capraro, R. M., & Capraro, M. M. (2014). Introducing STEM education: Implications for educating our teachers in the age of innovation. *Education in Science*, 39(171), 74–85. https://ngss.sdcoe.net/Evidence-Based-Practices/5E-Model-of-Instruction and https://www.al-monitor.com/originals/2018/12/iraq-illiteracy-education-culture.html#ixzz7vKKFMZN7 and https://www.undp.org/iraq/press-releases/new-study-supports-iraqi-private-sector-development

Dagher, Z. R., & BouJaoude, S. (2011). Science education in Arab states: Bright future or status quo? *Studies in Science Education*, 47(1), 73–101. doi:10.1080/03057267.2011.549622

Dickson, M., Fidalgo, P., & Cairns, D. (2019). The 'S' and 'T' in STEM: Integrating Science and Technology in Education in the UAE. In K. Gallagher (Ed.), *Education in the United Arab Emirates*. Springer. doi:10.1007/978-981-13-7736-5_6

Dickson, M., McMinn, M., & Cairns, D. (2023). *Gender in STEM Education in the Arab Gulf Countries* (1st ed. 2023). Springer. doi:10.1007/978-981-19-9135-6

Ferguson, C. (2008). *No End in Sight*. Public affairs.

Gardner, D. (1983). *A nation at risk: The imperative for educational reform. An open letter to the American people. Report to the nation and the secretary of education.* Government Printing Office.

House of Lords. (2012). *Higher education in science, technology, engineering and mathematics (STEM) subjects*. UK Parliament. https://publications.parliament.uk/pa/ld201213/ldselect/ldsctech/37/37.pdf

Institute of Economics and Peace (IEP). (n.d.). *Positive Peace: The Eight Pillars of Positive Peace*. IEP. https://www.visionofhumanity.org/the-eight-pillars-of-positive-peace/

Routledge. (2010). *Intelligence and National Security,* 25(1). Routledge Taylor and Frances Group.

Japan Gov. (2018). *Realizing Society 5.0. Islam, Ibrahim*. Japan Government.

Jo, H. S., Kim, H., & Heo, J. Y. (2012). Understanding of STEAM education in the school field (*Research Report No. OR 2012-02- 02*). Google Scholar. https://goo.gl/W9PuoU

Khalil, S. (2018). Iraq's educational system is dying. *Voices for Iraq Voices For All*. https://rawabetcenter.com/en/?p=6480.

Kim, H. N., & Myeong, J. O. (2009). The relationship between elementary science teaching efficacy and science affective characteristics of pre-service elementary teachers. *Journal of Educational Studies*, 40(2), 29–50.

Kjerfve, B. (2014). Op-ed: The State of Higher Education in the Middle East Documenting Change, challenges, and an undeniable opportunity. US News World Report.

Kovac, K. (2022). Baldwin Union Free School District Superintendent Shari L. Camhi in her district office. *Herald*. https://liherald.com/oceanside/stories/superintendent-shari-l-camhi-elected-president-of-the-school-superintendents-association,142879

Kulakoglu, B., & Kondakci, Y. (2023). STEM Education as Concept Borrowing Issue: Perspectives of School Administrators in Turkey. *ECNU Review of Education*, 6(1), 84–104. doi:10.1177/20965311221107390

World Learning. (2019). *How a Partnership is Paving the Way to STEM Education in Kurdistan*. World Learning. https://www.worldlearning.org/story/how-a-partnership-is-paving-the-way-to-stem-education-in-kurdistan/

Maltese, A. V., & Tai, R. H. (2010). Eyeballs in the fridge: Sources of early interest in science. *International Journal of Science Education*, *32*(5), 669–685. doi:10.1080/09500690902792385

Maltese, A. V., & Tai, R. H. (2011). Pipeline persistence: Examining the association of educational experiences with earned degrees in STEM among US students. *Science Education*, *95*(5), 877–907. doi:10.1002ce.20441

McCreath, H. E., Norris, K. C., Calderón, N. E., Purnell, D. L., Maccalla, N., & Seeman, T. E. (2017). Evaluating efforts to diversify the biomedical workforce: The role and function of the Coordination and Evaluation Center of the Diversity Program Consortium. *BMC Proceedings*, *11*(S12, Suppl. 12), 27. doi:10.118612919-017-0087-4 PMID:29375668

McMinn, M. (2023). Science is a Boy's Subject-Changing Perceptions in the Arabian Gulf. Gender in STEM Education in the Arab Gulf Countries. Springer.

Nouri, S. G. (2019). *The Course System in Iraq Between Theory and Practice: Analytical Study*. The University of Misan., doi:10.13140/RG.2.2.31599.18082

OCHA Iraq Humanitarian Bulletin. (2021). Government of Iraq National Plan to End Displacement. *Report*. file:///Users/jalobaidi/Downloads/may_2021_humanitarian_bulletin%20(1).pdf

Office of the Chief Scientist. (2014). *Science, technology, engineering, and mathematics: Australia's future*. Australian Government. https://www.chiefscientist.qov.au/sites/default/files/STEM AustraliasFuture Sept2014 Web.pdf

Office of the Press Secretary. (2009). *President Obama launches the "Educate to Innovate" campaign for excellence in science, technology, engineering &math (STEM)education*. Office of the Press Secretary.

Panorama Education. https://www.panoramaed.com/blog/comprehensive-guide-21st-century-skills

Pfiffner, P. (2010). *US Blunders in Iraq: De-Baathification and Disbanding the Army*.

President's Council of Advisors on Science and Technology (PCAST). (2012). *Report to the president, engage to excel: Producing one million additional colleges. graduates with degrees in Science, Technology, Engineering, and Mathematics.* US Government. https://obamawhitehouse.archives.gov/sites/defaul/files/microsites/ostp/pcast-engage-to-excel-final_2-25-12.pdf

Qureshi, S., Bradley, K., Vishnumolakala, V. R., Treagust, D. F., Southar, D. C., Mocerino, M., & Ojeil, J. (2016). Educational Reforms and Implementation of Student-Centered Active Learning in Science at Secondary and University Levels in Qatar. *Science Education International*, 27(3), 437.

Reeves, P. M., Bobrownicki, A., Bauer, M., & Graham, M. J. (2020). Communicating complex STEM program evaluation to diverse stakeholders. *CBE Life Sciences Education*, 19(2), es4. doi:10.1187/cbe.19-06-0108 PMID:32453678

Reliefweb. (2003). *Background Paper: Education in Iraq.* Relief Web. https://reliefweb.int/report/irag/background-paper-education-iraq

Saadoun, M. (2018). *Why has the illiteracy rate gone up in Iraq?* Al-Monitor. Al.

Sadoon, B., & Alnooria, M. (2018) Evaluating the college of Education Program in Iraq-Baghdad and Italy Florence in terms of ESL and TESOL Standards. *Form@re - Open Journal per la formazione in rete, 18*(3), 265-278. . file:///Users/jalobaidi/Downloads/3779-Article%20Text-3744-1-1-20190918.pdf doi:10.13128/formare-24224

Samira. (2019). Science, Technology, Engineering and Mathematics (STEM): Liberating Women in the Middle East. *World Journal of Education*, 9(3), 94-104.

Society 5.0, an Era of Societal and Technological Fusion. *Journal of Comparative & International Higher Education, 13*(1), pp. 44-65. DOI: Retrieve from https://files.eric.ed.gov/fulltext/EJ1294600.pdf doi:10.32674/jcihe.v13i1.1980

The future philosophical vision of higher education in Iraq. (2022). *Citation metadata.*

UNDP. MBRF. (2014). Arab knowledge report 2014: Youth and Localisation of Knowledge. Dubai, United Arab Emirates 2014

UNESCO. (1981) https://en.unesco.org/courier/november-1981

UNICEF Iraq Country Office. (October 2014). Summary, *Iraq Country Report on Out-of-School Children.* UNICEF. https://www.unicef.org/mena/media/6506/file/Iraq%20Country%20Report%20on%20OOSC%20Summary_EN.pdf%20.pdf

Wang, D. R.; Hajjar, David. P.; & Cole, Curtis. L. (2020). International Partnerships for the Development of Science, Technology, Engineering, Mathematics, and Medical Education of Middle Eastern Women. *International Journal of Higher Education, 9*(2). doi:10.5430/ijhe.v9n2p1

Wang, M.-T., Degol, J., & Ye, F. (2015). Math achievement is important, but task values are critical, too: Examining the intellectual and motivational factors leading to gender disparities in STEM careers. *Frontiers in Psychology, 6*, 36. doi:10.3389/fpsyg.2015.00036 PMID:25741292

Worldometer. (2022). *Elaboration of data*. United Nations Department of Economic and Social Affairs. www.worldometers.info

Yamada, Aki. (2021). Japanese Higher Education: The Need for STEAM in

KEY TERMS AND DEFINITIONS

21st Century Skills: Reflects status of both broader and specific knowledge, advanced communication skills, critical thinking qualities, intercultural communication competencies, professional skills, ethics, positive attitude, global citizenship, and social responsibility

Experiential Learning: It's learning by doing and participating to gain familiarity with the subject matter, obtain knowledge, develop new skills, and implement what you learned into action.

Information Management: It is a systematic process involving gathering information and data from various sources, sorting, and storing the information, and distributing the information to those who need or demand it.

Iraq Constitution: The amended constitution of Iraq has 144 articles and was approved by the Iraqi government and published in Iraqi Gazette No. 4012 ON December 28, 2005.

Model of Instructions: Refers to teaching and learning strategies, activities, and pedagogies that teachers utilize in and outside classrooms to execute learning objectives and measurable outcomes.

Professional Qualifications: Includes undergraduate and graduate academic degrees, specific certificates, advanced training, and skills related to the work or profession that someone can do.

STEM Management: Offering classes in Science, Technology, Engineering, and Mathematics on regular bases for students at the level of primary, middle, and secondary schools, throughout the academic year.

Chapter 6
Opportunities and Challenges of Introducing Digital Health Training in Medical and Health Sciences Education in Palestine

Mohammad J. Ghosheh
 https://orcid.org/0000-0002-6970-9777
Ghosheh Medical and Surgical Complex, Palestine

Ghadeer O. Ghosheh
Ghosheh Medical and Surgical Complex, Palestine

ABSTRACT

Over the past decade, there has been an increase in the spread of digital health tools in the Middle East and North Africa (MENA), including Palestine. This spread is changing the role of medical and health sciences students, which necessitates educational training to prepare a new generation of professionals. This chapter reviews the programs in Palestine in terms of offering classes in the three main areas in Digital Medicine, Artificial Intelligence and Robotics, and Genomics. Each of the areas is discussed in terms of state-of-the-art applications, opportunities and challenges that could be faced regarding its inclusion in Palestinian education programs. While many Palestinian universities offered classes that target computer skills, most programs lacked a focus on new applications that are projected to change the future of healthcare. The chapter concludes by discussing the promise of developing competencies in digital health on job opportunities and improving the Palestinian education indicators for medicine and health sciences on the local and international levels.

DOI: 10.4018/978-1-6684-6883-8.ch006

Introducing Digital Health Training in Medical, Health Sciences Education

INTRODUCTION

Over the past decade, there has been an unprecedented increase in the adoption of hospital information systems (HIS) and electronic health records (EHRs) systems worldwide. By using HIS systems, hospitals can manage internal and external operational aspects, patient data, and financial transactions related to patient encounters. EHRs, on the other hand, are the digital patient record, where all patient-level information, from demographics to diagnostic procedures and prescribed interventions, is recorded, similar to paper records (Birkhead et al., 2015). For example, in the United States alone, since 2015, more than 80% of medical facilities have adopted EHR systems (Henry et al., 2016). Recently, the increased adoption of digital health platforms such as EHR systems is spreading in low-middle-income countries (LMIC) (Syzdykova et al., 2017), like Palestine, where the national EHR system was first implemented in 2010. The increased adoption of EHRs and HIS systems presents a great opportunity for data-driven healthcare (Sun et al., 2012), clinical research (Cowie et al., 2017) and even machine learning for diagnostic and prognostic applications (Cowie et al., 2017, Kim et al., 2019), especially for understudied populations such as the Middle East and North Africa (MENA) countries, and Palestine specifically. Another area of health digitization that received significant attention from clinical practitioners during the pandemic is telemedicine (Portnoy et al., 2020).

With the spread of access to the internet and smartphones in rural areas, telemedicine offers great opportunities where patients get access to professional health services and communicate with their doctors without the need to travel, making healthcare more accessible for many low-income communities (Barbosa et al., 2021). Notwithstanding the promise of digital health technologies, most medical and health sciences educational curricula do not include digital health courses (Car et al., 2021), especially in Palestine. With no formal digital health training in health sciences education curricula, the utilization of new digital technologies remains suboptimal, limiting the financial benefits of medical providers, increasing the burden on health practitioners, and compromising patient experience and outcomes (Waseh et al., 2019). Despite the relatively young age of medical degree-granting universities in Palestine, there is a growing number of medical and health professionals (Kerr Winter et al., 2015). In 2021 alone, there are about 5000+ new health sciences graduates from various Palestinian universities and colleges, where specialities ranged from medicine to pharmacy, nursing and medical laboratory technology, yet available jobs remain limited. Introducing digital health training could open doors for new job opportunities on local, regional, and international levels for many health professionals. To this end, in this chapter, the aim is to analyze the current medical education curricula in Palestine and evaluate the opportunities and challenges in introducing digital health training in various health sciences specialities. While this chapter focuses on Palestine, many of the findings and challenges are relevant to neighbouring MENA countries, where there are similar financial and cultural backgrounds. Furthermore, studying the job prospects and career directions of healthcare can inform and highlight useful insights for building a strong education system across various levels in the MENA region.

The chapter is arranged as follows. We begin by introducing the background on the emergence of health informatics and digital health in Section 2, followed by a literature review on the existing studies investigating the higher education particularly, health majors in Palestine in Section 3. Section 4 presents the methodology followed in the paper for reviewing the curricula and choosing the digital health education areas. The rest of the paper discusses the current medical health sciences curricula in Palestine in light of the areas of digital health education. Finally, we conclude by summarising the major findings and evaluating the job opportunities and future outlook.

BACKGROUND

Over the past years, there has been a noticeable trend in the continuous and fast-paced development of many university-level educational curricula across disciplines (Des Marchais et al., 1992). The trend was catalyzed by the fast development and scalability of technology and digital tools and by considering how technology impacts the field and career path for the respective majors (Grimus, 2020). Medicine and health science disciplines were not excluded from these changes. Considering the emergence of new technologies at the point of care and research, the role of doctors and healthcare professionals is evolving beyond the scope of medical consultations (Moskowitz et al., 2015). As a part of this change, medical and health sciences curricula worldwide have introduced new courses to better prepare students for new career paths (Saba, 2001, Medicine, 2019).

For this reason, many medical and health sciences curricula now include courses in health research, statistics, and mathematics, some of which may even be required for the accreditation of medical programs (Miles et al., 2010, Houlden et al., 2004). Introducing these courses, which might not be at the heart of medical and health sciences, prepares the students for working with interdisciplinary teams and building a strong understanding of essential skills needed for excelling in their careers. More recently, some educational institutes introduced more specialized courses in digital health tools where students are introduced to electronic health records (Wald et al., 2014, Rajaram et al., 2020), biomedical informatics (Car et al., 2021, Mantel-Teeuwisse et al., 2021), and telemedicine (Waseh et al., 2019). The rest of the paper will discuss the impact of the development of digital health on medical and health sciences student training and education and the downstream impact on their job opportunities.

LITERATURE REVIEW

Modern medicine was introduced to Palestine in the early 1900s during the Ottoman period's final years. However, during the British mandate, not much progress was made in expanding hospital infrastructure, and healthcare remained primarily provided by religious missions and community organizations (Hashweh & Hashweh., 1999). The history of medical education in Palestine has been influenced by foreign powers and marked by significant events. Under Ottoman rule, formal education emerged in Palestine, delivered in Turkish to an Arabic-speaking population (Hashweh & Hashweh., 1999). British rule, starting in 1917, expanded the education system to meet the needs of the British Empire, but it also perpetuated power imbalances and limited Palestinian involvement (Habasch., 1999). During this time, there was no established medical education system, and medical services were primarily provided by charitable and foreign organizations (Dudin., 2008). The establishment of Israel disrupted Palestinian aspirations for educational autonomy, greatly impacting medical education. Occupation, displacement of medical professionals, restricted access to resources, movement restrictions, checkpoints, and attacks on healthcare facilities further hindered medical education and practice (Habasch., 1999).

Despite the political turmoil, Palestinians sent their students abroad to study medicine. In the late 1940s, a Palestinian medical association was founded, and a medical journal was published. The 1950s saw the need for healthcare development and professional training after the upheaval caused by the war and the events of 1948 (Habasch., 1999). Augusta Victoria Hospital played a crucial role in training physicians and nurses during this time. Non-governmental organizations also played a significant role in maintaining and expanding healthcare facilities since 1967, with Makassed Hospital in Jerusalem offering modern facilities for Palestinian physicians. By the early 1980s, conditions were favorable for the establishment of the first residency program in major medical and surgical specialities, producing graduates who continue to contribute to the Palestinian health system (Dudin., 2008).

After the Oslo Peace Accords in 1993, efforts were made to rebuild the medical education system in the occupied Palestinian territories. The Palestinian Ministry of Education, in collaboration with the Ministry of Health, aimed to prepare citizens for state formation and participation in the global information economy, including health-related institution building (Ramahi., 2015). The first degree-granting medical university was Al Quds University in Jerusalem, established in 1994 (Sweileh et al., 2013, Salamma et al., 2014), followed by Al-Azhar University and Al-Najah Universities in 1999, operating in Gaza and Nablus, respectively (Salamma et al., 2014). Since the establishment of these universities, the medical and health sciences educational landscape has evolved significantly.

However, challenges such as a shortage of qualified teachers, inadequate infrastructure, and reliance on foreign aid hindered progress (Ramahi., 2015). These obstacles also contributed to limited Palestinian control over medical education and further exacerbated the trend of doctors migrating to practice in developed foreign countries. To address these issues, modern teaching hospitals were linked to existing faculties of medicine, and a national training program was launched, with the Palestinian Medical Council. These efforts aimed to shape the future of medical education in Palestine (Ramahi., 2015).

METHODOLOGY

In this chapter, we intend to review the Palestinian medical and health sciences curricula offered by the degree-granting institutes in the West Bank and Gaza Strip in light of the various areas of digital health. The definition of digital health varies and is an active area of research that lacks a universal unified definition. Previous surveys and studies focused on the informatics component (Stellefson, Michael et al., 2011) where they lacked information on practical hardware developments that heavily impact specific medical sub-specialities. To this end, we adopt the NHS Topal Review classification for digital health technologies (Topol et al., 2019). The NHS Topol Review is a summary of an exhaustive study evaluating and preparing the healthcare workforce to deliver the digital future in light of the impact on education and potential impact in the next 20 years (Topol et al., 2019). This classification groups the areas of digital health into three main categories: Digital medicine, Artificial Intelligence & Robotics and Genomics, respectively (Topol et al., 2019). The report provides example use cases on each of the three areas with practical implications on job prospects, which include telemedicine, device training, virtual reality as well as health informatics, all of which align with previous studies conducted on Palestinian Medical professionals (Jabareen et al., 2020) . The final included areas in our chapter with some examples are shown in Figure 1.

Figure 1: Proposed areas of digital health education to be incorporated in Palestinian medical and health Sciences undergraduate training

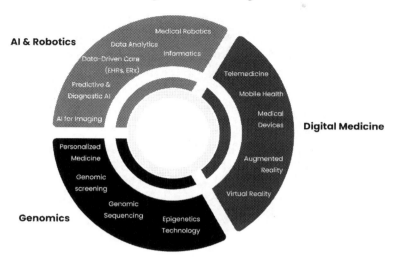

For this purpose, we evaluated the Palestinian universities with respect to the inclusion of the aforementioned topics for thee main specialities, Medicine, Nursing and Pharmacy, respectively.

While "healthcare professions" is a broader term that includes degree holders of more majors, the section focuses on these three majors since they represent the majority of health-related sciences graduates in Palestine. The information for each of the included university programs is primarily based on extensive browsing and keyword search of publicly available programs and university websites to ensure the latest and up-to-date program details. To the best of our knowledge, there are no surveys or reviews that summarize digital health education in Palestine. While there is limited information on programs in research databases, we searched Google Scholar to include additional information on program development, assessment, or evaluation of relevant courses in Palestinian universities. The search terms used were "BioInformatics", " Health Informatics", "Medical informatics", "Nursing informatics, "pharmacy informatics", "Digital Health", "Artificial Intelligence", " Robotics", and "Virtual Reality". Each of the university programs was evaluated in terms of the courses offered, course requirement type as well as the number of credit hours allocated to the courses.

RESULTS AND DISCUSSION

Given the nature of the research, we combine the findings and discussion in one section, where we report the findings and discuss the opportunities and challenges of introducing each of the areas of digital health education included in this study.

When reviewing the included universities with respect to the covered majors, we found that 8/11 universities had medicine programs, compared to 10/11 offered that nursing programs. Pharmacy, on the other hand, was only offered in 6/11 universities. The full list of the included universities and the covered majors are listed in Table 1. The eleven universities were reviewed in terms of providing courses in the ree main areas of digital health. In general, most universities provided courses that focused on digital literacy, biostatistics and general genomics, however very few programs focused on the new technologies and trends in healthcare. Each of the three areas is explained in its dedicated section below.

Table 1: A list of Palestinian universities and their offering of the included majors in this chapter, which are medicine and selected health sciences professions

University	City	Medicine	Nursing	Pharmacy
Al-Quds University	Jerusalem	✓	✓	✓
Hebron University	Hebron	✓	✓	✓
Palestine Polytechnic University	Hebron	✓	✓	
Bethlehem University	Bethlehem		✓	
Palestine Ahliya University	Bethlehem		✓	
An-Najah National University	Nablus	✓	✓	✓
The Arab American University	Jenin	✓	✓	✓
Birzeit University	Ramallah		✓	✓
Washington University of Health Sciences	Ramallah	✓		
Al-Azhar University	Gaza	✓	✓	✓
The Islamic University of Gaza	Gaza	✓	✓	

Digital Medicine

As defined by previous works, digital medicine refers to the " digital products and services that are intended for use in the diagnosis, prevention, monitoring and treatment of a disease, condition or syndrome" (Topol et al., 2019). Preparing for digital medicine areas, it is important to work on training the health workforce and upskilling them in aspects such as computer literacy, and related aspects. Palestinian universities were reviewed in terms of their readiness and inclusion of topics related to digital health. Included topics were chosen based on previous studies such as computer skills, health information systems and digital literacy. As shown in Table 2, only four (57.1%) of the included medical programs offered courses that target building basic computer skills among their students all of which were university requirements. Similarly, only five universities (50.0%) offer nursing programs, and four universities (66.6%) for pharmacy programs, taught courses in computer applications and skills. The number of credit hours allocated for each of the computer skills classes ranged between 2-3 credit hours across the three majors. While most universities offered computer science as a part of their university requirement, the "Computer Science for Medical Technology" course offered by Hebron University Pharmacy program, was the only one that offered computer science with a focus on medical technologies.

A sample class description of the included classes is shown below:

This course gives the student a general view of the computer in theory and practice. The student will implement the skills acquired in computer science in the computer lab practically on the computer under the supervision of the instructor.

- Fundamentals of Computer Science and Programming, AlAhliya Univesity

It is important to note that only two universities, Hebron University and Palestine Polytechnic University, offered medicine programs had courses that target more specific and clinical practice-related topics such as "Health Information Systems" and "Approaches & Standards of Exchaning Medical Data". The same courses offered for Hebron University Medicine students were also offered to Nursing students, which is considered the only program across all nursing schools in Palestine that tackled and prepared students in terms of digital literacy and familiarity with topics related to exchanging data and use of HIS systems.

While most universities offered classes that targeted digital literacy, none targeted new trends in medicine and nursing such as Telemedicine, Mobile Health and Virtual reality in healthcare. These statistics suggest an urgent need to address and improve the digital literacy and preparedness of healthcare professionals to meet the requirements of their future roles.

Table 2: Overview of offered courses that prepare students for Digital Health Applications in terms of the offered courses, requirement type and number of credit hours. Not applicable, is used for majors/programs not offered by the university. Not listed, refers to an offered major but with no reference to relevant digital health courses offered as per the university website.

	Offered Courses			Course Requirement Type			Number of Credits		
	Medicine	Nursing	Pharmacy	Medicine	Nursing	Pharmacy	Medicine	Nursing	Pharmacy
Al-Quds University	Computer Skills	Not listed	Not listed	Required	Not listed	Not listed	3	Not listed	Not listed
Hebron University	Computer Applications, Hospital Information System, Approaches & Standards of Exchanging Medical Data	Computer Applications, Hospital Information System, Approaches & Standards of Exchanging Medical Data	Computer Applications, Computer Science for Medical Technology	Required	Required	Required, Required	3	3,3,3,3	3,3
Palestine Polytechnic University	Health information systems	Computer Skills	Not Applicable	Elective	Requied, Required	Not Applicable	3	2,4	Not Applicable
Bethlehem University	Not Applicable	Not listed	Not Applicable	Not Applicable	Not listed	Not Applicable	Not Applicable	Not listed	Not Applicable
Palestine Ahliya University	Not Applicable	Fundementasl of Computer Science and Programming	Not Applicable	Not Applicable	Required	Not Applicable	Not Applicable	3	Not Applicable
An-Najah National University	Introduction to Computer Science and Skills	Introduction to Computer Science and Skills	Introduction to Computer Science and Skills	Required	Required	Required	2	2	2
The Arab American University	Computer Skills	Computer Skills	Computer Skills	Required	Required	Required	2	2	2
Birzeit University	Not Applicable	Not listed	Not listed	Not Applicable	Not listed	Not Applicable	Not listed	Not listed	Not listed
Washington University of Health Sciences	Not listed	Not Applicable	Not Applicable	Not listed	Not Applicable	Not Applicable	Not listed	Not Applicable	Not Applicable
Al-Azhar University	Not listed	Not listed	Computer Science	Not listed	Not listed	Required	Not listed	Not listed	3
The Islamic University of Gaza	Not listed	Not listed	Not Applicable	Not listed	Not listed	Not Applicable	Not listed	Not listed	Not Applicable

Introducing Digital Health Training in Medical, Health Sciences Education

In the following subsections, we discuss important applications of digital health and potential opportunities and challenges with incorporating such topics in medical and health sciences higher education curricula. While there are various use cases of digital medicine, we carefully chose the ones that reflect the impact of introducing training on clinical practice and healthcare delivery.

Data-Driven Care: Electronic Health Records And ePrescribing

With the spread of technology and computers worldwide, many healthcare facilities adopted hospital information systems where hospital transactions, finances, and patient information are stored (Xiao et al., 2018). This spread facilitated the transition from paper patient records to comprehensive electronic records, where all data and patient encounter information are stored in a comprehensive way, creating a wealth of longitudinal records (Adler-Milstein et al., 2013, Coorevits et al., 2013). Similarly, managing hospital transactions electronically allowed for keeping track of expenditures and opening the door to limiting financial spending and managing resources (Balaraman and Kosalram, 2013, Zhu et al., 2021). Furthermore, with an electronic system, it became possible to view the occupancy of beds and hospital performance, manage admission, discharge, and patient registration, as well as dynamically monitor the allocation of nurses and doctors, which could improve the utilisation of resources, especially in resource-constrained clinical settings.

The spread of HIS and EHR systems adoption did not exclude the MENA region and the Arab world. For example, several countries adopted HIS and EHR systems at their healthcare facilities. For example, the United Arab Emirates (UAE) adopted Cerner and Epic Systems, in government and private healthcare facilities, as a part of the National Unified Medical Record (NUMR) initiative (Harbi, 2021). Similar trends were noticed in government facilities in the Kingdom of Saudi Arabia, Jordan (Othman et al., 2015), and Kuwait (Alnashmi et al., 2022), all of which have increased the adoption of HIS and EHR systems. Similarly, in Palestine, the national deployment of the EHR system was completed in 2010, when the Palestinian Ministry of Health (PMOH) partnered with the USAID-funded Palestinian Health Sector Reform and Development Project to implement a computerized HIS for government facilities. The implementation of the chosen software Avicenna HIS was carried out by a local technology company. Currently, the system is deployed in more than 18+ facilities, including eight hospitals, the national blood bank and eight primary care clinics, across the West Bank and East Jerusalem.

The EHR/HIS system was well-perceived by most medical practitioners. However, its optimal usage is not achieved (Samara, 2021). There's a gap in technical competencies and knowledge in standard data reporting guidelines for reporting structured clinical data regarding diagnosis, prescriptions, procedural codes, clinical laboratory and vital signs. Particularly, diagnosis and procedure codes are often reported in standardized ways such as the International Classification of Diseases 10th Revision (ICD10) (Hirsch et al., 2016), the Current Procedural Terminology (CPT) code (Hirsch et al., 2015), and the Diagnosis Related Group (DRG), to allow for a unified way of reporting clinical findings and procedures worldwide. Although most EHR/HIS systems do not require doctors to memorize the codes but rather use lookup tables where doctors or healthcare professionals can search for the relevant code by search mechanism, using such systems still requires training. Training doctors and healthcare professionals to be familiar with such coding is vital to allow for the scalability of the work and avoid missing diagnoses and errors in coding (Silow-Carroll et al., 2012, Humphrey-Murto et al., 2022). Furthermore, there needs to be training on properly reporting unstructured data such as clinical notes, radiology, pathology and discharge notes, keeping in mind the mix of languages Arabic and English and terminology that might be used. Moreover, training needs to be conducted on how the data collection is carried out at different care setups, whether outpatient, inpatient, emergency or even ICU care.

Considering the increased adoption of EHRs and the promising potential of using the collected data for patient care, billing, and population research, there's a technical competency gap in the Palestinian Market. As reported by related studies in KSA, the major challenges in implementing and optimal utilization of HIS/EHR systems include the lack of computer competency, perceived ease and perceived usefulness of the introduced systems (Alqahtani et al., 2017). In a study conducted in governmental hospitals in Palestine and Jordan, 86% of healthcare professionals and doctors reported that they needed skills health informatics skills to monitor patients' diagnoses and treatment, with similar percentages of 84.5% and 83.4% for the need for training in using patient medical records and using medical records for clinical research, respectively (Jabareen et al., 2020). With these statistics, it becomes important to implement training programs to upskill the current healthcare professionals working at various institutions; however, this may face various challenges, such as limitations in governmental budgets and limited resources and time available at the overburdened medical facilities.

Therefore, it has been recommended worldwide to include training in undergraduate-level courses to ensure a minimum familiarity of the new generation of graduates (Moskowitz et al., 2015). Including lectures, research-based projects, and workshops on using electronic systems widely adopted in the government and private facilities will limit potential inefficiencies due to user frustration and lack of technical competencies in using electronic systems. Moreover, lack of training could lead to impaired quality of the collected data, resulting in poor research quality of care and data-driven research on the individual and population level in Palestine.

Palestinian medical residency programs are still in nascent stages, where many specialities do not have established programs for sub-specialisation (Kerr Winter et al., 2015). The lack of a wide range of options for medical specialisation causes many doctors to conduct their residencies abroad (Kerr Winter et al., 2015), where hospitals rely on residents for entering patient information into the system (Aylor et al., 2017). Considering this trend is a motivator to improve the quality of Palestinian medical students and strengthen their chances in regional and international residency training programs. Similarly, pharmacy students require training in using pharmacy inventory management, e-prescribing and e-dispensing systems (Mantel-Teeuwisse et al., 2021). Incorporating such training in formal training would lead to next-generation clinicians and healthcare professionals with contributions in biomedical innovation and effective, efficient care that serves the needs of Palestine, MENA countries and the world. Such initiatives require a redefinition of the role of a doctor and healthcare professionals, where their role involves contributing to the knowledge and understanding of diseases that impact the patient population, using technology tools that improve patient outcomes and experiences.

While incorporating many of these topics and training on using these systems in the education of medical, nursing and pharmacy students seems promising, there still remain challenges. One of the major challenges is the shortage of qualified professionals and faculty trained on using EHRs and ePrescribing/e-Dispensing systems in Palestine (Jabareen et al., 2020). This, however, can be addressed by designing curricula and workshops in collaboration with professionals from industry and practising clinicians where students could benefit from the practical and technical experience, which in return raises the qualifications of the Palestinian medical and healthcare professionals graduates. Another limitation is the compact and packed medical curriculum offered by most Palestinian universities and degree-granting institutions, making it difficult to add extra courses. However, this limitation could be addressed over multiple folds. First, most Palestinian universities have a two-month summer break, with limited internship opportunities for healthcare professionals. These two months could be utilized by the universities or partner institutions to provide hands-on experiences in digital health subjects, whether in hardware or software training. These training courses could be counted for credit, or they could offer extra accreditation that could be used to improve the medical student's profile and resumes. The other option could be offering elective courses in the fourth year, where the curriculum tends to be more flexible, and students are closer to making choices that impact their career path.

Telemedicine and Mobile Health

With the spread of internet access and smartphones worldwide, many healthcare services could be offered beyond the clinic's scope (Sood et al., 2016). Telemedicine gained increased interest during the coronavirus pandemic (Colbert et al., 2020), where patients could conduct teleconsultation remotely without the need to see the doctor in person. While some doctors and healthcare professionals were used to teleconsultations before the pandemic (Zha et al., 2020, Jumreornvong et al., 2020), the majority were not used to conducting consultations using a new medium. Similarly, Palestinian medical and healthcare professionals had no previous experience with telemedicine, leaving the Palestinian population with an unmet need during the pandemic. Due to the geopolitical situation in Palestine, travelling between provinces present a significant challenge for many patients to see specialists from other provinces under restrictions or those with closed city entrances.

Furthermore, many elderly and frail patients from rural areas are hard to move since they depend on other family members to follow up on their medical conditions. Telemedicine solutions could offer a potential solution that provides continuous care at a low cost by overcoming many financial barriers and dependencies on other family members. As one of the countries with the highest literacy rates in the MENA region, where literacy is as high as 97.2% (Ghazal et al., 2022), Palestine might be well suited for the elderly and younger generations to use new mediums of health services. Similarly, technical literacy for using various video/audio platforms is common, keeping in mind that many Palestinian families have relatives living abroad, which could make the elderly familiar with the use of online calls.

Despite this promise, training medical students and health science graduates to conduct remote medical consultations, report patient outcomes, and adhere to international patient safety and privacy guidelines is an untapped area of training in the Palestinian curriculum. Many international medical committees as well as those formed in neighbouring Arab countries, called for efforts to familiarize doctors and healthcare professionals with the main principles of conducting teleconsultations (Waseh and Dicker, 2018, Waseh et al., 2019). There has also been high interest expressed by health professionals in the region. For instance, Around 75.9% of doctors and healthcare professionals working in Palestine and Jordan expressed their need to be trained to conduct telemedicine (Jabareen et al., 2020). As doctors' and healthcare professionals' role is going beyond the clinic's scope and incorporating new modes of care, building the next generation of healthcare professionals requires training in using digital means for healthcare service delivery. For instance, incorporating modules as a part of existing classes that involve how to screen, diagnose and treat patients remotely would be valuable for students. Moreover, such modules could be included as a part of the residency and rotations for students in various specialities.

Other than telemedicine, various mobile health applications have been introduced in the region, where patients can view a centralized medical record, manage appointment bookings and keep track of prescriptions. One of the pioneering examples is that of the Kingdom of Saudi Arabia (KSA), "Tawakkalna" (AlGothami and Saeed, 2021). Training doctors and healthcare professionals on how to introduce patients to such digital solutions could positively impact the patient's experience and outcomes. Examples of subjects that could be covered include communication skills, patient privacy (Kayaalp, 2018), ethical data management (Knoppers and Thorogood, 2017), and consultations in the lack of physical examination. Moreover, Palestinian doctors with professional expertise in telemedicine could have exposure to opportunities beyond the scope of Palestine. For example, Palestinian medical graduates could serve patients from other countries in the MENA region, where Arabic is also the primary language of communication.

Immersive Technology In Health Education And Training

The evolving nature of digital technologies and the new means by which they are being integrated into health training and digital education (eLearning) worldwide has been evolving progressively. In this section, a new focus direction in the utilization of digital devices in medical and healthcare training and education in Palestine is discussed with examples in terms of challenges and opportunities. Immersive technologies such as augmented reality (AR), mixed reality (MR), and virtual reality (VR) are up-and-coming emerging technologies in the world of digital health training and education worldwide (Bremner et al., 2020).

VR Incorporates an immersive experience where the content is artificial, 100% digital, and computer generated. Users are expected to have a completely immersive experience that closely resembles real life (Ghanem et al., 2020). On the other hand, AR combines digital elements, sensory stimuli, sound, tactile, and other haptic stimuli with the real world, ultimately providing an enhanced version that can be presented to the viewer. Lastly, MR would combine the aforementioned technologies into one. The virtual and real-time environments in MR allow the user to interact in both real and virtual content. The definitions for the three often confused terms are provided in Table 2. In all three technologies, the observed environment interacts and changes around and in response to the user (Ghanem et al., 2020).

Table 3. Important definitions for immersive technologies in medical and health sciences education

Term	Definition
Virtual Reality (VR)	Interaction with an artificial computer-generated image
Augmented Reality (AR)	Interaction with a real-life computer-generated image
Mixed Reality (MR)	Interaction with a mix of real-life and artificial computer-generated image

The utilization of immersive technologies in training and education has been by and large gaining popularity and showing signs of progression and development internationally. It has been adopted in medical, military, gaming, and sports organizations effectively (Khan and Lippert, 2022). Yet, the current applications of immersive technologies in digital health training and education in the MENA region and particularly in Palestine are lagging. A few representations were immersive technologies such as VR was successfully implemented in Palestine, such as the "Palestine VR" virtual app that offers a 360-degree immersive tour of Palestine where you can walk the real cities of Palestine and experience life there (Pears and Konstantinidis, 2022). Despite its success, this model has not been replicated in any situation from an educational or training standpoint. Immersive technologies have been proven to be an effective tool for increasing competency and providing safer patient care. Additionally, it has been demonstrated to be linked to higher levels of student engagement, self-efficacy, and satisfaction. By simulating clinical circumstances in a realistic and experimental setting, and improving medical and surgical education (Khan and Lippert, 2022).

The implementation of immersive technologies such as AR, VR, and MR in Head-Mounted Displays (HMDs) will uncover new opportunities for teaching and training in Palestine. Their integration into health training and education in Palestine can be divided into both theoretical knowledge education and practical training education. With respect to theoretical knowledge education, recreating picture-perfect anatomical representations of the human body will allow students to experience real-life familiarity. Medical students can visualize the entire human body and construct accurate clinical correlations. Anatomical/pathological variations and abnormalities can also be visualized separately, further reinforcing the student's understanding of various anatomical pathologies. Similarly, dental students will be able to accurately visualize the oral cavity and correlate the various dental diseases with anatomical landmarks. Equally, nursing students will be able to visualize the relevant human anatomy regions, particularly the anatomical variations of blood vessels and adjacent structures. Compared to old-school teaching on cadavers, immersive technology delivers real-time feedback with lower risk and affordable cost. Owing to the situation in Palestine and amidst the limiting political situation where many restrictions prohibit the acquisition of cadavers by universities, the integration of such technologies can be of substantial benefit. Regarding pharmacy students, human physiology, drug pharmacokinetics/pharmacodynamics, and drug-drug interactions visualized on VR HMDs can be integrated and provided as part of the teaching curriculum to complement their studies.

On the other hand, practical training education can be developed through immersive technology by creating virtual patients to enhance the student's technical skills. Inserting a needle and drawing blood for nursing students, pulling out a tooth and inserting fillings for dental students, performing vascular interventions via inserting a wire or a port, and mimicking percutaneous interventions with tumor resection planning for medical students or surgical residents. This approach will enable the students to mimic real-life scenarios, practice their abilities and examine various outcomes in a risk-free setting (Venkatesan et al., 2021). In the future, its incorporation could help improve the healthcare providers' competency and technical skills and ultimately result in a more proficient multidisciplinary healthcare team (Ryan et al., 2022). In a systematic review study conducted by Barteit, S., et al, in 2021, Training with AR- and VR-based HMDs was perceived as salient, motivating, and engaging, indicating that they were effective for certain aspects of medical skills and knowledge learning and training . Therefore, immersive technologies can be seen as a valuable resource that has the potential to strengthen medical education and healthcare training in Palestine.

Immersive technologies, like all other digital technologies, have challenges and limitations. These include user attitude challenges, cost limitations, unaccustomedness to information technology devices, and most importantly cybersickness due to continuous eye strain and prolonged exposure (Khan and Lippert, 2022). A very crucial limitation that needs to be considered especially in classrooms and educational facilities is the potential interference with the cognitive and physical development of children. Finally, immersive technology can be like most technological inventions, addictive, and pose a threat to the social skill development in children. This is particularly important when considering the long periods of time that can be spent using such technology without engaging in real-life communication (Venkatesan et al., 2021).

Medical Device Training

Digital health training is currently a top priority for medical device manufacturers and other significant stakeholders in the industry. Medical device digital health training combines all mobile health applications, medical device data systems, medical image communication devices, radiological devices, and laboratory devices altogether. The incorporation of digital health training with these devices creates better access, lowers the costs of training, and increases the efficiency of such devices, such that more experienced individuals will be able to exploit the device beyond its current scope. The enormous and incessantly progressive innovation of biomedical devices and the excessive training that healthcare providers ought to be complemented with, however, are becoming very burdensome. In Palestine, due to the current geopolitical situation and the long-suffering instability of the region, restricted travel, and economic insecurity, the potential of constructing a decent training facility with high-end medical devices and equipment remains tortuous. However, sometimes hospitals and training facilities in Palestine receive a much-needed donation. An essential medical machine that has been lacking and, in much demand, or some equipment that was too expensive to get. But unfortunately, in many cases after the donation is received, the device sits unused for months before it gets wasted. This almost always happens due to the shortage of well-trained physicians, nurses, or technicians. Sometimes, a few employees are selected for a month-long training camp with an international training organization, with the intention of returning to work on the machine and helping develop the department. Unfortunately, however, in many cases after the return of the trained professionals, they end up working in the private sector or leave abroad due to the limited local opportunities, hurdling the potential and scalability of using such devices in academic medical centers and governmental facilities, This creates an injurious atmosphere and holds up any potential development. Furthermore, due to the lack of trained biomedical technicians and device engineers, improper machine fault diagnosis measures are implemented, which may further worsen the devices' performance and hamper their functionality. Definitively, with the introduction of digital health training and education, a big part of this problem can potentially be mitigated.

By actively utilizing tele-education students will be able to direct their training to their own learning interests freely and flexibly. This also eliminates the constraints of cost and travel for the students. Not only will they be able to develop their technical skills and expand their knowledge, but also offer them more networking opportunities and allow them to get in touch with experts in the field to further enhance their contribution and influence. Tele-educational programs and distance learning courses can be offered in advanced teaching facilities in Palestine. This is essential for building strong social interactions between colleagues in the same area of focus that can potentially reciprocate in real-world work. Tele-educational programs can comprise online discussion boards, video collaborations, online research, and real-time video training courses to increase the competencies of students and residents in using both hardware and software medical devices and tools (Upadhyay and Khandelwal, 2022). Students may also actively design their own problems and precisely target their areas of concern. Moreover, it provides the students with freedom and eliminates the current unfriendly learning environment by providing them with endless autonomy (Fracaro et al., 2022).

The implementation of immersive technology in medical device training has great potential, especially in Palestine. The attendance of sensory inputs on virtual patients using VR technology and applying it to medical machine training enhances realism and promotes a meaningful interaction (Burdea and Coiffet, 2003). Moreover, with the growing importance of developing healthier healthcare provider (HCP)-patient and HCP-HCP interactions, the utilization of a Virtual Objective Structured Clinical Exam (VOSCE) system will enable medical students to experience highly immersive interactions between patients and physicians using natural interaction methods. These features allow the system to train medical communication skills (Carmigniani and Furht, 2011). Another area of exploitation is in telerehabilitation. VR can be used to perform rehabilitation exercises at home or outside a medical facility without the direct supervision or physical presence of a healthcare provider (Speicher and Nebeling, 2019).

Artificial Intelligence and Robotics

Artificial Intelligence (AI) for health is gaining increased interest across the research and industry communities worldwide, where AI-based applications could be used to advance research and build clinical decision support systems (Aung et al., 2021). For instance, AI has been used for the early detection of diagnosis (Iqbal et al., 2021, Nichols et al., 2019), prediction of patient outcomes and deterioration (Peng et al., 2021, Veldhuis et al., 2022), admission to hospitals and even in generating radiology reports (Croon et al., 2022). In research, AI was used at the early stages of COVID-19 to better understand the disease's nature and indicators of deterioration (Arora et al., 2021). Other use cases include drug-repurposing and drug-discovery applications (Tanoli et al., 2021, Mohanty et al., 2021), where AI could identify potential drugs to treat new diseases. Another closley related field, is medical robotics where machines are programmed to do specialised tasks that help automate tasks in medical settings and conduct them with high precision.

For this digital health area, the included Palestinian universities were evaluated for including skills that prepare their students for new job roles that involved diffusion of AI & Robotics in clinical and allied health professions practice. The included skills needed to understand AI are very closely related to statistics and informatics, as well as classes that specialise in health informatics, data analytics and medical devices. As shown in Table 4, none of the universities offered required nor elective courses that directly target AI & Robotics applications in healthcare. Nevertheless, all included medical programs (8/8) offered courses in medical research, where some of the covered topics were research methods, biostatistics, and mathematics for health sciences. Similarly, all of the nursing programs (10/10) offered mandatory courses in research as a part of the nursing degree programs, where example courses were "Nursing Research" and "Biostatistics", and "Scientific Research for Health Professions". A similar trend was noticed in pharmacy programs, where (6/6) universities offered courses in research methodologies, mathematics and biostatistics. An example course description of the Biostatistics is shown to demonstrate the content offered in such courses.

This course introduces the methods of statistical data classification and presentation, as well as their collection, organization and analysis. It also introduces principles of probabilities, some probability distributions, and distribution of samples, testing of hypotheses, simple linear regression and correlation, analysis of variance. There will be also medical and biological applications on all of the aforementioned .

- Biostatistics for Medical and Health Sciences, The Arab American University

The number of credit hours allocated to such courses ranged between 2-8, where the varriance depended on the nature of the course and whether it was combined with other topics such as the case of "Behavioral Science & Epidemiology/Biostatistics" offered by Washington University of Health Sciences.

Out of all the programs two medicine schools, and two nursing schools offered classes in Health Informatics, which more directly tackle topics related to data analysis and AI. The number of credit hours allocated for the Health Informatics classes 2-3, all of which were faculty requirements. An example class description of the health Informatics class offered to medicine students is shown below:

This course aims to provide the student with an overview of current issues in health informatics and health information management applications. It also introduces the student to health information systems and technology related to the application of health information, health records, in addition to data analysis and retrieval.

- Health Informatics, The Arab American University

Table 4: Overview of offered courses that prepare students for AI & Robotics Applications in terms of the offered courses, requirement type and number of credit hours. Not applicable, is used for majors/programs not offered by the university. Not listed, refers to an offered major but with no reference to relevant digital health courses offered as per the university website. The star indicates a lack of description of the academic plan.

	Offered Courses			Course Requirement Type			Number of Credits		
	Medicine	Nursing	Pharmacy	Medicine	Nursing	Pharmacy	Medicine	Nursing	Pharmacy
Al-Quds University	Research Methodology and Biostatistics	Biostatistics for Health Professions,, Scientific Research for Health Professions, Health Informatics	Biostatistics	Required	Required, Elective	*	4	3, 3,2	*
Hebron University	Biostatistics for MS, Bioinformatics	Health Informatics, Biostatistics for Nursing	Biostatistics	Required	Elective College Required	Required	*	3,3	3
Palestine Polytechnic University	Biostatistics for MS, Bioinformatics	Biostatistics for Nursing, Methods of Health Research, Health Informatics,	Not Applicable	Required, Elective	Required, Required	Not Applicable	3,3	3	Not Applicable
Bethlehem University	Not Applicable	Introduction to Statistics	Not Applicable	Not Applicable	Required	Not Applicable	Not Applicable	3	Not Applicable
Palestine Ahliya University	Not Applicable	Scientific Methods & Statistics	Not Applicable	Not Applicable	Required	Not Applicable	Not Applicable	3	Not Applicable
An-Najah National University	Biostatistics for Medical and Health Sciences	Biostatistics for Nursing Students	Biostatistics for Medical and Health Sciences	Required	Required	Required	3	2	3
The Arab American University	Biostatistics for Medical Students, Health Informatics	Biostatistics	Biostatistics	Required	Required	Required	3, 2	2	3
Birzeit University	Not Applicable	Not listed	Introduction to Pharmacy/ Claculations, Biostatistics & Epidemiology	Not Applicable	Not listed	Required	Not Applicable	Not listed	2
Washington University of Health Sciences	Behavioral Science & Epidemiology/ Biostatistics	Not Applicable	Not Applicable	Required	Not Applicable	Not Applicable	8	Not Applicable	Not Applicable
Al-Azhar University	Biostatistics & Methodology Research	Mathematics for health sciences	Mathematics for health sciences, Biostatistics	Required	Required	Required	4	3	3,2
The Islamic University of Gaza	Research & Statistics	Biostatistics	Not Applicable	Required	Required	Not Applicable	3	*	Not Applicable

It is important to note that most of the aforementioned health informatics courses for nursing programs were offered by the departments in the universities that received funding from the HiCURE program, which is a project targeting the upskilling of health professionals by designing undergraduate courses that address the gap of lack of digital competencies, funded by ERASMUS. There were also a few studies documenting the development of some of the courses proposed as a part of the HiCURE project, such as adopting a case study approach for understanding EHRs (Al-Jabari et al., 2018). However, there is limited information on the impact of the introduced courses on student outcomes.

The need to introduce health informatics to cope with the fast-changing practice is a concern expressed and realized by Palestinian students in health sciences majors. Based on a survey conducted on students from Palestine and Jordan, 83% of students from the health sciences department were interested in learning health informatics (Khader et al., 2019). The same survey reported that 63% of students expressed interest in taking an undergraduate course in health informatics (Khader et al., 2019). Despite the high student interest, only 36% believed that their university provided a supportive environment for learning health informatics (Khader et al., 2019), leaving the students with an unmet need for learning health informatics and digital health. These statistics suggest a pressing need for incorporating digital health courses that better prepare health professionals for the new era of health sciences and medical practice.

In the following subsections, we discuss health informatics and AI research and Medical Robotics usecases and their respective impact on Palestinian university students.

Health Informatics and Artificial Intelligence Research

The scarcity of structured evidence in medicine and health science remains a bottleneck in discovering and understanding various pathologies and true disease prevalence worldwide. It is estimated that only 10-20% of clinical decisions are evidence (McGinnis et al., 2013). Despite many initiatives and speciality societies' efforts to establish evidence-based guidelines for care, it has been reported by multiple studies that about 50% of the guideline recommendations are based on experts' opinions and quantitive data and evidence (McGinnis et al., 2013). It is also essential to note that much of the current world evidence is positioned to target patients from high-income countries and the Western world in general, where most of the data come from (Ebrahim et al., 2013). This issue leaves low-middle income countries, including many countries in the MENA region, with limited care and clinical evidence that addresses their needs and suits their lifestyle and population specific-diseases and needs. In Palestine and several MENA countries, until recently, most of the medical data recorded in paper outpatient, inpatient and emergency data was collected on paper records and viewed by one physician at a time, which had a direct impact on creating the gap in care and fragmented evidence that serves the needs of the people from this region. The new adoption and aggregation of a structured way of collecting data could mitigate this gap by allowing Palestinian clinicians, scientists and healthcare professionals to participate in international research and create evidence-based societies that address the needs of our population.

The study of healthcare data using digital technologies to create knowledge and evidence is often referred to as health informatics (Mantas et al., 2010). With the new accumulation of health data from governmental and private healthcare facilities, Palestinian medical and health science researchers could build tools that improve their patient's experience, outcomes and understanding of the disease. For example, the centralized government database could be used to study the prevalence of genetic diseases on a population level and design initiatives targeting the population of interest (Casey et al., 2016, Gianfrancesco and Goldstein, 2021). Other example use cases could be related to optimizing the insurance coverage for diseases with low-cost interventions that could reduce the high disease burden (Heart et al., 2017). These initiatives become highly valued, especially when resources, be it financial or experienced professionals, are limited.

The increased adoption and low-cost hardware needed to train and deploy such AI software systems could open the doors for utilising them in low-resource clinical settings such as those in Palestine. To avoid a negative impact on the patient experience, medical and healthcare professionals require training to seamlessly integrate AI clinical decision support systems in current patient flows. Specifically, this requires training on an understanding of the implications of deploying AI systems, the promise, limitations, and other active areas of research, including trust, reliability, and other ethical issues. Other important training components are data protection, patient privacy, and ethics board approvals to work with patient data.

By incorporating courses that cover topics such as the principles of health informatics research, reporting guidelines, and basic data analysis techniques, the medical and healthcare professionals, students would be equipt with tools that allow them to build high-quality tools, develop strong evidence in novel applications in treatment effects, diagnosis, prognosis and public health. Introducing such components in the formal curricula of medical and health science degree-granting institutions will build the tools needed to allow the work of Palestinian universities to be published in high-impact scholarly venues driving the next generation of high-impact data-driven care. Moreover, this data-driven work could be used to drive decisions on where limited funding and resources could be allocated to make the most suitable impact on the population.

Medical Robotics

Another area that has become more widespread and is gaining a lot of popularity in the healthcare setting is medical robotics. The use of robots in pioneering hospitals, especially recently, has become a cornerstone for their development. By assisting the medical staff in operating rooms, intensive care units, or other risky settings, collaborative mobile robots can make excellent hospital aides (Speich and Rosen, 2004). Mobile robotic applications have developed into technologies that significantly improve quality of life and provide reliable people autonomy. Simplifying routine tasks, reducing the physical demands on physicians and healthcare workers by ensuring a more consistent process, and keeping a safe environment. Additionally, their use in surgical assistance, logistical task roles, and directly interacting with patients to offer directions and provide friendly interactions has been an area of advancement in the most renowned hospitals in the world (Troccaz et al., 2019). The integration of healthcare robotic technology into Palestinian hospitals holds the potential to revolutionize clinical workflows, augment medical and surgical interventions, and enhance medical training and education in local universities. However, the implementation of such technology necessitates comprehensive training in advanced medical and engineering techniques prior to adoption (Beasley, 2012). Furthermore, an environment that fosters seamless collaboration between healthcare practitioners and robotic systems is crucial. To facilitate this, training programs can incorporate immersive technologies, enabling practitioners to familiarize themselves with these systems and optimize their usage.

Genomics

Genomics, the study of an individual's genes and their relationship to health and disease, has emerged as a groundbreaking field in healthcare (Demmer & Waggoner., 2014). Recent advancements in genomics research and technology have significantly expanded our understanding of the genetic basis of diseases and treatment responses. This growing knowledge underscores the critical need to incorporate genomics into medical and health education, both globally and in Palestine, to meet the evolving demands of patient care and drive progress in personalized medicine (Nelson & McGuire., 2010).

Furthermore, technology has significantly contributed to the progress of genomics education in medical and professional health programs, revolutionizing the way students learn (Feero & Green., 2011). Through digital platforms and online resources, students now have unprecedented access to the latest genomics research and immersive learning experiences. For instance, virtual laboratories and simulation software offer students a hands-on opportunity to delve into genomic data analysis, comprehend genetic variations, and grasp the far-reaching implications of genomics in healthcare decision-making (Feero & Green., 2011). Moreover, the integration of bioinformatics tools and genomic data analysis software empowers students to employ computational approaches in studying intricate genetic diseases and identifying promising therapeutic targets (Persky & McBride., 2009). By harnessing technology, genomics education has been elevated to new heights, preparing students for the challenges and opportunities that lie ahead in the field of genomics (Persky & McBride., 2009).

The Palestinian universities were reviewed in terms of the inclusion of genomics-related courses in their medical and health-sciences curricula, and the results are shown in Table 5. All medical programs offered classes that covered genomics directly or indirectly. Specifically, 4/8 universities required genomics courses where they often referred to such courses as "Human Genetics" or "Medical Genetics". The four other medical programs universities offered courses in biology where they incorporated genetics, but not as an independent required course. A sample course description is shown below:

The course covers two parts; first part will include detailed description of nucleic acids chemistry, DNA replication and transcription. The mechanism of gene regulation at different levels will be emphasized. The basics of various mutations in genes will be discussed along with the various approaches to identify mutations and their effects. Special mechanisms used by eukaryotic cells to ensure gene diversity will also be discussed. The second part will provide students with a comprehensive view of the science of genetics. It covers the history and development of genetics, structure and function of gene, chromosomes and their anomalies, pattern of single gene inheritance, types and mechanisms of mutations. Gene therapy strategies and selected applications will be discussed as a central approach in inherited diseases therapy.

- *Molecular Biology & Genetics, Al Quds University*

Similarly, all nursing courses offered biology courses, however, only three universities offered courses with genetics as a main focus. Pharmacy programs were generally the least prepared for genomic courses inclusion in their curriculum. Only two universities with pharmacy programs, Al-Najah and The Arab American Universities, offered courses that targeted genomics and pharmacogenomics and their possible integration with biotechnology devices. The course description of the Human Genetics, Biotechnology Product courses is shown below:

This course deals with molecular and genetic biochemical technology with emphasis on medical uses of drugs manufactured by the biotechnological methods. This course will also deal with diseases treated with gene therapy.

- Human Genetics, Biotechnology Products, Al-Najah National University

These statistics necessitate raising awareness on the importance of incorporating classes and better preparing the new health sciences graduates for the new error of genomics in their practice. In the following section, we discuss more specific genomics applications and their implications for Palestine.

Table 5: Overview of offered courses that prepare students for Genomics Applications in terms of the offered courses, requirement type and number of credit hours. Not applicable, is used for majors/programs not offered by the university. Not listed, refers to an offered major but with no reference to relevant digital health courses offered as per the university website.

	Offered Courses			Course Requirement Type			Number of Credits		
	Medicine	Nursing	Pharmacy	Medicine	Nursing	Pharmacy	Medicine	Nursing	Pharmacy
Al-Quds University	Molecular Biology & Genetics	Biology for Health Professions	Not Listed	Required	Required	Not Listed	4	3	Not Listed
Hebron University	Medical Genetics	Biology for Nursing	General Biology	Required	Required	Required	2	3	3
Palestine Polytechnic University	Medical Genetics	Biology for Health Professions	Not Applicable	Required	Required	Not Applicable	3	3	Not Applicable
Bethlehem University	Not Applicable	Principles of Biology	Not Applicable	Not Applicable	Required	Not Applicable	Not Applicable	4	Not Applicable
Palestine Ahliya University	Not Applicable	Nursing Genomics	Not Applicable	Not Applicable	Required	Not Applicable	Not Applicable	2	Not Applicable
An-Najah National University	Human Genetics	Maternal Health Nursing 1: Obstetrics Genetics, Embryology	Human Genetics, Biotechnology Products	Required	Required	Speciality Optional Requirements	2	4	2, 3
The Arab American University	Medical Genetics	Genetics & Genomic Nursing	Genetics and Pharmacogenomics	Required	Required	Required	2	3	3
Birzeit University	Not Applicable	Not Listed	Not Listed	Not Applicable	Not Listed	Not Listed	Not Applicable	Not Listed	Not Listed
Washington University of Health Sciences	Biochemistry with Nutrition and Genetics	Not Applicable	Not Applicable	Required	Not Applicable	Not Applicable	8	Not Applicable	Not Applicable
Al-Azhar University	Molecular Biology & Genetics	General Biology	Cell Biology	Required	Required	Required	4	3	3
The Islamic University of Gaza	Medical Biology	Not Listed	Not Applicable	Required	Not Listed	Not Applicable	3	Not Listed	Not Applicable

From Precision Medicine to Pharmacogenomics

The importance of genomics in healthcare cannot be overstated. It has revolutionized the way we approach diagnosis, treatment, and prevention. By analyzing an individual's genomic information, healthcare professionals can gain valuable insights into their susceptibility to various diseases, their response to medications, and their predisposition to adverse drug reactions (Nelson & McGuire., 2010). This enables the delivery of tailored care, customized to each patient's unique genetic makeup.

Furthermore, genomics plays a pivotal role in identifying therapeutic targets, developing innovative treatments, and deepening our understanding of disease mechanisms (Demmer & Waggoner, 2014).

Efficiently implementing genomics in healthcare education is crucial to equip healthcare professionals with the knowledge and skills necessary to leverage genomic information effectively (Demmer & Waggoner, 2014). As future genomics applications have signficant overlap with technology, it is of vital importance to expose the new generation of medical and health sciences students to state-of-the-art applications such as epigentic technologies (Zheng et al., 2015). Integrating genomics into medical and health-related curricula empowers future healthcare providers to interpret and apply genomic data in clinical practice. This integration should span foundational courses, clinical training, and continuous professional development to ensure a comprehensive grasp of genomics (Nelson & McGuire, 2010). By staying abreast of the latest developments in genomics, healthcare professionals can contribute to improving patient outcomes, optimizing therapy, and reducing adverse events (Crellin et al., 2019).

In Palestine, as in many regions worldwide, the integration of genomics education in healthcare is of paramount importance. The need for pharmacogenomics education among pharmacists in the West Bank of Palestine highlights the significance of incorporating genomics into the local healthcare system (Jarrar et al., 2021). By providing pharmacists and other health professionals with genomics knowledge, Palestine can enhance patient care, minimize inter-individual variation in drug response, and contribute to the advancement of precision medicine. Integrating genomics education into medical and pharmacy school curricula, workshops, and continuing education programs can bridge the existing knowledge gap and empower healthcare professionals to make informed decisions based on genomic information (Jarrar et al., 2019).

In conclusion, genomics has become a pivotal discipline in healthcare, enabling personalized approaches to diagnosis, treatment, and prevention. Incorporating genomics education into medical and health curricula is essential to prepare healthcare professionals for the future of medicine (Crellin et al., 2019). By embracing genomics, healthcare professionals can harness its potential to deliver tailored care and optimize patient outcomes. In Palestine, the integration of genomics education is particularly vital as it equips health professionals with the skills necessary to leverage genomic information and contribute to the advancement of precision medicine in the region.

IMPACT ON THE JOB MARKET

As a part of scaling and improving the quality of the Palestinian medical and health sciences curricula, it's important to include practical training beyond the scope of the class. For instance, academia-industry partnership training for healthcare professionals could open new doors for opportunities in healthcare beyond services in medical facilities (Kourouklis et al., 2022, Buehler et al., 2013). Industry partnerships could help students practise and acquire new skills in the various areas of digital health services. For example, working closely with information technology (IT) companies could expose healthcare professionals to new digital technologies and modalities and make them up-to-date with cutting-edge technologies they could bring to their patients. Moreover, participating in internships, training and programs close to the industry will build a generation of medical entrepreneurs and introduce them to business and marketing skills they could utilize to build companies that address clinical problems and needs.

Industry training and internships could include careers in research on medical data collected from hospitals, community-based initiatives, predictive analytics solutions, or even building and validating medical devices, all of which provide healthcare graduates with hands-on experience that would make them better equipt for the next generation of patients and technology-enabled and data-driven care. In addition, industry partnerships could foster collaborations with students and healthcare professionals in hospitals in the private and public sectors, which would open the door for long-term collaborations that will drive the biomedical innovation sector in Palestine.

The various areas of digital health applications presented in previous sections present directions for new job opportunities and career paths for medical and health sciences graduates. By training the new generation of graduates to make the best out of the data collected in EHRs and e-Prescribing/e-Dispensing systems, the education system could open doors for new career opportunities, such as new roles in public health, health insurance, and government programs. Opening new job opportunities is of vital importance considering the large numbers of new graduates every year, with limited job opportunities in public and private facilities. By developing systematic awareness and competencies in informatics and technologies, Palestinian graduates could develop an edge that prepares them for working in interdisciplinary teams on advancing patient care, in both hardware and software. Not only does technology open new roles and job opportunities, but it could also make the traditional medical practice more efficient, by increasing productivity and reducing medical errors and unnecessary costs, which is of high relevance in low-resource clinical settings such as Palestine.

CONCLUSION

This chapter reviewed the digital-health-related courses offered for various Palestinian medical and health sciences programs. While most universities offered courses that work on improving digital literacy, research skills and genomics, however, the classes often did not focus on tailoring such skills to the needs of the healthcare practice. Furthermore, many new topics such as AI and Robotics, Telemedicine and biotechnology products were mostly missing from the curricula. These findings suggest a pressing need for awareness and work of policymakers.

In this chapter, the main aim was to direct the attention of policymakers, health strategists, educators, and public and private stakeholders to the importance of introducing digital health training towards improving the national and international education indicators for medicine and health sciences. Introducing such initiatives could give rise to new domains and job opportunities in the intersection of various STEM fields, including medical and health sciences and technology. Despite the high potential of the areas presented in previous sections, it is important to note that there is a need for enabling policies and guidance from regulators and governmental and educational bodies to incentivise universities and educators to introduce new courses.

Furthermore, by highlighting potential aspects to be included in digital health training, this work builds evidence that could guide funders and national and international organizations in directing funds that improve the quality of healthcare and health research in low-resource areas such as Palestine. While the focus of this work was Palestine, it is important to note that there exist similarities with several countries in the MENA region, making the presented findings relevant to neighbouring countries with similar educational systems and job markets

REFERENCES

Adler-Milstein, J., Salzberg, C., Franz, C., Orav, E. J., Newhouse, J. P., & Bates, D. W. (2013). Effect of electronic health records on health care costs: Longitudinal comparative evidence from community practices. *Annals of Internal Medicine*, *159*(2), 97–104. doi:10.7326/0003-4819-159-2-201307160-00004 PMID:23856682

Al-Jabari, M., Amro, B., Jabareen, H., Khadir, Y., & Taweel, A. (2018). Development of case study-based approach for learning undergraduate students to effectively understanding and use of ehr. *15th ACS/IEEE International Conference on Computer Systems and Applications*. IEEE.

Al Gothami, S. S., & Saeed, S. (2021). Digital transformation and usability: User acceptance of tawakkalna application during covid-19 in saudi arabia. In *Pandemic, Lockdown, and Digital Transformation* (pp. 95–109). Springer.

Alnashmi, M., Salman, A., AlHumaidi, H., Yunis, M., & Al-Enezi, N. (2022). Exploring the health information management system of kuwait: Lessons and opportunities. *Applied System Innovation*, *5*(1), 25. doi:10.3390/asi5010025

Alqahtani, A., Aljarullah, A. J., Crowder, R., & Wills, G. (2017). Barriers to the adoption of ehr systems in the kingdom of saudi arabia: An exploratory study using a systematic literature review. *Journal of Health Informatics in Developing Countries*, *11*(2).

Arora, G., Joshi, J., Mandal, R. S., Shrivastava, N., Virmani, R., & Sethi, T. (2021). Artificial intelligence in surveillance, diagnosis, drug discovery and vaccine development against covid19. *Pathogens (Basel, Switzerland)*, *10*(8), 1048. doi:10.3390/pathogens10081048 PMID:34451513

Aung, Y. Y., Wong, D. C., & Ting, D. S. (2021). The promise of artificial intelligence: A review of the opportunities and challenges of artificial intelligence in healthcare. *British Medical Bulletin*, *139*(1), 4–15. doi:10.1093/bmb/ldab016 PMID:34405854

Aylor, M., Campbell, E. M., Winter, C., & Phillipi, C. A. (2017). Resident notes in an electronic health record: A mixed-methods study using a standardized intervention with qualitative analysis. *Clinical Pediatrics*, *56*(3), 257–262. doi:10.1177/0009922816658651 PMID:27400934

Balaraman, P., & Kosalram, K. (2013). E-hospital management & hospital information systems-changing trends. *International Journal of Information Engineering & Electronic Business*, *5*(1), 50–58. doi:10.5815/ijieeb.2013.01.06

Barbosa, W., Zhou, K., Waddell, E., Myers, T., & Dorsey, E. R. (2021). Improving access to care: Telemedicine across medical domains. *Annual Review of Public Health*, *42*(1), 463–481. doi:10.1146/annurev-publhealth-090519-093711 PMID:33798406

Barteit, S., Lanfermann, L., Bärnighausen, T., Neuhann, F., & Beiersmann, C. (2021). Augmented, mixed, and virtual reality-based head-mounted devices for medical education: Systematic review. *JMIR Serious Games*, *9*(3), e29080. doi:10.2196/29080 PMID:34255668

Beasley, R. A. (2012). Medical robots: Current systems and research directions. *Journal of Robotics*, *2012*, 2012. doi:10.1155/2012/401613

Birkhead, G. S., Klompas, M., & Shah, N. R. (2015). Uses of electronic health records for public health surveillance to advance public health. *Annual Review of Public Health, 36*(1), 345–359. doi:10.1146/annurev-publhealth-031914-122747 PMID:25581157

Bremner, R., Gibbs, A., & Mitchell, A. R. (2020). The era of immersive health technology. *INNOVATIONS*.

Buehler, B., Ruggiero, R., & Mehta, K. (2013). Empowering community health workers with technology solutions. *IEEE Technology and Society Magazine, 32*(1), 44–52. doi:10.1109/MTS.2013.2241831

Burdea, G. C., & Coiffet, P. (2003). *Virtual reality technology*. John Wiley & Sons. doi:10.1162/105474603322955950

Car, L. T., Kyaw, B. M., Panday, R. S. N., van der Kleij, R., Chavannes, N., Majeed, A., Car, J., & ... . (2021). Digital health training programs for medical students: Scoping review. *JMIR Medical Education, 7*(3), e28275. doi:10.2196/28275 PMID:34287206

Carmigniani, J., & Furht, B. (2011). Augmented reality: an overview. Handbook of augmented reality, 3-46.

Casey, J. A., Schwartz, B. S., Stewart, W. F., & Adler, N. E. (2016). Using electronic health records for population health research: A review of methods and applications. *Annual Review of Public Health, 37*(1), 61–81. doi:10.1146/annurev-publhealth-032315-021353 PMID:26667605

Colbert, G. B., Venegas-Vera, A. V., & Lerma, E. V. (2020). Utility of telemedicine in the covid-19 era. *Reviews in Cardiovascular Medicine, 21*(4), 583–587. doi:10.31083/j.rcm.2020.04.188 PMID:33388003

Coorevits, P., Sundgren, M., Klein, G. O., Bahr, A., Claerhout, B., Daniel, C., Dugas, M., Dupont, D., Schmidt, A., Singleton, P., De Moor, G., & Kalra, D. (2013). Electronic health records: New opportunities for clinical research. *Journal of Internal Medicine, 274*(6), 547–560. doi:10.1111/joim.12119 PMID:23952476

Cowie, M. R., Blomster, J. I., Curtis, L. H., Duclaux, S., Ford, I., Fritz, F., Goldman, S., Janmohamed, S., Kreuzer, J., Leenay, M., Michel, A., Ong, S., Pell, J. P., Southworth, M. R., Stough, W. G., Thoenes, M., Zannad, F., & Zalewski, A. (2017). Electronic health records to facilitate clinical research. *Clinical Research in Cardiology; Official Journal of the German Cardiac Society, 106*(1), 1–9. doi:10.100700392-016-1025-6 PMID:27557678

Crellin, E., McClaren, B., Nisselle, A., Best, S., Gaff, C., & Metcalfe, S. (2019). Preparing medical specialists to practice genomic medicine: Education an essential part of a broader strategy. *Frontiers in Genetics*, *10*, 789. doi:10.3389/fgene.2019.00789 PMID:31572433

Croon, P., Selder, J., Allaart, C., Bleijendaal, H., Chamuleau, S., Hofstra, L., Išgum, I., Ziesemer, K. A., & Winter, M. M. (2022). Current state of artificial intelligence-based algorithms for hospital admission prediction in patients with heart failure: A scoping review. *European Heart Journal. Digital Health*, *3*(3), 415–425. doi:10.1093/ehjdh/ztac035 PMID:36712159

Demmer, L. A., & Waggoner, D. J. (2014). Professional medical education and genomics. *Annual Review of Genomics and Human Genetics*, *15*(1), 507–516. doi:10.1146/annurev-genom-090413-025522 PMID:24635717

Des Marchais, J., Bureau, M., Dumais, B., & Pigeon, G. (1992). From traditional to problem-based learning: A case report of complete curriculum reform. *Medical Education*, *26*(3), 190–199. doi:10.1111/j.1365-2923.1992.tb00153.x PMID:1614344

Dudin, A. (2008). *Medical Education in Palestine, past, present and future*. Research Gate.

Ebrahim, S., Pearce, N., Smeeth, L., Casas, J. P., Jaffar, S., & Piot, P. (2013). Tackling non-communicable diseases in low-and middle-income countries: Is the evidence from highincome countries all we need? *PLoS Medicine*, *10*(1), e1001377. doi:10.1371/journal.pmed.1001377 PMID:23382655

Feero, W. G., & Green, E. D. (2011). Genomics education for health care professionals in the 21st century. *Journal of the American Medical Association*, *306*(9), 989–990. doi:10.1001/jama.2011.1245 PMID:21900139

Fertleman, C., Aubugeau-Williams, P., Sher, C., Lim, A.-N., Lumley, S., Delacroix, S., & Pan, X. (2018). A discussion of virtual reality as a new tool for training healthcare professionals. *Frontiers in Public Health*, *6*, 44. doi:10.3389/fpubh.2018.00044 PMID:29535997

Fracaro, S. G., Glassey, J., Bernaerts, K., & Wilk, M. (2022). Immersive technologies for the training of operators in the process industry: A Systematic Literature Review. *Computers & Chemical Engineering*, *160*, 107691. doi:10.1016/j.compchemeng.2022.107691

Ghanem, D., Zahran, N., Saramah, J., Aboudi, A., Afaneh, W., & Musa, A. (2020). *VR Palestine - BuildPalestine*. BuildPalestine - a Global Community for Social Impact in Palestine. https://buildpalestine.com/project/vr-palestine/

Ghazal, H., Alshammari, A., Taweel, A., ElBokl, A., Nejjari, C., Alhuwail, D., AlThani, D., Al-Jafar, E., Wahba, H., Alrishidi, M., Hamdi, M., Househ, M., El-Hassan, O., Alnafrani, S., Kalhori, S. R. N., Emara, T., Alam, T., El Otmani Dehbi, Z., & Al-Shorbaji, N. (2022). Middle east and north african health informatics association (menahia). *Yearbook of Medical Informatics*, *31*(1), 354–364. doi:10.1055-0042-1742495

Gianfrancesco, M. A., & Goldstein, N. D. (2021). A narrative review on the validity of electronic health record-based research in epidemiology. *BMC Medical Research Methodology*, *21*(1), 1–10. doi:10.118612874-021-01416-5 PMID:34706667

Grimus, M. (2020). Emerging technologies: Impacting learning, pedagogy and curriculum development. Emerging technologies and pedagogies in the curriculum, 127–151.

Harbi, A. (2021). Health care expert's readiness to implement national unified medical records (numr) system in the united arab emirates; a qualitative study. *Informatica (Vilnius)*, *45*(5).

Hashweh, M., & Hashweh, M. (1999). *Higher education in Palestine: current status and recent developments.*

Heart, T., Ben-Assuli, O., & Shabtai, I. (2017). A review of phr, emr and ehr integration: A more personalized healthcare and public health policy. *Health Policy and Technology*, *6*(1), 20–25. doi:10.1016/j.hlpt.2016.08.002

Henry, J., Pylypchuk, Y., Searcy, T., and Patel, V. (2016). Adoption of electronic health record systems among us non-federal acute care hospitals: 2008–2015. *ONC data brief*, *35*, 1–9.

Hirsch, J., Nicola, G., McGinty, G., Liu, R., Barr, R., Chittle, M., & Manchikanti, L. (2016). Icd-10: History and context. *AJNR. American Journal of Neuroradiology*, *37*(4), 596–599. doi:10.3174/ajnr.A4696 PMID:26822730

Hirsch, J. A., Leslie-Mazwi, T. M., Nicola, G. N., Barr, R. M., Bello, J. A., Donovan, W. D., Tu, R., Alson, M. D., & Manchikanti, L. (2015). Current procedural terminology; a primer. *Journal of Neurointerventional Surgery*, *7*(4), 309–312. doi:10.1136/neurintsurg-2014-011156 PMID:24589819

Houlden, R. L., Raja, J. B., Collier, C. P., Clark, A. F., & Waugh, J. M. (2004). Medical students' perceptions of an undergraduate research elective. *Medical Teacher*, *26*(7), 659–661. doi:10.1080/01421590400019542 PMID:15763861

Humphrey-Murto, S., Makus, D., Moore, S., Watanabe Duffy, K., Maniate, J., Scowcroft, K., Buba, M., & Rangel, J. C. (2022). Training physicians and residents for the use of electronic health records—A comparative case study between two hospitals. *Medical Education*. PMID:36181382

Iqbal, M. J., Javed, Z., Sadia, H., Qureshi, I. A., Irshad, A., Ahmed, R., Malik, K., Raza, S., Abbas, A., Pezzani, R., & Sharifi-Rad, J. (2021). Clinical applications of artificial intelligence and machine learning in cancer diagnosis: Looking into the future. *Cancer Cell International*, *21*(1), 1–11. doi:10.118612935-021-01981-1 PMID:34020642

Jabareen, H., Khader, Y., & Taweel, A. (2020). Health information systems in jordan and palestine: The need for health informatics training. *Eastern Mediterranean Health Journal*, *26*(11), 1323–1330. doi:10.26719/emhj.20.036 PMID:33226099

Jarrar, Y., Mosleh, R., Hawash, M., & Jarrar, Q. (2019). Knowledge and attitudes of pharmacy students towards pharmacogenomics among universities in Jordan and west bank of Palestine. *Pharmacogenomics and Personalized Medicine*, *12*, 247–255. doi:10.2147/PGPM.S222705 PMID:31632127

Jarrar, Y., Musleh, R., Ghanim, M., AbuKhader, I., & Jarrar, Q. (2021). Assessment of the need for pharmacogenomics education among pharmacists in the West Bank of Palestine. *International Journal of Clinical Practice*, *75*(9), e14435. doi:10.1111/ijcp.14435 PMID:34191402

Jumreornvong, O., Yang, E., Race, J., and Appel, J. (2020). Telemedicine and medical education in the age of covid-19. *Academic Medicine*.

Kayaalp, M. (2018). Patient privacy in the era of big data. *Balkan Medical Journal*, *35*(1), 8–17. doi:10.4274/balkanmedj.2017.0966 PMID:28903886

Kerr Winter, B., Salamma, R. M., & Qabaja, K. A. (2015). Medical education in palestine. *Medical Teacher*, *37*(2), 125–130. doi:10.3109/0142159X.2014.971721 PMID:25333712

Khader, Y., Alzyoud, S., Jabareen, H., Awad, S., Rumeileh, N. A., Manasrah, N., Modallal, R., & Taweel, A. (2019). Students' perceptions of health informatics learning: A survey of jordanian and palestinian students in health-related disciplines. *Lancet*, *393*, S33. doi:10.1016/S0140-6736(19)30619-1

Khan, M. N. R., & Lippert, K. J. (2022). Immersive technologies in healthcare education. In *Intelligent Systems and Machine Learning for Industry* (pp. 115–138). CRC Press.

Kim, E., Rubinstein, S. M., Nead, K. T., Wojcieszynski, A. P., Gabriel, P. E., & Warner, J. L. (2019). The evolving use of electronic health records (ehr) for research. In *Seminars in radiation oncology* (pp. 354–361). Elsevier. doi:10.1016/j.semradonc.2019.05.010

Knoppers, B. M., & Thorogood, A. M. (2017). Ethics and big data in health. *Current Opinion in Systems Biology*, *4*, 53–57. doi:10.1016/j.coisb.2017.07.001

Kourouklis, A. P., Wu, X., Geyer, R. C., Exarchos, V., Nazari, T., Kaemmel, J., Magkoutas, K., Daners, M. S., Weisskopf, M., Maini, L., Roman, C., Iske, J., Pappas, G. A., Chen, M. J., Smid, C., Unbehaun, A., Meyer, A., Emmert, M., Ferrari, A., & Cesarovic, N. (2022). Building an interdisciplinary program of cardiovascular research at the swiss federal institute of technology–the etheart story. *iScience*, *25*(10), 105157. doi:10.1016/j.isci.2022.105157 PMID:36185369

Kyaw, B. M., Saxena, N., Posadzki, P., Vseteckova, J., Nikolaou, C. K., George, P. P., Divakar, U., Masiello, I., Kononowicz, A. A., Zary, N., & Tudor Car, L. (2019). Virtual reality for health professions education: Systematic review and meta-analysis by the digital health education collaboration. *Journal of Medical Internet Research*, *21*(1), e12959. doi:10.2196/12959 PMID:30668519

Mantas, J., Ammenwerth, E., Demiris, G., Hasman, A., Haux, R., Hersh, W., Hovenga, E., Lun, K., Marin, H., & Martin-Sanchez, F. (2010). Recommendations of the international medical informatics association (imia) on education in biomedical and health informatics. *Methods of Information in Medicine*, *49*(02), 105–120. doi:10.3414/ME5119 PMID:20054502

Mantel-Teeuwisse, A. K., Meilianti, S., Khatri, B., Yi, W., Azzopardi, L. M., Acosta G'omez, J., Gu¨lpınar, G., Bennara, K., & Uzman, N. (2021). Digital health in pharmacy education: Preparedness and responsiveness of pharmacy programmes. *Education Sciences*, *11*(6), 296. doi:10.3390/educsci11060296

McGinnis, J. M., Stuckhardt, L., Saunders, R., Smith, M., et al. (2013). *Best care at lower cost: the path to continuously learning health care in america*. Research Gate.

Medicine, S. (2019). *Stanford medicine 2020 health trends report: the rise of the datadriven physician*. Stanford Medicine.

Miles, S., Price, G. M., Swift, L., Shepstone, L., & Leinster, S. J. (2010). Statistics teaching in medical school: Opinions of practising doctors. *BMC Medical Education*, *10*(1), 1–8. doi:10.1186/1472-6920-10-75 PMID:21050444

Mohanty, S., Al Rashid, M. H., Mohanty, C., & Swayamsiddha, S. (2021). Modern computational intelligence based drug repurposing for diabetes epidemic. *Diabetes & Metabolic Syndrome*, *15*(4), 102180. doi:10.1016/j.dsx.2021.06.017 PMID:34186343

Moskowitz, A., McSparron, J., Stone, D. J., and Celi, L. A. (2015). Preparing a new generation of clinicians for the era of big data. *Harvard medical student review*, *2*(1), 24.

Nelson, E. A., & McGuire, A. L. (2010). The need for medical education reform: Genomics and the changing nature of health information. *Genome Medicine*, *2*(3), 1–3. doi:10.1186/gm139 PMID:20236478

Nichols, J. A., Herbert Chan, H. W., & Baker, M. A. (2019). Machine learning: Applications of artificial intelligence to imaging and diagnosis. *Biophysical Reviews*, *11*(1), 111–118. doi:10.100712551-018-0449-9 PMID:30182201

Othman, M., & Hayajneh, J. A. (2015). An integrated success model for an electronic health record: A case study of hakeem jordan. *Procedia Economics and Finance*, *23*, 95–103. doi:10.1016/S2212-5671(15)00526-2

Pears, M., & Konstantinidis, S. (2022). The future of immersive technology in global surgery education. *Indian Journal of Surgery*, *84*(1), 281–285. doi:10.100712262-021-02998-6 PMID:34230785

Peng, J., Zou, K., Zhou, M., Teng, Y., Zhu, X., Zhang, F., & Xu, J. (2021). An explainable artificial intelligence framework for the deterioration risk prediction of hepatitis patients. *Journal of Medical Systems*, *45*(5), 1–9. doi:10.100710916-021-01736-5 PMID:33847850

Persky, S., & McBride, C. M. (2009). Immersive virtual environment technology: A promising tool for future social and behavioral genomics research and practice. *Health Communication*, *24*(8), 677–682. doi:10.1080/10410230903263982 PMID:20183376

Portnoy, J., Waller, M., & Elliott, T. (2020). Telemedicine in the era of covid-19. *The Journal of Allergy and Clinical Immunology. In Practice*, *8*(5), 1489–1491. doi:10.1016/j.jaip.2020.03.008 PMID:32220575

Rajaram, A., Hickey, Z., Patel, N., Newbigging, J., & Wolfrom, B. (2020). Training medical students and residents in the use of electronic health records: A systematic review of the literature. *Journal of the American Medical Informatics Association : JAMIA*, *27*(1), 175–180. doi:10.1093/jamia/ocz178 PMID:31592531

Ramahi, H. (2015). *Education in Palestine: Current challenges and emancipatory alternative*, 1-51. Rosa Luxemburg Stiftung Regional Office Palestine.

Ryan, G. V., Callaghan, S., Rafferty, A., Higgins, M. F., Mangina, E., & McAuliffe, F. (2022). Learning Outcomes of Immersive Technologies in Health Care Student Education: Systematic Review of the Literature. *Journal of Medical Internet Research*, *24*(2), e30082. doi:10.2196/30082 PMID:35103607

Saba, V. (2001). Nursing informatics: Yesterday, today and tomorrow. *International Nursing Review*, *48*(3), 177–187. doi:10.1046/j.1466-7657.2001.00064.x PMID:11558693

Salamma, R., & Qabaja, K. (2014). Medical education in palestine. *Medical Teacher*, *37*(2), 125–130. PMID:25333712

Samara, M. (2021). *Enabling and Restricting Factors That Affect the Adoption of Electronic Health Records (EHRs) in the Palestinian Public Healthcare System.* [PhD thesis, An-Najah National University].

Silow-Carroll, S., Edwards, J. N., & Rodin, D. (2012). Using electronic health records to improve quality and efficiency: The experiences of leading hospitals. *Issue Brief (Commonwealth Fund)*, *17*(1), 40. PMID:22826903

Sood, M., Chadda, R. K., & Singh, P. (2016). Mobile health (mhealth) in mental health: Scope and applications in low-resource settings. *The National Medical Journal of India*, *29*(6), 341. PMID:28327483

Speich, J. E., & Rosen, J. (2004). Medical robotics. Encyclopedia of biomaterials and biomedical engineering, 983. Springer.

Speicher, M., Hall, B. D., & Nebeling, M. (2019, May). What is mixed reality? In *Proceedings of the 2019 CHI conference on human factors in computing systems* (pp. 1-15). Research Gate.

Stellefson, M. (2011). eHealth literacy among college students: a systematic review with implications for eHealth education. *Journal of medical Internet research 13*(4).

Sun, J., Hu, J., Luo, D., Markatou, M., Wang, F., Edabollahi, S., Steinhubl, S. E., Daar, Z., & Stewart, W. F. (2012). Combining knowledge and data driven insights for identifying risk factors using electronic health records. [American Medical Informatics Association.]. *AMIA ... Annual Symposium Proceedings - AMIA Symposium. AMIA Symposium*, *2012*, 901. PMID:23304365

Sweileh, W. M., Zyoud, S. H., Sawalha, A. F., Abu-Taha, A., Hussein, A., & Al-Jabi, S. W. (2013). Medical and biomedical research productivity from palestine, 2002–2011. *BMC Research Notes*, *6*(1), 1–5. doi:10.1186/1756-0500-6-41 PMID:23375070

Syzdykova, A., Malta, A., Zolfo, M., Diro, E., & Oliveira, J. L. (2017). Opensource electronic health record systems for low-resource settings: Systematic review. *JMIR Medical Informatics*, *5*(4), e8131. doi:10.2196/medinform.8131 PMID:29133283

Tanoli, Z., Vähä-Koskela, M., & Aittokallio, T. (2021). Artificial intelligence, machine learning, and drug repurposing in cancer. *Expert Opinion on Drug Discovery*, *16*(9), 977–989. doi:10.1080/17460441.2021.1883585 PMID:33543671

Topol, E. (2019). *Preparing the healthcare workforce to deliver the digital future Internet. NHS Health Education England*. Topol. https://topol.hee.nhs.uk/wp-content/uploads/HEE-Topol-Review-2019.pdf

Troccaz, J., Dagnino, G., & Yang, G. Z. (2019). Frontiers of medical robotics: From concept to systems to clinical translation. *Annual Review of Biomedical Engineering*, *21*(1), 193–218. doi:10.1146/annurev-bioeng-060418-052502 PMID:30822100

Upadhyay, A. K., & Khandelwal, K. (2022). Metaverse: The future of immersive training. *Strategic HR Review*, *21*(3), 83–86. doi:10.1108/SHR-02-2022-0009

Veldhuis, L. I., Woittiez, N. J., Nanayakkara, P. W., & Ludikhuize, J. (2022). Artificial intelligence for the prediction of in-hospital clinical deterioration: A systematic review. *Critical Care Explorations*, *4*(9), e0744. doi:10.1097/CCE.0000000000000744 PMID:36046062

Venkatesan, M., Mohan, H., Ryan, J. R., Schürch, C. M., Nolan, G. P., Frakes, D. H., & Coskun, A. F. (2021). Virtual and augmented reality for biomedical applications. *Cell Reports Medicine*, *2*(7), 100348. doi:10.1016/j.xcrm.2021.100348 PMID:34337564

Wald, H. S., George, P., Reis, S. P., & Taylor, J. S. (2014). Electronic health record training in undergraduate medical education: Bridging theory to practice with curricula for empowering patient-and relationship-centered care in the computerized setting. *Academic Medicine*, *89*(3), 380–386. doi:10.1097/ACM.0000000000000131 PMID:24448045

Waseh, S., & Dicker, A. (2018). Telemedicine and undergraduate medical education: Lessons in capacity building. *JMIR Medical Education*, *5*(1). doi:10.2196/12515

Waseh, S., & Dicker, A. P. (2019). Telemedicine training in undergraduate medical education: Mixed-methods review. *JMIR Medical Education*, *5*(1), e12515. doi:10.2196/12515 PMID:30958269

Xiao, C., Choi, E., & Sun, J. (2018). Opportunities and challenges in developing deep learning models using electronic health records data: A systematic review. *Journal of the American Medical Informatics Association : JAMIA*, *25*(10), 1419–1428. doi:10.1093/jamia/ocy068 PMID:29893864

Zha, A. M., Chung, L. S., Song, S. S., Majersik, J. J., & Jagolino-Cole, A. L. (2020). Training in neurology: adoption of resident teleneurology training in the wake of covid-19: telemedicine crash course. *Neurology*, *95*(9), 404–407. doi:10.1212/WNL.0000000000010029 PMID:32554768

Zheng, Y. G. (2015). Epigenetic technological applications. Academic Press.

Zhu, Y., Zhao, Y., Dou, L., Guo, R., Gu, X., Gao, R., & Wu, Y. (2021). The hospital management practices in chinese county hospitals and its association with quality of care, efficiency and finance. *BMC Health Services Research*, *21*(1), 1–8. doi:10.118612913-021-06472-7 PMID:33975605

ADDITIONAL READINGS

Dudin, A. (2008). *Medical Education in Palestine, past, present and future*.

Jabareen, H., Khader, Y., & Taweel, A. (2020). Health information systems in jordan and palestine: The need for health informatics training. *Eastern Mediterranean Health Journal*, *26*(11), 1323–1330. doi:10.26719/emhj.20.036 PMID:33226099

Salamma, R., & Qabaja, K. (2014). Medical education in palestine. *Medical Teacher*, *37*(2), 125–130. PMID:25333712

Samara, M. (2021). *Enabling and Restricting Factors That Affect the Adoption of Electronic Health Records (EHRs) in the Palestinian Public Healthcare System*. [PhD thesis, An-Najah National University].

Topol, E. (2019). *Preparing the healthcare workforce to deliver the digital future Internet*. NHS Health Education England. https://topol.hee.nhs.uk/wp-content/uploads/HEE-Topol-Review-2019.pdf (accessed 2019-06-22)

KEY TERMS AND DEFINITIONS

Artificial Intelligence (AI): A branch of computer science concerned with the development of software that is capable of carrying out tasks which, in most cases, call upon humans' intelligence. Example tasks include problemsolving, pattern recognition and decision making.

Digital Health: The use of digital technologies, such as electronic health records, mobile health applications, wearable devices, and telemedicine, to improve the delivery of healthcare services, enhance patient outcomes, and promote population health.

Genomics: The branch of molecular biology that studies the structure, function, mapping, and editing of genomes. It involves analyzing the complete set of an organism's genes and their interactions to understand genetic variations, heredity, and the role of genes in health and disease.

Health Sciences: A multidisciplinary field that encompasses the study, research, and application of knowledge in various healthcare-related disciplines, including medicine, nursing, pharmacy, and allied health professions.

Medicine: The science and practice that focuses on the diagnosis, treatment, and prevention of diseases and disorders in individuals, using a combination of medical knowledge, clinical skills, and therapeutic interventions.

Middle East North Africa (MENA): A region encompassing countries in North Africa and the Middle East, characterized by shared cultural, linguistic, and socioeconomic aspects.

Robotics: A branch of technology that deals with the design, construction, programming, and use of robots. Robotics involves the development of machines capable of performing tasks on their own or with human guidance, which are often used in health facilities for surgeries, rehabilitation and assistance to people with disabilities.

Chapter 7
Analyzing the Role of Popular Scientific Journalism in STEM and Turkey's Science Communication Model

Hasan Gürkan
Girona University, Spain & Istinye University, Turkey

Carmen Soler Echazarreta
Girona University, Spain

ABSTRACT

This study examines the contributions of popular science magazines in Turkey to STEM as a field and discusses science journalism's support of the STEM world. The study explores the rules and perspective of science journalism and discusses the contributions of this field to STEM and STEM literacy. In its discussion of the impact of popular science magazines on STEM literacy, the study encompasses magazines in Turkey that publish science journalism and popularize science, making it easier for the public to understand. The study's interviews reveal that popular science magazines deliberately construct gendered language to increase popular knowledge and awareness of this field. Finally, the study summarizes the goals for scientific publications and science journalism in Turkey seeking to promote STEM literacy: (i) preparing content that will strengthen the public's relationship with science, (ii) promoting the number and quality of scientific studies in Turkey, (iii) challenging political power to realize the role of science, and (iv) reducing fake news.

DOI: 10.4018/978-1-6684-6883-8.ch007

INTRODUCTION

Media is the main source of information people access to learn about science, medicine, and technology (Livingstone et al., 2008; Livingstone, 2003; Deuze, 2006). Science journalism is a specialized form of journalism that covers these fields (Guenther, 2019; Summ et al., 2016; Guenther et al., 2016). This kind of journalism is relatively new, having professionalized in the second half of the 20th century, and it is possible to see various approaches in its coverage of its subject matter.

There is abundant research (Guenther et al., 2019; Göpfert, 2008; Shachar, 2000; Cortinas-Rovira et al., 2015; Peters, 1995) criticizing science journalism and science journalists, focusing on science journalists' work and their reporting on scientific issues, as well as their relationship to scientists. In addition, science journalism seems to be in crisis due to increasing digitization and changing media landscapes (Guenther, 2019). Science journalism has been declining in some countries and many journalists have lost their jobs (Bauer et al., 2013). Evaluation of the quality and relevance of science journalism should be based on professional journalism ideology rather than scientific criteria, and this should define science journalism and how science journalism works best. Finally, though increasing digitization is changing the routines and practices of science journalists, these journalists can adapt to new media environments and maintain their essential role for society as the most relevant source of information about science, medicine, and technology (Burston et al., 2010).

Based on their own subjective values, journalists determine what is published according to the novelty, relevance and entertainment value of the content (Caple et al., 2013). Journalists' play a crucial role. This is why editors marginalize topics from science that blend with their perspectives and/or only put them on the front page when there is nothing to report other than business, politics and sports. Meaningful discussion of the topics of science journalism requires scientific thinking.

This study examines the contributions of popular science magazines in Turkey to STEM as a field and discusses how science journalism in Turkey supports the STEM world. The study explores the rules and perspective of science journalism and discusses the contributions of this field to STEM and STEM literacy. In its discussion of the impact of popular science magazines on STEM literacy, the study encompasses magazines in Turkey that publish science journalism and popularize science, making it easier for the public to understand.

MAIN FOCUS OF THE CHAPTER

This study considers the media as a force that influences and mobilizes the masses, journalism practices and science journalism in Turkey. Probing the rules and perspective of science reportage as a journalism specialty and discussing the contributions of this field to the STEM world frame the study.

Issues, Controversies, Problems

This study examines the contribution of scientific journalism in building interactive communication models with scientists and the public and to discuss the contribution of science journalism publications to STEM literacy. Disparities between the goals of science and journalism and the reflective roles of journalism cause problems in accuracy, leading to disagreements on the application of journalistic practices in science journalism. To show the importance of the conflicts between STEM and journalists, the study links the less interactive science communication model in Turkey with the immaturity of scientific journalism forms.

Magazines in Turkey that publish science journalism and popularize science include *Bilim Genç, Bilim ve Gelecek, Bilim ve Teknik, Bilim ve Ütopya, Herkes Için Bilim Teknoloji,* and *Popular Science*. The study includes these as well as *Bilim ve Ütopya* and *Herkes Için Bilim Teknoloj* magazines. The remaining magazines state that they do not include STEM-oriented content but instead only publish popular science.

The study is based on in-depth interviews with the editorial team in Turkey. The following questions are asked to the participants:

Table 1: The questions to be asked to the journalists

1. How would you describe science journalism in Turkey?
2. What can you say about STEM education in Turkey?
3. Do you think that enough attention is paid to the STEM field in Turkey?
4. What can you say about the popularization of science?
5. Do popular science-oriented journals help the STEM field to be understood, and how?
6. How is the STEM language constructed and coded in the content?
7. What is the impact of popular science journals and the science language they build and use on STEM literacy?
8. What do you think about the impact of popular science magazines on young people's career choices in the STEM field?
9. What do you think about the gender gap in STEM? If you believe there is a gap, what are the ways to overcome it? What role can journals publishing science journalism and popularizing science play in reducing this gap?

The stages of the research included

i. Researching and evaluating the relationship between STEM and popular science journalism,
ii. Determining the subjects to be interviewed in-depth and obtaining their commitments to the interviews,
iii. Compiling the interview results and analyzing similarities and differences in opinions adhering to the literature review,
iv. Preparing a model.

The study relies on the in-depth interview, a qualitative analysis method. In-depth interviewing entails intensive individual interviews with a small number of respondents to find out and analyze their perspectives on a particular idea (Boyce et al. 2006; Gürkan, 2019). Semi-structured interviews were undertaken with the three editors working at popular science magazines in Turkey. The participants were asked open-ended questions so the researchers could understand and analyze the relationship between STEM and science journalism in Turkey. The respondents are referred to as E1, E2, and E3.

The study of an issue is based on autoethnographic relations (Bleiker & Brigg, 2010: 792), which can provide explanations about more traditional-political values, beliefs and behaviors. This study strives to conduct meaningful, accessible, and evocative research based on personal and professional experiences to enable readers to understand the relationship between STEM and popular journalism. The findings part of the study, framed by using an in-depth interview technique, describes the media professionals' answers, experiences, perceptions, and perspectives within the scope of the questions posed to them.

General Approach on STEM

STEM consists of the first letters of "Science, Technology, Engineering and Mathematics" and describes the integration of these disciplines. STEM education is shaped from the interests and experiences of students and teachers. It teaches the knowledge and skills of a given field through integration with at least one other STEM discipline. STEM is an approach that covers the preschool education to higher education and is one of the crucial developments in education in the globalizing and rapidly developing world. STEM is an education system that allows individuals to apply their thinking skills to interdisciplinary challenges and enables individuals to develop simultaneously in more than one field (Arifin et al., 2021; Breiner et al., 2012; Jones et al., 2000; Campbell et al., 2018).

STEM, in this sense, can help a closer relationship can be established with daily life, and it can be determined which problem-based content to connect. In this respect, the fields of science, technology, engineering, and mathematics are brought together and tried to be integrated (Moore et al., 2015; Mpofu, 2020).

STEM in Turkey

In Turkey, national science and technology policies, 2003-2023 strategy document, STEM Education Turkey Report, Turkish Industrialists and Businessmen's Association Vision-2050 Turkey Report all acknowledge the need to raise individuals with knowledge and skills in STEM disciplines (Akgündüz et al., 2015). Studies have been carried out in Turkey in the field of STEM since 2005 and the number of studies been increasing since 2012 with studies conducted in state and private universities. The world's countries STEM achievements in education are evaluated using the widely known and internationally recognized TIMSS[1] and PISA[2] exams, which help countries to assess their education policies and make new investments in growing and expanding them.

The STEM movement in Turkey started in 2010, gaining rapid momentum with the inclusion of STEM in curricula as of 2017 and the Vision 2023 project. STEM has strategic importance in terms of increasing Turkey's international competitiveness as STEM innovation movements will help it become a country with a voice (Çorlu, 2012; Doğanay, 2018).

The FATIH Project[3], which supports STEM, aims to meet students' need to access scientific developments by utilizing information technologies. EBA[4] provided schools with interactive whiteboards, internet infrastructure, tablet computers, and electronic content. Though most students can access information technologies to develop the skills of inquiry, research, product creation, and invention, the goals of STEM practices, Turkey does not have a direct-action plan for STEM prepared by the Ministry of National Education. However, the 2015-2019 Strategic Plan includes goals for strengthening STEM. STEM objectives overlap to some extent with the objectives of the Technology and Design course (STEM Education Report, 2016).

Meanwhile, the Scientific and Technological Research Council of Turkey (TÜBİTAK)[5] included targets to support STEM practices in its 2011-2016 Science and Technology Development Plan (Baran et al., 2015; Pekbay, 2017: 16-17). TÜBİTAK also established science centers related to STEM (Pekbay, 2017: 17). Yet STEM-related studies and projects are not common in universities in Turkey (Çorlu, 2013; Pekbay, 2017: 17). Those involved in STEM-related initiatives include Hacettepe University, Istanbul Aydın University (Istanbul Aydın University STEM Lab) and Bahçeşehir University (BAUSTEM) (Pekbay, 2017).

Initiatives introduced to increase the STEM skills of teachers and prospective teachers through in-service training and to strengthen integrated teaching knowledge in faculties of education have not succeeded (MEB, 2016). The expression "21st-century skills" in relation to STEM is a stumbling block, as there is no clear definition of 21st-century skills, the goals of STEM, or the skills targeted by science programs in Turkey. The targeted skills largely overlap (Koştur, 2017: 63).

Science Journalism and the Role of the Science Journalists

Science journalists are the interface between scientists and the mainstream media. They report not only on science and research policy, but also clarify and classify new developments and. They present complex topics and introduce new findings – mainly from the natural, social and historical sciences and technology – for public consumption in a generally understandable, entertaining, and critical manner. Publication of scientific research results in academic journals is not science journalism, though these articles are often the foundation of science journalism reporting.

Molek-Kozakowska (2016) states that science journalism has turned into a discursive space where science-related content is made accessible to a broad public rather than a narrow elite. According to him, science journalism is produced by commercial media organizations taking advantage of the mass appeal of science news. As with other areas of popular journalism, science journalism includes prominent viewpoints, representations, or features of science considered by science editors to be attractive to audiences.

Popular science journalism is structured to appeal to audiences, follow current trends (in a commercial context), represent science, and make effective use of language in this representation. At this point, science journalism is affected by all of these features. Some researchers (Bowler, 2009; Broks, 2006) criticize the trivialization and simplification of science news. As Bauer and Gregory (2007) point out, this new science news is "saleable stories."

Science journalists are concerned with sourcing and writing science stories. They play an essential role in relations with the newspaper and broadcasting companies and should advise on stories that overlap or relate to science (Williams & Clifford, 2010). The scope of the role of science journalist may vary by publisher.

Murcott (2009) says a science journalist must sell stories to the editor and show why specific scientific research is necessary and worth reporting. In this respect, the sources of science stories can be divided into two broad categories: journalists reveal the documents sent to themselves for consideration. The other is more significant than the previous one.

There are claims that the field of science journalism, like other fields, is heavily dependent on press releases (Davies, 2009). Williams and Clifford (2010) highlight the science journalist's relationship with his editor as critical element to the job. A journalist's job is to broadcast to a broad audience; therefore, s/he needs to focus on a readership and then her/his editors. The editor is the gatekeeper for the broader audience at this point. The journalist must convince her/his editor for anyone who wants to get the science story in the media. Science journalism reflects the fact that this role is all the more important for journalists who want to communicate with the world, given the often-complex nature of scientific discourse and the increasing centrality of science in controversial and heavily politicized policy debates surrounding how we should live sustainably and healthily.

FINDINGS AND DISCUSSIONS

This study uses the in-depth interview research technique to collect, assemble and edit the data. This technique also reveales the role of a gatekeeper and forces researchers to rely on the criterion of synchronicity. Finally, the in-depth interview technique enables us to identify the critical points in the explored STEM and science journalism relationship. In addition, the information obtained from the editors was articulated with STEM and science journalism issues.

The interviews yielded the following topics for discussion:

- The Relationship between Science Journalism and STEM
- Popularizing Science
- The Relationship between Popular Magazines and STEM
- The Constructed STEM Language
- Popular Science Magazines and STEM Career Choices

- STEM, Gender and Popular Science Magazines

The Relationship Between Science Journalism and STEM

Mass media are the mechanisms that most easily and rapidly connect the public to science. Science journalism plays an important role in this. While science journalism can be defined as the activity of reporting about science, a science journalist communicates science through all kinds of media, such as newspapers, television, and blogs (Bauer et al., 2013; Cassany et al., 2018) and journalism is the "key" word in establishing communication between the public and science (Lynch et al., 2014. 480). The work of communicating science through the media is referred to as "science journalism," "science reporting," and "science journalism" (Bauer et al., 2013; Fahy & Lisbet, 2011). Science journalists, who ensure that science is popularized, perceived and understood by large masses, also play an essential role in making the STEM field known. E1, one of the editors interviewed, defines the relationship between science journalism and STEM in Turkey as follows:

"Science journalism in Turkey should be defined according to the fields in which it is practiced. Science journalism in science journals has an editorial weight. It evaluates the topics it deals with, including current developments, according to historical and possible future developments and reflects them to the readers in a certain depth. Science journalism on television and in newspapers is more about reporting news that has made or is likely to impact the international and national arena. With the widespread use of the internet and social media in the last ten years, science journalism on the internet is concerned with both bringing what is popular to the public and processing the topics it covers through an editorial filter as much as possible. In addition, Turkey is a country with world-class science, technology, engineering, and mathematics scientists. However, since Turkey still needs a science strategy or policy and still has problems with the most fundamental laws of science, such as evolution, achievements are limited to certain institutions or individuals, and efforts cannot be concentrated at a single point. Quantitative achievements cannot lead to qualitative leaps."

E2 said the following about the relationship between science journalism and STEM in Turkey:

"Science journalism is informing people about the work of scientists in a way that they can understand and accurately. In a sense, it reflects their research in the media. However, it is difficult to say that science journalism is practiced in Turkey. The number of popular science publications is shallow, shows this. There are several

reasons for this: (i) Society's relationship with science is weak, (ii) scientific studies are not widespread in Turkey, (iii) political powers still need to fully grasp the role of science in the development of a country. This, in turn, constitutes a major obstacle in creating the conditions and ecosystem necessary for the production of science and technology. Freedoms, democracy, autonomous universities, and institutions free from political interference, the right incentives, etc., are sine qua non for this... When all these factors come together, science journalism becomes a field that needs to be given more importance. In addition, there is no comprehensive science journalism education as in other countries. This situation brings with it a need for more emphasis on STEM education. This is partly related to the qualitative decline in our education system in recent years. The fact that we are far behind in comparison with other countries in the PISA research conducted every three years for 15-year-old students is the most concrete indicator of this. The research results on reading comprehension, math, and science literacy are dismal. Likewise, the low number of correct answers to math and science questions in university entrance exams shows this. The foundations of STEM education must be laid in primary education and pre-school. There is much to be done to develop 'curiosity and questioning' in children. Countries that care about this are paving the way with science centers and striking changes in education curricula. The spread of science centers in Turkey is a process that has just begun. It is an important step, but more is needed on its own."

Popularizing Science

In the 19th century ordinary people became interested in science, science became popularized, and people began to see the effects of scientific and technological developments in their own lives. Bridging the worlds of ordinary people and scientists and facilitating the general public's access to science through a mechanism of communication has been a priority of developed countries and has thus a priority of science and media. With the increasing importance and centrality of science in the 20th century, public understanding of science has also gained importance over time. Since the 1990s science communication has started to take shape, especially in industrialized Western countries. In relation to this E1 states that the popularization of science is correct and appropriate and says the following:

"Especially in conditions where superstition, sophistry, and bigotry are institutionalized, whether science is popular or specialized, it is beneficial for Turkey and humanity as a whole. However, when science is an activity that remains popular and is not deepened, Turkey will not have a science agenda, and we will only talk about "shocking" scientific developments or the scientific achievements of other nations. Science will only have meaningful and lasting achievements if it

is popularized in line with Turkey's science agenda and integrated into it. The way to do this is through a minimum understanding of the history of science, philosophy of science, and enlightenment thought."

On the other hand, E2 stated that the world's rapid digitalization and giant steps in science and technology have also popularized science:

"Science news started to appear more frequently in newspapers and televisions. People started to follow and understand the science and technology behind the developments that affect and even shape their daily lives. We need to take advantage of this positive picture and make popular science more continuous. In this respect, science magazines and popular science publishing should be supported and made more widespread. For example, we have been trying to do this with the weekly magazine Herkese Bilim Teknoloji, which we have published for over six years. This is why we named it Herkese Bilim Teknoloji; we aimed to be accessible to all segments and everywhere. The magazine's readership and feedback show that our magazine has undertaken a critical task in bringing science to the public."

The Relationship Between Popular Magazines and STEM

In the 19th century, the low cost and accessibility of magazines and newspapers popularized science among the masses who settled in cities. With the introduction of the popular press, many followed what was happening in the world, including scientific developments. As a result, the authors of science communication openly targeted the general public (Bucchi, 1998: 2). On this subject, E1 points out that popular science-oriented magazines have an essential function in bringing people together and understanding the STEM field, especially with young audiences.

"Those who want to pursue an academic career and specialize in science are the regular readers of popular science magazines. These are the embodied core of Turkey's science consciousness. If it were not for the culture and environment created by popular science magazine publishing (one of the most fundamental elements in the formation of this environment is, of course, the authors), today, the STEM field would be limited to a purely academic-technical endeavor. This institutionalization does not go beyond the closed-circuit network of some experts. On the other hand, science journalism is the most qualified and, in this sense, the most important channel that transfers energy from academia to society. It is essential as it enlightens the society on the topics it deals with, improves its knowledge repertoire, integrates academics with the society, and is also a science school."

E2 stated that popular journals contribute to the STEM field:

"We include the success stories of scientists as well as their research. How did they get to this point? What did they do? From the most famous Nobel scientists to young scientists to our researchers... It is important and stimulating to convey the latest science and technology news in a way that readers can understand. All the feedback we receive confirms this. Math, medicine, philosophy, archeology, nutrition science, brain research... All of these make STEM tangible rather than a perception."

The Constructed STEM Language

The media's language and communication style are important. A short, concise, striking, and attention-grabbing message is essential, as is powerful visual material. Media language is the most effective tool for creating perception today. These perceptions often mix medium and message and they can override the truth. E1 says the constructed STEM language is intended to arouse the curiosity of the average reader and promote understanding without compromising the content.

"Despite all the distance covered by science literacy, the STEM field can still be seen as incomprehensible, complex, and inaccessible. For this reason, more important than language and style, it is more or less important to integrate what science, technology, engineering, and mathematics mean for humanity into the content. Popular science magazines and the language of science they create, and use have paved the way for STEM literacy. This path has influenced and contributed to many fields, from publishing houses to highly clicked science websites and video channels. Of course, it is no longer possible to talk about a one-sided influence in today's complex and intertwined publishing world. Everyone feeds off each other, but historically speaking, the role of popular science magazines is undeniable."

E2 stated that the news in popular science publishing occurs spontaneously in the content of the news, and this is what should be conveyed in the presentation of the news and E2 said:

"When we look at the backgrounds of people who are oriented towards the STEM field, we see that popular science magazines have a significant impact on all of them. They convey this in interviews and interviews. For a while, TÜBİTAK Science and Technology magazine and CUMHURİYET Science and Technology magazine greatly contributed greatly. I think this has been strengthened by magazines like ours and science news that are becoming more and more prominent on social media."

Popular Science Magazines and STEM Career Choices

Integrated STEM education intends to equip young people with 21st-century skills, direct them to science and engineering-related professions, and build the knowledge society of the future (Moore et al., 2015; Pleasants & Olson, 2019). Experts agree that the integration of science, technology, engineering, and mathematics will bridge different disciplines, harness the power of mathematics to accelerate discoveries, and bring together dispersed data sets in creative ways to solve problems and provide meaningful solutions (NSF, 2020). Regarding the effects of popular science magazines on young people's career choices in the STEM field, E1 said,

"I think that popular science magazines highly influence a young reader both in the department he/she will go to at university, the academic career he/she intends to pursue, and his/her business career. This should not be considered only as a concrete result. The habits of thought gained by popular science magazines play a vital role in determining what kind of life path young people will take. Understanding the world, the country, people, and oneself through science and material reality, knowing and recognizing oneself..."

E2 said popular magazines positively affect young people's career choices and stated,

"I think that young people who constantly follow popular science magazines are one step ahead in their decisions."

STEM, Gender, and Popular Science Magazines

Popular science magazines play an essential role in creating a balance between STEM and gender relations. Although the language varies from medium to medium, popular science magazine discourse and news content that support gender equality in STEM introduce an incentive. E1 said the gender gap in STEM is an issue that should be evaluated according to the gender gap in society, stating,

"As far as I know, the ratio of men and women in universities in Turkey is better than in many developed countries. The reason for this is the achievements of the Republican culture despite all the destruction and the encouragement of girls to study despite all the negativities. There is a social-economic and ideological phenomenon underlying this. We need to look at development from this point; otherwise, if it were a purely material criterion, we would expect gender equality to be positive in many oil-rich Gulf countries. Of course, this does not mean that there is no

gender discrimination in STEM. The way to overcome the situation in question is through an education system and government incentives that will encourage and direct our female citizens to STEM. Science journalism is especially responsible for highlighting women scientists and publicizing their achievements widely. So are popular science magazines, but one of the duties of magazines is to give more space to women writers, but basically to exhibit an approach and understanding within the framework of equality between women and men because, in an environment where women are imprisoned, men are not free either. In this environment, one leg of science will always be missing."

On the other hand, E2 stated these related to the subject:

"Unfortunately, there is gender inequality both in STEM education and in pursuing a career in STEM. It is important to provide information that encourages girls in STEM education. There are various campaigns on this issue. However, popular science magazines are also important in this respect. Success stories of women in STEM fields can be featured more, and the difficulties they face and how they overcome them can be included. Role models are important. Another issue is the low number of women in STEM careers, and they are giving up over the years. Institutional mechanisms and incentives may be needed in this regard."

Given these collected findings, the study formulated a structural equation model of scientific publications and science journalism in Turkey towards STEM literacy:

Figure 1: A structural equation model of scientific publications and science journalism

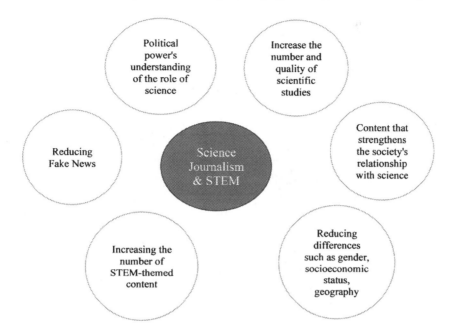

According to this model, while STEM and science journalism are at the center, on the other hand, policymakers' understanding of the role of science should be systematic, the number and quality of scientific studies should be increased, the content that strengthens the relationship of society with science should be produced, differences such as gender, socioeconomic status, geography should be reduces, the number of STEM-themed content should be increased and fake needs to be reduced.

CONCLUSION

The media is focused on STEM-oriented publishing and building a STEM-oriented language. Yet women are underrepresented in the content of STEM topics. Media organizations must ensure that women are well represented in all research areas, particularly in STEM fields, and that conditions are right for maximum research impact.

Popular science publications aim to combine science with STEM by constructing a specifically gender-oriented language to increase knowledge and awareness on this subject. In addition, it is essential to take into account the structural equation model mentioned in the study, especially for the scientific publications and science journalism in Turkey, in terms of STEM literacy, popularizing science and making it easier for the public to understand:

To prepare and present content that will strengthen society's relationship with science,
To increase the number and quality of scientific studies in Turkey,
Political power making decisions that recognize the role of science,
Reducing fake news,

The inequality in ownership, accessibility, and usability of information technologies due to differences such as gender, socioeconomic status, geography, etc., which is called the digital divide, stands as a reality in Turkey,

The content that appears in the print media and is considered "science and technology communication" focuses on health and technology. While the public is generally interested in health and technology news, there needs to be an enormous gap in areas such as astronomy, science, and mathematics.

Although science communication's contribution to STEM has increased qualitatively and quantitatively, problems remain in how science meets the public. In the public's engagement with science, scientific field discussions occur before decisions are made. The distance between science and the public has been great due to the late establishment of structures to regulate the relationship between science and the public; the fact that once established, the relationship between science and the public has been maintained mainly through magazines and other media aimed at popularizing science; and other activities have not been as widespread as hoped. It is crucial to understand science communication as a field that needs to be supported and regulated in public policies (Dursun, 2010).

The structure and dynamics of the media, one of the leading actors of science communication, need to do more for the public's understanding of science or the public's connection with science in Turkey. In the context of science communication in Turkey, the issue is not whether media professionals report science and technology uncritically but whether they report them sufficiently. First, there is the issue of whether science journalism is recognized as a specialty; second there is the issue of how science journalism is positioned vis-à-vis other types of knowledge (e.g., metaphysical knowledge, esoteric knowledge, faith, etc.). To address these problems; and to pave the way for the democratization of science communication; and to align STEM with the society's approach to science, further research and investment in this field are needed.

ACKNOWLEDGMENT

This study has received funding from the Maria Zambrano Grant for the attraction of international talent in Spain.

REFERENCES

Akgündüz, D., Aydeniz, M., Çakmakçı, G., Çavaş, B., Çorlu, M., Öner, T., & Özdemir, S. (2015). *STEM Eğitimi Türkiye Raporu: "Günümüz modası mı yoksa gereksinim mi?"*. İstanbul Aydın Üniversitesi STEM Merkezi.

Alan, B. (2017). *Fen bilgisi öğretmen adaylarının bütünleşik öğretmenlik bilgilerinin desteklenmesi: STEM uygulamalarına hazırlama eğitimi*. Yüksek Lisans Tezi, Fırat Üniversitesi, Eğitim Bilimleri Enstitüsü.

Arifin, N., & Mahmud, S. (2021). A Systematic Literature Review of Design Thinking Application in STEM Integration. *Creative Education*, *12*(7), 1558–1571. doi:10.4236/ce.2021.127118

Baharin, N. H., Kamarudin, N., & Manaf, U. K. (2018). Integrating STEM Education Approach in Enhancing Higher Order Thinking Skills. *International Journal of Academic Research in Business & Social Sciences*, *8*(7). doi:10.6007/IJARBSS/v8-i7/4421

Baran, E., & Canbazoğlu-Bilici, S. ve Mesutoğlu, C. (2015). Fen, teknoloji, mühendislik ve matematik (FeTeMM) spotu geliştirme etkinliği. [ATED]. *Araştırma Temelli Etkinlik Dergisi*, *5*(2), 60–69.

Bauer, M. W., & Gregory, J. (2007). From journalism to corporate communication in postwar Britain. In M. W. Bauer & M. Bucchi (Eds.), *Journalism, Science and Society: Science Communication between News and Public Relations* (pp. 33–52). Routledge.

Bauer, M. W., Howard, S., Romo, R., Yulye, J., Massarani, L., & Amorim, L. (2013) Global science journalism report: working conditions & practices, professional ethos and future expectations. Our learning series. Science and Development Network, London, UK.

Borrego, M., & Henderson, C. (2014). Increasing the Use of Evidence-Based Teaching in STEM Higher Education: A Comparison of Eight Change Strategies. *Journal of Engineering Education*, *103*(2), 220–252. doi:10.1002/jee.20040

Bowler, P. (2009). *Science for All: The Popularization of Science in Early Twentieth Century*. Chicago University Press. doi:10.7208/chicago/9780226068664.001.0001

Boyce, C.; Neale, P. (2006). *Conducting In-Depth Interviews: A Guide for Designing and Conducting In-Depth-Interviews for Evaluation Input*. Watertown: Pathfinder International.

Breiner, J. M., Harkness, S. S., Johnson, C. C., & Koehler, C. M. (2012). What Is STEM? A Discussion about Conceptions of STEM in Education and Partnerships. *School Science and Mathematics*, *112*(1), 3–11. doi:10.1111/j.1949-8594.2011.00109.x

Brigg, M., & Bleiker, R. (2010). Autoethnographic international relations: Exploring the self as a source of knowledge. *Review of International Studies*, *36*(3), 779–798. doi:10.1017/S0260210510000689

Broks, P. (2006). *Understanding Popular Science*. Open University Press.

Bucchi, M. (1998). *Science and the Media: Alternative Routes in Scientific Communication*. Routledge. doi:10.4324/9780203263839

Burston, J., Dyer-Witheford, N., & Hearn, A. (2010). Digital labour: Workers, authors, citizens. *Ephemera*, *10*(3/4), 214–221.

Campbell, C., Speldewinde, C., Howitt, C., & MacDonald, A. (2018). STEM Practice in the Early Years. *Creative Education*, *9*(1), 11–25. doi:10.4236/ce.2018.91002

Caple, H., & Bednarek, M. (2013). *Delving into the discourse: approaches to news values in journalism studies and beyond (Publisher's version)*. Reuters Institute for the Study of Journalism.

Cassany, R., Cortinas, S., & Elduque, A. (2018). Communicating Science: The Profile of Science Journalists in Spain. *Merdia Education Research Journal*, *17*(55), 9–17. doi:10.3916/C55-2018-01

Çorlu, M. S. (2012). *A pathway to STEM education: Investigating pre-service mathematics and science teachers at Turkish universities in terms of their understanding of mathematics used in science*. [Doctoral Dissertation, Texas A&M University, College Station].

Cortiñas-Rovira, S., Alonso-Marcos, F., Pont-Sorribes, C., & Escribà-Sales, E. (2015). Science journalists' perceptions and attitudes to pseudoscience in Spain. *Public Understanding of Science (Bristol, England)*, *24*(4), 450–465. doi:10.1177/0963662514558991 PMID:25471350

Davies, N. (2009). *Flat Earth News*. Vintage Books.

Deuze, M. (2006). Participation, Remediation, Bricolage: Considering Principal Components of a Digital Culture. *The Information Society*, 22(2), 63–75. doi:10.1080/01972240600567170

Doğanay, K. (2018). *Probleme dayalı stem etkinlikleriyle gerçekleştirilen bilim fuarlarının ortaokul öğrencilerinin fen bilimleri dersi akademik başarılarına ve fen tutumlarına etkisi*. Yüksek Lisans Tezi, Kastamonu Üniversitesi, Fen Bilimleri Enstitüsü, Kastamonu.

Dursun, Ç. (2010). Dünyada Bilim İletişiminin Gelisimi ve Farklı Yaklaşımlar: Toplum İçin Bilimden Toplumda Bilime. *Kurgu Online International Journal of Communication Studies*, 2, 1–31.

Eğitim, R. (2016). *STEM*. MEB. http://yegitek.meb.gov.tr/STEM_Egitimi_Raporu.pdf, Accessed Date: 21.09.2022.

Fahy, D., & Nisbet, M. C. (2011). The Science Journalist Online: Shifting Roles and Emerging Practices. *Journalism*, 12(7), 778–793. doi:10.1177/1464884911412697

Göpfert, W. (2008). The strength of PR and the weakness of science journalism. In M. W. Bauer & M. Bucchi (Eds.), *Jounalism, Science and Society*. Routledge.

Guenther, L. (2019). *Science Journalism*. Oxford: Oxford research encyclopedia of communication.

Guenther, L. (2019). Homeostasis and novelty as concepts for science journalism: A re-interpretation of the selection and depiction of scientific issues in the media. In P. Katz & L. Avraamidou (Eds.), *Stability and change in science education – meeting basic learning needs. Homeostasis and novelty in teaching and learning* (pp. 85–102). Brill Sense.

Guenther, L., & Weber, A. (2019). Science, journalism, and the language of (un) certainty: A review of science journalists' use of language in reports on science. In D. R. Gruber & L. C. Olman (Eds.), *The Routledge Handbook of Language and Science*. Routledge. doi:10.4324/9781351207836-5

Gürkan, H. (2019). The Experiences of Women Professionals in the Film Industry in Turkey: A Gender Based Study. *Acta Universitatis Sapientia-Film and Media Studies Journal*, 16(1), 205–219. doi:10.2478/ausfm-2019-0011

Jones, M. G., Howe, A., & Rua, M. J. (2000). Gender Differences in Students' Experiences, Interests and Attitudes toward Science and Scientists. *Science Education*, 84(2), 180–192. doi:10.1002/(SICI)1098-237X(200003)84:2<180::AID-SCE3>3.0.CO;2-X

Koştur, H. (2017). FeTeMM eğitiminde bilim tarihi uygulamaları: El-Cezerî örneği. *Başkent University Journal of Education*, *4*(1), 61–73.

Livingston, S., Van Couvering, E., & Thumim, N. (2008). Converging Traditions of Research on Media and Information Literacies: Disciplinary, Critical, and Methodological Issues. In J. Coiro, M. Knobel, C. Lankshear, & D. J. Leu (Eds.), *Handbook of Research on New Literacies*. Routledge.

Livingstone, S. (2003) The changing nature and uses of media literacy. (Media@ LSE electronic working papers (4)). Media@lse, London School of Economics and Political Science, London, UK.

Malik, R.S. (2018). Educational Challenges in 21st Century and Sustainable Development. *Journal of Sustainable Development Education and Research*.

MEB - YEĞİTEK Milli Eğitim Bakanlığı - Yenilik ve Eğitim Teknolojileri Genel Müdürlüğü. (2016). *STEM eğitimi raporu*. MEB.

Molek-Kozakowska, K. (2016). Framing Disease, Ageing and Death in Popular Science Journalism. *Brno Studies in English.*, *42*(1), 49–69. doi:10.5817/BSE2016-1-3

Moore, T.J., Johnson, C.C., Peters-Burton, E., & Guzey, S.S. (2021). The Need for a STEM Road Map. *STEM Road Map 2.0*. Research Gate.

Moore, T. J., Tank, K. M., Glancy, A. W., & Kersten, J. A. (2015). NGSS and the landscape of engineering in K-12 state science standards. *Journal of Research in Science Teaching*, *52*(3), 296–318. doi:10.1002/tea.21199

Mpofu, V. (2020). A Theoretical Framework for Implementing STEM Education. *Theorizing STEM Education in the 21st Century*.

Murcott, T. (2009). Science journalism: Toppling the priesthood. *Nature*, *459*(7250), 1054–1055. doi:10.1038/4591054a PMID:19553976

National Science Foundation. (2020). *STEM education for the future: A visioning report*. NSF. https://www.nsf.gov/ehr/Materials/STEM%20Education%20for%20the%20Future%20-%202020%20Visioning%20Report.pdf, 20.10.2022.

Pekbay, C. (2017). *Fen, teknoloji, matematik ve mühendislik etkinliklerinin ortaokul öğrencileri üzerindeki etkileri*. Doktora Tezi, Hacettepe Üniversitesi, Eğitim Bilimleri Enstitüsü.

Peters, H. P. (1995). The interaction of journalists and scientific experts: Co-operation and conflict between two professional cultures. *Media Culture & Society*, *17*(1), 31–48. doi:10.1177/016344395017001003

Pleasants, J., & Olson, J. K. (2019). What is engineering? Elaborating the nature of engineering for K-12 education. *Science Education, 103*(1), 145–166. doi:10.1002ce.21483

Shachar, O. (2000). Spotlighting women scientists in the press: Tokenism in science journalism. *Public Understanding of Science (Bristol, England), 9*(4), 347–358. doi:10.1088/0963-6625/9/4/301

Williams, A., & Clifford, S. (2010). *Mapping the field: A political economic account of specialist science news journalism in the UK national media.* Report funded by the Department for Business, Innovation and Skills and commissioned by the Expert Group on Science and the Media. https://www.cardiff.ac.uk/jomec/research/researchgroups/risk scienceandhealth/fundedprojects/mappingscience.html, Accessed Date: 05.10.2022

KEY TERMS AND DEFINITIONS

Popularization of Science: The global growth of the appeal of science and technology positions itself as an alternative strategy for improving access to scientific knowledge and education. This is supported by scientific policy through the promotion of relevant programs and projects.

STEM Activities: Activities in which children measure their science and engineering knowledge in the experiment and production phase of a project, followed by presentation. Within STEM activities, children also gain knowledge and ideas about physics, mathematics, space science, technology literacy, and engineering skills.

STEM in Education: STEM (Science, Technology, Engineering, Mathematics) education is an approach that covers all grade levels from preschool to higher education. It intends to enable students to take an interdisciplinary approach to problem-solving and to develop knowledge and skills through a new-generation approach to education.

The Importance of Science Journalism: Science journalism is one of the primary responsibilities of the chain of communication and interpretation of scientific news, innovation, or progress to society.

ENDNOTES

[1] Survey research aimed at evaluating the knowledge and skills that students have acquired in the fields of mathematics and science. It is a project of the International Association for the Evaluation of Educational Achievement (IEA).

[2] The PISA Exam measures the science, mathematics, and reading skills of 15-year-old students and their practice of using this information in daily life.

[3] A project defined as "Movement to Increase Opportunities and Improve Technology (FATIH)" in November 2010 in Turkey, aiming to increase student achievement through the effective use of technology in schools.

[4] EBA, the Education Information Network, is a system prepared by the Ministry of National Education in Turkey that serves as a social education platform. It provides and facilitates free education by supporting the lessons of every student that cannot receive special education.

[5] TÜBİTAK is an institution of the Ministry of Industry and Technology aiming to promote, direct and popularize science and technology in Turkey. It is subject to private law provisions.

Chapter 8
STEAM Education in an Online Modality:
Teaching and Learning Tradeoff – A Case Study

Mohamed El Nagdi
https://orcid.org/0000-0001-7787-0870
American University in Cairo, Egypt

Gihan Osman
American University in Cairo, Egypt

Heba EL-Deghaidy
https://orcid.org/0000-0002-0681-4334
American University in Cairo, Egypt

ABSTRACT

This chapter investigates the status of one of the online programs at a not-for-profit university in Egypt offering professional development diplomas to school teachers and leaders. The program focuses on a STEAM online modality track. To explore the program, both graduates and instructors teaching in the online modality program were part of this research. Two main instruments were designed and administered: one was a focus group discussion with instructors in addition to individual interviews with 9 graduates. The research utilized a case study approach and data were analyzed using thematic analysis. Findings show areas of strength in the program design and delivery. Learners were clearly impacted by the online modality, although for some it started as a shock then gradually improved as they too started to replicate instructors' scaffolding and interdisciplinary design with their students. Recommendations were provided related to the start of the program to include more guidance and the final practicum course where it turned out to be an opportunity for innovative thinking.

DOI: 10.4018/978-1-6684-6883-8.ch008

INTRODUCTION

In this chapter, an online program focusing on teachers' professional development in STEM education is explored. This program is probably the first of its kind in Egypt and the Arab region where a STEM/STEAM education (will be used interchangeably in this chapter) preparation program is provided in an online modality. The sections below highlight why STEM education is important in the Arab region and specifically in Egypt and how higher education institutions are catering for the need to provide qualified teachers enacting innovative pedagogies. The move towards online teaching and learning is discussed with emphasis on the best practices and challenges of using the online modality in higher education, background and context of the program investigated is explained, the data collection and analysis is laid out, and finally the findings are categorized and discussed.

Science, Technology, Engineering, and Mathematics (STEM) education has been at the forefront of educational reform initiatives since the 1990s with the United States of America (USA) as a pioneer (Breiner et al., 2012). Later, the STEM movement has gradually expanded to different parts of the world; the Arab world was no exception (Freeman et al., 2019). STEM education has come into existence because of several economic and educational motives in the USA like competing with other countries across the world in educational achievement especially in mathematics and science and raising students interest in STEM fields especially engineering (Bybee, 2013); the needs for STEM in the Arab world were slightly different. BouJaoude (2020) identified several needs to promote pre-college STEM education in the Arab world including the need for a STEM literate citizen who can embark on developing technologically and scientific research using cutting edge technological and engineering tools. With Egypt at the forefront of the Arab world in regards to the STEM approach, many Arab countries joined including Saudi Arabia, Kuwait, Emirates whose educational policy considers STEM as a policy priority to attract, retain and prepare students in STEM fields of study and profession (Kayan-Fadlelmula, 2022). The Arab Gulf Council Countries (GCC) have developed plans to introduce STEM education in their pre-college systems as a means for creating a sustainable knowledge-based economy and produce a skilled workforce capable of meeting the demands of modern society (Kayan-Fadlelmula, 2022). At the Higher Education level, The American University in Cairo, and Ain Shams universities in Egypt started introducing teacher preparation programs for STEM schools (BouJaoude, 2020).

STEM experience in Egypt started when the first two STEM schools were established in specific locations in Egypt namely Giza and Cairo in 2011 and 2012 respectively (Rissmann-Joyce & El Nagdi, 2013; El Nagdi & Roehrig, 2020). The United States Agency for International Development (USAID) funded Egypt's

STEM project and provided assistance for these schools in curriculum development and teacher preparation. This helped early cohorts of teachers enroll in an induction program and ongoing onsite professional development (Rissmann-Joyce & El Nagdi, 2013).

Currently, there are 23 schools with an intention to expand in as many Egyptian cities as possible as a result of the noticeable impact of and call for the STEM schools (Egypt Ministry of Education and Technical Education, 2023). This expansion has naturally called for a need for teachers with certain qualities to enact the needed STEM pedagogies; teachers who are open minded, flexible, critical thinkers and believe in student centeredness, etc (El Nagdi, et al., 2018; Fulton & Britton, 2011). Teachers for the STEM schools were hired from existing secondary teachers' pools who are on top of their jobs for periods from 5 to 20 years. Naturally, teachers with these qualities are not easy to find in a highly traditional centralized education system (Rissmann-Joyce & El Nagdi, 2013)

A not-for-profit university in Egypt initiated a teacher professional education program focusing on STEAM education (with the Arts included) within its previously running Professional Educator Diploma (PED) program (EL-Deghaidy & El Nagdi, 2023). The STEAM Track in the PED program, recognized by the Supreme Council of Universities in Egypt as providing a professional educator diploma came to life in 2013 and aimed to prepare aspiring teachers and enhance practices of existing teachers to work in STEM schools affiliated with the Ministry of Education and Technical Education (MoE&TE) and/or private schools. The program provided a robust scheme that supported the idea of integration and multidisciplinarity and provided teachers with innovative teaching and learning practices that are essential to teach effectively within STE(A)M contexts (EL-Deghaidy & El Nagdi, 2023).

The need to go online with innovative practices had been in the mind of the program developers for a long time; however, the Covid-19 lockdown accelerated going online with participants left with this modality as the only option. Here we have to differentiate between 'emergency remote teaching' that happened due to the lockdown and the 'fully online PED'. The former was a replacement for the Face to Face (F2F) modality while the latter was a carefully and intentionally designed online learning modality.

The STEAM PED started in 2012/2013 in its initial F2F modality. From 2017 plans for scalability in terms of expansion in size and quality were discussed to provide opportunities for participants to enroll in the program from areas beyond those in Cairo in terms of outreach. With steady steps, the planning and design of the STEAM PED online included input from experts in the field and instructional designers. The design process was informed by the following guidelines:

- The online experience should be of the same quality and quantity (number of courses and weeks per course) to the F2F on campus experience;
- Activities and assignments should pave the way for students to achieve the same learning outcomes of the F2F modality while maintaining rigor and quality of the experience with modified versions that suit the online modality.
- Course materials to be provided through a friendly to use LMS for students' independent navigation with guided support from the instructors when needed.
- Instructors are to be informed of the unique nature of the online modality, and trained on how to facilitate, design and assess online instruction as well as guide and support online students.
- Learning is designed to be self-paced through asynchronous learning experiences.

The online modality was launched in 2020 close to the announcement of the closure of all educational institutions due to the Covid-19 lockdown in March 2020, which marked the World Health Organization's announcement of Covid-19 Pandemic. With this online modality completing its third year, it is high time to look back, reflect, and assess this modality. The online modality started with 13 participants in 2020 and up till its 11th semester offering a total of 396 participants have enrolled in the program since its launch. 44 students have completed the programs and graduated from the online program (based on data from the program records).

In this research, the authors, who were an integral part of the whole design and review process, sought to investigate aspects related to the STEAM online modality track from both the learners' and the instructors' points of view. The purpose of this research is to investigate the structure of the STEAM online track courses, the implementation of these courses, the challenges, and successes of the program for institutional development and research. The research is guided by the following research questions:

1- What are both instructors' and learners' perspectives of the STEAM online modality versus the F2F modality?
2- What impact does the STEAM online modality have on learners' classroom teaching practices?
3- How can the STEAM online program be improved from both the instructors and learners' perspectives?

Literature Review and Theoretical Background

Online learning was technically in action in the mid-1990s in response to several factors including, but not restricted to, advances in communication technology, wider spread of the internet, with other socio-economic factors that called for higher education graduates along with a more competitive world and increasing population (Bach et al., 2006). In this sense, technology can be seen not only as an impetus for change, but also one of the tools for education reform and the continuing efforts to provide quality education in a mass higher education world (Bach et al., 2007; Dennis, 2012; Mulla et al., 2023). Yet the widespread expansion of this modality has taken great momentum in the first two decades of the 21st century with emphasis on the same century's skills with the number of internet users surpassing 5.3 billion (Statista).

Massive Open Online Courses (MOOC) came as a new vent for those who will never have an educational experience with such reputable education institutions for economic and travel reasons (Valentina, 2022). Reputable and well-established universities and educational institutions started to provide some of their courses for those who can have an internet connection and be able to communicate using the language the courses were provided in (Dennis (2012). Such online offerings are growing and expanding throughout the whole world including the Arab region (Zalat et al., 2021). Platforms like Edraak and Almentor, though not representing higher education institutions and not fully free, provide models of MOOCs in the Arab region. The need for online learning in higher educational institutions have been aggravated in the era of Covid-19; it was the sole option to offer educational content while ensuring the most possible social distance.

Online teaching has been used to refer to replacing the human direct interaction between students and teachers in a physical classroom by a virtual class where teachers and students communicate and do all teaching and learning activities physically separated but closely communicating through different modes of contact (Brinthaupt et al, .2011). The three key areas for successful online teaching are: methods of fostering student engagement, stimulating intellectual development, and building rapport with students when teaching online (Brinthaupt et al., 2011; Reeves & Pedulla, 2013). Based on Ken Bain seminal book (2004) book *What the Best College Teachers Do,* Brinthaupt and colleagues (2011) came up with a list of effective teaching practices that online teachers should do to achieve these three areas as follows:

(1) **Fostering student engagement**
    - Create a community of learners
    - Foster student-to-faculty and student-to-student interaction
    - Judicious and strategic use of humor

- Creative and engaging use of videos, chats, podcasts, wikis, and discussion forums
- Use blogs to facilitate reflective thinking, collaborative learning, and knowledge construction

(2) **Stimulating intellectual development**
- Create natural critical learning environments
- Generate provocative acts, questions, statements
- Reflect on students" inaccurate and incomplete preconceptions or mental models
- Use technology to create engaging and authentic content

(3) **Building rapport with students**
- Understand one"s student population and determine the amount of help needed
- Let students get to know their teacher
- Use introductory video or other self-disclosure resources
- Keep written records of communication that include relevant student information
- Be flexible with deadlines and due dates
- Provide individualized feedback on assignments and activities (p.519)

Teaching Presence (TP) is highly needed especially in online teaching and learning. TP as a code was generated mainly by learners and elaborated further by the instructors as it seems to be of significant importance that indicates the relationship between students and their instructors, especially in online learning contexts. This is exemplified in how instructors not only provide content, but through the design that happens before the course and constant support during the course, this all directs students to meaningful learning experiences (Anderson et al., 2001).

Logistically speaking, Verdana and Thurman (2019) collected and analyzed definitions of online teaching and concluded that though there are many definitions to the concept, there are still common grounds: these common grounds can be summarized as follows:

- "Learning organized or delivered through web-based or internet based technologies
- Use of the internet to enhance interaction
- Use of the internet to enhance the learning environment
- Use of information and communication technologies
- Technology-based learning
- Audio/video CD-ROM, pre-2000 era" (p.295).

She' and colleagues (2019) outlined the educator's role in an online environment as a facilitator who "may provide many different functions such as, supporting students learning, delivering online teaching, student assessment and preparing learning materials." (p.19). Denis et al., (2004) describe the online educator as one "who interacts directly with learners to support their learning process when they are separated from the tutor in time and place for some or all of these direct interactions" (Denis et al., 2004, p. 3).

Online Teaching in the Arab World

Online teaching and learning has been studied widely but intensively in the last few years due to the expansion of the modality and opportunities it provides for wider populations including the Arab world and the Middle East and North Africa (MENA) region. These studies examine both opportunities and challenges in an attempt to understand the mechanism and provide guidelines for better performance (Lei & SO, 2021; She' et al., 2019).

Though there was an overwhelming acceptance of online teaching in some Arab countries especially during the pandemic (Zalat et al., 2021), teaching online has been a steep learning curve for faculty members teaching higher education in several Arab countries (Mulla et al., 2023; Zalat et al., 2021). These challenges include lack of ability to meet learners' expectations; absence of online teaching and learning as a culture; lack of incentives for faculty members to engage in online teaching; not being prepared with best practices to teach online; and the logistic and resources issues like insufficient/ unstable internet connectivity, inadequate computer labs, lack of computers/ laptops, and technical problems (Zalat et al., 2021; Mulla, 2022).

Soliman and colleagues (2022) in their study of MBA and DBA programs in Egypt, found out that students' satisfaction with online education is influenced by several factors, including their resources and talents. Student initiative was discovered to play a moderating role in the effects of student, instructor, and institution factors on students' satisfaction with online education. This research is being carried out during the COVID-19 outbreak to see how online instruction affects student achievement.

Ismail and colleagues (2016) described online learning in Egypt as still in its infancy. However, during Covid-19, this has developed into a well-defined phenomenon. Faculty members at Arab Higher education institutions are getting readier for online teaching mainly in domains like evaluating students' achievements and limitations, problem-solving skills, information technology and computer skills, monitoring and motivating techniques, communication, and class management skills (Khtere et al., 2021).

STEAM in Online Formats

Baucum and Capraro (2021) have reported the change in students' STEM perceptions in two different informal learning environments: an online STEM camp and a face-to-face (FTF) STEM camp; they found out that both camps produce similar outcomes regarding STEM field and career perceptions. This suggests that STEM camps, both online and in-person, can improve students' perceptions of the STEM fields and of STEM careers.

Yildrim (2023) discussed the experience of providing an online professional development STEM program (OPDP) to preschool teachers and found a positive effect on these teachers in regards to "STEM education content knowledge, pedagogy knowledge, professional skills, and STEM teaching (creativity, collaboration, etc.)" (p.24). For these OPDPs to be successful, educators, and program designers need to focus on teachers' needs and providing required technological infrastructure that teachers may need (Yidrim, 2023).

Background (PED STEAM Track as Teachers' Preparation in an Online Environment)

STEM education has been linked to project-based learning and instruction, hands-on work, and direct interaction between teachers and students and students among themselves. Turning this into an online learning environment would be perilous and a challenge (Dede et al., 2016). In the online modality of the PED STEAM track (Professional Educator Diploma, n.d) and in order to avoid this, the program developers created multiple pathways and opportunities for learners to interact through tools and activities. Examples include several discussion forums in each course, differentiated assessment tasks with both collaborative and individual modes to enable participants to form a community of learners in an online modality with learners from different disciplines while designing their group interdisciplinary STEAM units (Brinthaupt et al., 2011). Therefore, learners had several opportunities to interact with each other on different occasions. Instructors used both rare synchronous meetings for both the orientation to the program's content and its modality in addition to support and scaffold the learning journey all along the program's six courses.

One of the key challenges in the design and offering of the online modality was the practicum course offered at the end of the program which forms one of the cornerstones of this program; providing a practicum course in which learners plan, teach, and provide feedback to each other in a critical friends' framework has always been a challenge even in the on-campus F2F modality. For this to happen, the course was designed in a manner that allowed students to:

- Reflect on their previous experience in the other five courses in an attempt to consolidate and review their understanding of STEAM philosophy and principles as well as their challenges in this journey.
- Support circles were created to give them an opportunity to regularly meet each week to discuss an issue in their teaching or school.
- In a group work format, plan a customized unit to be delivered during the course which is the real challenge; teachers wonder how they can teach a STEAM lesson in a virtual and distance learning environment. Different options were provided by the instructors of this course, but the most inspiring were the suggestions and implementations of the course learners. Learners are given different options: to record the session in their classes, teach an online lesson to students or fellow teachers, etc. This shows how flexible the program is.
- The role of instructors is crucial in this as their role is more as facilitators: encouraging and motivating students and providing feedback and utilizing the various online tools such as discussion threads.

While existing literature examines the nature and impact of online learning and teaching mostly from learners' perspectives and minor work from instructors' perspectives, this study included voices of both. Here we examine the nature, success, and challenges of the program from both the students and instructors' sides.

RESEARCH METHODS

An exploratory case study was used in this study. The purpose of this study was to explore the nature, impact, successes, challenges, and recommendations of online modality of a STEAM Track PED provided by a non-for-profit university in Egypt. The case study design is a good match for the nature and purpose of the study given the clear boundaries and context of the program and its participants: learners, instructors, designers, and leadership (Yin, 2014). In this case, the main contributors are the instructors of the course and learners who have completed the program. The learners in the program are mostly teachers or aspiring teachers and will be referred to through this paper as learners.

Data Collection

The sources of data for this study are semi structured interviews with learners, and a focus discussion with instructors. Interview and Focus group discussion FGD protocols can be found in Appendix 1. The criteria for contacting participating learners were those who have had a full experience with the program and still mindful of its details; those who have recently graduated from the program in the academic years 2022 and 2023. A message was sent from the authors to all prospective participants (around 50 learners) and 10 of them replied positively but 9 showed up in the interviews. In regards to participating instructors, the authors invited all instructors who were currently teaching in the online program at the time of the study. The first two authors facilitated the discussion of the focus group. The interviews were done in English and Arabic. Institutional Review Board (IRB) approval was obtained prior to collecting the data.

Both interviews with participants and FGD with the course instructors were done via Zoom recorded meetings. Consent for participating in research recording was granted at the beginning of the interview and FGDs. Two interviews were conducted in Arabic for ease of input on the part of the participants. The other eight interviews were done in English. Each author conducted a set of interviews that lasted from 30-40 minutes. The FGD with instructors was done in English. Following are two tables of the participants in both the FGD and the interviews.

Table 1. Instructors who participated in the focus group discussion

Name*	Experience in teaching in general	Academic Degree	Experience in online teaching in the track
Mohsen	10	PhD	3 years
Mary	10	PhD	2 years
Hany	7	MA	1 year

* Names are pseudonyms

Table 2. Learners interviewed

Name**	Teaching experience	Date of graduation from the program	discipline they are teaching
Rania	6 years	Summer 2022	Science
Rahma	7 years	Spring 2023	Science
M Hamdy	14 years	Spring 2022	Maths
M Fahmy	15 years	Spring 2023	Biology
Amira	10 Years	Spring 2023	Science
Mona	7 years	Spring 2023	Science
Hala	25 years	Spring 2022	History
Nesreen	7 years	Spring 2021	Library studies
Awatef	24 years	Summer 2022	English

** Names are pseudonyms

Data Analysis

The recorded focus group discussion with the course instructors was listened to by the three authors several times. The authors spent some time familiarizing themselves with the data. Then each one of them came up with a set of themes emerging from the discussion (Saldana, 2013). The themes were compared and there was an agreement regarding the following list: Course flexibility and organization, detailed and rigorous material, gender equity and agency friendly mode, challenges include how to cope with students' different readiness levels, how to deal with frustration resulting from lack of regular meeting, suggestions to use more videos than readings.

The recorded interviews with the graduates of the program were analyzed separately by the authors. Each author wrote an immediate summary of the input of each participant highlighting the key responses. Key responses were then categorized into codes and later clustered into themes after a discussion among the authors. The generated themes from the responses included: asynchronous shock, equity (the only pathway for several teachers who cannot reach the program on campus), instruction issues, courses organization, administration issues, transformative impact, and several suggestions to improve the program.

The common key aspects between the instructors and the learners can be elucidated as follows.

Findings

Based on the data analysis of the input by the learners and instructors, a vivid image of the program in its entirety is provided including, the content, organization, instruction, impact, and challenges is provided. Recommendations from both learners and instructors are forewarned as well. The themes are first categorized per participants' role; learners or instructors. Then the themes from the instructors were added whenever pertinent to the learners' themes. Following are the themes based on the learners' input and the thoughts shared by the instructors. The themes gave answers to the three research questions regarding the program's impact, perspectives on the online teaching and learning, and recommendations for improvement.

Positive Impact

Interviewed students noted how their experience in the STEAM track online modality had a positive impact on their teaching in their different contexts. Rania, who is teaching in the Kingdom of Saudi Arabia (KSA), mentioned that the units she developed throughout the program's different courses were so beneficial in her work; she maintained " I use one of the units we developed in the program. It was excellent. Students liked it. I need to repeat it. All school staff/parents are amazed". Amira, who had no prior experience in STEM teaching, seconded Rania's opinion. She said that "the program gave me a new (different) perspective in teaching. It helped me develop the independent learner in me. It changed my views on the ways of thinking, and how to deal with students". Amira started to propose to her school leadership how to start a STEAM program in the school. Hala, who had a certificate of education, had a new perspective on the program; she rated the program and the experience "excellent. The PED provided me with a holistic experience from teaching to assessing. I never expected to learn to do the things I did by the end of the program, even the theories of learning that I knew from my BA degree, I learnt from differently and so much better." Nesreen added "I really got to know types of assessment, design an integrated unit, state objectives, learning theories. All these were excellent points that I am applying in my current teaching, especially that I receive a detailed plan but now I can design my own lessons and activities." M Hamdy, who is a teacher in an Egyptian STEM school, referred to a different dimension. He thought that this program may not add new things to him as a teacher in a STEM school for 8 years, but "when I joined, I was surprised by the new things I learned like unit development. This helped me a lot after finishing the diploma; I became so meticulous and stopped students memorizing answers to questions before the exam which is against STEM (philosophy). I started to insist that students make citations for project work by asking them where they get their

STEAM Education in an Online Modality

information from." Rahma emphasized the need to help students reflect on their learning, one of the most important things she learned from the online program; "My teaching before the diploma was the traditional way; I knew nothing about the engineering design process, (alternative) assessment, use of technology; but after the diploma I became so different. I started to encourage students to reflect on how they learn. Traditionally we neglect students' reflection, but now this is different."

Content, Organization, and Layout

This positive impact did not happen without a price; the program's content, instructional methods, and organization were among the aspects students referred to that helped them gain that positive experience. Awatef described the program's content as "so rich; it provided a bank of activities to apply, how to manage the class, how to design a unit that needed deep research, using inquiry-based learning as an approach as students can define what they can learn." The course layout and organization were learner friendly. All learners who participated in the interviews expressed their satisfaction with this. Some participants like Hala, however, thought that some of the readings are "difficult and rich (in information) and time consuming." The same concern was shared by the instructors; Mohsen mentioned in the FDG that "some readings are so hard for the teachers to digest." He therefore suggested "using more videos and visuals instead."

Instruction and Teaching Presence

The role of the instructors in the online program is crucial. They provide constant support and feedback and try to provide the best environment possible that reduces the stress on the online learners while supporting and guiding learners. Instructors' presence can be observed from the learners' input. Nesreen, for example, stressed that "the online experience was great and having all the material and activities all uploaded on Moodle was extremely helpful and organized". She also highlighted immensely the "role of the instructors and the support and guidance provided especially in the first courses in this online experience." Awatef mentioned that she "learned how to help her students and provide effective feedback from her experience with the instructors." From the instructor's perspective Mohsen stressed that the challenge learners had is not the content itself, but rather on how the content was presented. 'Learners learn from the feedback provided by instructors. We give them the opportunity to give feedback on their received feedback to see how they think about things and how they internalized certain points and concepts'. Mary, another instructor in the program, followed up on this point that 'creating the power dynamics in online environments is challenging but once a pattern is established things get better'.

Equity and Advocacy

Several learners reiterated the fact that they "would never have this opportunity, were it just F2F." Amira said that" I live in KSA and it would have been impossible to join this diploma face to face." Mona echoed Amira's thoughts. Learners from Alexandria and Upper Egypt said the same. Mary, an instructor in the program, described the value of the online modality as a means to create equity and advocacy in society; she stated that "as a woman you can't possibly join such courses while you have your own job, and you know the other rules society dictated on you as a woman and then find some time in the evening to travel to a different location in order to take professional development. From an advocacy point of view, what I noticed is that for a lot of women this was their only chance to be included." She added that "I think, and having this online modality, it means that certain voices will be heard, and that certain people will be included."

Challenges of Online Modality and Recommendations

The Asynchronous Shock

When teachers/learners join this program, they have in mind the typical synchronous Zoom meetings that instructors would have with them every session. However, on the first day of the course instructors are entitled to tell them that this course is asynchronous. "This was a shock to me." This sentence was heard from almost all learners in the interviews. Mona said "Nobody told us we are meeting instructors every session"; Nesreen and M Fathy had the same opinion:" We felt frustrated." This may have happened because of a misunderstanding of concepts of synchronous and asynchronous when they had an orientation meeting with the track coordinators. This shock never lasted forever. Learners got the support needed from instructors to overcome this situation. M Fathy maintained that "I like the asynchronous nature; it is convenient to my learning style, my commitments etc." based on the FGD, participants shared another challenge: when learners start the practicum course where they are entitled to teach, and they teach many times because they teach a unit they are asked to work together as a group to teach a unit of like 5 lessons. So, we have them teaching more than one lesson, and they need to find students and resources to be used by their students to do hands-on work to produce a solution to a problem. Instructors provide a safe and supportive and flexible environment to safeguard integrity and learning while accepting the different options and scenarios the learners may have to overcome the issues regarding doing practicum in a fully online mode.

Instructors and learners have shared some common recommendations to improve the program. Hany, an instructor in the program, suggested that we design more meaningful, more authentic tasks to suit the online modality, not just discussion forums" Mohsen, another instructor recommended more "Peer to peer reviews- more videos and less readings."

Learners ask for more clarity in the orientation session, more live synchronous sessions with instructors, less readings and more videos as well. They think that they need to have a firsthand experience in real STEM schools either by visiting or watching what really happens in such schools.

DISCUSSION

Developing an online version of the F2F STEAM education program for teachers has been one of the targets of the educational studies program at a non-for-profit university in Egypt. This move coincides with the ever-increasing tendency to rely on internet-based education and respond to the increasing needs by learners who may have no option to attend the on-campus option (Brinthaupt et al., 2011 & Dede, et al., 2016; Lei & SO, 2021). The program was designed and delivered just prior to the Covid-19 lockdown but that lockdown accelerated the spread and adoption of the modality (Bach et al., 2006). The participants in this study shared their thoughts on describing and reflecting on their experience in this program as providing their critique. One of the major findings was the positive impact of the online modality (Singh & Thurman, 2019; She' et al., 2019). The impact of the online modality was seen as not less than the F2F one (Brinthaupt et al., 2011 & Dede, et al., 2016); learners gained not only content knowledge but skills and attitudes as well (EL-Deghaidy & El Nagdi, 2023; Back et al., 2006). The role of the educator was seen as more than just to deliver information but a facilitator and a guide on the side fostering student engagement, stimulating intellectual development, and building rapport with students

(Denis et al., 2004; Brinthaupt et al., 2011 & Dede, et al., 2016). Teachers' presence was reflected on how instructors are there for their students though not meeting them every session in a live meeting through feedback, discussion, support and questions (Anderson et al., 2001). Providing everybody an access to quality and needed education is another feature of online modality that was seen very clearly in this study where various learners mentioned that they would not have had such an opportunity except through the online modality (Baucum & Capraro, 2021). Like all endeavors in education, nothing is perfect. The issues raised in this study by both learners and instructors provide an opportunity for development and improvement. Helping instructors to have more presence by helping them have better tools to monitor group work, designing different assessments than just designing units, more support at the beginning of the program, providing clear instructions and orientation, increasing visuals and videos are recommendations that would enhance the online modality's impact. With the strong points outlined in this study including content, interaction, pedagogies and online tools used by instructors, and the smooth sequence, the effective design of learning activities, feedback and scaffolding, being understanding and supportive instructors, learners ask for more monitoring of group work to create a real sense of professional community.

CONCLUSION

This study explored the online modality of a STEAM program provided by a non for profit university in Egypt. Learners and instructors in the program provided their input regarding the program's nature, strengths, challenges, impact and their recommendations to improve the program. The program was found to be having a strong positive impact on graduates professionally; graduates expressed how they transformed their teaching practices and introduced interdisciplinary STEAM ideas in their classes, and how the online modality provided an equitable opportunity to people who would not have that opportunity otherwise due to distance, time constraints and their daily work duties.

REFERENCES

Anderson, T., Rourke, L., Garrison, R., & Archer, W. (2001). Assessing teaching presence in a computer conferencing context. *Online Learning : the Official Journal of the Online Learning Consortium*, 5(2), 1–17. doi:10.24059/olj.v5i2.1875

Bach, S., Haynes, P., & Lewis, J. (2006). *Online learning and teaching in higher education*, McGraw-Hill Education. https://ebookcentral.proquest.com/lib/aucegypt/detail.action?docID=316249

Bain, K. (2004). *What the best college teachers do*. Harvard University Press.

Baucum, M., & Capraro, R. (2021). A system for equity: Enhancing STEM education during a pandemic. *Journal of Research in Innovative Teaching & Learning Emerald Publishing.*, 14(3), 365–377. doi:10.1108/JRIT-12-2020-0087

Bekir, Y. (2023). Preparation of preschool teachers during the COVID-19 pandemic: An online professional development program in STEM education. *Research in Science & Technological Education*, 1–37. doi:10.1080/02635143.2023.2209855

BouJaoude, S. (2020). STEM Education in the Arab Countries. In *STEM in Science Education and S in STEM*. Brill. doi:10.1163/9789004446076_010

Breiner, J. M., Johnson, C. C., Harkness, S. S., & Koehler, C. M. (2012). What is STEM? A discussion about conceptions of STEM in education and partnerships. *School Science and Mathematics*, *112*(1), 3–11. doi:10.1111/j.1949-8594.2011.00109.x

Brinthaupt, T. M., Fisher, L. S., Gardner, J. G., Raffo, D. M., & Woodward, J. B. (2011). What the best online teachers should do. *Journal of Online Learning and Teaching*, *7*(4), 515–524.

Bybee, R. W. (2013). *The case for STEM education: challenges and opportunities*. National Science Teachers Association.

Dede, C., Eisenkraft, A., Frumin, K., & Hartley, A. (Eds.). (2016). *Teacher learning in the digital age: Online professional development in STEM education*. Harvard Education Press.

Denis, B., Watland, P., Pirotte, S., & Verday, N. (2004). Roles and competencies of the e-tutor. Networked Learning 2004: A Research Based Conference on Networked Learning and Lifelong Learning. *Proceedings of the Fourth International Conference*, (pp. 150–157). ORBI. https://orbi.uliege.be/bitstream/2268/12722/1/DENIS_WATLAND_PIROTTE_VERDAY_Roles_and_competencies_of_the_tutor_30_03_2009.pdf

Egypt Ministry of Education and Technical Education. (n.d.). وزارة التربية والتعليم - الصفحة الرئيسية. MOE. https://moe.gov.eg/en/stem/

EL-Deghaidy. H., & El Nagdi, M. (2023). To STEAM or Not to STEAM: Is It a Matter of Professional Development or Professional Creation? In: Al-Balushi, S.M., Martin-Hansen, L., Song, Y. (eds) Reforming Science Teacher Education Programs in the STEM Era. Palgrave Studies on Leadership and Learning in Teacher Education. Palgrave Macmillan, Cham. doi:10.1007/978-3-031-27334-6_6

El Nagdi, M., Leammukda, F., & Roehrig, G. (2018). Developing identities of STEM teachers at emerging STEM schools. *International Journal of STEM Education*, *5*(1), 36. doi:10.118640594-018-0136-1 PMID:30631726

El Nagdi, M., & Roehrig, G. (2020). Identity evolution of STEM teachers in Egyptian STEM schools in a time of transition: A case study. *International Journal of STEM Education*, 7(1), 1–16. doi:10.118640594-020-00235-2

Freeman, B., Marginson, S., & Tytler, R. (2019). An international view of STEM education. In *STEM Education 2.0* (pp. 350–363). Brill. doi:10.1163/9789004405400_019

Fulton, K., & Britton, T. (2011). *STEM Teachers in Professional Learning Communities: From Good Teachers to Great Teaching*. National Commission on Teaching and America's Future.

Goglio, V. (2022). *The diffusion and social implications of MOOCs: A comparative study of the USA and Europe*. Taylor and Francis.

Ismail, N., Kinchin, G., & Edwards, J. (2016). Investigating continuing professional development provided for Egyptian higher education online tutors. *International Journal of Enhanced Research in Educational Development*, 4 (2), 7-14.

Kayan-Fadlelmula, F., Sellami, A., Abdelkader, N., & Umer, S. (2022). A systematic review of STEM education research in the GCC countries: Trends, gaps and barriers. *International Journal of STEM Education*, 9(1), 1–24. doi:10.118640594-021-00319-7

Lei, S. I., & Amy, S. I. S. (2021). Online Teaching and Learning Experiences During the COVID-19 Pandemic – A Comparison of Teacher and Student Perceptions. *Journal of Hospitality & Tourism Education*, 33(3), 148–162. doi:10.1080/10963758.2021.1907196

Mulla, T., Munir, S., & Mohan, V. (2023). An exploratory study to understand faculty members' perceptions and challenges in online teaching. *International Review of Education*, 69(1-2), 73–99. doi:10.100711159-023-10002-4 PMID:37313288

Online courses in Arabic (n.d.). Edraak. https://www.edraak.org/en/

Professional educator diploma program. (n.d.) AUC School of Humanities and Social Sciences. https://huss.aucegypt.edu/departments/educational-studies/professional-educator-diploma

Reeves, T. D., & Pedulla, J. (2013). Bolstering the impact of online professional development for teachers. *Journal of Educational Research & Policy Studies*, 1, 50–66. https://files.eric.ed.gov/ fulltext/ED545314.pdf

Rissmann-Joyce, S., & El Nagdi, M. (2013). A case study: Egypt's first STEM schools: Lessons learned. *Proceeding of the Global Summit on Education*, (pp. 11-12). Research Gate.

Saldaña, J. (2013). *The coding manual for qualitative researchers* (2nd ed.). SAGE.

Shé, N., Farrell, C., Brunton, O., Costello, J., Donlon, E., Trevaskis, E., & Eccles, S. (2019). *Teaching online is different: critical perspectives from the literature.* Dublin City University. doi:10.5281/zenodo.3479402

Singh, V., & Thurman, A. (2019). How Many Ways Can We Define Online Learning? A Systematic Literature Review of Definitions of Online Learning (1988-2018). *American Journal of Distance Education*, *33*(4), 289–306. doi:10.1080/08923647.2019.1663082

Soliman, C., Salman, D. & GamalEldin, G.O. (2022). Students' perceptions of online learning in higher education during COVID-19: an empirical study of MBA and DBA students in Egypt. *Futur Bus J, 8* (45). doi:10.1186/s43093-022-00159-z

The Statistics Portal. (n.d.). Statista. https://www.statista.com/statistics/273018/number-of-internet-users-worldwide/

Yin, R. K. (2014). *Case Study Research: Design and Methods* (5th ed.). SAGE Publications.

Zalat, M. M., Hamed, M. S., & Bolbol, S. A. (2021). The experiences, challenges, and acceptance of elearning as a tool for teaching during the COVID-19 pandemic among university medical staff. *PLoS One*, *16*(3), e0248758. doi:10.1371/journal.pone.0248758 PMID:33770079

Appendix 1

Focus Discussion Prompts and Questions with Instructors
1. How long have you been teaching in this program f2f and/or online?
2. Did you participate in the design of this program?
3. What was your teaching expectations before teaching this program?
4. How was it different from your f2f teaching experience?
5. How was the program design different from your expectations?
6. What strong points do you see in this program?
7. What points of improvement do you think the program people in charge should be working on?
8. If compared to a f2f experience, how can you see its impact on learners in terms of the depth of learning, engagement, access, ease of learning?
9. How do you see the course's design and arrangement of materials?
10. Are there any suggestions for better design and/or delivery?
11. Please describe the process you use in teaching in this program
12. What successes did you make as you teach in this track online modality?
13. What challenges did you have? Why?
14. How can we overcome these challenges?

Appendix 2

Interview Questions with learners
1. How long have you been teaching?
2. Do you have any previous STEAM learning experience prior to f2f or online?
3. What was your expectations before joining this program?
4. How was it different from other previous experiences if any?
5. How was it different from your expectations?
6. What strong points do you see in this program?
7. What points of improvement do you think the program people in charge should be working on?
8. If compared to a f2f experience, is there any difference in the depth of learning, engagement, access, ease of learning?
9. How do you see the course's design and arrangement of materials?
10. Are there any suggestions for better design and/or delivery?

Chapter 9
Teachers' Perceptions Towards the Implementation of STEM Education in the State of Kuwait

Abrar Almoosa
Kuwait Foundation for Advancement of Sciences, Kuwait

ABSTRACT

Recent long-term policy plans in the MENA region stress the growing importance of transitioning to 21st-century skills and pursuing sustainable development objectives through the preparation of highly skilled nationals holding credentials in STEM fields that align with current and future labor market demands. Despite multiple educational reforms, national and international indicators of student performance still demonstrate insignificant improvement in MENA students' achievement. This study explored the current status of STEM education in Kuwait from the teachers' perceptions. A qualitative research design was used, with semi-structured interviews as the main data collection method. The results showed that teachers had generally positive perceptions of STEM education and believed that it is important for the learners and their future careers. However, several challenges were identified including the curriculum and instructional strategies. The findings suggest that adopting new curriculums and teachers training are important towards successful implementation of STEM education.

DOI: 10.4018/978-1-6684-6883-8.ch009

INTRODUCTION

Education refers to the process of acquiring knowledge, skills, values, beliefs, and habits through various forms of learning and instruction. It is a fundamental human right and plays a crucial role in personal, social, and economic development. The ultimate goal of education is to enable individuals to lead fulfilling and productive lives and to contribute to their communities and the world at large. According to Batdi, Talan, and Semerci (2019), the increasing economic, social, scientific, and technological developments in recent years have heightened the demand for individuals who possess collaborative, reasonable, creative, questioning, and innovative skills, enabling them to work harmoniously in group settings (p. 382).

STEM education is accepted as one of the largest educational movements in recent years (Ozkan & Topsakal, 2021, p.442). Yet, to driving innovation and economic growth STEM fields (Science, Technology, Engineering, and Mathematics) are at the forefront of technological and scientific advancements and play a critical role in driving economic growth and competitiveness. STEM is a multi-disciplinary holistic approach that aims to teach students integrally in science, technology, engineering, and mathematics disciplines (Ozkan & Topsakal, 2021, p.442). STEM knowledge and skills are essential in addressing global challenges such as climate change, food and water security, and healthcare to solve global challenges and set long term strategic plans to be prepared for the future as the world becomes more technologically advanced, STEM skills and knowledge will become increasingly important for individuals and society to thrive in the future. In addition, STEM education is a great investment to empower the students and occupy them with the 21st century skills and competencies such as critical thinking and problem-solving.

STEM is an interdisciplinary field that encompasses a range of subjects and disciplines that are crucial for innovation, economic growth, and problem-solving in the modern world. The purpose of this type of education is to remove the distinction among disciplines, to create a single discipline and thus, to educate a generation who question, research, produce and make inventions throughout the whole education process starting from pre-school until higher education as noted by Batdi, Talan and Semerci (2019, p.383). STEM education provides students with the skills and knowledge they need to succeed in a rapidly changing and increasingly technological society. It includes subjects such as physics, biology, chemistry, computer science, mathematics, and engineering, and emphasizes hands-on learning and critical thinking.

General Overview About STEM in Kuwait

Educators in Kuwait are making efforts to drive a change and implement new instructional strategies as meeting the generation needs and interest is the base for successful and complete education. Yet, the struggle is with the national curriculums and the obstacles that the educational community is facing regardless the requests to change the curriculums and update them. Kuwait did not make a significant progress in the field of Science, Technology, Engineering, and Mathematics (STEM) in recent years. There are a limited number of STEM initiatives and programs overall in Kuwait and most of the initiatives come from the private sector to promote STEM education and encourage young people to pursue careers in these fields. Most of these initiatives are conducted as a non-formal and informal learning that promote STEM education and career development through enrichment content.

The Ministry of Education in Kuwait has not made it a priority to enhance the STEM curriculum in schools or provide students with the necessary resources to excel in these subjects or specifically train teachers to implementing teaching and learning strategies that teach STEM education. On the other side, there is a lack in investments in research and development in STEM fields.

Yet, in recent years, there is an increase in the awareness of the importance of STEM amongst the Kuwaiti educators and teachers with shy attempts to apply instructional methods to focus on STEM. On the other side, the Kuwaiti government continues to invest in STEM majors for the university level, specifically in providing scholarship to increase in the number of students pursuing degrees and careers in STEM fields. the development of the STEM sector to attract more talent and build a knowledge-based economy.

Objective

The objective of this chapter is to contribute to the body of the existing STEM literature by exploring factors that influence teachers' participation in STEM in Kuwait. The intention is to also identify the gaps in STEM education research in Kuwait. This chapter presents the current status and challenges in implementing STEM education in Kuwait.

STEM Education Challenges

In Kuwait, some of the specific challenges facing STEM education are financial, technical and educational. When it comes to the financials, despite being a wealthy country, investment in STEM education in Kuwait is relatively low compared to other countries, leading to insufficient resources and funding for STEM initiatives. Implementing STEM education often requires a significant investment in technology and equipment, which many schools may not have access to. Technical challenges vary from the availability of high tech-resources to access to technology for teachers and students.

For the educational challenges, the outdated curricula and/or curriculum development is possessing a major challenge in implementing STEM education. Developing a comprehensive STEM curriculum that meets educational standards can be a challenging and time-consuming process. In addition, teacher training is important to effectively incorporate technology and hands-on learning into the classrooms.

This study will focus on the educational challenges as follows:

1- Outdated curricula: Kuwait's curricula often struggle to keep up with the latest technological advancements, which can limit students' exposure to cutting-edge technology and limits the teachers for implementing STEM education. The integration of diverse disciplines into the educational milieu is crucial in facilitating a more robust and impactful learning experience for students. By establishing a bridge between these subjects, students will not only acquire a vast repository of knowledge, but they will also cultivate a range of advanced competencies and skills that will serve them for a lifetime. Regrettably, the current situation in Kuwait is marked by a noticeable disconnect between different academic disciplines. Furthermore, many educators lack the in-depth expertise required to employ the most effective teaching methodologies and techniques in the classroom.
2- Limited teacher training: The acronym STEM (Science, Technology, Engineering, and Mathematics) is a well-known concept among educators within the field in Kuwait, however, it appears that many of them lack the necessary expertise and competencies to effectively integrate it into their pedagogical practices. There is a pressing need for professional development opportunities to enhance the instructional capabilities of these educators and provide them with up-to-date teaching strategies. There exists a scarcity of teachers who possess the requisite training and qualifications, which has the potential to impede the standard of STEM education.

Methodology

The present chapter employed a qualitative research design to explore the experiences and perceptions of teachers regarding STEM Education in Kuwait. The following subsections describe the research design, participant selection, data collection, and data analysis.

Research Design

This research adopted a qualitative research design to uncover the rich, in-depth experiences and understandings of the teachers. The design was chosen to gain a comprehensive understanding of the status of STEM education in Kuwait's schools.

Participant Selection

A purposive sampling technique was used to select participants for the study. A total of 10 middle school's teachers were selected teaching science subject. The participants were recruited from several schools through referrals. The inclusion criteria were being a local Kuwaiti teacher teaching science subject.

Data Collection

Data was collected through semi-structured, in-depth interviews, which involved asking participants open-ended questions related to their experiences and perceptions of STEM education in Kuwait. The interviews were audio-recorded and lasted between 45-60 minutes. An interview guide was used to ensure consistency and to cover key topics. The interviews were conducted in a private setting to ensure comfort and confidentiality.

Data Analysis

The data collected from the semi-structured interviews was analyzed using a thematic analysis approach. This involved reviewing the transcripts and identifying common themes and patterns in the participants' responses. The themes were then organized and coded, and a narrative was developed to provide an in-depth understanding of the experiences and perceptions of teachers regarding STEM education in Kuwait. The transcripts of the interviews were analyzed using a thematic analysis approach. Thematic analysis involves identifying, coding, and categorizing patterns and themes in the data. The process of analysis involved several steps, including transcribing the interviews, reading the transcripts multiple times, identifying themes, and coding the data.

In conclusion, this chapter employed a qualitative research design to explore the experiences and perceptions of teachers regarding STEM Education in Kuwait. The research design, participant selection, data collection, and data analysis methods were carefully chosen to provide a rich and in-depth understanding of the experiences and perceptions of the participants. The methodology section described the steps taken to conduct this research using a qualitative research design. The study aimed to uncover the experiences and perceptions of teachers regarding STEM education through semi-structured interviews. The ethical considerations, such as informed consent and confidentiality, were also discussed.

RESULTS

The results of this qualitative research are based on the in-depth interviews with 10 teachers from different schools. The interviews were conducted to explore the challenges and experiences of teachers in implementing STEM education in the classroom. -

The analysis revealed two major themes: (1) teacher training and (2) updated curriculum.

1. Teacher Training: Several teachers expressed that they had limited training in STEM subjects and felt unprepared to teach these subjects effectively. They reported feeling the need for more comprehensive professional development opportunities to improve their confidence and competence in teaching STEM.
2. Updated Curriculum: Teachers also indicated that the existing curriculum was outdated and not aligned with worldwide educational standards and technological advancements. They emphasized the need for a revised and updated curriculum that is engaging and relevant to students' interests and future careers.

These themes were consistent across all 10 teachers interviewed, indicating that teacher training and updated curriculum are critical areas of concern for successful implementation of STEM education in the classroom.

To further explore the theme of teacher training, participants were asked about the type of professional development opportunities they would like to receive. Most teachers expressed an interest in hands-on workshops and practical training in the use of technology and instructional strategies or techniques for teaching STEM effectively and successfully that meets the learning outcomes. It has been also reported the necessary for ongoing support from the school management and opportunities for collaboration with other STEM teachers in public and private schools locally, regionally or on the international level.

Regarding the theme of updated curriculum, teachers expressed and described the urgent need to update the curriculum and adopt information that is relevant to the students' realty and current changes in the world. Additionally, there is a need for a more integrated and interdisciplinary approach to teaching STEM. They emphasized the importance of incorporating real-world problems, connect to the reality in utilizing cases and situations and relevant examples into the curriculum to make it more engaging and relevant for students.

The results of this study highlight the importance of teacher training and updated curriculum for effective implementation of STEM education in the classroom. Research showed that sustaining and expanding the development of 21st Century skills can be taught and enhanced through the integration of curricula (Matinez, 2022). The findings from this research provide valuable insights for educators, administrators, and policy makers and to assist them in their efforts to implement STEM education in Kuwait to prepare students for the future.

Discussion

STEM education, which encompasses the subjects of Science, Technology, Engineering, and Mathematics, plays a critical role in preparing students for the challenges of the modern world. It equips them with the essential knowledge and skills needed to thrive in an increasingly complex and technology-driven society. By fostering a multidisciplinary approach, STEM education encourages students to think critically, solve problems, collaborate, and innovate, all of which are crucial in today's rapidly evolving global landscape.

However, despite the undeniable significance of STEM education, there are several challenges that hinder its effective implementation in many countries, including Kuwait. One major challenge is the lack of qualified and trained educators who are proficient in delivering STEM curricula. Teaching STEM subjects requires specialized expertise and pedagogical skills that go beyond traditional teaching methods. It is imperative to invest in professional development programs for teachers to enhance their understanding of STEM concepts, instructional strategies, and the integration of technology in the classroom.

In addition to the challenges mentioned above, another significant concern in STEM education is the availability of resources and funding. Providing access to up-to-date equipment, technology, and materials for hands-on learning experiences can be costly for educational institutions (Miller, Peterson, & Williams, 2021). Limited resources may hinder the implementation of practical, inquiry-based activities that are essential for fostering critical thinking and problem-solving skills among students.

Moreover, a shortage of qualified STEM teachers poses a considerable obstacle to effective STEM education (Baker & Turner, 2019). Recruiting and retaining highly skilled educators who possess both subject expertise and effective pedagogical practices can be challenging. Without well-trained teachers, the delivery of engaging and innovative STEM instruction becomes difficult, impacting students' overall learning experiences.

Addressing these challenges requires a comprehensive approach that involves collaboration between policymakers, educators, and stakeholders. Ensuring adequate funding and resource allocation for STEM programs is vital to provide students with the necessary tools and opportunities for hands-on learning (Miller et al., 2021). Professional development programs and incentives for teachers can help attract and retain qualified educators in the STEM field, fostering a strong and competent teaching workforce (Baker & Turner, 2019).

Additionally, integrating real-world applications and problem-solving activities into the curriculum can enhance students' engagement and understanding of STEM concepts (Smith et al., 2020). Encouraging partnerships between educational institutions and industry professionals can also provide students with valuable exposure to real-world STEM practices and potential career paths.

By acknowledging and actively addressing these challenges, the field of STEM education can evolve to better meet the needs of students and equip them with the skills necessary for success in a rapidly advancing technological and scientific world.

To address these challenges and enhance the quality of STEM education, it is crucial to provide ongoing professional development opportunities for teachers. This can help them to improve their instructional competencies, increase their proficiency in hands-on, experiential learning techniques, and develop the skills necessary to integrate STEM education into the broader curriculum. "Research indicates that teacher education and professional development need to be of sufficient quality and quantity to affect change in teaching practices" (Matinez, 2022, p13).

It is evident that the implementation of STEM education in Kuwait is characterized by a dearth of practical experience, as students are frequently presented with a theoretical curriculum that offers limited opportunities for hands-on learning.: In order to effectively incorporate STEM education into the broader curriculum, it may necessitate a collaborative and harmonized approach between educators from diverse subjects as interdisciplinary integration is what it needed along with new updated curriculums.

In addition, for a quality of STEM education, it is imperative to provide ongoing professional development opportunities for teachers to improve their instructional competencies and increase their proficiency in hands-on, experiential learning techniques. In conclusion, while STEM education is critical for preparing students for the future, it is important to address the challenges that hinder its effective implementation. By providing ongoing teacher training and support, we can help to ensure that students receive a well-rounded, engaging STEM education that prepares them for the challenges of the modern world.

FUTURE RESEARCH DIRECTIONS

The results of this research highlight the importance of addressing teacher training and updated curriculum for effective implementation of STEM education in the classroom. However, this research was limited in scope and additional research is needed to fully understand the challenges and opportunities in STEM education.

Future research could focus on:

1. Examining the impact of comprehensive teacher training programs on teachers' confidence and competence in teaching STEM subjects.
2. Exploring the process of curriculum revision and updating, including the involvement of teachers and other stakeholders in the process.
3. Conducting a larger-scale study with a more diverse sample of teachers to understand the challenges and opportunities in STEM education across different regions and school contexts.
4. Evaluating the effectiveness of integrated and interdisciplinary approaches to teaching STEM in the classroom.

Considering the identified challenges, teacher training programs need to be designed and implemented to address the needs of STEM teachers. These programs should be comprehensive and provide hands-on workshops and practical training in the use of technology and instructional strategies for teaching STEM. Additionally, ongoing support and opportunities for collaboration with other STEM teachers can help to build teachers' confidence and competence in teaching STEM subjects.

Regarding updated curriculum, it is crucial for schools and educational institutions to engage in a collaborative and ongoing process of curriculum revision and updating. This process should involve teachers and other stakeholders, such as subject matter experts and industry professionals, to ensure that the curriculum is relevant and up to date. Furthermore, the curriculum should be designed to be integrated and interdisciplinary, incorporating real-world problems and relevant examples to make STEM subjects engaging and relevant for students.

In conclusion, the results of this study underscore the need for a comprehensive and integrated approach to improving STEM education in the classroom. Addressing the identified challenges of teacher training and updated curriculum is critical for ensuring that students receive a high-quality STEM education that prepares them for success in the 21st century. As Batdi, Talan, and Semerci (2029) pointed out, STEM education had a positive impact on students due to such reasons as offering the opportunity for team work, solidarity, cooperation and collaboration, developing communication, decision-making, leadership and feeling of achievement (p.394).

Future research should continue to explore these important areas to inform and improve STEM education practices."

CONCLUSION

In conclusion, the overall of this chapter is to fill the gap in the current literature mainly in STEM education in Kuwait and to learn from the teachers' perspectives by conducting qualitative research to explore the perceptions of teachers from the field of education in Kuwait. The outcomes and results of this research contribute to the educational field in Kuwait by providing evidence and insights about the status in the educational setting and highlight the challenges, need and gaps. However, it is important to note that this chapter has some limitations, such as the small sample size, which might affect the overall findings of the study. It is highly recommended that future research should aim to replicate this research with a larger sample size and include a more diverse population to increase the external validity of the results. considering these findings, we recommend that further research to be conducted in this area to gain a deeper understanding.

RECOMMENDATIONS

Based on the conducted research and the literature review, implementing STEM education in Kuwait's Ministry of Education (MOE) would have numerous benefits for students and the country as it is a significant step towards a sustainable education. Yet, with all the current efforts and shy attempts of teachers and educators, MOE is required to take major decisions to officially implement STEM education.

This chapter recommends that part of the process is to foster partnerships with industry and collaborate with technological companies and engineering firms to accommodate the teachers with the appropriate instructional tools to provide students with real-world experience. Additionally, it holds great significance for the Ministry of Education (MOE) to continually update the curriculum in line with the latest advancements in the field. By implementing these recommendations, the MOE can assist to promote STEM education and ensure that teachers and students in Kuwait have the knowledge and skills necessary to succeed in a rapidly changing world.

"The affiliation listed in this research paper simply reflects the current professional position of the author and should not be interpreted as any type of affiliation or support from the organization regarding the research and its results. The study is based solely on the author's expertise, and the organization is not involved or

influence over the research process. No funding from any public, commercial, or non-profit sources was received for this research."

REFERENCES

Achat-Mendes, C., Anfuso, C., Johnson, C., & Shepler, B. (2020). Learning, leaders, and STEM skills: adaptation of the supplemental instruction model to improve STEM education and build transferable skills in undergraduate courses and beyond: STEM supplemental instruction. *Journal of STEM Education: Innovations and Research*, *20*(2). https://www.jstem.org/jstem/index.php/JSTEM/article/view/2418/2135

Anisimova, T., Sabirova, F., Shatunova, O., Bochkareva, T., & Vasilev, V. (2022). The Quality of Training Staff for the Digital Economy of Russia within the Framework of STEAM Education: Problems and Solutions in the Context of Distance Learning. *Education Sciences*, *12*(2), 87. doi:10.3390/educsci12020087

Batdi, V., Talan, T., & Semerci, C. (2019). Meta-Analytic and Meta-Thematic Analysis of STEM Education. International Journal of Education in Mathematics. *Science and Technology*, *7*(4), 382–399.

Belbase, S., Mainali, B. R., Kasemsukpipat, W., Tairab, H., Gochoo, M., & Jarrah, A. (2022). At the dawn of science, technology, engineering, arts, and mathematics (STEAM) education: Prospects, priorities, processes, and problems. *International Journal of Mathematical Education in Science and Technology*, *53*(11), 2919–2955. doi:10.1080/0020739X.2021.1922943

Bertrand, M. G., & Namukasa, I. K. (2020). STEAM education: Student learning and transferable skills. *Journal of Research in Innovative Teaching & Learning*, *13*(1), 43–56. doi:10.1108/JRIT-01-2020-0003

Erstad, O., Kjällander, S., & Järvelä, S. (2021). Facing the challenges of 'digital competence' a Nordic agenda for curriculum development for the 21st century. *Nordic Journal of Digital Literacy*, *16*(2), 77–87. doi:10.18261/issn.1891-943x-2021-02-04

Imron, A., Wiyono, B. B., Hadi, S., Gunawan, I., Abbas, A., Saputra, B. R., & Perdana, D. B. (2020, November). Teacher professional development to increase teacher commitment in the era of the ASEAN Economic Community. In *2nd Early Childhood and Primary Childhood Education (ECPE 2020)* (pp. 339-343). Atlantis Press. doi:10.2991/assehr.k.201112.059

Kang, N. H. (2019). A review of the effect of integrated STEM or STEAM (science, technology, engineering, arts, and mathematics) education in South Korea. *Asia-Pacific Science Education*, *5*(1), 1–22. doi:10.118641029-019-0034-y

Kayan-Fadlelmula, F., Sellami, A., Abdelkader, N., & Umer, S. (2022). A systematic review of STEM education research in the GCC countries: Trends, gaps and barriers. *International Journal of STEM Education*, *9*(1), 1–24. doi:10.118640594-021-00319-7

Lavicza, Z., Weinhandl, R., Prodromou, T., Anđić, B., Lieban, D., Hohenwarter, M., Fenyvesi, K., Brownell, C., & Diego-Mantecón, J. M. (2022). Developing and evaluating educational innovations for STEAM education in rapidly changing digital technology environments. *Sustainability (Basel)*, *14*(12), 7237. doi:10.3390u14127237

Lee, I., & Perret, B. (2022, June). Preparing High School Teachers to Integrate AI Methods into STEM Classrooms. *Proceedings of the AAAI Conference on Artificial Intelligence*, *36*(11), 12783–12791. doi:10.1609/aaai.v36i11.21557

Li, J., Luo, H., Zhao, L., Zhu, M., Ma, L., & Liao, X. (2022). Promoting STEAM education in primary school through cooperative teaching: A design-based research study. *Sustainability (Basel)*, *14*(16), 10333. doi:10.3390u141610333

Margot, K. C., & Kettler, T. (2019). Teachers' perception of STEM integration and education: A systematic literature review. *International Journal of STEM Education*, *6*(1), 1–16. doi:10.118640594-018-0151-2

Martinez, C. (2022). Developing 21st century teaching skills: A case study of teaching and learning through project-based curriculum. *Cogent Education*, *9*(1), 2024936. doi:10.1080/2331186X.2021.2024936

Muxiddinovna, A. Z. (2022). The Place and Importance of Steam Educational Technology in Preschool Education. *Journal of Pedagogical Inventions and Practices*, *11*, 3–5.

National Academies of Sciences, Engineering, and Medicine. (2020). *The inclusion of women in STEM in Kuwait and the United States: Proceedings of a workshop*. National Academies Press.

Ozkan, G., & Umdu Topsakal, U. (2021). Investigating the effectiveness of STEAM education on students' conceptual understanding of force and energy topics. *Research in Science & Technological Education*, *39*(4), 441–460. doi:10.1080/02635143.2020.1769586

Park, W., & Cho, H. (2022). The interaction of history and STEM learning goals in teacher-developed curriculum materials: Opportunities and challenges for STEAM education. *Asia Pacific Education Review*, *23*(3), 457–474. doi:10.100712564-022-09741-0

Stehle, S. M., & Peters-Burton, E. E. (2019). Developing student 21st Century skills in selected exemplary inclusive STEM high schools. *International Journal of STEM Education*, *6*(1), 1–15. doi:10.118640594-019-0192-1

Tytler, R. (2020). STEM education for the twenty-first century. *Integrated approaches to STEM education: An international perspective*, 21-43. Research Gate.

Wu, C. H., Liu, C. H., & Huang, Y. M. (2022). The exploration of continuous learning intention in STEAM education through attitude, motivation, and cognitive load. *International Journal of STEM Education*, *9*(1), 1–22. doi:10.118640594-022-00346-y

Chapter 10
Reimagining Curriculum:
Responding to Qatari Culture Through Mathematics

Summer Bateiha
Virginia Commonwealth University School of the Arts in Qatar, Qatar

Sadia Mir
Virginia Commonwealth University School of the Arts in Qatar, Qatar

ABSTRACT

The authors of this chapter propose that the decolonization of Western course content and teaching practice is one of the necessary next steps to build a more equitable and inclusive mathematics curriculum in Qatar. Decolonization of curriculum and pedagogy involves a multilayered process including recognition of constraints placed upon curriculum and pedagogy, a disruption of these constraints, and a creation of alternatives. In this chapter, the authors outline three areas of concern: non-Eurocentric representation, single ways of learning, and elitism in mathematics; and offers pedagogical strategies as a roadmap forward towards decolonization of mathematics curriculum. This is followed by a description of a series of workshops designed for and held with teachers in the community. Finally, the authors present data about teacher perceptions of adopting culturally relevant storytelling as a tool for math education when combined with best practices in mathematics pedagogy.

DOI: 10.4018/978-1-6684-6883-8.ch010

Reimagining Curriculum

INTRODUCTION

In traditional classroom settings, mathematics is typically taught using lectures, where the teacher stands at the front of the room and provides procedural instructions to students on how to solve problems. This teaching method by and large is based on demonstrating examples similar to those students will encounter in the homework assignment. For example:

To find a common denominator, find the least common multiple (LCM) of the denominators.
Then, use the LCM as the common denominator. Now, add the numerators and keep the same denominator.

$\frac{2}{3} + \frac{5}{6}$

In most educational systems, mathematics is still taught this way. Students practice problems individually and are evaluated based on how accurately they follow the taught procedures. The teaching focuses on abstract symbols, numbers, and formulas and contains little to no use of context except when word problems may be introduced at the end of a lesson. Even then, students are often taught to disregard much of the context and search for keywords and numbers to complete the problem in a way similar to the examples previously provided. The context in these word problems is often superficial, irrelevant to students' realities, and does not affect and orient the readers' feelings about the content.

In recent years, some schooling systems have been shifting instruction to include more meaningful problem-solving through story problems like the one below, in an attempt to make mathematics more accessible and less prescribed:

Oscar ate $\frac{2}{3}$ of his pizza and John $\frac{5}{6}$ of his pizza. How much did they eat all together?

However, even with this shift, this type of context remains superficial and reflective of Western perspectives and activities, ignoring diverse cultural and social backgrounds and realities. These types of problems exclude and disadvantage students from non-Eurocentric cultures (LittleBear, 2000). And even in non-Western communities, when changes are made to problems in an attempt to make them more relevant, such as changing names from Western to local (ex. Oscar to Omar), the attempts are often superficial and do not address the underlying cultural bias in the content. Moreover, students are often not provided with sufficient time and resources to explore and develop solutions that are personal and meaningful to them. However,

Reimagining Curriculum

what if mathematics started to reflect non-Western cultures in more meaningful ways and incorporated multidisciplinary approaches like this:

Each evening for Iftar, Jassim's parents put fresh food on the table in the tent in front of their house. The food was for anyone who was hungry. Night after night, the air was full of heartfelt "thank yous."

One evening as his parents prepared the meals, Jassim looked down at all of his candy from Garangao. He knew what he wanted to do. He separated his candy into two equal piles, and placed them on the table beside the rest of the food. At the end of the night, he looked excitedly at the table. He saw that ⅔ of one pile, and ⅚ of the other pile were taken.

How much candy did he give away all together?

Figure 1. Illustration by Shouq Rahim Poor

Reimagining Curriculum

What happens to students' sense of self within the curriculum? Is a problem such as this one more inviting to a Middle Eastern student? Is learner motivation and engagement affected?

Indeed, earlier research has indicated the value of harnessing learner affect in the teaching of mathematics (Attard et al., 2016), an important element of the proposed research here. Qatar's K-12 mathematics curriculum has been adopted from various international educational models, including those of the United States of America, the United Kingdom, and other Western countries. Therefore, the curriculum and pedagogy are Western in nature, delivering a colonized form of mathematics to students who may not be able to relate to or engage with this content. The authors of this chapter propose that decolonization of Western course content and teaching practice are necessary next steps to build a more equitable and inclusive curriculum in Qatar. In order to align with international standards, Decolonization of curriculum and pedagogy involves a multilayered process including recognition of constraints placed upon curriculum and pedagogy, a disruption of these constraints, and a creation of alternatives (Shahjahan et al, 2021). In this chapter, the authors outline three areas of concern: Eurocentric representation, single ways of learning, and elitism in mathematics.

The authors offer pedagogical strategies as a roadmap forward towards the decolonization of mathematics curriculum. These strategies include harnessing the potential of diverse literature and the function of storytelling in the mathematics classroom. There is a perception within mathematics education that literacy specialists should focus on texts and literacies that are currently used in the classroom rather than suggest alternative texts and literacies, such as essays, poems, or stories (Draper et al., 2005, p. 43). This view suggests that although there are pedagogical benefits for the use of such new forms of literature in the classroom, they may not be well-suited to communicate mathematical concepts and activities. The authors of this chapter are interested in countering this argument by seeking an integrative collaborative approach which adheres to the pedagogical potential of multiple disciplines. Another strategy towards decolonization is to develop a critical and self-reflective teaching practice that, as part of its best practices, connects mathematics to the "big ideas" that form our social world, concretizes mathematics for students and supports students developing autonomous critical thinking skills. The authors outline the delivery and reception of a series of professional development workshops offered to teachers in Qatar that target such areas of mathematics education and reflect upon how adopting culturally responsive storytelling combined with best practices can lead toward a math curriculum with equity at its core.

BACKGROUND

Western Colonization in Mathematics

Eurocentric Representation

How has colonization manifested in mathematics education? The authors of this chapter propose three effects of colonization on the current mathematics curriculum. The first ramification is the lack of representation of non-Western people, whether through historical accounts or through curricular contexts. Mathematics textbooks and historical accounts of the development of mathematics often reflect a belief about the subject as universal and unbiased. These accounts contain a great deal of information about European mathematicians, who wrote about and distributed mathematical knowledge, such as Gaus, Euler, Descartes, Euclid and Pythagoras, depicting an orthodox view of mathematics (Gangolli, 1999).

According to Gangolli, the orthodox view is that:

- The beginnings of deductive mathematics in antiquity were in Greece. Greek investigators (mainly in the period from about 600 B.C. to 300 A.D.) gave a logical basis to the subject.
- After the "Greek miracle," there was a period of stagnation, the so-called dark ages, of a thousand years or more.
- At the end of the dark ages, there was a rediscovery of Greek learning that led to the Renaissance in the 15th and 16th centuries. The foundations of modern mathematics were laid during the Renaissance.
- The post-Renaissance development of mathematics, from the 17th century onwards, took place essentially in Europe. (p. 10)

However, this view disregards the contributions of many non-Western civilizations that contributed greatly to the formation of modern mathematics before, during, and after the "dark ages." These include cultures such as the Middle East, West Asia, China, India and pre-Columbian America (Gangolli). For example, according to Anderson (2006):

Euclid – the so-called 'father' of plane geometry – spent 21 years studying and translating mathematic tracts in Egypt. Pythagoras also spent years studying philosophy and science in Egypt, and possibly journeyed East to India and/or Persia, where he 'discovered' the so-called Pythmatical documents (c. 800-500 B.C.). How could a theorem whose proof was recorded in Babylonian documents dating 1,000 years before he was born be attributed to Pythagoras? (p. 44)

According to Bateiha (2016, p. 72):

This system of instruction perpetuates ideologies that impose and reward Western contributions over all other societal groups. Students from cultures outside the West are expected to study this Westernized discipline of mathematics with complete disregard of their own historical cultural mathematical ideas and contributions. This is particularly poignant in locations around the world where Western expat faculty members teach Western-based mathematics to non-Western students in their own homelands.

This view and depiction of mathematics as Eurocentric, when coupled with Western context word-problems, creates a mathematical environment bereft of Middle Eastern culture for students in Qatar.

What occurs when students do not see themselves in the curriculum they consume? Symbolic annihilation is a term first coined by George Gerbner in 1976 to describe the absence of representation, limited, or underrepresentation, of some group of people in the media, and can be understood in the social sciences to be a means of maintaining social inequality. "Representation in the fictional world signifies social existence; absence means symbolic annihilation." (Gerbner and Gross 182). The symbolic world created through the wide range of media, for example, film and tv, literature, advertising and song, defines social values, issues and status. This symbolic world can effectively support or challenge existing hegemonic structures of a society. Without diverse and inclusive storytelling, people, groups or communities whose stories are not told or are limited, face risk of societal erasure. Gaye Tuchman (1978) who focused her research on symbolic representation of women in US mass media, further defined this concept as a process that effectively omits, trivializes and condemns groups through the stories that are told. Eurocentrism in mathematics curriculum is a form of symbolic annihilation.

A Single Way of Learning

A second consequence of colonization in mathematics is the reinforcement of a one-size-fits-all, individualistic approach where students are taught formulas and procedures without emphasis on creative problem-solving or conceptual understanding. In other words, the typical classroom environment involves a lecture-style presentation of rules and step-by-step instructions, followed by repetitive exercises for individual work. Mathematics is presented as ready-made to be handed down from an authority figure. Unlike other subjects where students may be asked to think creatively and come up with their own ideas, mathematics is often presented as fixed, dry, unimaginative and repetitive. Typically, students are not given much time to grapple with unresolved issues, nor are they encouraged to explore problems from multiple perspectives or use different solutions methods. Students are rarely encouraged to work with others to come up with innovative strategies and understandings. This lack of opportunities for students to work collaboratively, analyze problems from multiple perspectives, and develop their own ideas, leads to a fragmented view of mathematics as a set of memorized rules instead of a logical and interconnected system of ideas.

Unfortunately, even teachers of mathematics often view the subject as just a set of rules and procedures (Bateiha & Reeder, 2014; Muir & Livy, 2012). For some students, success in their classrooms is often determined by students who obey and imitate, rather than demonstrate independent thought and problem-solving skills. Other students succeed because of their access to resources outside of the classroom that help them expand their knowledge. This creates an environment where students do not take ownership of their learning and wait for explicit guidance, rather than using their own reasoning and logical thinking. This teaching approach undermines students' confidence in their own abilities to do mathematics and become autonomous thinkers (Marchionda, Bateiha, Autin, 2014). In this system, students learn to play a school game in that they do not take the initiative to tackle their work on their own, and there is little regard for whether or not what they are being asked to do makes sense or is logical. Educators often talk about creating critical and innovative thinkers to lead the world into a better future, but construct an environment where they reward those who do not question what they are asked to do. According to De Corte, Verschaffel, & Greer (2000),

[I]t is not so much a cognitive deficit that causes pupils' abstention from sense making when doing arithmetic word problems in a typical school setting. To the contrary they are rather acting in accordance with the "rules of the game" which they belie[ve] to regulate the interactive ritual in which they are involved (p. 68).

This way of doing mathematics leads many students to believe that they are incapable of doing mathematics on their own, and that they need to be told how to do it by a more knowledgeable person (Bateiha, 2016). This develops a belief in students and teachers that mathematics is something reserved for certain gifted individuals. The teacher is needed to solve problems and students are not given opportunities to discover what they are capable of doing on their own or through group work. Non-Western forms of knowledge construction, such as working collectively and learning through storytelling, are often disregarded and undervalued. This can be particularly harmful to students from underprivileged cultures who lack access to resources that offer additional assistance, such as the guidance of tutors or successfully-educated family members, and may lead to internalized negative beliefs about their ability to do mathematics. (Little Bear, 2000; Porier, 2007).

Elitism in Mathematics

A third repercussion of colonization has also been perpetuating a perception of mathematics as an elitist and detached subject. School often depicts mathematics as something mysterious and disconnected from students' everyday lives. Mathematics is presented with abstract symbols, formulas, and equations and is learned in a mechanistic fashion. Real-life activities, for example that students are engaged in, are absent even though these connections are very much present. Research suggests that connecting mathematics to students' lived experiences and culture can enhance their understanding and create a natural progression from concrete to abstract concepts (Widada, Herawaty, & Lubis, 2018). By presenting mathematics as a subject that is divorced from real-world applications, students are less likely to appreciate its relevance and importance in their daily lives. It is plucked from obscurity. When mathematics is linked to contexts, students are more able to build conceptual understanding of the material that will last as they progress through courses.

An example of elitism in mathematics can be seen in a paper Haris (1987) wrote about the similarity between knitting the heel of a sock and an engineering task of modeling a right-angled cylindrical pipe. Although both tasks require mathematical problem-solving skills, the knitting task is often regarded as a routine domestic chore primarily associated with women, while the pipe task is considered an engineering problem tackled by expert academics. According to Bateiha (2016), this differentiation highlights the presence of inherent sexism within formal educational conditioning. This type of elitism creates a particular image around mathematics that leads many to believe that they do not know how to do mathematics, even when they are engaging in mathematical tasks naturally in their lived experiences.

There are many more examples of this elitism that creates a divide between mathematics in an academic setting versus mathematics in life. In 1976, Spradbery documented the struggles of a group of teenagers who, despite receiving extensive remedial help, were unable to perform basic mathematical operations in school, but "kept and raced pigeons…[w]eighing, measuring, timing, using map scales, buying, selling, interpreting timetables, devising schedules, calculating probabilities and average" (p. 273) outside of school. These students "left school 'hating everyfink what goes on in maffs' [*sic*]" (p. 237). They perceived the mathematics in the classroom as something different and separate from the complex mathematics being performed in their extracurricular activities. This elitism devalues students' natural abilities to do mathematics and jumps to mathematics as abstraction in a way that portrays the subject as mystical and inaccessible. This particularly effects students from certain backgrounds, races, and genders, here again, where access to resources such as tutors or academically privileged families is limited (Powell & Frankenstein, 1997). A paper written by Ezeife noted that,

[O]ne of the reasons advanced for the high dropout rate and poor performance in examinations by the few aboriginal students who enroll in mathematics or science is that mathematics and science taught in school is bereft of aboriginal cultural and environmental content...American Indian students' capacity to learn mathematics is influenced by language, culture, and learning style. However, the methods by which mathematics is typically presented do not take into consideration these factors. (Davidson as cited by Ezeife, 2002, p. 177)

Establishing a Decolonizing Practice

How can these effects of colonization be addressed in mathematics education? As a whole, decolonization is an act of delinking from the hegemonic narrative of Western civilization, and it is engaged with building knowledge that supersedes the current predominance of Western knowledge (Mignolo, 2011). One method to decolonize a curriculum involves creating course content and multimodal lessons that invites students to engage with the plurality of their own diverse histories and lived experiences. The authors argue for the use of storytelling to allow for such engagement and to challenge existing hegemonic structures found in society, and those that are perpetuated within mathematics education. Storytelling has been a part of the fabric of Arab culture and society, and is "likely the oldest form of teaching, allowing generations of humans to share cultural knowledge to be remembered over time" (Landrum et al., 2019, p. 247). Humans use stories to make sense of the world (Bruner, 1990); they serve as a foundation for humans to create their sense of self and identity, "through narrative, we construct, reconstruct, in some ways reinvent today and tomorrow" (Bruner, 2002, p. 93).

Stories typically revolve around one or two protagonists who journey through a sequence of events, grapple with a central conflict, and reach a resolution. Within this expedition, the main characters often undergo some form of personal growth, and navigate and negotiate their way through their social world. As a pedagogical strategy, the use of story offers opportunities for students to create meaning collaboratively, to unpack a story's message, meaning and purpose, and to collectively decipher social values and structures. Utilizing stories in the classroom, among other outcomes, help learners understand "one's place in the world" (Gallo, 2007, p. 110), "forge a sense of interconnectedness and community" (Stallworth et al., p. 478), increase knowledge retention (Locket and Jones, 2009, p. 176) and support imaginative development. (Ellis, 1997, p. 21). Culturally-responsive literature can promote social bonding.

Research demonstrates that to achieve basic cultural identity, individuals must feel a sense of "belonging or connection to one's larger culture" (Ting-Toomey, 2005, p. 215). A diverse symbolic world created by diverse literature can both promote and support such belonging.

Outside of the classroom, storytelling can serve as a means to create and share cultural knowledge. In particular, within Arab culture, storytelling is steeped in rich cultural heritage and history, and as a cultural practice, transmits knowledge, wisdoms, belief systems, and traditions from one generation to the next. The authors argue that there is a place for this type of storytelling within the classroom walls to connect culture and curriculum in both practice and content, and that this integration can produce a nuanced curriculum that is more attuned and responsive to Arab students' lived experiences and complex realities.

In Haida Gwaii, a rural community in British Columbia, Canada, an Indigenous storywork in mathematics education project delivers curriculum founded upon values of "respect, responsibility, reverence and reciprocity" (Archibald et al, 2019, p. 119) with an aim to develop interconnectivity between teachers, students and community, and to build a curriculum honoring culturally-responsive consciousness and practices. Embedded stories were built upon existing Indigenous knowledge and wisdom, local culture and community, and served as a means to "give expression to Aboriginal philosophies, world views, and social relations" (Castellano, 2000, p.23). In this mathematics educational model, a central tenet was to create a curriculum that is deeply inclusive of Indigenous knowledge and ways of being, and one that connects mathematics to culture and place. This learner-centered and culturally-responsive approach offers a counter-practice to Western ideas of how to create and pursue knowledge. On storytelling, "the point about the stories is not that they simply tell a story, or tell a story simply. These new stories contribute to a collective story in which every indigenous person has a place" (Smith, 1999, p.144). In contrast to one-size-fits-all approaches to curriculum and instruction, decolonizing and culturally responsive pedagogy recognizes cultural background as one factor that can shape how students learn and engage differently within educational spaces, and it seeks relevant curricular content, instructional techniques, and community-building strategies.

METHODOLOGY

Culturally-Responsive Curricular Content

The authors of this chapter first addressed the effects of colonization through the creation of culturally responsive stories as a means to disrupt current storytelling trends and offer an alternative. Their first attempt was to write the children's book,

Spring Bloom: A Math Adventure Story. The authors aimed to offer a story that connected a mathematical concept to Arab culture and place, and to infuse cultural values and sensibilities into the narrative. *Spring Bloom* (see Figure 1) tells the story of two Arab siblings, Aliya and Zade, who help a young falcon reunite with his family at the spring bloom annual event. Aliya, Zade and the young falcon must solve a series of riddles to obtain a secret password to the event. The riddles ask the protagonists to problem-solve based on the mathematical concept of place value, and are based on geographical knowledge of the desert. The setting takes place in the mangroves, an accurate Middle Eastern topography. The story incorporates culturally representative motifs and imagery. The characters engage with their geographic landscape including specific flora and fauna. These narrative choices aim to move past surface descriptive cultural representation to one that is more dynamic and layered. In terms of values messaging, the story also encourages young readers to reflect upon empathy, collaborative team work, community, and social behavior.

Figure 2. Spring Bloom cover

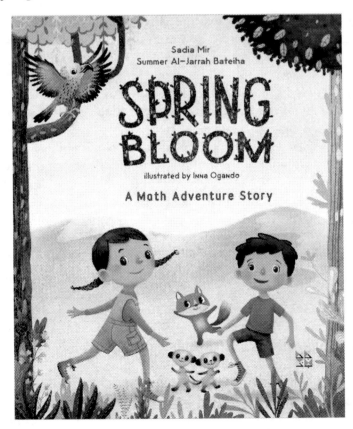

Reimagining Curriculum

Figure 3. Visualization of place value

To reiterate, literature in the mathematics classroom can be effective as a pedagogical tool due to its concreteness, specificity and narrative organization (Finkel, 2000). Readers are able to immerse themselves in the imaginative world of the story; this narrative transportation lends to an immersive experience (Green & Brook, 2000). Research shows that narrative presentation supports memory recall and retention of words over rote memorization (Bower & Clark, 1969). In a story reading circle with the target age group (6–7-year-old children), the authors read *Spring Bloom* to observe its effectiveness to engage children in mathematics. The young learners were given manipulatives and a numbers grid to work out the math problems found in the story. At the end of the reading, students commented on the experience:

- "adventurous," "fun," "mischievous"
- "Are we going to do the math?"
- "Is the party over?"
- "It felt fun, but we also learned math at the same time."

We could see a potential for positive learning outcomes as a result of the culturally-responsive narrative presentation of the mathematical concept. In the first year of publication, *Spring Bloom* won first-place awards including one in the category of education. At this point, propelled by the book's positive reception, the authors began experimenting with the use of different story forms in the mathematics curriculum and for different age groups. The authors and their research team that comprised of one mathematics education faculty, one literature and writing faculty, and one design faculty and four art and design undergraduate students, created culturally-based math vignettes as per the following:

Original Math Problem:

To divide fractions, convert mixed numbers to improper fractions. Then, invert the second fraction. Now, multiply across the numerators and across the denominators, and simplify the resulting fraction.

½ ÷ 4 ½

Traditional Word Problem:

A pizza is cut into five pieces. Four of the pieces are the same size, and the fifth piece is half the size of each of the others. What fraction of the pizza is the smallest piece?

Culturally Relevant Story and Visualization:

Figure 4. Fraction Problem Illustration by Ghada Ali

It is Ramadan. The sky is clear except for the bright orange and yellow setting sun which marks the breaking of fast. All across the city, families sit down for Iftar.

In one home, Ali watches his mother cut the perfectly round kunafeh, his favorite dessert. His mother cuts five pieces, one for each member of the family. Four of the pieces are the same size, and the fifth piece is ½ the size of each of the others. Ali gets the smallest piece and exclaims, "It's so small!" His mother looks at him with a smile. She knows his eyes are bigger than his stomach. "We must all be grateful for the food we eat, Ali." She continues, "Ok, let's play a game. If you can answer the next question, and if you are still hungry, I will share my piece with you." Ali nods. "Here is the question: What fraction of the kunafeh is the smallest piece?"

Teacher Workshops

The authors facilitated a series of professional development workshops that offered an opportunity for teachers in Qatar to come together to investigate nontraditional math pedagogy and consider the use of multimodal (storytelling, interactive, culturally relevant) approaches in mathematics education. The mathematics concepts focused on middle grades topics that included geometry, algebra, integers, and proportional reasoning. The researchers used problem posing, math manipulatives, storytelling, illustrations, and fluency activities to demonstrate best practices in mathematics education that could be used in a Middle Eastern context. Teachers used hands-on mathematics manipulatives and worked in groups to solve these problems experientially and shared their perceptions of these teaching methods. A component of these workshops revolved around the introduction of the culturally-based mathematical vignettes designed by the research team which centered upon Arab culture and contextualized mathematical concepts in real-life scenarios. Teachers were also provided with mathematics children literature such as *Spring Bloom: A Mathematics Adventure Story*, *Two of Everything* by Lily Toy Hong, *Grandfather Tang's Story* by Ann Tompert, *One Grain of Rice* by Charlotte Dumaresq Hunt, and *Fractions in Disguise* by Edward Einhom. The workshops also consisted of data collection via teacher surveys (pre and post workshop).

Twenty-three teachers attended the workshops from schools across Qatar. Teachers came from various cultural backgrounds, which included the Middle East, North America, and the United Kingdom. The workshops spanned five days that fell on the weekend: two days were in Fall 2021, two days in Spring 2022 and one day in Fall 2022. Teachers were solicited through an open call emailed to English-speaking international schools across Qatar and through social media channels, i.e., Instagram, Facebook and WhatsApp.

The authors recognized the importance in designing workshops where participants were vital to the research outcomes. Teachers participated in the construction of ideas, as active participants, in line with constructivist theories of learning (von Glasersfeld, 1998). Just as the authors hoped to emphasize to the teachers the importance of students constructing their own knowledge in the mathematics classroom, teachers were the learners and creators in the workshops. In particular, it was vital to have the teachers share their own knowledge, and inform and shape the direction of activities alongside the researchers. Although the researchers had outlined prompts, the workshop emerged organically based on the participation of the educators. To accomplish these objectives, trust was paramount. Core strategies for developing trust included engaging perspectives and expertise, and reserving ample time for discussion at every step of the process. Also, receiving input from participants on their teaching realities via pre and post surveys and discussion-based activities was key to deeper understanding of research findings. An aim was for the math teachers to take ownership of whichever aspects of multimodal teaching practices resonated, and to then share such knowledge to other educators in their networks.

Data Collection and Analysis

Qualitative and quantitative data were collected from participants through pre and post workshop surveys, and from researcher reflections on the workshops. Data collection also included researcher observational notes taken during the workshops. One researcher sat at the back of the room and transcribed discussions between participants. The other researcher, who facilitated the workshops, provided reflections of her experience during the workshops. For this chapter, qualitative data are presented.

The researchers analyzed the data through interpretivism, a major paradigm in educational research (Bunniss & Kelly, 2010; Humphrey, 2013), which centers on the idea that

our capacity for consciousness in relation to ourselves, others and the world is the distinguishing mark of our humanity, so we conduct our affairs in accordance with our motives, meanings, life-goals and self-concepts, and we co-create cultures with shared patterns of feeling, thinking, believing and doing. This reconfigures our epistemological orientation since the only way of understanding the social world is to draw from the well of our own humanity in order to make sense of the other person or community from the inside out. (Humphrey, 2013, p. 7)

Fundamental to interpretive research is the acknowledgment of its subjective nature, in particular, researcher subjectivity. Interpretive educational research serves as a method to offer purposeful reflection and continued investigation of reality, which is complex, nuanced, and contains the researcher's subjectivity. In this type of research, investigators must consider their own positionality, histories, and worldviews when engaging in data analysis.

In the context of teacher professional development, interpretive inquiry engages the researchers in the process of critical questioning, where they must consider the identities and experiences of both the participants and themselves. The researchers in this study are women who are Western-trained university educators. One researcher is an Arab-American mathematics education professor who has lived in the Middle East for 18 years, while the second researcher is a Pakistani-Canadian English professor who has lived in the Middle East for 12 years. It is through the particular lenses of these researchers that data were interpreted and analyzed.

RESULTS

All respondents expressed an interest for more professional development in a similar vein. A teacher remarked, "I am very grateful for your time and the knowledge you so engagingly imparted." Another teacher noted that this was the best teacher development workshop she had attended in her 20 years in Qatar. The reasons for this enthusiasm seemed to revolve around some particular themes for the teachers. Those were discovering they had a procedural rather than conceptual understanding of the curriculum, realizing the importance of storytelling for engaging students emotionally in mathematics, and recognizing the importance of integrating culture into the mathematics curriculum.

Several teachers made newfound realizations about their lack of conceptual understanding behind the procedures they teach. For example, one teacher commented,"[Y]ou proved to me that my knowledge of math is largely procedural… I am not aware of much of the concepts behind the procedural math."

Many teachers also commented on the usefulness and benefit of "cross-curricular integration with literacy" to create more dynamic mathematics lessons. Along this line, one teacher observed that although they integrated storytelling as a teaching method in other content areas, doing similar in mathematics had not occurred to them prior to the workshop. This participant reflected on the connection between mathematics and story: "[As] humans we are story driven. Context is very important to us. Furthermore, context actually trumps process: given a certain context, certain assumptions materialize, which in turn forces the process to adapt."

One teacher expressed:

Mathematics is a human endeavor. The big ideas in math specifically, easily translate to big ideas in life. I feel the purpose of education is to both help students grow into their jobs, and to allow the same students to be human vehicles that would solve our social concerns, and bring new healthy ideas to the world. I feel if we teach math the way that was presented in this workshop, it is possible to do both. In a sense math allows the liberal arts and sciences, and the technical sciences to connect to each other. All disciplines intersect at the big ideas.

When asked if teachers used storytelling as a mode of teaching mathematics, some participants identified a lack of resources and shortage of time. However, when teachers were given the packet of culturally relevant mathematical stories, they expressed enthusiasm for numerous reasons. Having these types of resources in the math classroom demonstrated a viable way to integrate local culture, another subject they were required to teach; this integration could save time. The teachers could also envision these curricular materials serving as a bridge for students between themselves and the content, helping them connect and relate to the subject matter.

When asked what was the most useful part of the workshop, one participant responded: "I feel the entire workshop was useful." This participant went on to state that allowing teachers to use the manipulatives experientially as if they were students rather than show-and-tell different methods, was transformative. "Having us go through the actual methods and using the teaching tools as a group was very effective in getting us to appreciate how to implement the tools in our classrooms." The researchers received requests to expand further into Qatar's educational communities.

DISCUSSION

Who is the curriculum designed for? Whose voices, experiences and values are supported? Which voices and experiences are missing and to what effect? How can instructors, as a community of practice, challenge existing effects of colonization in mathematics education? This study reinforces the need for visibility in mathematics education where learners "see themselves" in the curriculum they consume, where the curriculum actively challenges continued Eurocentrism and Western-focused contexts, and the teaching of mathematics shifts away from the perception of an elite discipline entrenched in procedural rules. Whereas the authors do not attempt to generalize their findings, they recognize the impact these effects can have on learners outside of these boundaries and who belong to other cultural communities, as demonstrated by their research in the target Qatari context.

Through this research, the authors consider how a culturally-responsive curriculum, coupled with best teaching practices, presents a potential to transform the classroom

Reimagining Curriculum

into a holistic learning environment that centers on the humanity of the learners. The authors propose that the use of storytelling to share, keep and construct knowledge, and teaching practices that encourage creativity and independence of thought in learners, is a way forward in mathematics education. A curriculum that embeds indigenous and culturally responsive themes can offer deep learning by connecting students to their value. This approach can take mathematical problem-solving beyond abstract equations into meaningful exercises. This curriculum lends to the inclusion of their own cultural mathematical ideas and contributions, which paints a more accurate picture of the historical development of the field of mathematics.

How can we implement such educational change? This research study highlights the potential of a multi-pronged collaboration between researchers, educators and the community which it serves. This vital cultural representation contributes to outputs that evolve from within the community, rather than outputs made about and for them. For our project, this included researchers from mathematics education, literature and creative writing, and art and design, and undergraduate art and design students, some of whom were members of the local Qatari community. The teacher workshops moved the research further within the educational communities. Similar to the research aims, the co-collaboration is based on principles of equity and inclusion. This research encouraged the authors to further develop and articulate their understandings of community-engaged research practice, and demonstrated how creative research, through the co-construction of a multidisciplinary mathematics curriculum with the communities it serves, can be transformative.

The data collected in research such as this one can be used to further shape what histories, experiences and narratives are shared in the classroom, and can be used to disrupt existing inequitable representation and offer alternative ways of teaching. The authors of this chapter acknowledge that this is only a glimpse of the totality of what occurred in the creation and execution of the ongoing project. This study is one of what would need to be an ongoing series of research endeavors that could lead to substantive change.

This collaborative research project is a part of the *Multimodal Mathematics Research Lab: Storytelling, Interactivity and Cultural Relevance* and is supported by a Virginia Commonwealth University School of the Arts Research Lab grant.

REFERENCES

Anderson, S. (2006). Historical, cultural, and social implications of mathematics. In E. Gutstein & B. Peterson (Eds.), *Rethinking mathematics: teaching social justice by the number* (pp. 43–44). Rethinking Schools.

Archibald, J., Nicol, C., & Yovanovich, J. (2019). Transformative education for Aboriginal mathematics learning: Indigenous storywork as methodology. In J. Archibald, J. Lee-Morgan, & J. De Santolo (Eds.), *Decolonizing Research: Indigenous Storywork as Methodology* (pp. 118–142). Zed Books.

Attard, C., Ingram, N., Forgasz, H., Leder, G., & Grootenboer, P. (2016). Mathematics education and the affective domain. In J. Bobis, J. Way, C. Attard, J. Anderson, H. McMaster, & K. Cartwright (Eds.), *Research in Mathematics Education in Australasia 2012-2015*. Springer. doi:10.1007/978-981-10-1419-2_5

Bateiha, S. (2016). Creating space for critical consciousness in the mathematics classroom. In L. Seawright & A. Hodges (Eds.), *Learning across borders: International and transnational education*. Cambridge Scholars Press. https://www.cambridgescholars.com/product/978-1-4438-8583-6

Bateiha, S., & Reeder, S. (2014). Transforming perceptions of elementary preservice teachers' mathematical knowledge for and through social understanding. *RIEJS: International Journal of Education for Social Justice, 3*(1), 71–86.

Bear, L. L. (2000). Jagged worldviews colliding. *Reclaiming Indigenous voice and vision, 77*.

Bower, G. H., & Clark, M. C. (1969). Narrative stories as mediators for serial learning. *Psychonomic Science, 14*(4), 181–182. doi:10.3758/BF03332778

Bruner, J. S. (1990). *Acts of meaning*. Harvard University Press.

Bruner, J. S. (2002). *Making stories: Law, literature, life*. Farrar, Straus and Giroux.

Bunniss, S., & Kelly, D. R. (2010). Research paradigms in medical education research. *Medical Education, 44*(4), 358–366. doi:10.1111/j.1365-2923.2009.03611.x PMID:20444071

Castellano, M. B. (2000). Updating Aboriginal traditions of knowledge. In G. Dei, B. Hall, & D. Rosenberg (Eds.), *Indigenous Knowledges in Global Contexts: Multiple Readings of Our World* (pp. 21–36). University of Toronto Press.

De Corte, E., Verschaffel, L., & Greer, B. (2000, November). Connecting mathematics problem solving to the real world. In *Proceedings of the International Conference on Mathematics Education into the 21st Century: Mathematics for living* (pp. 66-73). IEEE.

Draper, R. J., Broomhead, P., Jensen, A. P., Siebert, D. N., & Jeffrey, D. (2005). Aims and criteria for collaboration in content-area classrooms. In R. J. Draper & G. P. Broomhead (Eds.), *Re)imagining content-area literacy instruction*. Teachers College Press.

Ellis, B. F. (1997). Why Tell Stories? *Storytelling Magazine*, 9(1), 21–23.

Ezeife, A. (2002). Mathematics and culture nexus: The interactions of culture and mathematics in an aboriginal classroom. *International Education Journal*, 3(3), 176–187. Retrieved January 1, 2009, from http://ehlt.flinders.edu.au/education/iej/articles/v3n3/Ezeife/paper.pdf

Finkel, D. L. (2000). *Teaching with your mouth shut*. Boynton/Cook.

Gallo, D. (2007). Making time for literature with Middle Eastern perspectives. *English Journal*, 96(3), 110–113. doi:10.2307/30047310

Gangolli, R. (1999). *Asian contributions to mathematics*. Portland Public Schools Geocultural Baseline Essay Series.

Gerbner, G., & Gross, L. (2017). Living with television: The violence profile. In *The Fear of Crime* (pp. 169–195). Routledge. doi:10.4324/9781315086613-10

Green, M. C., & Brock, T. C. (2000). The role of transportation in the persuasiveness of public narratives. *Journal of Personality and Social Psychology*, 79(5), 701–721. doi:10.1037/0022-3514.79.5.701 PMID:11079236

Haris, M. (1987). An example of traditional women's work as a mathematics resource. *For the Learning of Mathematics*, 7(3), 26–28.

Humphrey, C. (2013). A paradigmatic map of professional education research. *Social Work Education*, 32(1), 3–16. doi:10.1080/02615479.2011.643863

Koss, M. D. (2015). Diversity in contemporary picturebooks: A content analysis. *Journal of Children's Literature*, 41(1), 32–42.

Landrum, R. E., Brakke, K., & McCarthy, M. A. (2019). The pedagogical power of storytelling. *Scholarship of Teaching and Learning in Psychology*, 5(3), 247–253. doi:10.1037tl0000152

Larrick, N. (1965, September 11). The all-White world of children's books. *Saturday Review*, pp. 63–65, 84–85.

Marchionda, H., Bateiha, S., & Autin, M. (2014). The effects of instruction on developing autonomous learners in a college statistics class. *Annual Perspectives in Mathematics Education*. National Council of Teachers of Mathematics: Using Research to Improve Instruction.

Mignolo, W. (2011). *The Darker Side of Western Modernity: Global Futures, Decolonial Options*. Duke University Press.

Muir, T., & Livy, S. (2012). What do they know? A comparison of pre-service teachers' and in-service teachers' decimal mathematical content knowledge. *International Journal for Mathematics Teaching and Learning*, 1-15.

Poirier, L. (2007). Teaching mathematics and the Inuit community. *Canadian Journal of Math. Science & Technology Education*, 7(1), 53–67.

Powell, B., & Frankenstein, M. (Eds.). (1997). *Ethnomathematics: Challenging Eurocentrism in Mathematics Education*. State University of New York Press.

Shahjahan, R. A., Estera, A. L., Surla, K. L., & Edwards, K. T. (2022). "Decolonizing" curriculum and pedagogy: A comparative review across disciplines and global higher education contexts. *Review of Educational Research*, 92(1), 73–113. doi:10.3102/00346543211042423

Smith, L. T. (1999). *Decolonizing methodologies: Research and Indigenous peoples*. Zed Books.

Spradbery, J. (1976). Conservative pupils? Pupil resistance to curriculum innovation in mathematics. In G. Witty and M. Young (Eds.), Explorations in the Politics of School Knowledge (pp. 236-243). Driffeld: Nafferton.

Stallworth, B. J., Gibbons, L., & Fauber, L. (2006). It's not on the list: An exploration of teachers' perspectives on using multicultural literature. *Journal of Adolescent & Adult Literacy*, 49(6), 478–489. doi:10.1598/JAAL.49.6.3

Taylor, P. C., & Medina, M. (2011). Educational research paradigms: From positivism to pluralism. *College Research Journal*, 1(1), 1–16.

Ting-Toomey, S. (2005). Identity negotiation theory: Crossing cultural boundaries. In W. B. Gudykunst (Ed.), *Theorizing about intercultural communication* (pp. 211–233). Sage Publications Ltd.

Tuchman, G. (1978). The symbolic annihilation of women by the mass media. In G. Tuchman, A. K. Daniels, & J. Benet (Eds.), *Hearth and home: Images of women in the mass media* (pp. 3–38). Oxford University Press.

Von Glasersfeld, E. (1998). Cognition, construction of knowledge, and teaching. In *Constructivism in science education* (pp. 11–30). Springer. doi:10.1007/978-94-011-5032-3_2

Widada, W., Herawaty, D., & Lubis, A. N. M. T. (2018, September). Realistic mathematics learning based on the ethnomathematics in Bengkulu to improve students' cognitive level. [). IOP Publishing.]. *Journal of Physics: Conference Series*, *1088*(1), 012028. doi:10.1088/1742-6596/1088/1/012028

KEY TERMS AND DEFINITIONS

Culturally Responsive Pedagogy: A teaching approach that recognizes cultural background as one factor that can shape how students learn and engage differently within educational spaces, and seeks relevant curricular content, instructional techniques, and community-building strategies.

Decolonizing Curriculum: Course content and multimodal lessons that reflect the plurality of diverse histories and lived experiences of marginalized and historically oppressed communities.

Eurocentrism: A worldview that reinforces and favors Western ideas and civilization over those of non-Western cultural groups.

Hegemony: The dominance of one group's ways of knowing over other social groups, often imposing political, cultural, social, historical perspectives.

Interpretivism: A paradigm in educational research which is founded on the idea that reality is socially constructed, and we perceive such reality based on our subjective experiences.

Multimodal Mathematics: Multiple and diverse ways of learning mathematics including, but not limited to, storytelling, interactivity, and employing culturally-relevant instructional strategies.

Symbolic Annihilation: The absence of representation, limited, or underrepresentation, of some group of people in the media, which can be understood in the social sciences as a means of maintaining social inequality.

Compilation of References

Abulibdeh, E. S., & Hassan, S. S. S. (2011). E-learning interactions, information technology self efficacy and student achievement at the University of Sharjah, UAE. *Australasian Journal of Educational Technology*, 27(6). doi:10.14742/ajet.926

Achat-Mendes, C., Anfuso, C., Johnson, C., & Shepler, B. (2020). Learning, leaders, and STEM skills: adaptation of the supplemental instruction model to improve STEM education and build transferable skills in undergraduate courses and beyond: STEM supplemental instruction. *Journal of STEM Education: Innovations and Research*, 20(2). https://www.jstem.org/jstem/index.php/JSTEM/article/view/2418/2135

Adler-Milstein, J., Salzberg, C., Franz, C., Orav, E. J., Newhouse, J. P., & Bates, D. W. (2013). Effect of electronic health records on health care costs: Longitudinal comparative evidence from community practices. *Annals of Internal Medicine*, 159(2), 97–104. doi:10.7326/0003-4819-159-2-201307160-00004 PMID:23856682

Ajzen, I., & Madden, T. J. (1986). Prediction of goal-directed behavior: Attitudes, intentions, and perceived behavioral control. *Journal of Experimental Social Psychology*, 22(5), 453–474. doi:10.1016/0022-1031(86)90045-4

Akgündüz, D., Aydeniz, M., Çakmakçı, G., Çavaş, B., Çorlu, M., Öner, T., & Özdemir, S. (2015). *STEM Eğitimi Türkiye Raporu: "Günümüz modası mı yoksa gereksinim mi?"*. İstanbul Aydın Üniversitesi STEM Merkezi.

Akgündüz, D., & Ertepınar, H. (2015). *Stem Eğitimi Türkiye Raporu, Günün Modası mı Yoksa Gereksinim mi?* Scala.

Al Azmeh, S. (2019). The relationship between e-learning service and student satisfaction a case study at the Syrian virtual university (SVU). *Business. Management in Education*, 17(0), 49–71. doi:10.3846/bme.2019.7451

Al Gothami, S. S., & Saeed, S. (2021). Digital transformation and usability: User acceptance of tawakkalna application during covid-19 in saudi arabia. In *Pandemic, Lockdown, and Digital Transformation* (pp. 95–109). Springer.

Alan, B. (2017). *Fen bilgisi öğretmen adaylarının bütünleşik öğretmenlik bilgilerinin desteklenmesi: STEM uygulamalarına hazırlama eğitimi.* Yüksek Lisans Tezi, Fırat Üniversitesi, Eğitim Bilimleri Enstitüsü.

Alayyar, G. M., Aljeeran, R. K., & Almodaires, A. A. (2018). Information and Communication Technology and Educational Policies in Primary and Secondary Education in the Middle East and North African (MENA) Region. *Springer International Handbooks of Education, 1–21.* Springer. doi:. doi:10.1007/978-3-319-53803-7_91

Albugamis, S., & Vian, A. (2015). Success factors for ICT implementation in Saudi Secondary schools: From the perspective of ICT directors head teachers, teachers and students [IJEDICT]. *International Journal of Education and Development Using Information and Communication Technology, 11*(1), 36–54.

Alexander, R. (2005). Culture, dialogue and learning: Notes on an emerging pedagogy (Keynote Address). *10th International Conference: Education, Culture and Cognition: intervening for growth, International Association for Cognitive Education and Psychology (IACEP).* University of Durham, United Kingdom.

Alexander, R. (2008). In Education for all, the quality imperative and the problem of pedagogy. Consortium for Research on Educational Access. Transitions and Equity.

Alfarah, M. & Bosco, A. (2016). The role of icts in rebuilding education in areas of armed conflicts: the syrian case. *Edulearn.* . doi:10.21125/edulearn.2016.0359

Alghamdi, A. A. (2022). Exploring early childhood teachers' beliefs about STEAM education in Saudi Arabia. *Early Childhood Education Journal.* doi:10.100710643-021-01303-0

Alghamdi, A. K. H., Al Ghamdi, K. S., & Kim, S. Y. (2022). Epidemiology in middle school science curricula: A COVID-19 pre–post intervention. *Journal of Science Education and Technology, 31*(5), 583–593. doi:10.100710956-022-09975-y PMID:35730014

Alghamdi, J., Mostafa, F., & Abubshait, A. (2022). Exploring technology readiness and practices of kindergarten student-teachers in Saudi Arabia: A mixed-methods study. *Education and Information Technologies, 27*(6), 7851–7868. doi:10.100710639-022-10920-0 PMID:35233174

Al-Hinai, M., Al-Balushi, S.M. & Ambusaidi, A. (2020). The effectiveness of engineering design in developing engineering habits of mind among eight grade students in Sultanate of Oman. *Journal of Education & Psychological Studies* (Oman), *14*(2), 362-380. doi:10.24200/jeps.vol14iss2pp362-380

Al-Hosni, A., Al-Balushi, S. M., Ambusaidi, A., & Alkharusi, H. (2022). ((accepted). The effectiveness of teaching using a phone application based on the gamification approach in developing the motivation for achievement among fourth-grade students in light of the Corona pandemic (Covid-19). [University of Jordan]. *Studies: Educational Sciences.*

Al-Jabari, M., Amro, B., Jabareen, H., Khadir, Y., & Taweel, A. (2018). Development of case study-based approach for learning undergraduate students to effectively understanding and use of ehr. *15th ACS/IEEE International Conference on Computer Systems and Applications*. IEEE.

Alkharusi, A. (2020). *Perceptions of teachers and students participating in the STEM OMAN program*. [Unpublished Master's Thesis, Sultan Qaboos University. Muscat, Sultanate of Oman].

Almgadmi, N. Y. (2018). *Use of ICT in Secondary Schools in Libya: A Teachers' Perspective*. [Master's thesis, Eastern Mediterranean University (EMU)-Doğu Akdeniz Üniversitesi (DAÜ)].

Alnashmi, M., Salman, A., AlHumaidi, H., Yunis, M., & Al-Enezi, N. (2022). Exploring the health information management system of kuwait: Lessons and opportunities. *Applied System Innovation*, 5(1), 25. doi:10.3390/asi5010025

Alomari, A. M. (2009). Investigating online learning environments in a web-based math course in Jordan. [IJEDICT]. *International Journal of Education and Development Using Information and Communication Technology*, 5(3), 19–36.

Alotaibi, W. H., & Alghamdi, A. K. H. (2022). Teaching 21st century skills in Saudi Arabia with attention to elementary science reading habits. *Education Sciences*, 12(6), 392. doi:10.3390/educsci12060392

Alqahtani, A., Aljarullah, A. J., Crowder, R., & Wills, G. (2017). Barriers to the adoption of ehr systems in the kingdom of saudi arabia: An exploratory study using a systematic literature review. *Journal of Health Informatics in Developing Countries*, 11(2).

Alqiam, H. A. A. (2021). The challenges facing primary school students in Jordan in learning math online during the Coronavirus Crisis. *Journal of Arts, Literature. Humanities and Social Sciences*, 64. doi:10.33193/JALHSS.64.2021.421

Alshref, M. H., Abas, H., & Abu Bakar, N. A. (2021). The adoption of ICT in Libyan Higher Education Institutions (lheis): Theoretical models and challenges. *Journal of Physics: Conference Series*, 1897(1), 012003. doi:10.1088/1742-6596/1897/1/012003

Al-Shukaili, A., Shahat, M.A., & Said, S. I. (2023). *Level of including the fields of Science, Technology, Engineering, Art, and Mathematics (STEAM) in the Omani Science Curricula content for Grades 5–8*. [Submitted for publication]

Alsmadi, K. M., Al-Marashdeh, B., Alzaqebah, M., Jaradat, G., Alghamdi, F. A., Rami, M., Alshabanah, M., Alrajhi, D., Alkhaldi, H., Aldhafferi, N., Alqahtani, A., Badawi, U. A., & Tayfour, M. (2021). Digitalization of learning in Saudi Arabia during the COVID-19 outbreak: A survey. *Informatics in Medicine Unlocked*, 25, 100632. doi:10.1016/j.imu.2021.100632 PMID:34150983

Al-Wakeel, S. (2001). Innovation in computer education. Curriculum for the computerization of Saudi Arabia: A model for developing countries. In *Proceedings from Frontiers in Education Conference* (vol.3, pp. 2–7).

Compilation of References

Alyami, R. (2014). Educational Reform in the Kingdom of Saudi Arabia: Tatweer Schools as a Unit of Development. *Literacy Information and Computer Education Journal, 5*(2), 1515–1524. doi:10.20533/licej.2040.2589.2014.0202

Alzubi, K. A. (2022). The effect of teaching mathematics supported by e-learning platforms on the students' mathematical skills in a college course in Jordan. [IJET]. *International Journal of Emerging Technologies in Learning, 17*(12), 269–275. doi:10.3991/ijet.v17i12.30049

Ambusaidi, A., Al-Harthi, A., & Al-Shuhaimi, A. (2015). *Science teachers' beliefs in the Sultanate of Oman towards science and technology and engineering and mathematics (STEM) and their relationship to some variables*. The 1st Excellent Conference in Teaching & Learning in Science and Mathematics. King Saud University, Riyadh, Saudi Arabia.

Anandarajan, M., Igbaria, M., & Anakwe, U. P. (2002). IT acceptance in a less-developed country: A motivational factor perspective. *International Journal of Information Management, 22*(1), 47–65. doi:10.1016/S0268-4012(01)00040-8

Anderson, S. (2006). Historical, cultural, and social implications of mathematics. In E. Gutstein & B. Peterson (Eds.), *Rethinking mathematics: teaching social justice by the number* (pp. 43–44). Rethinking Schools.

Anderson, T., Rourke, L., Garrison, R., & Archer, W. (2001). Assessing teaching presence in a computer conferencing context. *Online Learning : the Official Journal of the Online Learning Consortium, 5*(2), 1–17. doi:10.24059/olj.v5i2.1875

Andersson, A., & Gronlund, A. (2009). A Conceptual Framework for E-Learning in Developing Countries: A Critical Review of Research Challenges. *The Electronic Journal on Information Systems in Developing Countries, 38*(1), 1–16. doi:10.1002/j.1681-4835.2009.tb00271.x

Anisimova, T., Sabirova, F., Shatunova, O., Bochkareva, T., & Vasilev, V. (2022). The Quality of Training Staff for the Digital Economy of Russia within the Framework of STEAM Education: Problems and Solutions in the Context of Distance Learning. *Education Sciences, 12*(2), 87. doi:10.3390/educsci12020087

Archibald, J., Nicol, C., & Yovanovich, J. (2019). Transformative education for Aboriginal mathematics learning: Indigenous storywork as methodology. In J. Archibald, J. Lee-Morgan, & J. De Santolo (Eds.), *Decolonizing Research: Indigenous Storywork as Methodology* (pp. 118–142). Zed Books.

Arifin, N., & Mahmud, S. (2021). A Systematic Literature Review of Design Thinking Application in STEM Integration. *Creative Education, 12*(7), 1558–1571. doi:10.4236/ce.2021.127118

Arora, G., Joshi, J., Mandal, R. S., Shrivastava, N., Virmani, R., & Sethi, T. (2021). Artificial intelligence in surveillance, diagnosis, drug discovery and vaccine development against covid19. *Pathogens (Basel, Switzerland), 10*(8), 1048. doi:10.3390/pathogens10081048 PMID:34451513

Arslan, S. Y., & Arastaman, G. (2021). Dünyada Stem Politikaları: Türkiye İçin Çıkarımlar ve Öneriler. *Nevşehir Hacı Bektaş Veli Üniversitesi SBE Dergisi*, *11*(2), 894–910. doi:10.30783/nevsosbilen.903115

Arvan, L. (1998). The SCALE efficiency projects. *Journal of Asynchronous Learning Networks*, *2*, 2.

Attard, C., Ingram, N., Forgasz, H., Leder, G., & Grootenboer, P. (2016). Mathematics education and the affective domain. In J. Bobis, J. Way, C. Attard, J. Anderson, H. McMaster, & K. Cartwright (Eds.), *Research in Mathematics Education in Australasia 2012-2015*. Springer. doi:10.1007/978-981-10-1419-2_5

Aung, Y. Y., Wong, D. C., & Ting, D. S. (2021). The promise of artificial intelligence: A review of the opportunities and challenges of artificial intelligence in healthcare. *British Medical Bulletin*, *139*(1), 4–15. doi:10.1093/bmb/ldab016 PMID:34405854

Ay, K., & Seferoğlu, S. S. (2021). Farklı ülkelerin STEM eğitimi politikalarının incelenmesi ve Türkiye için çıkarımlar. *Erzincan Üniversitesi Eğitim Fakültesi Dergisi*, *23*(1), 82–105. doi:10.17556/erziefd.669988

Aylor, M., Campbell, E. M., Winter, C., & Phillipi, C. A. (2017). Resident notes in an electronic health record: A mixed-methods study using a standardized intervention with qualitative analysis. *Clinical Pediatrics*, *56*(3), 257–262. doi:10.1177/0009922816658651 PMID:27400934

Azmi, F. M., & Khoshaim, H. B. (2021). The COVID-19 pandemic and the challenges of E-assessment of calculus courses in higher education: A case study in Saudi Arabia. *International Journal of Learning. Teaching and Educational Research*, *20*(3), 265–281. doi:10.26803/ijlter.20.3.16

Bach, S., Haynes, P., & Lewis, J. (2006). *Online learning and teaching in higher education*, McGraw-Hill Education. https://ebookcentral.proquest.com/lib/aucegypt/detail.action?docID=316249

Badmus, O., & Jita, L. (2022). What is Next for Africa's Youthful and Useful Population? STREAM Education for Global Inclusivity. *Journal of Culture and Values in Education*, *5*(2), 32–46. doi:10.46303/jcve.2022.18

Baharin, N. H., Kamarudin, N., & Manaf, U. K. (2018). Integrating STEM Education Approach in Enhancing Higher Order Thinking Skills. *International Journal of Academic Research in Business & Social Sciences*, *8*(7). doi:10.6007/IJARBSS/v8-i7/4421

Bahri, H., El Mlili, N., Akande, O. N., Abdel-ilah, K., & Madrane, M. (2021). Dataset of Moroccan nursing students' intention to use and accept information and communication technologies and social media platforms for learning. *Data in Brief*, *37*, 107230. doi:10.1016/j.dib.2021.107230 PMID:34179321

Bain, K. (2004). *What the best college teachers do*. Harvard University Press.

Balaraman, P., & Kosalram, K. (2013). E-hospital management & hospital information systems-changing trends. *International Journal of Information Engineering & Electronic Business*, *5*(1), 50–58. doi:10.5815/ijieeb.2013.01.06

Compilation of References

Baran, E., & Canbazoğlu-Bilici, S. ve Mesutoğlu, C. (2015). Fen, teknoloji, mühendislik ve matematik (FeTeMM) spotu geliştirme etkinliği. [ATED]. *Araştırma Temelli Etkinlik Dergisi*, *5*(2), 60–69.

Baran, E., Canbazoğlu-Bilici, S., Mesutoğlu, C., & Ocak, C. (2016). Moving STEM Beyond Schools: Students' Perceptions About an Out-of-School STEM Education Program. *International Journal of Education in Mathematics. Science and Technology*, *4*(1), 9–19. doi:10.18404/ijemst.71338 PMID:27453919

Barbosa, W., Zhou, K., Waddell, E., Myers, T., & Dorsey, E. R. (2021). Improving access to care: Telemedicine across medical domains. *Annual Review of Public Health*, *42*(1), 463–481. doi:10.1146/annurev-publhealth-090519-093711 PMID:33798406

Barteit, S., Lanfermann, L., Bärnighausen, T., Neuhann, F., & Beiersmann, C. (2021). Augmented, mixed, and virtual reality-based head-mounted devices for medical education: Systematic review. *JMIR Serious Games*, *9*(3), e29080. doi:10.2196/29080 PMID:34255668

Batdi, V., Talan, T., & Semerci, C. (2019). Meta-Analytic and Meta-Thematic Analysis of STEM Education. International Journal of Education in Mathematics. *Science and Technology*, *7*(4), 382–399.

Bateiha, S. (2016). Creating space for critical consciousness in the mathematics classroom. In L. Seawright & A. Hodges (Eds.), *Learning across borders: International and transnational education*. Cambridge Scholars Press. https://www.cambridgescholars.com/product/978-1-4438-8583-6

Bateiha, S., & Reeder, S. (2014). Transforming perceptions of elementary preservice teachers' mathematical knowledge for and through social understanding. *RIEJS: International Journal of Education for Social Justice*, *3*(1), 71–86.

Baucum, M., & Capraro, R. (2021). A system for equity: Enhancing STEM education during a pandemic. *Journal of Research in Innovative Teaching & Learning Emerald Publishing.*, *14*(3), 365–377. doi:10.1108/JRIT-12-2020-0087

Bauer, M. W., Howard, S., Romo, R., Yulye, J., Massarani, L., & Amorim, L. (2013) Global science journalism report: working conditions & practices, professional ethos and future expectations. Our learning series. Science and Development Network, London, UK.

Bauer, M. W., & Gregory, J. (2007). From journalism to corporate communication in postwar Britain. In M. W. Bauer & M. Bucchi (Eds.), *Journalism, Science and Society: Science Communication between News and Public Relations* (pp. 33–52). Routledge.

Baytak, A. (2014). Metropolitan Law: A Sociological Perspective. Daily Sabah. https://www.dailysabah.com/opinion/2014/05/13/metropolitan-law-a-sociological-perspective

Baytak, A. Tarman, B., & Duman, H. (2013). Does Fatih Project Ensure Social Justice In Education: Looking In Depth *II. Uluslararası Sosyal Bilgiler Eğitimi Sempozyumu (USBES II)* 26-28 April 2013 Aksaray.

Baytak, A. (2009). *Reforms for Technology Integration into education*. Bilisim Teknolojileri Işığında Eğitim Kongresi.

Bear, L. L. (2000). Jagged worldviews colliding. *Reclaiming Indigenous voice and vision, 77*.

Beasley, R. A. (2012). Medical robots: Current systems and research directions. *Journal of Robotics, 2012*, 2012. doi:10.1155/2012/401613

Beck, K. H., & Treiman, K. A. (1996). The relationship of social context of drinking, perceived social norms, and parental influence to various drinking patterns of adolescents. *Addictive Behaviors, 21*(5), 633–644. doi:10.1016/0306-4603(95)00087-9 PMID:8876762

Bekir, Y. (2023). Preparation of preschool teachers during the COVID-19 pandemic: An online professional development program in STEM education. *Research in Science & Technological Education*, 1–37. doi:10.1080/02635143.2023.2209855

Belbase, S., Mainali, B. R., Kasemsukpipat, W., Tairab, H., Gochoo, M., & Jarrah, A. (2022). At the dawn of science, technology, engineering, arts, and mathematics (STEAM) education: Prospects, priorities, processes, and problems. *International Journal of Mathematical Education in Science and Technology, 53*(11), 2919–2955. doi:10.1080/0020739X.2021.1922943

Bertrand, M. G., & Namukasa, I. K. (2020). STEAM education: Student learning and transferable skills. *Journal of Research in Innovative Teaching & Learning, 13*(1), 43–56. doi:10.1108/JRIT-01-2020-0003

Binmohsen, S. A., & Abrahams, I. (2022). Science teachers' continuing professional development: Online vs face-to-face. *Research in Science & Technological Education, 40*(3), 291–319. doi:10.1080/02635143.2020.1785857

Bircan, M. A., Köksal, Ç., & Cımbız, A. T. (2019). Examining The Stem Centres in Turkey and Stem Centre Model Proposal. *Kastamonu Education Journal, 27*(3), 1033–1045. doi:10.24106/kefdergi.2537

Birkhead, G. S., Klompas, M., & Shah, N. R. (2015). Uses of electronic health records for public health surveillance to advance public health. *Annual Review of Public Health, 36*(1), 345–359. doi:10.1146/annurev-publhealth-031914-122747 PMID:25581157

Bodner, G. (1986). Constructivism: A Theory of Knowledge. *Journal of Chemical Education, 63*(10), 873. doi:10.1021/ed063p873

Borrego, M., & Henderson, C. (2014). Increasing the Use of Evidence-Based Teaching in STEM Higher Education: A Comparison of Eight Change Strategies. *Journal of Engineering Education, 103*(2), 220–252. doi:10.1002/jee.20040

BouJaoude, S. (2020). STEM Education in the Arab Countries. In *STEM in Science Education and S in STEM*. Brill. doi:10.1163/9789004446076_010

Bower, G. H., & Clark, M. C. (1969). Narrative stories as mediators for serial learning. *Psychonomic Science, 14*(4), 181–182. doi:10.3758/BF03332778

Compilation of References

Bowler, P. (2009). *Science for All: The Popularization of Science in Early Twentieth Century*. Chicago University Press. doi:10.7208/chicago/9780226068664.001.0001

Boyce, C.; Neale, P. (2006). *Conducting In-Depth Interviews: A Guide for Designing and Conducting In-Depth-Interviews for Evaluation Input*. Watertown: Pathfinder International.

Brahim, N., Mohamed, B., Abdelwahed, N., Ahmed, L., Radouane, K., Khalid, S., & Mohammed, T. (2014). The use of the internet in Moroccan high schools mathematics teaching: State and Perspectives. *Procedia: Social and Behavioral Sciences*, *116*, 5175–5179. doi:10.1016/j.sbspro.2014.01.1095

Bransford, J. D., Brown, A. L., & Cocking, R. R. (2000). *How People Learn: Brain, Mind, Experience, and School*. National Academy Press.

Breiner, J. M., Harkness, S. S., Johnson, C. C., & Koehler, C. M. (2012). What Is STEM? A Discussion about Conceptions of STEM in Education and Partnerships. *School Science and Mathematics*, *112*(1), 3–11. doi:10.1111/j.1949-8594.2011.00109.x

Bremner, R., Gibbs, A., & Mitchell, A. R. (2020). The era of immersive health technology. *INNOVATIONS*.

Brigg, M., & Bleiker, R. (2010). Autoethnographic international relations: Exploring the self as a source of knowledge. *Review of International Studies*, *36*(3), 779–798. doi:10.1017/S0260210510000689

Brinthaupt, T. M., Fisher, L. S., Gardner, J. G., Raffo, D. M., & Woodward, J. B. (2011). What the best online teachers should do. *Journal of Online Learning and Teaching*, *7*(4), 515–524.

Broks, P. (2006). *Understanding Popular Science*. Open University Press.

Bruner, J. S. (1990). *Acts of meaning*. Harvard University Press.

Bruner, J. S. (2002). *Making stories: Law, literature, life*. Farrar, Straus and Giroux.

Bucchi, M. (1998). *Science and the Media: Alternative Routes in Scientific Communication*. Routledge. doi:10.4324/9780203263839

Buehler, B., Ruggiero, R., & Mehta, K. (2013). Empowering community health workers with technology solutions. *IEEE Technology and Society Magazine*, *32*(1), 44–52. doi:10.1109/MTS.2013.2241831

Bukhatowa, B. Porter, A. & Nelson, M. I. (2010). *Emulating the Best Technology in Teaching and Learning Mathematics: Challenges Facing Libyan Higher Education* (Working Paper). https://ro.uow.edu.au/cssmwp/97

Bunniss, S., & Kelly, D. R. (2010). Research paradigms in medical education research. *Medical Education*, *44*(4), 358–366. doi:10.1111/j.1365-2923.2009.03611.x PMID:20444071

Burdea, G. C., & Coiffet, P. (2003). *Virtual reality technology*. John Wiley & Sons. doi:10.1162/105474603322955950

Burston, J., Dyer-Witheford, N., & Hearn, A. (2010). Digital labour: Workers, authors, citizens. *Ephemera*, *10*(3/4), 214–221.

Bybee, R. W. (2010). What is STEM education? *Science*, *329*(5995), 996–997. doi:10.1126cience.1194998 PMID:20798284

Bybee, R. W. (2013). *The case for STEM education: challenges and opportunities*. National Science Teachers Association.

Campbell, C., Speldewinde, C., Howitt, C., & MacDonald, A. (2018). STEM Practice in the Early Years. *Creative Education*, *9*(1), 11–25. doi:10.4236/ce.2018.91002

Caple, H., & Bednarek, M. (2013). *Delving into the discourse: approaches to news values in journalism studies and beyond (Publisher's version)*. Reuters Institute for the Study of Journalism.

Car, L. T., Kyaw, B. M., Panday, R. S. N., van der Kleij, R., Chavannes, N., Majeed, A., Car, J., & ... . (2021). Digital health training programs for medical students: Scoping review. *JMIR Medical Education*, *7*(3), e28275. doi:10.2196/28275 PMID:34287206

Carmigniani, J., & Furht, B. (2011). Augmented reality: an overview. Handbook of augmented reality, 3-46.

Casey, J. A., Schwartz, B. S., Stewart, W. F., & Adler, N. E. (2016). Using electronic health records for population health research: A review of methods and applications. *Annual Review of Public Health*, *37*(1), 61–81. doi:10.1146/annurev-publhealth-032315-021353 PMID:26667605

Cassany, R., Cortinas, S., & Elduque, A. (2018). Communicating Science: The Profile of Science Journalists in Spain. *Merdia Education Research Journal*, *17*(55), 9–17. doi:10.3916/C55-2018-01

Castellano, M. B. (2000). Updating Aboriginal traditions of knowledge. In G. Dei, B. Hall, & D. Rosenberg (Eds.), *Indigenous Knowledges in Global Contexts: Multiple Readings of Our World* (pp. 21–36). University of Toronto Press.

Çavaş, P., Ayar, A., & Gürcan, G. (2020). Türkiye'de STEM eğitimi üzerine yapılan araştırmaların durumu üzerine bir çalışma. *Van Yüzüncü Yıl Üniversitesi Eğitim Fakültesi Dergisi*, *17*(1), 823–854. doi:10.33711/yyuefd.751853

Chevallard, Y. (1992). Fundamentals of didactics: Perspectives made by an anthropological approach. *Research in Mathematics Education*, *12*(1), 73–112.

Chong, Y. S., & Quek, A. H. (2022). Navigating the Contemporary Rites of Passage: A Typology of STEM Professional Identity Transition. *Research in Social Sciences and Technology*, *7*(3), 86–100. doi:10.46303/ressat.2022.19

Colbert, G. B., Venegas-Vera, A. V., & Lerma, E. V. (2020). Utility of telemedicine in the covid-19 era. *Reviews in Cardiovascular Medicine*, *21*(4), 583–587. doi:10.31083/j.rcm.2020.04.188 PMID:33388003

Compilation of References

Coorevits, P., Sundgren, M., Klein, G. O., Bahr, A., Claerhout, B., Daniel, C., Dugas, M., Dupont, D., Schmidt, A., Singleton, P., De Moor, G., & Kalra, D. (2013). Electronic health records: New opportunities for clinical research. *Journal of Internal Medicine*, *274*(6), 547–560. doi:10.1111/joim.12119 PMID:23952476

Çorlu, M. S. (2012). *A pathway to STEM education: Investigating pre-service mathematics and science teachers at Turkish universities in terms of their understanding of mathematics used in science*. [Doctoral Dissertation, Texas A&M University, College Station].

Cortiñas-Rovira, S., Alonso-Marcos, F., Pont-Sorribes, C., & Escribà-Sales, E. (2015). Science journalists' perceptions and attitudes to pseudoscience in Spain. *Public Understanding of Science (Bristol, England)*, *24*(4), 450–465. doi:10.1177/0963662514558991 PMID:25471350

Cowie, M. R., Blomster, J. I., Curtis, L. H., Duclaux, S., Ford, I., Fritz, F., Goldman, S., Janmohamed, S., Kreuzer, J., Leenay, M., Michel, A., Ong, S., Pell, J. P., Southworth, M. R., Stough, W. G., Thoenes, M., Zannad, F., & Zalewski, A. (2017). Electronic health records to facilitate clinical research. *Clinical Research in Cardiology; Official Journal of the German Cardiac Society*, *106*(1), 1–9. doi:10.100700392-016-1025-6 PMID:27557678

Crellin, E., McClaren, B., Nisselle, A., Best, S., Gaff, C., & Metcalfe, S. (2019). Preparing medical specialists to practice genomic medicine: Education an essential part of a broader strategy. *Frontiers in Genetics*, *10*, 789. doi:10.3389/fgene.2019.00789 PMID:31572433

Croon, P., Selder, J., Allaart, C., Bleijendaal, H., Chamuleau, S., Hofstra, L., Išgum, I., Ziesemer, K. A., & Winter, M. M. (2022). Current state of artificial intelligence-based algorithms for hospital admission prediction in patients with heart failure: A scoping review. *European Heart Journal. Digital Health*, *3*(3), 415–425. doi:10.1093/ehjdh/ztac035 PMID:36712159

Cziesielski, M. J. (2020). Andragogy: The Art of Effectively Teaching Adults. *Limnology and Oceanography Bulletin*, *29*(1), 29–30. doi:10.1002/lob.10358

DAI. (2019). *DAI's Sakil Malik presents recommendations for improving STEM education in Oman*. DAI. https://www.dai.com/news/dais-sakil-malik-presents-recommendations-for-improving-stem-education-in-oman#:~:text=To%20improve%20STEM%20education%20in,organizations%20as%20well%20as%20schools

DAI. (2022). *Oman—Corporate Social Investment Science, Technology, Engineering, and Mathematics (CSI STEM) Program*. DAI. https://www.dai.com/our-work/projects/oman-corporate-social-investment-science-technology-engineering-and-mathematics-csi-stem-program

Davies, N. (2009). *Flat Earth News*. Vintage Books.

De Corte, E., Verschaffel, L., & Greer, B. (2000, November). Connecting mathematics problem solving to the real world. In *Proceedings of the International Conference on Mathematics Education into the 21st Century: Mathematics for living* (pp. 66-73). IEEE.

Dede, C., Eisenkraft, A., Frumin, K., & Hartley, A. (Eds.). (2016). *Teacher learning in the digital age: Online professional development in STEM education*. Harvard Education Press.

Demmer, L. A., & Waggoner, D. J. (2014). Professional medical education and genomics. *Annual Review of Genomics and Human Genetics*, *15*(1), 507–516. doi:10.1146/annurev-genom-090413-025522 PMID:24635717

Denis, B., Watland, P., Pirotte, S., & Verday, N. (2004). Roles and competencies of the e-tutor. Networked Learning 2004: A Research Based Conference on Networked Learning and Lifelong Learning. *Proceedings of the Fourth International Conference*, (pp. 150–157). ORBI. https://orbi.uliege.be/bitstream/2268/12722/1/DENIS_WATLAND_PIROTTE_VERDAY_Roles_and_competencies_of_the_tutor_30_03_2009.pdf

Des Marchais, J., Bureau, M., Dumais, B., & Pigeon, G. (1992). From traditional to problem-based learning: A case report of complete curriculum reform. *Medical Education*, *26*(3), 190–199. doi:10.1111/j.1365-2923.1992.tb00153.x PMID:1614344

Deuze, M. (2006). Participation, Remediation, Bricolage: Considering Principal Components of a Digital Culture. *The Information Society*, *22*(2), 63–75. doi:10.1080/01972240600567170

Dewey, J. (1916). *Democracy and Education: An Introduction to the Philosophy of Education*. Free Press.

Dewey, J. (1993). *How We Think: A Restatement of the Relation of Reflective Thinking to the Educative Process*. D. C. Heath.

Dhurgham, A., Kadhim, T. A., Qasim, R. M., & Abid, A. (2011). E-learning in Iraq: Challenges and Opportunities. *International Conference on Teaching and Learning Education*. Research Gate.

Disterveg, A. (1956). *Rukovodstvo k obrazovaniyu nemeskix uchiteley. Izbranniye pedagogicheskiye sochineniye* [A guide to the education of German teachers. Selected pedagogical essays]. Uchpegdiz.

Doğan, İ. (2019). *STEM etkinliklerinin 7. sınıf öğrencilerinin bilimsel süreç becerilerine, fen ve STEM tutumlarına ve elektrik enerjisi ünitesindeki başarılarına etkisi.* [Doctoral thesis, Balıkesir University], tez.yok.gov.tr/

Doğanay, K. (2018). *Probleme dayalı stem etkinlikleriyle gerçekleştirilen bilim fuarlarının ortaokul öğrencilerinin fen bilimleri dersi akademik başarılarına ve fen tutumlarına etkisi*. Yüksek Lisans Tezi, Kastamonu Üniversitesi, Fen Bilimleri Enstitüsü, Kastamonu.

Draper, R. J., Broomhead, P., Jensen, A. P., Siebert, D. N., & Jeffrey, D. (2005). Aims and criteria for collaboration in content-area classrooms. In R. J. Draper & G. P. Broomhead (Eds.), *Re) imagining content-area literacy instruction*. Teachers College Press.

Dudin, A. (2008). *Medical Education in Palestine, past, present and future*. Research Gate.

Durmuşoğlu, M. C., & Yıldız Taşdemir, C. (2022). Determining the parent education preferences and needs of parents with children in preschool education institutions in Turkey. *Theory and Practice in Child Development*, *2*(1), 1–21. doi:10.46303/tpicd.2022.7

Compilation of References

Dursun, Ç. (2010). Dünyada Bilim İletişiminin Gelisimi ve Farklı Yaklaşımlar: Toplum İçin Bilimden Toplumda Bilime. *Kurgu Online International Journal of Communication Studies*, 2, 1–31.

Durucu, A. S. (2022). *Öğretmenlerin Stem+S İçin Sorgulamaya Dayali Öğretim Öz-Yeterlilikleri İle 21.Yy. Becerileri Öğretimi Arasindaki İlişkinin İncelenmesi*. [Master Thesis, Gaziantep University], tez.yok.gov.tr/

Ebrahim, S., Pearce, N., Smeeth, L., Casas, J. P., Jaffar, S., & Piot, P. (2013). Tackling non-communicable diseases in low-and middle-income countries: Is the evidence from highincome countries all we need? *PLoS Medicine*, *10*(1), e1001377. doi:10.1371/journal.pmed.1001377 PMID:23382655

EDUSIMSTEAM. (2022). *Fostering STEAM Education in Schools*. Edusimsteam. https://edusimsteam.eba.gov.tr/en/home/

Eğitim, R. (2016). *STEM*. MEB. http://yegitek.meb.gov.tr/STEM_Egitimi_Raporu.pdf, Accessed Date: 21.09.2022.

Ekici, S., & Yılmaz, B. (2013). FATİH Projesi Üzerine Bir Değerlendirme. *Türk Kütüphaneciliği,27*(2), 317-339. https://dergipark.org.tr/en/pub/tk/issue/48832/622078

El Hammoumi, S., Zerhane, R., & Janati Idrissi, R. (2022). The impact of using interactive animation in biology education at Moroccan universities and students' attitudes towards animation and ICT in general. *Social Sciences & Humanities Open*, *6*(1), 100293. doi:10.1016/j.ssaho.2022.100293

El Jaoussi, Z., & Al Achhab, S. (2013). *The mathematics in Moroccan universities. 1st Annual International Interdisciplinary Conference*, Azores, Portugal.

El Nagdi, M., Leammukda, F., & Roehrig, G. (2018). Developing identities of STEM teachers at emerging STEM schools. *International Journal of STEM Education*, *5*(1), 36. doi:10.118640594-018-0136-1 PMID:30631726

El Nagdi, M., & Roehrig, G. (2020). Identity evolution of STEM teachers in Egyptian STEM schools in a time of transition: A case study. *International Journal of STEM Education*, *7*(1), 1–16. doi:10.118640594-020-00235-2

Elayyan, S., & Al-Mazroi, Y. (2020). Obstacles that limit the implementation of STEM approach in science education from teachers' point view. *Journal of Educational and Psychological Sciences*, *4*(2), 57–74.

Elayyan, S., & Al-Shizawi, F. (2019). Teachers' perceptions of integrating STEM in Omani schools. *International Journal of Education*, *8*(1), 16–21. doi:10.34293/education.v8i1.1136

EL-Deghaidy. H., & El Nagdi, M. (2023). To STEAM or Not to STEAM: Is It a Matter of Professional Development or Professional Creation? In: Al-Balushi, S.M., Martin-Hansen, L., Song, Y. (eds) Reforming Science Teacher Education Programs in the STEM Era. Palgrave Studies on Leadership and Learning in Teacher Education. Palgrave Macmillan, Cham. doi:10.1007/978-3-031-27334-6_6

Elkhayma, R. (2021). Distant Learning in Morocco: Examining students' attitudes and motivation at the tertiary level. *International Journal of English Literature and Social Sciences, 6*(3), 001–009. . doi:10.22161/ijels.63.1

Ellis, B. F. (1997). Why Tell Stories? *Storytelling Magazine, 9*(1), 21–23.

Erbilgin, E., & Şahin, B. (2021). The Effects of a Professional Development Program for Technology Integrated Algebra Teaching. *Research in Educational Policy and Management, 3*(2), 1–21. doi:10.46303/repam.2021.4

Ergül, A. (2020). 2012-2018 yılları arasında Türkiye'de gerçekleştirilen STEM eğitimi konulu lisansüstü tezlerin incelenmesi. *Mediterranean Journal of Educational Research, 14*(31), 393–421. doi:10.29329/mjer.2020.234.19

Eroğlu, S., & Bektaş, O. (2016). STEM eğitimi almış fen bilimleri öğretmenlerinin STEM temelli ders etkinlikleri hakkındaki görüşleri. *Eğitimde Nitel Araştırmalar Dergisi, 4*(3), 43–67.

Erstad, O., Kjällander, S., & Järvelä, S. (2021). Facing the challenges of 'digital competence' a Nordic agenda for curriculum development for the 21st century. *Nordic Journal of Digital Literacy, 16*(2), 77–87. doi:10.18261/issn.1891-943x-2021-02-04

Ezeife, A. (2002). Mathematics and culture nexus: The interactions of culture and mathematics in an aboriginal classroom. *International Education Journal, 3*(3), 176–187. Retrieved January 1, 2009, from http://ehlt.flinders.edu.au/education/iej/articles/v3n3/Ezeife/paper.pdf

Fahim, J., Brammer, D., & Elass, R. (2017, April 20). *Experiences of creating e-learning programs in the Middle East.* Middle East Institute. https://www.mei.edu/publications/experiences-creating-e-learning-programs-middle-east

Fahy, D., & Nisbet, M. C. (2011). The Science Journalist Online: Shifting Roles and Emerging Practices. *Journalism, 12*(7), 778–793. doi:10.1177/1464884911412697

Feero, W. G., & Green, E. D. (2011). Genomics education for health care professionals in the 21st century. *Journal of the American Medical Association, 306*(9), 989–990. doi:10.1001/jama.2011.1245 PMID:21900139

Feldman, J., & Mcphee, D. (2008). *The science of learning and the art of teaching* (1st ed.). Thomson Delmar Cengage Learning.

Fertleman, C., Aubugeau-Williams, P., Sher, C., Lim, A.-N., Lumley, S., Delacroix, S., & Pan, X. (2018). A discussion of virtual reality as a new tool for training healthcare professionals. *Frontiers in Public Health, 6*, 44. doi:10.3389/fpubh.2018.00044 PMID:29535997

Finkel, D. L. (2000). *Teaching with your mouth shut.* Boynton/Cook.

Fracaro, S. G., Glassey, J., Bernaerts, K., & Wilk, M. (2022). Immersive technologies for the training of operators in the process industry: A Systematic Literature Review. *Computers & Chemical Engineering, 160*, 107691. doi:10.1016/j.compchemeng.2022.107691

Freeman, B., Marginson, S., & Tytler, R. (2019). An international view of STEM education. In *STEM Education 2.0* (pp. 350–363). Brill. doi:10.1163/9789004405400_019

Fulton, K., & Britton, T. (2011). *STEM Teachers in Professional Learning Communities: From Good Teachers to Great Teaching*. National Commission on Teaching and America's Future.

Gallo, D. (2007). Making time for literature with Middle Eastern perspectives. *English Journal*, *96*(3), 110–113. doi:10.2307/30047310

Gangolli, R. (1999). *Asian contributions to mathematics*. Portland Public Schools Geocultural Baseline Essay Series.

Gedeon, S. & Al-Qasem, L. (2019). *Jordan's ICT Sector Analysis* and *Strategy* for *Sectoral Improvement*: GIZ *Jordan*. Employment-oriented MSME Promotion Project (MSME).

Gerbner, G., & Gross, L. (2017). Living with television: The violence profile. In *The Fear of Crime* (pp. 169–195). Routledge. doi:10.4324/9781315086613-10

Ghanem, D., Zahran, N., Saramah, J., Aboudi, A., Afaneh, W., & Musa, A. (2020). *VR Palestine - BuildPalestine*. BuildPalestine - a Global Community for Social Impact in Palestine. https://buildpalestine.com/project/vr-palestine/

Ghazal, H., Alshammari, A., Taweel, A., ElBokl, A., Nejjari, C., Alhuwail, D., AlThani, D., Al-Jafar, E., Wahba, H., Alrishidi, M., Hamdi, M., Househ, M., El-Hassan, O., Alnafrani, S., Kalhori, S. R. N., Emara, T., Alam, T., El Otmani Dehbi, Z., & Al-Shorbaji, N. (2022). Middle east and north african health informatics association (menahia). *Yearbook of Medical Informatics*, *31*(1), 354–364. doi:10.1055-0042-1742495

Gherbi, M. (2015). ICT and the reality in Algeria. *International Academic Conference on Education, Teaching and E-learning*, (IAC-ETeL 2015), Prague, Volume: ISBN 978-80-88085-01-0

Gianfrancesco, M. A., & Goldstein, N. D. (2021). A narrative review on the validity of electronic health record-based research in epidemiology. *BMC Medical Research Methodology*, *21*(1), 1–10. doi:10.118612874-021-01416-5 PMID:34706667

Goglio, V. (2022). *The diffusion and social implications of MOOCs: A comparative study of the USA and Europe*. Taylor and Francis.

Gökçe Tekin, Ö. (2022). *Ortaokul Ve Lise Öğrencilerinin Stem Öz-Yeterlik Algıları Ve Kariyer İlgileri İle Problem Çözme Becerileri*. [Doctoral Thesis, İnönü Üniversitesi].

Gökcül, M. (2022). *Türkiye'de Stem Eğitimine Yönelik Öğretmen Yetiştirme Uygulamalarinin Değerlendirilmesi*. [Doctoral Thesis, Gazi University]. tez.yok.gov.tr/

Göpfert, W. (2008). The strength of PR and the weakness of science journalism. In M. W. Bauer & M. Bucchi (Eds.), *Jounalism, Science and Society*. Routledge.

Greenberg, D. (1987). Teaching Justice through Experience. *Journal of Experiential Education*, *10*(1), 46–47. doi:10.1177/105382598701000112

Green, M. C., & Brock, T. C. (2000). The role of transportation in the persuasiveness of public narratives. *Journal of Personality and Social Psychology, 79*(5), 701–721. doi:10.1037/0022-3514.79.5.701 PMID:11079236

Grimus, M. (2020). Emerging technologies: Impacting learning, pedagogy and curriculum development. Emerging technologies and pedagogies in the curriculum, 127–151.

Guenther, L. (2019). *Science Journalism*. Oxford: Oxford research encyclopedia of communication.

Guenther, L. (2019). Homeostasis and novelty as concepts for science journalism: A re-interpretation of the selection and depiction of scientific issues in the media. In P. Katz & L. Avraamidou (Eds.), *Stability and change in science education – meeting basic learning needs. Homeostasis and novelty in teaching and learning* (pp. 85–102). Brill Sense.

Guenther, L., & Weber, A. (2019). Science, journalism, and the language of (un)certainty: A review of science journalists' use of language in reports on science. In D. R. Gruber & L. C. Olman (Eds.), *The Routledge Handbook of Language and Science*. Routledge. doi:10.4324/9781351207836-5

Gürkan, H. (2019). The Experiences of Women Professionals in the Film Industry in Turkey: A Gender Based Study. *Acta Universitatis Sapientia-Film and Media Studies Journal, 16*(1), 205–219. doi:10.2478/ausfm-2019-0011

Hajji, A. K. (2018). ICT in Education System: Comparing Morocco and Korea. *Sun Moon Islam Center., 7*, 2018.

Hamdy, A. (2007). *ICT in Education in Libya. Survey of ICT and education in Africa: Libya Country Report*. Libya Government.

Harbi, A. (2021). Health care expert's readiness to implement national unified medical records (numr) system in the united arab emirates; a qualitative study. *Informatica (Vilnius), 45*(5).

Haris, M. (1987). An example of traditional women's work as a mathematics resource. *For the Learning of Mathematics, 7*(3), 26–28.

Hashweh, M., & Hashweh, M. (1999). *Higher education in Palestine: current status and recent developments*.

Heart, T., Ben-Assuli, O., & Shabtai, I. (2017). A review of phr, emr and ehr integration: A more personalized healthcare and public health policy. *Health Policy and Technology, 6*(1), 20–25. doi:10.1016/j.hlpt.2016.08.002

Henry, J., Pylypchuk, Y., Searcy, T., and Patel, V. (2016). Adoption of electronic health record systems among us non-federal acute care hospitals: 2008–2015. *ONC data brief, 35*, 1–9.

Hirsch, J. A., Leslie-Mazwi, T. M., Nicola, G. N., Barr, R. M., Bello, J. A., Donovan, W. D., Tu, R., Alson, M. D., & Manchikanti, L. (2015). Current procedural terminology; a primer. *Journal of Neurointerventional Surgery, 7*(4), 309–312. doi:10.1136/neurintsurg-2014-011156 PMID:24589819

Hirsch, J., Nicola, G., McGinty, G., Liu, R., Barr, R., Chittle, M., & Manchikanti, L. (2016). Icd-10: History and context. *AJNR. American Journal of Neuroradiology*, *37*(4), 596–599. doi:10.3174/ajnr.A4696 PMID:26822730

Hişmi, E. (2022). *Stem Etkinliklerinin İlkokul Öğrencilerindeki Stem'e İlişkin Tutumlar, Akademik Başarı, Problem Çözme ve Sosyal Beceri Geliştirme Süreci Açısından İncelenmesi.* [Doctoral Thesis, Çukurova University]. tez.yok.gov.tr/

Ho, H. C. Y., Poon, K.-T., Chan, K. K., Cheung, S. K., Datu, J. A., & Tse, C. Y. (2023). Promoting preservice teachers' psychological and pedagogical competencies for online learning and teaching: The T.E.A.C.H. program. *Computers &amp. Computers & Education*, *195*, 104725. doi:10.1016/j.compedu.2023.104725

Houlden, R. L., Raja, J. B., Collier, C. P., Clark, A. F., & Waugh, J. M. (2004). Medical students' perceptions of an undergraduate research elective. *Medical Teacher*, *26*(7), 659–661. doi:10.1080/01421590400019542 PMID:15763861

Humphrey, C. (2013). A paradigmatic map of professional education research. *Social Work Education*, *32*(1), 3–16. doi:10.1080/02615479.2011.643863

Humphrey-Murto, S., Makus, D., Moore, S., Watanabe Duffy, K., Maniate, J., Scowcroft, K., Buba, M., & Rangel, J. C. (2022). Training physicians and residents for the use of electronic health records—A comparative case study between two hospitals. *Medical Education*. PMID:36181382

Imron, A., Wiyono, B. B., Hadi, S., Gunawan, I., Abbas, A., Saputra, B. R., & Perdana, D. B. (2020, November). Teacher professional development to increase teacher commitment in the era of the ASEAN Economic Community. In *2nd Early Childhood and Primary Childhood Education (ECPE 2020)* (pp. 339-343). Atlantis Press. doi:10.2991/assehr.k.201112.059

Iqbal, M. J., Javed, Z., Sadia, H., Qureshi, I. A., Irshad, A., Ahmed, R., Malik, K., Raza, S., Abbas, A., Pezzani, R., & Sharifi-Rad, J. (2021). Clinical applications of artificial intelligence and machine learning in cancer diagnosis: Looking into the future. *Cancer Cell International*, *21*(1), 1–11. doi:10.118612935-021-01981-1 PMID:34020642

Ismail, N., Kinchin, G., & Edwards, J. (2016). Investigating continuing professional development provided for Egyptian higher education online tutors. *International Journal of Enhanced Research in Educational Development*, *4* (2), 7-14.

Jabareen, H., Khader, Y., & Taweel, A. (2020). Health information systems in jordan and palestine: The need for health informatics training. *Eastern Mediterranean Health Journal*, *26*(11), 1323–1330. doi:10.26719/emhj.20.036 PMID:33226099

Jarrar, Y., Mosleh, R., Hawash, M., & Jarrar, Q. (2019). Knowledge and attitudes of pharmacy students towards pharmacogenomics among universities in Jordan and west bank of Palestine. *Pharmacogenomics and Personalized Medicine*, *12*, 247–255. doi:10.2147/PGPM.S222705 PMID:31632127

Jarrar, Y., Musleh, R., Ghanim, M., AbuKhader, I., & Jarrar, Q. (2021). Assessment of the need for pharmacogenomics education among pharmacists in the West Bank of Palestine. *International Journal of Clinical Practice, 75*(9), e14435. doi:10.1111/ijcp.14435 PMID:34191402

Jones, M. G., Howe, A., & Rua, M. J. (2000). Gender Differences in Students' Experiences, Interests and Attitudes toward Science and Scientists. *Science Education, 84*(2), 180–192. doi:10.1002/(SICI)1098-237X(200003)84:2<180::AID-SCE3>3.0.CO;2-X

Jouicha, A. I., Berrada, K., Bendaoud, R., Machwate, S, Miraoui, A. & Burgos, D. (2020). Starting MOOCs in African University: The Experience of Cadi Ayyad University, Process, Review, Recommendations, and Prospects. *IEEE Access*. IEEE. . doi:10.1109/ACCESS.2020.2966762

Jumreornvong, O., Yang, E., Race, J., and Appel, J. (2020). Telemedicine and medical education in the age of covid-19. *Academic Medicine*.

Kang, N. H. (2019). A review of the effect of integrated STEM or STEAM (science, technology, engineering, arts, and mathematics) education in South Korea. *Asia-Pacific Science Education, 5*(1), 1–22. doi:10.118641029-019-0034-y

Kansanen, P., & Meri, M. (1999). The didactic relation in the teaching-studying-learning process. *TNTEE Publications., 2*, 107–116.

Karabulut, H., Tosunbayraktar, G., & Kariper, A. (2022). Ortaokul Öğrencilerinin Beceri Temelli (Yeni Nesil) Fen Bilimleri Sorularına Yönelik Görüşlerinin İncelenmesi. *Akdeniz Üniversitesi Eğitim Fakültesi Dergisi, 1*(2), 301-320. https://dergipark.org.tr/en/pub/akuned/issue/73080/1190147

Karadaş, Ö. F. (2021). *Fen Bilimleri Öğretmenleri Ve Stem Uygulamaları: Tercih Gerekçeleri, Sorunlar ve Çözüm Önerileri.* [Master Thesis, Kırşehir Ahi Evran University]. tez.yok.gov.tr/

Kayaalp, M. (2018). Patient privacy in the era of big data. *Balkan Medical Journal, 35*(1), 8–17. doi:10.4274/balkanmedj.2017.0966 PMID:28903886

Kaya, D., & Ok, G. (2021). Problems encountered by mathematics and science teachers in classrooms where Syrian students under temporary protection status are educated and suggestions for solution. *International Journal of Contemporary Educational Research, 8*(1), 111–127. doi:10.33200/ijcer.774094

Kaya, M. (2022). The First Life Studies Curriculum in the History of the Turkish Republic and the Influence of John Dewey. *Journal Of Curriculum Studies Research, 4*(2), 59–88. doi:10.46303/jcsr.2022.13

Kayan-Fadlelmula, F., Sellami, A., Abdelkader, N., & Umer, S. (2022). A systematic review of STEM Education research in the GCC countries: Trends, gaps and barriers. *International Journal of STEM Education, 9*(1), 2. doi:10.118640594-021-00319-7

Kenan, T., Pislaru, C., Elzawi, A., & Restoum, M. (2013). Improving the effectiveness of collaborative learning processes in Libyan Higher Education. *8th International Conference for Internet Technology and Secured Transactions* (ICITST-2013) (pp. 411- 416). IEEE.

Compilation of References

Kerello, C. (2021). *Mathics - strengthening mathematics education by the use of icts in Morocco.* Centrale Nantes. https://www.ec-nantes.fr/erasmus/key-action-2-cooperation-for-innovation-and-the-exchange-of-good-practices/mathics-strengthening-mathematics-education-by-the-use-of-icts-in-morocco

Kerr Winter, B., Salamma, R. M., & Qabaja, K. A. (2015). Medical education in palestine. *Medical Teacher, 37*(2), 125–130. doi:10.3109/0142159X.2014.971721 PMID:25333712

Keteci, H. E. (2021). *Çevrim İçi Stem Uygulamalarının (E-Stem) Öğrencilerin Kavram Öğrenmeleri Ve Bilimsel Süreç Becerilerine Etkisi.* [Master Thesis, Marmara University]. tez.yok.gov.tr/

Kewalramani, S., Adams, M., & Cooper, R. (2022). STEM professional learning: Supports and tensions with the Kingdom of Saudi Arabian teachers' immersion experiences in Australian schools. *Teachers and Teaching, 28*(4), 398–419. doi:10.1080/13540602.2022.2062736

Khader, Y., Alzyoud, S., Jabareen, H., Awad, S., Rumeileh, N. A., Manasrah, N., Modallal, R., & Taweel, A. (2019). Students' perceptions of health informatics learning: A survey of jordanian and palestinian students in health-related disciplines. *Lancet, 393*, S33. doi:10.1016/S0140-6736(19)30619-1

Khalaf, B., & Zin, M. Z. (2018). Traditional and Inquiry-Based Learning Pedagogy: A Systematic Critical Review. *International Journal of Instruction, 11*(4), 545–564. doi:10.12973/iji.2018.11434a

Khan, M. B., & Khan, M. K. (2020). Research, innovation and entrepreneurship in Saudi Arabia [Routledge.]. *Vision (Basel)..*

Khan, M. N. R., & Lippert, K. J. (2022). Immersive technologies in healthcare education. In *Intelligent Systems and Machine Learning for Industry* (pp. 115–138). CRC Press.

Kim, E., Rubinstein, S. M., Nead, K. T., Wojcieszynski, A. P., Gabriel, P. E., & Warner, J. L. (2019). The evolving use of electronic health records (ehr) for research. In *Seminars in radiation oncology* (pp. 354–361). Elsevier. doi:10.1016/j.semradonc.2019.05.010

Kingdom of Saudi Arabia. (2022). *Vision 2030 Overview.* Vision 2030. https://www.vision2030.gov.sa/

Knoppers, B. M., & Thorogood, A. M. (2017). Ethics and big data in health. *Current Opinion in Systems Biology, 4*, 53–57. doi:10.1016/j.coisb.2017.07.001

Knowles, M. S. (1980). *The modern practice of adult education: From pedagogy to andragogy.* Association Press.

Koss, M. D. (2015). Diversity in contemporary picturebooks: A content analysis. *Journal of Children's Literature, 41*(1), 32–42.

Koştur, H. (2017). FeTeMM eğitiminde bilim tarihi uygulamaları: El-Cezerî örneği. *Başkent University Journal of Education, 4*(1), 61–73.

Kourouklis, A. P., Wu, X., Geyer, R. C., Exarchos, V., Nazari, T., Kaemmel, J., Magkoutas, K., Daners, M. S., Weisskopf, M., Maini, L., Roman, C., Iske, J., Pappas, G. A., Chen, M. J., Smid, C., Unbehaun, A., Meyer, A., Emmert, M., Ferrari, A., & Cesarovic, N. (2022). Building an interdisciplinary program of cardiovascular research at the swiss federal institute of technology–the etheart story. *iScience*, *25*(10), 105157. doi:10.1016/j.isci.2022.105157 PMID:36185369

Kozma, R. B. (2008). Comparative analysis of policies for ICT in education. In J. Voogt & G. Knezek (Eds.), *International handbook of information technology in primary and secondary education* (pp. 1083–1096). Springer. doi:10.1007/978-0-387-73315-9_68

Kusmaryono, I. (2014). The importance of mathematical power in mathematics learning. *International Conference on Mathematics, Science, and Education*.

Kyaw, B. M., Saxena, N., Posadzki, P., Vseteckova, J., Nikolaou, C. K., George, P. P., Divakar, U., Masiello, I., Kononowicz, A. A., Zary, N., & Tudor Car, L. (2019). Virtual reality for health professions education: Systematic review and meta-analysis by the digital health education collaboration. *Journal of Medical Internet Research*, *21*(1), e12959. doi:10.2196/12959 PMID:30668519

Landrum, R. E., Brakke, K., & McCarthy, M. A. (2019). The pedagogical power of storytelling. *Scholarship of Teaching and Learning in Psychology*, *5*(3), 247–253. doi:10.1037tl0000152

Larrick, N. (1965, September 11). The all-White world of children's books. *Saturday Review*, pp. 63–65, 84–85.

Lavicza, Z., Weinhandl, R., Prodromou, T., Anđić, B., Lieban, D., Hohenwarter, M., Fenyvesi, K., Brownell, C., & Diego-Mantecón, J. M. (2022). Developing and evaluating educational innovations for STEAM education in rapidly changing digital technology environments. *Sustainability (Basel)*, *14*(12), 7237. doi:10.3390u14127237

Lee, I., & Perret, B. (2022, June). Preparing High School Teachers to Integrate AI Methods into STEM Classrooms. *Proceedings of the AAAI Conference on Artificial Intelligence*, *36*(11), 12783–12791. doi:10.1609/aaai.v36i11.21557

Lei, S. I., & Amy, S. I. S. (2021). Online Teaching and Learning Experiences During the COVID-19 Pandemic – A Comparison of Teacher and Student Perceptions. *Journal of Hospitality & Tourism Education*, *33*(3), 148–162. doi:10.1080/10963758.2021.1907196

Li, J., Luo, H., Zhao, L., Zhu, M., Ma, L., & Liao, X. (2022). Promoting STEAM education in primary school through cooperative teaching: A design-based research study. *Sustainability (Basel)*, *14*(16), 10333. doi:10.3390u141610333

Livingstone, S. (2003) The changing nature and uses of media literacy. (Media@LSE electronic working papers (4)). Media@lse, London School of Economics and Political Science, London, UK.

Livingston, S., Van Couvering, E., & Thumim, N. (2008). Converging Traditions of Research on Media and Information Literacies: Disciplinary, Critical, and Methodological Issues. In J. Coiro, M. Knobel, C. Lankshear, & D. J. Leu (Eds.), *Handbook of Research on New Literacies*. Routledge.

Compilation of References

Luscinski, A. (2018). Best practices in adult online learning. *Dissertation Abstracts International. A, The Humanities and Social Sciences.*

Maashi, K. M., Kewalramani, S., & Alabdulkareem, S. A. (2022). Sustainable professional development for STEM teachers in Saudi Arabia. *Eurasia Journal of Mathematics, Science and Technology Education*, *18*(12), em2189. doi:10.29333/ejmste/12597

Machwate, S., Echajari, L., Bendaoud, R., Berrada, K., & Daadaoui, L. (2023). *Pedagogical Innovation Centres*. Precursor for Research in Educational Sciences Promotion in Moroccan Higher Education. doi:10.2991/978-2-38476-036-7_4

Madani, R. A. (2020). Teaching Challenges and Perceptions on STEM Implementation for Schools in Saudi Arabia. *European Journal of STEM Education*, *5*(1), 03. https://doi.org/ doi:10.20897/ejsteme/8468

Makki, S. & Hanna, K.Y. (2011). Iraq ICT Situation and its effect on Iraq Rebuilding: Study, Analysis, and Suggestion. *Journal of Madenat Alelem college*, *3*(2), 57-70.

Malik, R.S. (2018). Educational Challenges in 21st Century and Sustainable Development. *Journal of Sustainable Development Education and Research.*

Mantas, J., Ammenwerth, E., Demiris, G., Hasman, A., Haux, R., Hersh, W., Hovenga, E., Lun, K., Marin, H., & Martin-Sanchez, F. (2010). Recommendations of the international medical informatics association (imia) on education in biomedical and health informatics. *Methods of Information in Medicine*, *49*(02), 105–120. doi:10.3414/ME5119 PMID:20054502

Mantel-Teeuwisse, A. K., Meilianti, S., Khatri, B., Yi, W., Azzopardi, L. M., Acosta G'omez, J., Gu¨lpınar, G., Bennara, K., & Uzman, N. (2021). Digital health in pharmacy education: Preparedness and responsiveness of pharmacy programmes. *Education Sciences*, *11*(6), 296. doi:10.3390/educsci11060296

Maralli, S. (2019). Harf inkilâbi'nin uygulanmasi ve birtakim etkileri. *Eskişehir Osmangazi Üniversitesi Tarih Dergisi*, *2*(1), 112-131. https://dergipark.org.tr/en/pub/esogutd/issue/46078/546953

Marchionda, H., Bateiha, S., & Autin, M. (2014). The effects of instruction on developing autonomous learners in a college statistics class. *Annual Perspectives in Mathematics Education.* National Council of Teachers of Mathematics: Using Research to Improve Instruction.

Margot, K. C., & Kettler, T. (2019). Teachers' perception of STEM integration and education: A systematic literature review. *International Journal of STEM Education*, *6*(1), 1–16. doi:10.118640594-018-0151-2

Martinez, C. (2022). Developing 21st century teaching skills: A case study of teaching and learning through project-based curriculum. *Cogent Education*, *9*(1), 2024936. doi:10.1080/2331186X.2021.2024936

Marzano, R. (2001) Analyzing two assumptions underlying the scoring of classroom assessments. SuDoc (ED 1.310/2:447169).

Matar, N., Hunaiti, Z., Halling, S., & Matar, Š. (2010). E-learning acceptance and challenges in the Arab Region. In S. Abdallah & F. Albadri (Eds.), *ICT acceptance, investment and organization: Cultural practices and values in the arab world* (pp. 184–200). Information Science Reference. doi:10.4018/978-1-60960-048-8.ch013

McGinnis, J. M., Stuckhardt, L., Saunders, R., Smith, M., et al. (2013). *Best care at lower cost: the path to continuously learning health care in america*. Research Gate.

MEB - YEĞİTEK Milli Eğitim Bakanlığı - Yenilik ve Eğitim Teknolojileri Genel Müdürlüğü. (2016). *STEM eğitimi raporu*. MEB.

MEB. (2019). *Kazanim Merkezli Stem Uygulamalari*. T.C. MEB Özel Öğretim Kurumları Genel Müdürlüğü.

MEB. (2022). *Kız Çocuklarının Okullaşma Oranları Rekor Seviyeye Ulaştı*. MEB. https://www.meb.gov.tr/kiz-cocuklarinin-okullasma-oranlari-rekor-seviyeye-ulasti/haber/27958/tr

MEB. (2023). *Fatih Projesi*. MEB. http://fatihprojesi.meb.gov.tr/

Medicine, S. (2019). *Stanford medicine 2020 health trends report: the rise of the datadriven physician*. Stanford Medicine.

Mehanna, W. (2004). E-pedagogy: The pedagogies of e-learning. *Research in Learning Technology*, *12*(3). Advance online publication. doi:10.3402/rlt.v12i3.11259

Menchaca, M., & Khwaldeh, N. (2014). Barriers to utilizing ICT in education in Jordan. *International Journal on E-Learning*, *13*, 127–155.

Merriam, S. B., & Caffarella, R. S. (1991). *Learning in adulthood: a comprehensive guide*. Jossey-Bass Publishers.

Mignolo, W. (2011). *The Darker Side of Western Modernity: Global Futures, Decolonial Options*. Duke University Press.

Miles, R., Al-Ali, S., Charles, T., Hill, C., & Bligh, B. (2021). Technology enhanced learning in the MENA region: Introduction to the special issue. *Issue 1.2 Technology Enhanced Learning in the MENA Region*, *1*(2). doi:10.21428/8c225f6e.df527b9d

Miles, S., Price, G. M., Swift, L., Shepstone, L., & Leinster, S. J. (2010). Statistics teaching in medical school: Opinions of practising doctors. *BMC Medical Education*, *10*(1), 1–8. doi:10.1186/1472-6920-10-75 PMID:21050444

Ministry of Education. (2021). *STEM Oman Overview of external undergraduate scholarships*. . Ministry of Education Ministry of Higher Education, Research and Innovation (2020-2021). https://heac.gov.om/media/doc/DE001_2021.pdf

Compilation of References

Ministry of Higher Education, Research and Innovation. (2022). *Information and data about STEM program at the Ministry of Higher Education, Research and Innovation.* [Unpublished requested report]. Muscat, Sultanate of Oman. Ministry of Higher Education, Research and Innovation. https://www.moheri.gov.om/InnerPage.aspx?id=612cd2b4-f14c-4f48-9dc0-1fa809efe308&culture=en

Mitra, S. (2007). *Sugata Mitra: Kids Can Teach Themselves* [Video File]. TED. https://www.ted.com/talks/sugata_mitra_shows_how_kids_teach_themselves

Mödritscher, F. (2006). E-Learning Theories in Practice: A Comparison of three Methods. *Journal of Universal Science and Technology of Learning*, 0(0), 3–18.

Mohanty, S., Al Rashid, M. H., Mohanty, C., & Swayamsiddha, S. (2021). Modern computational intelligence based drug repurposing for diabetes epidemic. *Diabetes & Metabolic Syndrome*, 15(4), 102180. doi:10.1016/j.dsx.2021.06.017 PMID:34186343

Molek-Kozakowska, K. (2016). Framing Disease, Ageing and Death in Popular Science Journalism. *Brno Studies in English.*, 42(1), 49–69. doi:10.5817/BSE2016-1-3

Moore, T.J., Johnson, C.C., Peters-Burton, E., & Guzey, S.S. (2021). The Need for a STEM Road Map. *STEM Road Map 2.0*. Research Gate.

Moore, T. J., Tank, K. M., Glancy, A. W., & Kersten, J. A. (2015). NGSS and the landscape of engineering in K-12 state science standards. *Journal of Research in Science Teaching*, 52(3), 296–318. doi:10.1002/tea.21199

Morin, A. (2012). Encyclopedia of Human Behavior. Inner Speech. 436–443. doi:10.1016/B978-0-12-375000-6.00206-8

Moskowitz, A., McSparron, J., Stone, D. J., and Celi, L. A. (2015). Preparing a new generation of clinicians for the era of big data. *Harvard medical student review*, 2(1), 24.

Mpofu, V. (2020). A Theoretical Framework for Implementing STEM Education. *Theorizing STEM Education in the 21st Century*.

Muilenburg, L. Y., & Berge, Z. L. (2005). Student barriers to online learning: A factor analytic study. *Distance Education*, 26(1), 29–48. doi:10.1080/01587910500081269

Muir, T., & Livy, S. (2012). What do they know? A comparison of pre-service teachers' and in-service teachers' decimal mathematical content knowledge. *International Journal for Mathematics Teaching and Learning*, 1-15.

Mulla, T., Munir, S., & Mohan, V. (2023). An exploratory study to understand faculty members' perceptions and challenges in online teaching. *International Review of Education*, 69(1-2), 73–99. doi:10.100711159-023-10002-4 PMID:37313288

Mullis, I. V. S., Martin, M. O., Foy, P., & Hooper, M. (2016). *TIMSS 2015 International Results in Mathematics*. Boston College, TIMSS & PIRLS International Study Center. http://timssandpirls.bc.edu/timss2015/international-results/

Murcott, T. (2009). Science journalism: Toppling the priesthood. *Nature*, *459*(7250), 1054–1055. doi:10.1038/4591054a PMID:19553976

Mutlu, S. (1995). Population of Turkey by ethnic groups and provinces. *New Perspectives on Turkey*, *12*, 33–60. doi:10.1017/S0896634600001138 PMID:12290933

Muxiddinovna, A. Z. (2022). The Place and Importance of Steam Educational Technology in Preschool Education. *Journal of Pedagogical Inventions and Practices*, *11*, 3–5.

National Academies of Sciences, Engineering, and Medicine. (2020). *The inclusion of women in STEM in Kuwait and the United States: Proceedings of a workshop.* National Academies Press.

National Science Foundation. (2020). *STEM education for the future: A visioning report.* NSF. https://www.nsf.gov/ehr/Materials/STEM%20Education%20for%20the%20Future%20-%20 2020%20Visioning%20Report.pdf, 20.10.2022.

Nelson, E. A., & McGuire, A. L. (2010). The need for medical education reform: Genomics and the changing nature of health information. *Genome Medicine*, *2*(3), 1–3. doi:10.1186/gm139 PMID:20236478

Nichols, J. A., Herbert Chan, H. W., & Baker, M. A. (2019). Machine learning: Applications of artificial intelligence to imaging and diagnosis. *Biophysical Reviews*, *11*(1), 111–118. doi:10.100712551-018-0449-9 PMID:30182201

Okwara, V., & Henrik Pretorius, J. P. (2023). The STEAM vs STEM Educational Approach: The Significance of the Application of the Arts in Science Teaching for Learners' Attitudes Change. *Journal of Culture and Values in Education*, *6*(2), 18–33. doi:10.46303/jcve.2023.6

Olgun, Ş. (2021). *Fetemm Kapsamında Yaygın Eğitimde Robotik Kodlama Dersi Alan Fen Bilgisi Öğretmenliği Öğrencilerinin Görüşlerine İlişkin Durum Çalışması.* [Master Thesis, Necmettin Erbakan University]. tez.yok.gov.tr/

Oman Educational Portal. (2018). *The national strategy for education 2040.* Oman. https://www.educouncil.gov.om/downloads/Ts775SPNmXDQ.pdf

Oman Educational Portal. (2020). *Objectives of national week for STEM sciences.* MOE. https://home.moe.gov.om/region/stem2021/page-prog

Oman Observer. (2018). First phase of STEM Oman' launched in six public schools. *Oman Observer.* https://www.Omanobserver.om/article/61954/Local/first-phase-of-stem-Oman-launched-in-six-public-schools

Oman Observer. (2019). 915 Students sign for STEM. *Oman Observer.* https://www.Omanobserver.om/article/38014/Local/915-students-sign-up-for-stem

Oman Observer. (2019a). Ministry of Education launches new educational platform. *Oman Observer.* https://www.Omanobserver.om/article/21617/Main/ministry-of-education-launches-new-educational-platform

Compilation of References

Oman Observer. (2021). National science week STEM begins with online events. *Oman Observer.* https://www.Omanobserver.om/article/1784/Local/national-science-week-stem-begins-with-online-events

Oman Observer. (2021). Science week observed with focus on environment. *Oman Observer.* https://www.Omanobserver.om/article/1558/Local/science-week-observed-with-focus-on-environment

Online courses in Arabic (n.d.). Edraak. https://www.edraak.org/en/

Othman, M., & Hayajneh, J. A. (2015). An integrated success model for an electronic health record: A case study of hakeem jordan. *Procedia Economics and Finance, 23*, 95–103. doi:10.1016/S2212-5671(15)00526-2

Ouajdouni, A., Chafik, K., & Boubker, O. (2021). Measuring e-learning systems success: Data from students of higher education institutions in Morocco. *Data in Brief, 35*, 106807. doi:10.1016/j.dib.2021.106807 PMID:33604428

Oxford Business Group. (2021). *Interview with: Rahma bint Ibrahim Al Mahrooqi, Minister for Higher Education, Research and Innovation (MoHERI)*. OBG. https://oxfordbusinessgroup.com/views/rahma-bint-ibrahim-al-mahrooqi-minister-higher-education-research-and-innovation-moheri

Ozkan, G., & Umdu Topsakal, U. (2021). Investigating the effectiveness of STEAM education on students' conceptual understanding of force and energy topics. *Research in Science & Technological Education, 39*(4), 441–460. doi:10.1080/02635143.2020.1769586

Park, W., & Cho, H. (2022). The interaction of history and STEM learning goals in teacher-developed curriculum materials: Opportunities and challenges for STEAM education. *Asia Pacific Education Review, 23*(3), 457–474. doi:10.100712564-022-09741-0

Pears, M., & Konstantinidis, S. (2022). The future of immersive technology in global surgery education. *Indian Journal of Surgery, 84*(1), 281–285. doi:10.100712262-021-02998-6 PMID:34230785

Pearson. (2016). *Building STEM capability in Saudi Arabia [web log]*. Pearson. https://middleeast.pearson.com/Blogsocialmedia/blog/2016/11/building-stem-capability-in-saudi-arabia.html

Pekbay, C. (2017). *Fen, teknoloji, matematik ve mühendislik etkinliklerinin ortaokul öğrencileri üzerindeki etkileri*. Doktora Tezi, Hacettepe Üniversitesi, Eğitim Bilimleri Enstitüsü.

Peng, J., Zou, K., Zhou, M., Teng, Y., Zhu, X., Zhang, F., & Xu, J. (2021). An explainable artificial intelligence framework for the deterioration risk prediction of hepatitis patients. *Journal of Medical Systems, 45*(5), 1–9. doi:10.100710916-021-01736-5 PMID:33847850

Persky, S., & McBride, C. M. (2009). Immersive virtual environment technology: A promising tool for future social and behavioral genomics research and practice. *Health Communication, 24*(8), 677–682. doi:10.1080/10410230903263982 PMID:20183376

Peters, H. P. (1995). The interaction of journalists and scientific experts: Co-operation and conflict between two professional cultures. *Media Culture & Society*, *17*(1), 31–48. doi:10.1177/016344395017001003

Pew, S. (2007). Andragogy and Pedagogy as Foundational Theory for Student Motivation in Higher Education. *InSight: A Journal of Scholarly Teaching*, 2. . doi:10.46504/02200701pe

Pleasants, J., & Olson, J. K. (2019). What is engineering? Elaborating the nature of engineering for K-12 education. *Science Education*, *103*(1), 145–166. doi:10.1002ce.21483

Poirier, L. (2007). Teaching mathematics and the Inuit community. *Canadian Journal of Math. Science & Technology Education*, *7*(1), 53–67.

Pollard, A. (2002). Readings for Reflective Teaching. (2ndEd.). London, UK: Continuum International Publishing Group.

Portnoy, J., Waller, M., & Elliott, T. (2020). Telemedicine in the era of covid-19. *The Journal of Allergy and Clinical Immunology. In Practice*, *8*(5), 1489–1491. doi:10.1016/j.jaip.2020.03.008 PMID:32220575

Powell, B., & Frankenstein, M. (Eds.). (1997). *Ethnomathematics: Challenging Eurocentrism in Mathematics Education*. State University of New York Press.

Professional educator diploma program. (n.d.) AUC School of Humanities and Social Sciences. https://huss.aucegypt.edu/departments/educational-studies/professional-educator-diploma

Qaddour, K., & Husain, S. (2022). *Syria's education crisis: a sustainable approach after 11 years of conflict*. Middle East Institute.

Rachal, J. R. (2002). Andragogy's detectives: A critique of the present and proposal for the future. *Adult Education Quarterly*, *52*(3), 210–227. doi:10.1177/0741713602052003004

Raddad, B. & Etlib, A. & Nuseir, N. (2018). *Implementing e-learning in the Libyan Open University*. Research Gate.

Rajaram, A., Hickey, Z., Patel, N., Newbigging, J., & Wolfrom, B. (2020). Training medical students and residents in the use of electronic health records: A systematic review of the literature. *Journal of the American Medical Informatics Association : JAMIA*, *27*(1), 175–180. doi:10.1093/jamia/ocz178 PMID:31592531

Ramahi, H. (2015). *Education in Palestine: Current challenges and emancipatory alternative*, 1-51. Rosa Luxemburg Stiftung Regional Office Palestine.

Rashty, D. (1999). *Traditional learning vs. eLearning*. Dostopno na.

Rebolj, V. (2009). E-education between pedagogical and didactic theory and practice. *Organizacija*, *42*(1), 10–16. doi:10.2478/v10051-008-0027-1

Compilation of References

Reeves, T. D., & Pedulla, J. (2013). Bolstering the impact of online professional development for teachers. *Journal of Educational Research & Policy Studies, 1*, 50–66. https://files.eric.ed.gov/fulltext/ED545314.pdf

Riskulova, K., & Yuldashova, U. (2020). The role of didactics in teaching process. *Theoretical & Applied Science.*, *85*(5), 786–792. doi:10.15863/TAS.2020.05.85.146

Rissmann-Joyce, S., & El Nagdi, M. (2013). A case study: Egypt's first STEM schools: Lessons learned. *Proceeding of the Global Summit on Education*, (pp. 11-12). Research Gate.

Russell, A. L., & Greenberg, D. A. (2008). *Turning learning right side up: Putting education back on track*. Wharton School Pub.

Ryan, G. V., Callaghan, S., Rafferty, A., Higgins, M. F., Mangina, E., & McAuliffe, F. (2022). Learning Outcomes of Immersive Technologies in Health Care Student Education: Systematic Review of the Literature. *Journal of Medical Internet Research, 24*(2), e30082. doi:10.2196/30082 PMID:35103607

Saba, V. (2001). Nursing informatics: Yesterday, today and tomorrow. *International Nursing Review, 48*(3), 177–187. doi:10.1046/j.1466-7657.2001.00064.x PMID:11558693

Saldaña, J. (2013). *The coding manual for qualitative researchers* (2nd ed.). SAGE.

Samara, M. (2021). *Enabling and Restricting Factors That Affect the Adoption of Electronic Health Records (EHRs) in the Palestinian Public Healthcare System*. [PhD thesis, An-Najah National University].

Schmidt, S., Dickerson, J. & Kisling, E. (2010). From Pedagogy to Andragogy: Transitioning Teaching and Learning in the Information Technology Classroom. *Integrating Adult Learning and Technologies for Effective Education: Strategic Approaches*. 63-81. . doi:10.4018/978-1-61520-694-0.ch004

Schneuwly, B. (2011). *Subject Didactics: An Academic Field Related to the Teacher Profession and Teacher Education*. JSTOR. . doi:10.2307/j.ctvhktksh.20

Serdyukov, P. (2015). Does Online Education Need a Special Pedagogy? *CIT. Journal of Computing and Information Technology, 23*(1), 61–74. doi:10.2498/cit.1002511

Serin, H. (2022). Challenges and opportunities of e-learning in secondary school in Iraq. *International Journal of Social Sciences &Educational Studies.*

Shachar, O. (2000). Spotlighting women scientists in the press: Tokenism in science journalism. *Public Understanding of Science (Bristol, England), 9*(4), 347–358. doi:10.1088/0963-6625/9/4/301

Shah, R. (2021). Revisiting Concept Definition and Forms of Pedagogy. *IJARIIE-ISSN(O)*-2395-4396.

Shahat, M. A., & Al-Amri, M. (2023). Science teacher preparation in Oman: Strengths and shortcomings related to STEM education. In S. Al-Balushi, L. Martin, & Y. Song (Eds.), *Reforming science teacher education programs in the STEM Era: International practices*. Springer. doi:10.1007/978-3-031-27334-6_10

Shahat, M. A., Al-Balushi, S. M., & Al-Amri, M. (2022). Investigating pre-Service science teachers' self-efficacy beliefs for teaching science through engineering design processes. *Interdisciplinary Journal of Environmental and Science Education, 18*(4), e2291. doi:10.21601/ijese/12121

Shahat, M. A., Al-Balushi, S. M., & Al-Amri, M. (2023). Measuring preservice science teachers' performance on engineering design process tasks: Implications for fostering STEM education. *Arab Gulf Journal of Scientific Research*. doi:10.1108/AGJSR-12-2022-0277

Shahjahan, R. A., Estera, A. L., Surla, K. L., & Edwards, K. T. (2022). "Decolonizing" curriculum and pedagogy: A comparative review across disciplines and global higher education contexts. *Review of Educational Research, 92*(1), 73–113. doi:10.3102/00346543211042423

Shatunova, O., Anisimova, T., Sabirova, F., & Kalimullina, O. (2019). Steam as an innovative educational technology. *Journal of Social Studies Education Research, 10*(2), 131–144.

Shé, N., Farrell, C., Brunton, O., Costello, J., Donlon, E., Trevaskis, E., & Eccles, S. (2019). *Teaching online is different: critical perspectives from the literature*. Dublin City University. doi:10.5281/zenodo.3479402

Silow-Carroll, S., Edwards, J. N., & Rodin, D. (2012). Using electronic health records to improve quality and efficiency: The experiences of leading hospitals. *Issue Brief (Commonwealth Fund), 17*(1), 40. PMID:22826903

Simuth, J., & Schuller, S. I. (2012). Principles for e-pedagogy. *Procedia: Social and Behavioral Sciences, 46*, 4454–4456. doi:10.1016/j.sbspro.2012.06.274

Singh, V., & Thurman, A. (2019). How Many Ways Can We Define Online Learning? A Systematic Literature Review of Definitions of Online Learning (1988-2018). *American Journal of Distance Education, 33*(4), 289–306. doi:10.1080/08923647.2019.1663082

Smith, K., Lancaster, G., & Johnson, L. (2019). *Exploring Saudi Arabian teachers' changing understandings of STEM education*. pp. 377-389. Paper presented at Asian Conference on Education 2019, Tokyo, Japan. https://papers.iafor.org/proceedings/conference-proceedings-ace2019/

Smith, L. T. (1999). *Decolonizing methodologies: Research and Indigenous peoples*. Zed Books.

Soliman, C., Salman, D. & GamalEldin, G.O. (2022). Students' perceptions of online learning in higher education during COVID-19: an empirical study of MBA and DBA students in Egypt. *Futur Bus J, 8* (45). doi:10.1186/s43093-022-00159-z

Sood, M., Chadda, R. K., & Singh, P. (2016). Mobile health (mhealth) in mental health: Scope and applications in low-resource settings. *The National Medical Journal of India, 29*(6), 341. PMID:28327483

Compilation of References

Sousa, D. (2014). *How the Brain Learns Mathematics.* Korwin.

Speich, J. E., & Rosen, J. (2004). Medical robotics. Encyclopedia of biomaterials and biomedical engineering, 983. Springer.

Speicher, M., Hall, B. D., & Nebeling, M. (2019, May). What is mixed reality? In *Proceedings of the 2019 CHI conference on human factors in computing systems* (pp. 1-15). Research Gate.

Spradbery, J. (1976). Conservative pupils? Pupil resistance to curriculum innovation in mathematics. In G. Witty and M. Young (Eds.), Explorations in the Politics of School Knowledge (pp. 236-243). Driffeld: Nafferton.

Stairs, A. (1995). Learning processes and teaching roles in Native education: Cultural base and cultural brokerage. In M. Battiste & J. Barman (Eds.), *First Nations education in Canada: The circle unfolds.* University of British Columbia Press.

Stallworth, B. J., Gibbons, L., & Fauber, L. (2006). It's not on the list: An exploration of teachers' perspectives on using multicultural literature. *Journal of Adolescent & Adult Literacy, 49*(6), 478–489. doi:10.1598/JAAL.49.6.3

Stehle, S. M., & Peters-Burton, E. E. (2019). Developing student 21st Century skills in selected exemplary inclusive STEM high schools. *International Journal of STEM Education, 6*(1), 1–15. doi:10.118640594-019-0192-1

Stellefson, M. (2011). eHealth literacy among college students: a systematic review with implications for eHealth education. *Journal of medical Internet research 13*(4).

STEM School. (2015). *İstanbul Aydın Üniversitesi Stem Okulu.* STEM. http://stemokulu.com/

Sulaiman, T. T. (2023). A systematic review on factors influencing learning management system usage in Arab Gulf countries. *Education and Information Technologies.* Advance online publication. doi:10.100710639-023-11936-w PMID:37361806

Sultanov, T. M. (2022). Traditional and Progressive Pedagogical Approaches in Primary Education. *International Journal of Innovative Research in Science, Engineering and Technology, 11*, 2343–2346. doi:10.15680/IJIRSET.2022.1102052

Sun, J., Hu, J., Luo, D., Markatou, M., Wang, F., Edabollahi, S., Steinhubl, S. E., Daar, Z., & Stewart, W. F. (2012). Combining knowledge and data driven insights for identifying risk factors using electronic health records. [American Medical Informatics Association.]. *AMIA ... Annual Symposium Proceedings - AMIA Symposium. AMIA Symposium, 2012*, 901. PMID:23304365

Sweileh, W. M., Zyoud, S. H., Sawalha, A. F., Abu-Taha, A., Hussein, A., & Al-Jabi, S. W. (2013). Medical and biomedical research productivity from palestine, 2002–2011. *BMC Research Notes, 6*(1), 1–5. doi:10.1186/1756-0500-6-41 PMID:23375070

Syzdykova, A., Malta, A., Zolfo, M., Diro, E., & Oliveira, J. L. (2017). Opensource electronic health record systems for low-resource settings: Systematic review. *JMIR Medical Informatics, 5*(4), e8131. doi:10.2196/medinform.8131 PMID:29133283

Tanoli, Z., V˝ah˝a-Koskela, M., & Aittokallio, T. (2021). Artificial intelligence, machine learning, and drug repurposing in cancer. *Expert Opinion on Drug Discovery*, *16*(9), 977–989. doi:10.10 80/17460441.2021.1883585 PMID:33543671

Tarman, B. (2016). Innovation and Education. *Research in Social Sciences and Technology*, *1*(1). doi:10.46303/ressat.01.01.4

Taylor, P. C., & Medina, M. (2011). Educational research paradigms: From positivism to pluralism. *College Research Journal*, *1*(1), 1–16.

Thair, K., & Marini, O. (2012). *A development of an ICT transformation framework for Iraqi schools (ICTIS). Proceedings National Graduate Conference 2012 (NatGrad2012)*. Universiti Tenaga Nasional, Putrajaya Campus.

The Statistics Portal. (n.d.). Statista. https://www.statista.com/statistics/273018/number-of-internet-users-worldwide/

Thowfeek, M. H., & Jaafar, A. (2011). Pedagogical approach to design an e-learning courseware. *2011 International Conference on Pattern Analysis and Intelligence Robotics*. IEEE. 10.1109/ICPAIR.2011.5976927

Ting-Toomey, S. (2005). Identity negotiation theory: Crossing cultural boundaries. In W. B. Gudykunst (Ed.), *Theorizing about intercultural communication* (pp. 211–233). Sage Publications Ltd.

Toker Gökçe, A. & Yıldırım, D. (2019). Öğretmenlerin STEM eğitiminde yaşadığı sorunlar ve çözümleri. *14. Uluslararası Eğitim Yönetimi Kongresi Tam Metin Bildiri Kitabı*, 45-50.

Topol, E. (2019). *Preparing the healthcare workforce to deliver the digital future Internet. NHS Health Education England*. Topol. https://topol.hee.nhs.uk/wp-content/uploads/HEE-Topol-Review-2019.pdf

Troccaz, J., Dagnino, G., & Yang, G. Z. (2019). Frontiers of medical robotics: From concept to systems to clinical translation. *Annual Review of Biomedical Engineering*, *21*(1), 193–218. doi:10.1146/annurev-bioeng-060418-052502 PMID:30822100

Tsakeni, M. (2022). STEM Education Practical Work in Remote Classrooms: Prospects and Future Directions in the Post-Pandemic Era. *Journal of Culture and Values in Education*, *5*(1), 144–167. doi:10.46303/jcve.2022.11

Tuchman, G. (1978). The symbolic annihilation of women by the mass media. In G. Tuchman, A. K. Daniels, & J. Benet (Eds.), *Hearth and home: Images of women in the mass media* (pp. 3–38). Oxford University Press.

TÜSİAD. (2017). *2023'e doğru Türkiye'de STEM gereksinimleri*. Tusaid. https://www.tusiadstem.org/images/raporlar/2017/STEM-Raporu-V7.pdf

Tytler, R. (2020). STEM education for the twenty-first century. *Integrated approaches to STEM education: An international perspective*, 21-43. Research Gate.

Compilation of References

Upadhyay, A. K., & Khandelwal, K. (2022). Metaverse: The future of immersive training. *Strategic HR Review*, *21*(3), 83–86. doi:10.1108/SHR-02-2022-0009

Veldhuis, L. I., Woittiez, N. J., Nanayakkara, P. W., & Ludikhuize, J. (2022). Artificial intelligence for the prediction of in-hospital clinical deterioration: A systematic review. *Critical Care Explorations*, *4*(9), e0744. doi:10.1097/CCE.0000000000000744 PMID:36046062

Venkatesan, M., Mohan, H., Ryan, J. R., Schürch, C. M., Nolan, G. P., Frakes, D. H., & Coskun, A. F. (2021). Virtual and augmented reality for biomedical applications. *Cell Reports Medicine*, *2*(7), 100348. doi:10.1016/j.xcrm.2021.100348 PMID:34337564

Venkatesh, V., Morris, M. G., Davis, G. B., & Davis, F. D. (2003). User acceptance of information technology: Toward a unified view. *Management Information Systems Quarterly*, *27*(3), 425–478. doi:10.2307/30036540

Von Glasersfeld, E. (1998). Cognition, construction of knowledge, and teaching. In *Constructivism in science education* (pp. 11–30). Springer. doi:10.1007/978-94-011-5032-3_2

Vygotsky, L. (1978). Interaction between learning and development. *Readings on the development of children*, *23*(3), 34-41.

Wald, H. S., George, P., Reis, S. P., & Taylor, J. S. (2014). Electronic health record training in undergraduate medical education: Bridging theory to practice with curricula for empowering patient-and relationship-centered care in the computerized setting. *Academic Medicine*, *89*(3), 380–386. doi:10.1097/ACM.0000000000000131 PMID:24448045

Waseh, S., & Dicker, A. (2018). Telemedicine and undergraduate medical education: Lessons in capacity building. *JMIR Medical Education*, *5*(1). doi:10.2196/12515

Weber, A. S., & Hamlaoui, S. (2018). *E-learning in the Middle East and North Africa (MENA) region*. Springer International Publishing. doi:10.1007/978-3-319-68999-9

Widada, W., Herawaty, D., & Lubis, A. N. M. T. (2018, September). Realistic mathematics learning based on the ethnomathematics in Bengkulu to improve students' cognitive level. [). IOP Publishing.]. *Journal of Physics: Conference Series*, *1088*(1), 012028. doi:10.1088/1742-6596/1088/1/012028

Williams, A., & Clifford, S. (2010). *Mapping the field: A political economic account of specialist science news journalism in the UK national media*. Report funded by the Department for Business, Innovation and Skills and commissioned by the Expert Group on Science and the Media. https://www.cardiff.ac.uk/jomec/research/researchgroups/riskscienceandhealth/fundedprojects/mappingscience.html, Accessed Date: 05.10.2022

Wilson, L., & Sipe, St. (2014). A Comparison of Active Learning and Traditional Pedagogical Styles in a Business Law Classroom. *Journal of Legal Studies Education*, *31*(1), 89–105. Advance online publication. doi:10.1111/jlse.12010

Wu, C. H., Liu, C. H., & Huang, Y. M. (2022). The exploration of continuous learning intention in STEAM education through attitude, motivation, and cognitive load. *International Journal of STEM Education*, 9(1), 1–22. doi:10.118640594-022-00346-y

Xiao, C., Choi, E., & Sun, J. (2018). Opportunities and challenges in developing deep learning models using electronic health records data: A systematic review. *Journal of the American Medical Informatics Association : JAMIA*, 25(10), 1419–1428. doi:10.1093/jamia/ocy068 PMID:29893864

Yaman, F., & Aşılıoğlu, B. (2022). Öğretmenlerin Stem Eğitimine Yönelik Farkındalık, Tutum Ve Sınıf İçi Uygulama Özyeterlik Algılarının İncelenmesi. *Milli Eğitim Dergisi*, 51(234), 1395–1416. doi:10.37669/milliegitim.845546

Yamani, H. (2014). E-learning in Saudi Arabia. *Journal of Information Technology and Application in Education*, 3(4), 169. doi:10.14355/jitae.2014.0304.10

Yıldırım, B., & Altun, Y. (2015). STEM Eğitim ve Mühendislik Uygulamalarının Fen Bilgisi Laboratuar Dersindeki Etkilerinin İncelenmesi. *El-Cezerî Fen ve Mühendislik Dergisi*, 2(2), 28–40.

Yıldırım, H., & Gelmez-Burakgazi, S. (2020). Türkiye'de STEM eğitimi konusunda yapılan çalışmalar üzerine bir araştırma: Meta-sentez çalışması. *Pamukkale Üniversitesi Eğitim Fakültesi Dergisi*, 50, 291–314. doi:10.9779/pauefd.590319

Yılmaz, A., Gülgün, C., Çetinkaya, M., & Doğanay, K. (2018). Initiatives and new trends towards stem education in Turkey. *Journal of Education and Training Studies*, 6(11a), 1–10. doi:10.11114/jets.v6i11a.3795

Yin, R. K. (2014). *Case Study Research: Design and Methods* (5th ed.). SAGE Publications.

Zalat, M. M., Hamed, M. S., & Bolbol, S. A. (2021). The experiences, challenges, and acceptance of elearning as a tool for teaching during the COVID-19 pandemic among university medical staff. *PLoS One*, 16(3), e0248758. doi:10.1371/journal.pone.0248758 PMID:33770079

Zha, A. M., Chung, L. S., Song, S. S., Majersik, J. J., & Jagolino-Cole, A. L. (2020). Training in neurology: adoption of resident teleneurology training in the wake of covid-19: telemedicine crash course. *Neurology*, 95(9), 404–407. doi:10.1212/WNL.0000000000010029 PMID:32554768

Zheng, Y. G. (2015). Epigenetic technological applications. Academic Press.

Zhu, Y., Zhao, Y., Dou, L., Guo, R., Gu, X., Gao, R., & Wu, Y. (2021). The hospital management practices in chinese county hospitals and its association with quality of care, efficiency and finance. *BMC Health Services Research*, 21(1), 1–8. doi:10.118612913-021-06472-7 PMID:33975605

Zoric, V. (2019). *History of Education as a Scientific Pedagogical Discipline and a Teaching Subject – Past*. Present and Perspectives.

Related References

To continue our tradition of advancing academic research, we have compiled a list of recommended IGI Global readings. These references will provide additional information and guidance to further enrich your knowledge and assist you with your own research and future publications.

Aburezeq, I. M., & Dweikat, F. F. (2017). Cloud Applications in Language Teaching: Examining Pre-Service Teachers' Expertise, Perceptions and Integration. *International Journal of Distance Education Technologies*, *15*(4), 39–60. doi:10.4018/IJDET.2017100103

Acharjya, B., & Das, S. (2022). Adoption of E-Learning During the COVID-19 Pandemic: The Moderating Role of Age and Gender. *International Journal of Web-Based Learning and Teaching Technologies*, *17*(2), 1–14. https://doi.org/10.4018/IJWLTT.20220301.oa4

Adams, J. L., & Thomas, S. K. (2022). Non-Linear Curriculum Experiences for Student Learning and Work Design: What Is the Maximum Potential of a Chat Bot? In S. Ramlall, T. Cross, & M. Love (Eds.), *Handbook of Research on Future of Work and Education: Implications for Curriculum Delivery and Work Design* (pp. 299–306). IGI Global. https://doi.org/10.4018/978-1-7998-8275-6.ch018

Adera, B. (2017). Supporting Language and Literacy Development for English Language Learners. In J. Keengwe (Ed.), *Handbook of Research on Promoting Cross-Cultural Competence and Social Justice in Teacher Education* (pp. 339–354). Hershey, PA: IGI Global. doi:10.4018/978-1-5225-0897-7.ch018

Ahamer, G. (2017). Quality Assurance for a Developmental "Global Studies" (GS) Curriculum. In I. Management Association (Ed.), Educational Leadership and Administration: Concepts, Methodologies, Tools, and Applications (pp. 438-477). Hershey, PA: IGI Global. https://doi.org/ doi:10.4018/978-1-5225-1624-8.ch023

Ahamer, G. (2017). Quality Assurance for a Developmental "Global Studies" (GS) Curriculum. In I. Management Association (Ed.), Educational Leadership and Administration: Concepts, Methodologies, Tools, and Applications (pp. 438-477). Hershey, PA: IGI Global. https://doi.org/ doi:10.4018/978-1-5225-1624-8.ch023

Akayoğlu, S., & Seferoğlu, G. (2019). An Analysis of Negotiation of Meaning Functions of Advanced EFL Learners in Second Life: Negotiation of Meaning in Second Life. In M. Kruk (Ed.), *Assessing the Effectiveness of Virtual Technologies in Foreign and Second Language Instruction* (pp. 61–85). IGI Global. https://doi.org/10.4018/978-1-5225-7286-2.ch003

Akella, N. R. (2022). Unravelling the Web of Qualitative Dissertation Writing!: A Student Reflects. In A. Zimmerman (Ed.), *Methodological Innovations in Research and Academic Writing* (pp. 260–282). IGI Global. https://doi.org/10.4018/978-1-7998-8283-1.ch014

Alegre de la Rosa, O. M., & Angulo, L. M. (2017). Social Inclusion and Intercultural Values in a School of Education. In S. Mukerji & P. Tripathi (Eds.), *Handbook of Research on Administration, Policy, and Leadership in Higher Education* (pp. 518–531). Hershey, PA: IGI Global. doi:10.4018/978-1-5225-0672-0.ch020

Alexander, C. (2019). Using Gamification Strategies to Cultivate and Measure Professional Educator Dispositions. *International Journal of Game-Based Learning*, *9*(1), 15–29. https://doi.org/10.4018/IJGBL.2019010102

Anderson, K. M. (2017). Preparing Teachers in the Age of Equity and Inclusion. In I. Management Association (Ed.), Medical Education and Ethics: Concepts, Methodologies, Tools, and Applications (pp. 1532-1554). Hershey, PA: IGI Global. doi:10.4018/978-1-5225-0978-3.ch069

Awdziej, M. (2017). Case Study as a Teaching Method in Marketing. In D. Latusek (Ed.), *Case Studies as a Teaching Tool in Management Education* (pp. 244–263). Hershey, PA: IGI Global. doi:10.4018/978-1-5225-0770-3.ch013

Bakos, J. (2019). Sociolinguistic Factors Influencing English Language Learning. In N. Erdogan & M. Wei (Eds.), *Applied Linguistics for Teachers of Culturally and Linguistically Diverse Learners* (pp. 403–424). IGI Global. https://doi.org/10.4018/978-1-5225-8467-4.ch017

Related References

Banas, J. R., & York, C. S. (2017). Pre-Service Teachers' Motivation to Use Technology and the Impact of Authentic Learning Exercises. In L. Tomei (Ed.), *Exploring the New Era of Technology-Infused Education* (pp. 121–140). Hershey, PA: IGI Global. doi:10.4018/978-1-5225-1709-2.ch008

Barton, T. P. (2021). Empowering Educator Allyship by Exploring Racial Trauma and the Disengagement of Black Students. In C. Reneau & M. Villarreal (Eds.), *Handbook of Research on Leading Higher Education Transformation With Social Justice, Equity, and Inclusion* (pp. 186–197). IGI Global. https://doi.org/10.4018/978-1-7998-7152-1.ch013

Benhima, M. (2021). Moroccan English Department Student Attitudes Towards the Use of Distance Education During COVID-19: Moulay Ismail University as a Case Study. *International Journal of Information and Communication Technology Education, 17*(3), 105–122. https://doi.org/10.4018/IJICTE.20210701.oa7

Beycioglu, K., & Wildy, H. (2017). Principal Preparation: The Case of Novice Principals in Turkey. In I. Management Association (Ed.), Educational Leadership and Administration: Concepts, Methodologies, Tools, and Applications (pp. 1152-1169). Hershey, PA: IGI Global. https://doi.org/ doi:10.4018/978-1-5225-1624-8.ch054

Bharwani, S., & Musunuri, D. (2018). Reflection as a Process From Theory to Practice. In M. Khosrow-Pour, D.B.A. (Ed.), Encyclopedia of Information Science and Technology, Fourth Edition (pp. 1529-1539). Hershey, PA: IGI Global. doi:10.4018/978-1-5225-2255-3.ch132

Bhushan, A., Garza, K. B., Perumal, O., Das, S. K., Feola, D. J., Farrell, D., & Birnbaum, A. (2022). Lessons Learned From the COVID-19 Pandemic and the Implications for Pharmaceutical Graduate Education and Research. In C. Ford & K. Garza (Eds.), *Handbook of Research on Updating and Innovating Health Professions Education: Post-Pandemic Perspectives* (pp. 324–345). IGI Global. https://doi.org/10.4018/978-1-7998-7623-6.ch014

Bintz, W., Ciecierski, L. M., & Royan, E. (2021). Using Picture Books With Instructional Strategies to Address New Challenges and Teach Literacy Skills in a Digital World. In L. Haas & J. Tussey (Eds.), *Connecting Disciplinary Literacy and Digital Storytelling in K-12 Education* (pp. 38–58). IGI Global. https://doi.org/10.4018/978-1-7998-5770-9.ch003

Bohjanen, S. L., Cameron-Standerford, A., & Meidl, T. D. (2018). Capacity Building Pedagogy for Diverse Learners. In J. Keengwe (Ed.), *Handbook of Research on Pedagogical Models for Next-Generation Teaching and Learning* (pp. 195–212). Hershey, PA: IGI Global. doi:10.4018/978-1-5225-3873-8.ch011

Brewer, J. C. (2018). Measuring Text Readability Using Reading Level. In M. Khosrow-Pour, D.B.A. (Ed.), *Encyclopedia of Information Science and Technology, Fourth Edition* (pp. 1499-1507). Hershey, PA: IGI Global. doi:10.4018/978-1-5225-2255-3.ch129

Brookbanks, B. C. (2022). Student Perspectives on Business Education in the USA: Current Attitudes and Necessary Changes in an Age of Disruption. In A. Zhuplev & R. Koepp (Eds.), *Global Trends, Dynamics, and Imperatives for Strategic Development in Business Education in an Age of Disruption* (pp. 214–231). IGI Global. doi:10.4018/978-1-7998-7548-2.ch011

Brown, L. V., Dari, T., & Spencer, N. (2019). Addressing the Impact of Trauma in High Poverty Elementary Schools: An Ecological Model for School Counseling. In K. Daniels & K. Billingsley (Eds.), *Creating Caring and Supportive Educational Environments for Meaningful Learning* (pp. 135–153). IGI Global. https://doi.org/10.4018/978-1-5225-5748-7.ch008

Brown, S. L. (2017). A Case Study of Strategic Leadership and Research in Practice: Principal Preparation Programs that Work – An Educational Administration Perspective of Best Practices for Master's Degree Programs for Principal Preparation. In V. Wang (Ed.), *Encyclopedia of Strategic Leadership and Management* (pp. 1226–1244). Hershey, PA: IGI Global. doi:10.4018/978-1-5225-1049-9.ch086

Brzozowski, M., & Ferster, I. (2017). Educational Management Leadership: High School Principal's Management Style and Parental Involvement in School Management in Israel. In V. Potocan, M. Üngan, & Z. Nedelko (Eds.), *Handbook of Research on Managerial Solutions in Non-Profit Organizations* (pp. 55–74). Hershey, PA: IGI Global. doi:10.4018/978-1-5225-0731-4.ch003

Cahapay, M. B. (2020). Delphi Technique in the Development of Emerging Contents in High School Science Curriculum. *International Journal of Curriculum Development and Learning Measurement*, 1(2), 1–9. https://doi.org/10.4018/IJCDLM.2020070101

Camacho, L. F., & Leon Guerrero, A. E. (2022). Indigenous Student Experience in Higher Education: Implementation of Culturally Sensitive Support. In P. Pangelinan & T. McVey (Eds.), *Learning and Reconciliation Through Indigenous Education in Oceania* (pp. 254–266). IGI Global. https://doi.org/10.4018/978-1-7998-7736-3.ch016

Cannaday, J. (2017). The Masking Effect: Hidden Gifts and Disabilities of 2e Students. In P. Dickenson, P. Keough, & J. Courduff (Eds.), *Preparing Pre-Service Teachers for the Inclusive Classroom* (pp. 220–231). Hershey, PA: IGI Global. doi:10.4018/978-1-5225-1753-5.ch011

Related References

Cederquist, S., Fishman, B., & Teasley, S. D. (2022). What's Missing From the College Transcript?: How Employers Make Sense of Student Skills. In Y. Huang (Ed.), *Handbook of Research on Credential Innovations for Inclusive Pathways to Professions* (pp. 234–253). IGI Global. https://doi.org/10.4018/978-1-7998-3820-3.ch012

Cockrell, P., & Gibson, T. (2019). The Untold Stories of Black and Brown Student Experiences in Historically White Fraternities and Sororities. In P. Hoffman-Miller, M. James, & D. Hermond (Eds.), *African American Suburbanization and the Consequential Loss of Identity* (pp. 153–171). IGI Global. https://doi.org/10.4018/978-1-5225-7835-2.ch009

Cohen, M. (2022). Leveraging Content Creation to Boost Student Engagement. In T. Driscoll III, (Ed.), *Designing Effective Distance and Blended Learning Environments in K-12* (pp. 223–239). IGI Global. https://doi.org/10.4018/978-1-7998-6829-3.ch013

Contreras, E. C., & Contreras, I. I. (2018). Development of Communication Skills through Auditory Training Software in Special Education. In M. Khosrow-Pour, D.B.A. (Ed.), Encyclopedia of Information Science and Technology, Fourth Edition (pp. 2431-2441). Hershey, PA: IGI Global. doi:10.4018/978-1-5225-2255-3.ch212

Cooke, L., Schugar, J., Schugar, H., Penny, C., & Bruning, H. (2020). Can Everyone Code?: Preparing Teachers to Teach Computer Languages as a Literacy. In J. Mitchell & E. Vaughn (Eds.), *Participatory Literacy Practices for P-12 Classrooms in the Digital Age* (pp. 163–183). IGI Global. https://doi.org/10.4018/978-1-7998-0000-2.ch009

Cooley, D., & Whitten, E. (2017). Special Education Leadership and the Implementation of Response to Intervention. In F. Topor (Ed.), *Handbook of Research on Individualism and Identity in the Globalized Digital Age* (pp. 265–286). Hershey, PA: IGI Global. doi:10.4018/978-1-5225-0522-8.ch012

Cosner, S., Tozer, S., & Zavitkovsky, P. (2017). Enacting a Cycle of Inquiry Capstone Research Project in Doctoral-Level Leadership Preparation. In I. Management Association (Ed.), Educational Leadership and Administration: Concepts, Methodologies, Tools, and Applications (pp. 1460-1481). Hershey, PA: IGI Global. doi:10.4018/978-1-5225-1624-8.ch067

Crawford, C. M. (2018). Instructional Real World Community Engagement. In M. Khosrow-Pour, D.B.A. (Ed.), Encyclopedia of Information Science and Technology, Fourth Edition (pp. 1474-1486). Hershey, PA: IGI Global. doi:10.4018/978-1-5225-2255-3.ch127

Crosby-Cooper, T., & Pacis, D. (2017). Implementing Effective Student Support Teams. In P. Dickenson, P. Keough, & J. Courduff (Eds.), *Preparing Pre-Service Teachers for the Inclusive Classroom* (pp. 248–262). Hershey, PA: IGI Global. doi:10.4018/978-1-5225-1753-5.ch013

Curran, C. M., & Hawbaker, B. W. (2017). Cultivating Communities of Inclusive Practice: Professional Development for Educators – Research and Practice. In C. Curran & A. Petersen (Eds.), *Handbook of Research on Classroom Diversity and Inclusive Education Practice* (pp. 120–153). Hershey, PA: IGI Global. doi:10.4018/978-1-5225-2520-2.ch006

Dass, S., & Dabbagh, N. (2018). Faculty Adoption of 3D Avatar-Based Virtual World Learning Environments: An Exploratory Case Study. In I. Management Association (Ed.), Technology Adoption and Social Issues: Concepts, Methodologies, Tools, and Applications (pp. 1000-1033). Hershey, PA: IGI Global. https://doi.org/ doi:10.4018/978-1-5225-5201-7.ch045

Davison, A. M., & Scholl, K. G. (2017). Inclusive Recreation as Part of the IEP Process. In C. Curran & A. Petersen (Eds.), *Handbook of Research on Classroom Diversity and Inclusive Education Practice* (pp. 311–330). Hershey, PA: IGI Global. doi:10.4018/978-1-5225-2520-2.ch013

DeCoito, I. (2018). Addressing Digital Competencies, Curriculum Development, and Instructional Design in Science Teacher Education. In M. Khosrow-Pour, D.B.A. (Ed.), Encyclopedia of Information Science and Technology, Fourth Edition (pp. 1420-1431). Hershey, PA: IGI Global. https://doi.org/ doi:10.4018/978-1-5225-2255-3.ch122

DeCoito, I., & Richardson, T. (2017). Beyond Angry Birds™: Using Web-Based Tools to Engage Learners and Promote Inquiry in STEM Learning. In I. Levin & D. Tsybulsky (Eds.), *Digital Tools and Solutions for Inquiry-Based STEM Learning* (pp. 166–196). Hershey, PA: IGI Global. doi:10.4018/978-1-5225-2525-7.ch007

Delmas, P. M. (2017). Research-Based Leadership for Next-Generation Leaders. In R. Styron Jr & J. Styron (Eds.), *Comprehensive Problem-Solving and Skill Development for Next-Generation Leaders* (pp. 1–39). Hershey, PA: IGI Global. doi:10.4018/978-1-5225-1968-3.ch001

Demiray, U., & Ekren, G. (2018). Administrative-Related Evaluation for Distance Education Institutions in Turkey. In K. Buyuk, S. Kocdar, & A. Bozkurt (Eds.), *Administrative Leadership in Open and Distance Learning Programs* (pp. 263–288). Hershey, PA: IGI Global. doi:10.4018/978-1-5225-2645-2.ch011

Related References

Dickenson, P. (2017). What do we Know and Where Can We Grow?: Teachers Preparation for the Inclusive Classroom. In P. Dickenson, P. Keough, & J. Courduff (Eds.), *Preparing Pre-Service Teachers for the Inclusive Classroom* (pp. 1–22). Hershey, PA: IGI Global. doi:10.4018/978-1-5225-1753-5.ch001

Ding, Q., & Zhu, H. (2021). Flipping the Classroom in STEM Education. In J. Keengwe (Ed.), *Handbook of Research on Innovations in Non-Traditional Educational Practices* (pp. 155–173). IGI Global. https://doi.org/10.4018/978-1-7998-4360-3.ch008

Dixon, T., & Christison, M. (2021). Teaching English Grammar in a Hybrid Academic ESL Course: A Mixed Methods Study. In K. Kelch, P. Byun, S. Safavi, & S. Cervantes (Eds.), *CALL Theory Applications for Online TESOL Education* (pp. 229–251). IGI Global. https://doi.org/10.4018/978-1-7998-6609-1.ch010

Donne, V., & Hansen, M. (2017). Teachers' Use of Assistive Technologies in Education. In L. Tomei (Ed.), *Exploring the New Era of Technology-Infused Education* (pp. 86–101). Hershey, PA: IGI Global. doi:10.4018/978-1-5225-1709-2.ch006

Donne, V., & Hansen, M. A. (2018). Business and Technology Educators: Practices for Inclusion. In I. Management Association (Ed.), Business Education and Ethics: Concepts, Methodologies, Tools, and Applications (pp. 471-484). Hershey, PA: IGI Global. https://doi.org/ doi:10.4018/978-1-5225-3153-1.ch026

Dos Santos, L. M. (2022). Completing Student-Teaching Internships Online: Instructional Changes During the COVID-19 Pandemic. In M. Alaali (Ed.), *Assessing University Governance and Policies in Relation to the COVID-19 Pandemic* (pp. 106–127). IGI Global. https://doi.org/10.4018/978-1-7998-8279-4.ch007

Dreon, O., Shettel, J., & Bower, K. M. (2017). Preparing Next Generation Elementary Teachers for the Tools of Tomorrow. In M. Grassetti & S. Brookby (Eds.), *Advancing Next-Generation Teacher Education through Digital Tools and Applications* (pp. 143–159). Hershey, PA: IGI Global. doi:10.4018/978-1-5225-0965-3.ch008

Durak, H. Y., & Güyer, T. (2018). Design and Development of an Instructional Program for Teaching Programming Processes to Gifted Students Using Scratch. In J. Cannaday (Ed.), *Curriculum Development for Gifted Education Programs* (pp. 61–99). Hershey, PA: IGI Global. doi:10.4018/978-1-5225-3041-1.ch004

Egorkina, E., Ivanov, M., & Valyavskiy, A. Y. (2018). Students' Research Competence Formation of the Quality of Open and Distance Learning. In V. Mkrttchian & L. Belyanina (Eds.), *Handbook of Research on Students' Research Competence in Modern Educational Contexts* (pp. 364–384). Hershey, PA: IGI Global. doi:10.4018/978-1-5225-3485-3.ch019

Ekren, G., Karataş, S., & Demiray, U. (2017). Understanding of Leadership in Distance Education Management. In I. Management Association (Ed.), Educational Leadership and Administration: Concepts, Methodologies, Tools, and Applications (pp. 34-50). Hershey, PA: IGI Global. https://doi.org/ doi:10.4018/978-1-5225-1624-8.ch003

Elmore, W. M., Young, J. K., Harris, S., & Mason, D. (2017). The Relationship between Individual Student Attributes and Online Course Completion. In K. Shelton & K. Pedersen (Eds.), *Handbook of Research on Building, Growing, and Sustaining Quality E-Learning Programs* (pp. 151–173). Hershey, PA: IGI Global. doi:10.4018/978-1-5225-0877-9.ch008

Ercegovac, I. R., Alfirević, N., & Koludrović, M. (2017). School Principals' Communication and Co-Operation Assessment: The Croatian Experience. In I. Management Association (Ed.), Educational Leadership and Administration: Concepts, Methodologies, Tools, and Applications (pp. 1568-1589). Hershey, PA: IGI Global. https://doi.org/ doi:10.4018/978-1-5225-1624-8.ch072

Everhart, D., & Seymour, D. M. (2017). Challenges and Opportunities in the Currency of Higher Education. In K. Rasmussen, P. Northrup, & R. Colson (Eds.), *Handbook of Research on Competency-Based Education in University Settings* (pp. 41–65). Hershey, PA: IGI Global. doi:10.4018/978-1-5225-0932-5.ch003

Farmer, L. S. (2017). Managing Portable Technologies for Special Education. In V. Wang (Ed.), *Encyclopedia of Strategic Leadership and Management* (pp. 977–987). Hershey, PA: IGI Global. doi:10.4018/978-1-5225-1049-9.ch068

Farmer, L. S. (2018). Optimizing OERs for Optimal ICT Literacy in Higher Education. In J. Keengwe (Ed.), *Handbook of Research on Mobile Technology, Constructivism, and Meaningful Learning* (pp. 366–390). Hershey, PA: IGI Global. doi:10.4018/978-1-5225-3949-0.ch020

Ferguson, B. T. (2019). Supporting Affective Development of Children With Disabilities Through Moral Dilemmas. In S. Ikuta (Ed.), *Handmade Teaching Materials for Students With Disabilities* (pp. 253–275). IGI Global. doi:10.4018/978-1-5225-6240-5.ch011

Fındık, L. Y. (2017). Self-Assessment of Principals Based on Leadership in Complexity. In I. Management Association (Ed.), Educational Leadership and Administration: Concepts, Methodologies, Tools, and Applications (pp. 978-991). Hershey, PA: IGI Global. https://doi.org/ doi:10.4018/978-1-5225-1624-8.ch047

Related References

Flor, A. G., & Gonzalez-Flor, B. (2018). Dysfunctional Digital Demeanors: Tales From (and Policy Implications of) eLearning's Dark Side. In I. Management Association (Ed.), The Dark Web: Breakthroughs in Research and Practice (pp. 37-50). Hershey, PA: IGI Global. https://doi.org/ doi:10.4018/978-1-5225-3163-0.ch003

Floyd, K. K., & Shambaugh, N. (2017). Instructional Design for Simulations in Special Education Virtual Learning Spaces. In T. Kidd & L. Morris Jr., (Eds.), *Handbook of Research on Instructional Systems and Educational Technology* (pp. 202–215). Hershey, PA: IGI Global. doi:10.4018/978-1-5225-2399-4.ch018

Freeland, S. F. (2020). Community Schools: Improving Academic Achievement Through Meaningful Engagement. In R. Kronick (Ed.), *Emerging Perspectives on Community Schools and the Engaged University* (pp. 132–144). IGI Global. https://doi.org/10.4018/978-1-7998-0280-8.ch008

Ghanbarzadeh, R., & Ghapanchi, A. H. (2019). Applied Areas of Three Dimensional Virtual Worlds in Learning and Teaching: A Review of Higher Education. In I. Management Association (Ed.), *Virtual Reality in Education: Breakthroughs in Research and Practice* (pp. 172-192). IGI Global. https://doi.org/10.4018/978-1-5225-8179-6.ch008

Giovannini, J. M. (2017). Technology Integration in Preservice Teacher Education Programs: Research-based Recommendations. In M. Grassetti & S. Brookby (Eds.), *Advancing Next-Generation Teacher Education through Digital Tools and Applications* (pp. 82–102). Hershey, PA: IGI Global. doi:10.4018/978-1-5225-0965-3.ch005

Good, S., & Clarke, V. B. (2017). An Integral Analysis of One Urban School System's Efforts to Support Student-Centered Teaching. In J. Keengwe & G. Onchwari (Eds.), *Handbook of Research on Learner-Centered Pedagogy in Teacher Education and Professional Development* (pp. 45–68). Hershey, PA: IGI Global. doi:10.4018/978-1-5225-0892-2.ch003

Guetzoian, E. (2022). Gamification Strategies for Higher Education Student Worker Training. In C. Lane (Ed.), *Handbook of Research on Acquiring 21st Century Literacy Skills Through Game-Based Learning* (pp. 164–179). IGI Global. https://doi.org/10.4018/978-1-7998-7271-9.ch009

Hamidi, F., Owuor, P. M., Hynie, M., Baljko, M., & McGrath, S. (2017). Potentials of Digital Assistive Technology and Special Education in Kenya. In C. Ayo & V. Mbarika (Eds.), *Sustainable ICT Adoption and Integration for Socio-Economic Development* (pp. 125–151). Hershey, PA: IGI Global. doi:10.4018/978-1-5225-2565-3.ch006

Hamim, T., Benabbou, F., & Sael, N. (2022). Student Profile Modeling Using Boosting Algorithms. *International Journal of Web-Based Learning and Teaching Technologies, 17*(5), 1–13. https://doi.org/10.4018/IJWLTT.20220901.oa4

Henderson, L. K. (2017). Meltdown at Fukushima: Global Catastrophic Events, Visual Literacy, and Art Education. In R. Shin (Ed.), *Convergence of Contemporary Art, Visual Culture, and Global Civic Engagement* (pp. 80–99). Hershey, PA: IGI Global. doi:10.4018/978-1-5225-1665-1.ch005

Hudgins, T., & Holland, J. L. (2018). Digital Badges: Tracking Knowledge Acquisition Within an Innovation Framework. In I. Management Association (Ed.), Wearable Technologies: Concepts, Methodologies, Tools, and Applications (pp. 1118-1132). Hershey, PA: IGI Global. https://doi.org/ doi:10.4018/978-1-5225-5484-4.ch051

Hwang, R., Lin, H., Sun, J. C., & Wu, J. (2019). Improving Learning Achievement in Science Education for Elementary School Students via Blended Learning. *International Journal of Online Pedagogy and Course Design, 9*(2), 44–62. https://doi.org/10.4018/IJOPCD.2019040104

Jančec, L., & Vodopivec, J. L. (2019). The Implicit Pedagogy and the Hidden Curriculum in Postmodern Education. In J. Vodopivec, L. Jančec, & T. Štemberger (Eds.), *Implicit Pedagogy for Optimized Learning in Contemporary Education* (pp. 41–59). IGI Global. https://doi.org/10.4018/978-1-5225-5799-9.ch003

Janus, M., & Siddiqua, A. (2018). Challenges for Children With Special Health Needs at the Time of Transition to School. In I. Management Association (Ed.), Autism Spectrum Disorders: Breakthroughs in Research and Practice (pp. 339-371). Hershey, PA: IGI Global. doi:10.4018/978-1-5225-3827-1.ch018

Jesus, R. A. (2018). Screencasts and Learning Styles. In M. Khosrow-Pour, D.B.A. (Ed.), Encyclopedia of Information Science and Technology, Fourth Edition (pp. 1548-1558). Hershey, PA: IGI Global. doi:10.4018/978-1-5225-2255-3.ch134

John, G., Francis, N., & Santhakumar, A. B. (2022). Student Engagement: Past, Present, and Future. In S. Ramlall, T. Cross, & M. Love (Eds.), *Handbook of Research on Future of Work and Education: Implications for Curriculum Delivery and Work Design* (pp. 329–341). IGI Global. https://doi.org/10.4018/978-1-7998-8275-6.ch020

Karpinski, A. C., D'Agostino, J. V., Williams, A. K., Highland, S. A., & Mellott, J. A. (2018). The Relationship Between Online Formative Assessment and State Test Scores Using Multilevel Modeling. In M. Khosrow-Pour, D.B.A. (Ed.), Encyclopedia of Information Science and Technology, Fourth Edition (pp. 5183-5192). Hershey, PA: IGI Global. doi:10.4018/978-1-5225-2255-3.ch450

Related References

Kats, Y. (2017). Educational Leadership and Integrated Support for Students with Autism Spectrum Disorders. In I. Management Association (Ed.), Educational Leadership and Administration: Concepts, Methodologies, Tools, and Applications (pp. 101-114). Hershey, PA: IGI Global. https://doi.org/ doi:10.4018/978-1-5225-1624-8.ch007

Kaya, G., & Altun, A. (2018). Educational Ontology Development. In M. Khosrow-Pour, D.B.A. (Ed.), Encyclopedia of Information Science and Technology, Fourth Edition (pp. 1441-1450). Hershey, PA: IGI Global. doi:10.4018/978-1-5225-2255-3.ch124

Keough, P. D., & Pacis, D. (2017). Best Practices Implementing Special Education Curriculum and Common Core State Standards using UDL. In P. Dickenson, P. Keough, & J. Courduff (Eds.), *Preparing Pre-Service Teachers for the Inclusive Classroom* (pp. 107–123). Hershey, PA: IGI Global. doi:10.4018/978-1-5225-1753-5.ch006

Kilburn, M., Henckell, M., & Starrett, D. (2018). Factors Contributing to the Effectiveness of Online Students and Instructors. In M. Khosrow-Pour, D.B.A. (Ed.), Encyclopedia of Information Science and Technology, Fourth Edition (pp. 1451-1462). Hershey, PA: IGI Global. doi:10.4018/978-1-5225-2255-3.ch125

Koban Koç, D. (2021). Gender and Language: A Sociolinguistic Analysis of Second Language Writing. In E. Hancı-Azizoglu & N. Kavaklı (Eds.), *Futuristic and Linguistic Perspectives on Teaching Writing to Second Language Students* (pp. 161–177). IGI Global. https://doi.org/10.4018/978-1-7998-6508-7.ch010

Konecny, L. T. (2017). Hybrid, Online, and Flipped Classrooms in Health Science: Enhanced Learning Environments. In I. Management Association (Ed.), Flipped Instruction: Breakthroughs in Research and Practice (pp. 355-370). Hershey, PA: IGI Global. https://doi.org/ doi:10.4018/978-1-5225-1803-7.ch020

Kupietz, K. D. (2021). Gaming and Simulation in Public Education: Teaching Others to Help Themselves and Their Neighbors. In N. Drumhiller, T. Wilkin, & K. Srba (Eds.), *Simulation and Game-Based Learning in Emergency and Disaster Management* (pp. 41–62). IGI Global. https://doi.org/10.4018/978-1-7998-4087-9.ch003

Kwee, C. T. (2022). Assessing the International Student Enrolment Strategies in Australian Universities: A Case Study During the COVID-19 Pandemic. In M. Alaali (Ed.), *Assessing University Governance and Policies in Relation to the COVID-19 Pandemic* (pp. 162–188). IGI Global. https://doi.org/10.4018/978-1-7998-8279-4.ch010

Lauricella, S., & McArthur, F. A. (2022). Taking a Student-Centred Approach to Alternative Digital Credentials: Multiple Pathways Toward the Acquisition of Microcredentials. In D. Piedra (Ed.), *Innovations in the Design and Application of Alternative Digital Credentials* (pp. 57–69). IGI Global. https://doi.org/10.4018/978-1-7998-7697-7.ch003

Llamas, M. F. (2019). Intercultural Awareness in Teaching English for Early Childhood: A Film-Based Approach. In E. Domínguez Romero, J. Bobkina, & S. Stefanova (Eds.), *Teaching Literature and Language Through Multimodal Texts* (pp. 54–68). IGI Global. https://doi.org/10.4018/978-1-5225-5796-8.ch004

Lokhtina, I., & Kkese, E. T. (2022). Reflecting and Adapting to an Academic Workplace Before and After the Lockdown in Greek-Speaking Cyprus: Opportunities and Challenges. In A. Zhuplev & R. Koepp (Eds.), *Global Trends, Dynamics, and Imperatives for Strategic Development in Business Education in an Age of Disruption* (pp. 126–148). IGI Global. https://doi.org/10.4018/978-1-7998-7548-2.ch007

Lovell, K. L. (2017). Development and Evaluation of Neuroscience Computer-Based Modules for Medical Students: Instructional Design Principles and Effectiveness. In J. Stefaniak (Ed.), *Advancing Medical Education Through Strategic Instructional Design* (pp. 262–276). Hershey, PA: IGI Global. doi:10.4018/978-1-5225-2098-6.ch013

Maher, D. (2019). The Use of Course Management Systems in Pre-Service Teacher Education. In J. Keengwe (Ed.), *Handbook of Research on Blended Learning Pedagogies and Professional Development in Higher Education* (pp. 196–213). IGI Global. https://doi.org/10.4018/978-1-5225-5557-5.ch011

Makewa, L. N. (2019). Teacher Technology Competence Base. In L. Makewa, B. Ngussa, & J. Kuboja (Eds.), *Technology-Supported Teaching and Research Methods for Educators* (pp. 247–267). IGI Global. https://doi.org/10.4018/978-1-5225-5915-3.ch014

Mallett, C. A. (2022). School Resource (Police) Officers in Schools: Impact on Campus Safety, Student Discipline, and Learning. In G. Crews (Ed.), *Impact of School Shootings on Classroom Culture, Curriculum, and Learning* (pp. 53–70). IGI Global. https://doi.org/10.4018/978-1-7998-5200-1.ch004

Related References

Marinho, J. E., Freitas, I. R., Leão, I. B., Pacheco, L. O., Gonçalves, M. P., Castro, M. J., Silva, P. D., & Moreira, R. J. (2022). Project-Based Learning Application in Higher Education: Student Experiences and Perspectives. In A. Alves & N. van Hattum-Janssen (Eds.), *Training Engineering Students for Modern Technological Advancement* (pp. 146–164). IGI Global. https://doi.org/10.4018/978-1-7998-8816-1.ch007

McCleskey, J. A., & Melton, R. M. (2022). Rolling With the Flow: Online Faculty and Student Presence in a Post-COVID-19 World. In S. Ramlall, T. Cross, & M. Love (Eds.), *Handbook of Research on Future of Work and Education: Implications for Curriculum Delivery and Work Design* (pp. 307–328). IGI Global. https://doi.org/10.4018/978-1-7998-8275-6.ch019

McCormack, V. F., Stauffer, M., Fishley, K., Hohenbrink, J., Mascazine, J. R., & Zigler, T. (2018). Designing a Dual Licensure Path for Middle Childhood and Special Education Teacher Candidates. In D. Polly, M. Putman, T. Petty, & A. Good (Eds.), *Innovative Practices in Teacher Preparation and Graduate-Level Teacher Education Programs* (pp. 21–36). Hershey, PA: IGI Global. doi:10.4018/978-1-5225-3068-8.ch002

McDaniel, R. (2017). Strategic Leadership in Instructional Design: Applying the Principles of Instructional Design through the Lens of Strategic Leadership to Distance Education. In V. Wang (Ed.), *Encyclopedia of Strategic Leadership and Management* (pp. 1570–1584). Hershey, PA: IGI Global. doi:10.4018/978-1-5225-1049-9.ch109

McKinney, R. E., Halli-Tierney, A. D., Gold, A. E., Allen, R. S., & Carroll, D. G. (2022). Interprofessional Education: Using Standardized Cases in Face-to-Face and Remote Learning Settings. In C. Ford & K. Garza (Eds.), *Handbook of Research on Updating and Innovating Health Professions Education: Post-Pandemic Perspectives* (pp. 24–42). IGI Global. https://doi.org/10.4018/978-1-7998-7623-6.ch002

Meintjes, H. H. (2021). Learner Views of a Facebook Page as a Supportive Digital Pedagogical Tool at a Public South African School in a Grade 12 Business Studies Class. *International Journal of Smart Education and Urban Society*, *12*(2), 32–45. https://doi.org/10.4018/IJSEUS.2021040104

Melero-García, F. (2022). Training Bilingual Interpreters in Healthcare Settings: Student Perceptions of Online Learning. In J. LeLoup & P. Swanson (Eds.), *Handbook of Research on Effective Online Language Teaching in a Disruptive Environment* (pp. 288–310). IGI Global. https://doi.org/10.4018/978-1-7998-7720-2.ch015

Meletiadou, E. (2022). The Use of Peer Assessment as an Inclusive Learning Strategy in Higher Education Institutions: Enhancing Student Writing Skills and Motivation. In E. Meletiadou (Ed.), *Handbook of Research on Policies and Practices for Assessing Inclusive Teaching and Learning* (pp. 1–26). IGI Global. https://doi.org/10.4018/978-1-7998-8579-5.ch001

Memon, R. N., Ahmad, R., & Salim, S. S. (2018). Critical Issues in Requirements Engineering Education. In I. Management Association (Ed.), Computer Systems and Software Engineering: Concepts, Methodologies, Tools, and Applications (pp. 1953-1976). Hershey, PA: IGI Global. doi:10.4018/978-1-5225-3923-0.ch081

Mendenhall, R. (2017). Western Governors University: CBE Innovator and National Model. In K. Rasmussen, P. Northrup, & R. Colson (Eds.), *Handbook of Research on Competency-Based Education in University Settings* (pp. 379–400). Hershey, PA: IGI Global. doi:10.4018/978-1-5225-0932-5.ch019

Mense, E. G., Griggs, D. M., & Shanks, J. N. (2018). School Leaders in a Time of Accountability and Data Use: Preparing Our Future School Leaders in Leadership Preparation Programs. In E. Mense & M. Crain-Dorough (Eds.), *Data Leadership for K-12 Schools in a Time of Accountability* (pp. 235–259). Hershey, PA: IGI Global. doi:10.4018/978-1-5225-3188-3.ch012

Mense, E. G., Griggs, D. M., & Shanks, J. N. (2018). School Leaders in a Time of Accountability and Data Use: Preparing Our Future School Leaders in Leadership Preparation Programs. In E. Mense & M. Crain-Dorough (Eds.), *Data Leadership for K-12 Schools in a Time of Accountability* (pp. 235–259). Hershey, PA: IGI Global. doi:10.4018/978-1-5225-3188-3.ch012

Mestry, R., & Naicker, S. R. (2017). Exploring Distributive Leadership in South African Public Primary Schools in the Soweto Region. In I. Management Association (Ed.), Educational Leadership and Administration: Concepts, Methodologies, Tools, and Applications (pp. 1041-1064). Hershey, PA: IGI Global. doi:10.4018/978-1-5225-1624-8.ch050

Monaghan, C. H., & Boboc, M. (2017). (Re)Defining Leadership in Higher Education in the U.S. In V. Wang (Ed.), *Encyclopedia of Strategic Leadership and Management* (pp. 567–579). Hershey, PA: IGI Global. doi:10.4018/978-1-5225-1049-9.ch040

Morall, M. B. (2021). Reimagining Mobile Phones: Multiple Literacies and Digital Media Compositions. In C. Moran (Eds.), *Affordances and Constraints of Mobile Phone Use in English Language Arts Classrooms* (pp. 41-53). IGI Global. https://doi.org/10.4018/978-1-7998-5805-8.ch003

Related References

Mthethwa, V. (2022). Student Governance and the Academic Minefield During COVID-19 Lockdown in South Africa. In M. Alaali (Ed.), *Assessing University Governance and Policies in Relation to the COVID-19 Pandemic* (pp. 255–276). IGI Global. https://doi.org/10.4018/978-1-7998-8279-4.ch015

Muthee, J. M., & Murungi, C. G. (2018). Relationship Among Intelligence, Achievement Motivation, Type of School, and Academic Performance of Kenyan Urban Primary School Pupils. In M. Khosrow-Pour, D.B.A. (Ed.), Encyclopedia of Information Science and Technology, Fourth Edition (pp. 1540-1547). Hershey, PA: IGI Global. https://doi.org/ doi:10.4018/978-1-5225-2255-3.ch133

Naranjo, J. (2018). Meeting the Need for Inclusive Educators Online: Teacher Education in Inclusive Special Education and Dual-Certification. In D. Polly, M. Putman, T. Petty, & A. Good (Eds.), *Innovative Practices in Teacher Preparation and Graduate-Level Teacher Education Programs* (pp. 106–122). Hershey, PA: IGI Global. doi:10.4018/978-1-5225-3068-8.ch007

Nkabinde, Z. P. (2017). Multiculturalism in Special Education: Perspectives of Minority Children in Urban Schools. In J. Keengwe (Ed.), *Handbook of Research on Promoting Cross-Cultural Competence and Social Justice in Teacher Education* (pp. 382–397). Hershey, PA: IGI Global. doi:10.4018/978-1-5225-0897-7.ch020

Nkabinde, Z. P. (2018). Online Instruction: Is the Quality the Same as Face-to-Face Instruction? In J. Keengwe (Ed.), *Handbook of Research on Digital Content, Mobile Learning, and Technology Integration Models in Teacher Education* (pp. 300–314). Hershey, PA: IGI Global. doi:10.4018/978-1-5225-2953-8.ch016

Nugroho, A., & Albusaidi, S. S. (2022). Internationalization of Higher Education: The Methodological Critiques on the Research Related to Study Overseas and International Experience. In H. Magd & S. Kunjumuhammed (Eds.), *Global Perspectives on Quality Assurance and Accreditation in Higher Education Institutions* (pp. 75–89). IGI Global. https://doi.org/10.4018/978-1-7998-8085-1.ch005

Nulty, Z., & West, S. G. (2022). Student Engagement and Supporting Students With Accommodations. In P. Bull & G. Patterson (Eds.), *Redefining Teacher Education and Teacher Preparation Programs in the Post-COVID-19 Era* (pp. 99–116). IGI Global. https://doi.org/10.4018/978-1-7998-8298-5.ch006

O'Connor, J. R. Jr, & Jackson, K. N. (2017). The Use of iPad® Devices and "Apps" for ASD Students in Special Education and Speech Therapy. In Y. Kats (Ed.), *Supporting the Education of Children with Autism Spectrum Disorders* (pp. 267–283). Hershey, PA: IGI Global. doi:10.4018/978-1-5225-0816-8.ch014

Okolie, U. C., & Yasin, A. M. (2017). TVET in Developing Nations and Human Development. In U. Okolie & A. Yasin (Eds.), *Technical Education and Vocational Training in Developing Nations* (pp. 1–25). Hershey, PA: IGI Global. doi:10.4018/978-1-5225-1811-2.ch001

Pack, A., & Barrett, A. (2021). A Review of Virtual Reality and English for Academic Purposes: Understanding Where to Start. *International Journal of Computer-Assisted Language Learning and Teaching*, *11*(1), 72–80. https://doi.org/10.4018/IJCALLT.2021010105

Pashollari, E. (2019). Building Sustainability Through Environmental Education: Education for Sustainable Development. In L. Wilson, & C. Stevenson (Eds.), *Building Sustainability Through Environmental Education* (pp. 72-88). IGI Global. https://doi.org/10.4018/978-1-5225-7727-0.ch004

Paulson, E. N. (2017). Adapting and Advocating for an Online EdD Program in Changing Times and "Sacred" Cultures. In I. Management Association (Ed.), *Educational Leadership and Administration: Concepts, Methodologies, Tools, and Applications* (pp. 1849-1876). Hershey, PA: IGI Global. https://doi.org/doi:10.4018/978-1-5225-1624-8.ch085

Petersen, A. J., Elser, C. F., Al Nassir, M. N., Stakey, J., & Everson, K. (2017). The Year of Teaching Inclusively: Building an Elementary Classroom for All Students. In C. Curran & A. Petersen (Eds.), *Handbook of Research on Classroom Diversity and Inclusive Education Practice* (pp. 332–348). Hershey, PA: IGI Global. doi:10.4018/978-1-5225-2520-2.ch014

Pfannenstiel, K. H., & Sanders, J. (2017). Characteristics and Instructional Strategies for Students With Mathematical Difficulties: In the Inclusive Classroom. In C. Curran & A. Petersen (Eds.), *Handbook of Research on Classroom Diversity and Inclusive Education Practice* (pp. 250–281). Hershey, PA: IGI Global. doi:10.4018/978-1-5225-2520-2.ch011

Phan, A. N. (2022). Quality Assurance of Higher Education From the Glonacal Agency Heuristic: An Example From Vietnam. In H. Magd & S. Kunjumuhammed (Eds.), *Global Perspectives on Quality Assurance and Accreditation in Higher Education Institutions* (pp. 136–155). IGI Global. https://doi.org/10.4018/978-1-7998-8085-1.ch008

Related References

Preast, J. L., Bowman, N., & Rose, C. A. (2017). Creating Inclusive Classroom Communities Through Social and Emotional Learning to Reduce Social Marginalization Among Students. In C. Curran & A. Petersen (Eds.), *Handbook of Research on Classroom Diversity and Inclusive Education Practice* (pp. 183–200). Hershey, PA: IGI Global. doi:10.4018/978-1-5225-2520-2.ch008

Randolph, K. M., & Brady, M. P. (2018). Evolution of Covert Coaching as an Evidence-Based Practice in Professional Development and Preparation of Teachers. In V. Bryan, A. Musgrove, & J. Powers (Eds.), *Handbook of Research on Human Development in the Digital Age* (pp. 281–299). Hershey, PA: IGI Global. doi:10.4018/978-1-5225-2838-8.ch013

Rell, A. B., Puig, R. A., Roll, F., Valles, V., Espinoza, M., & Duque, A. L. (2017). Addressing Cultural Diversity and Global Competence: The Dual Language Framework. In L. Leavitt, S. Wisdom, & K. Leavitt (Eds.), *Cultural Awareness and Competency Development in Higher Education* (pp. 111–131). Hershey, PA: IGI Global. doi:10.4018/978-1-5225-2145-7.ch007

Richards, M., & Guzman, I. R. (2020). Academic Assessment of Critical Thinking in Distance Education Information Technology Programs. In I. Management Association (Ed.), *Learning and Performance Assessment: Concepts, Methodologies, Tools, and Applications* (pp. 1-19). IGI Global. https://doi.org/10.4018/978-1-7998-0420-8.ch001

Riel, J., Lawless, K. A., & Brown, S. W. (2017). Defining and Designing Responsive Online Professional Development (ROPD): A Framework to Support Curriculum Implementation. In T. Kidd & L. Morris Jr., (Eds.), *Handbook of Research on Instructional Systems and Educational Technology* (pp. 104–115). Hershey, PA: IGI Global. doi:10.4018/978-1-5225-2399-4.ch010

Roberts, C. (2017). Advancing Women Leaders in Academe: Creating a Culture of Inclusion. In S. Mukerji & P. Tripathi (Eds.), *Handbook of Research on Administration, Policy, and Leadership in Higher Education* (pp. 256–273). Hershey, PA: IGI Global. doi:10.4018/978-1-5225-0672-0.ch012

Rodgers, W. J., Kennedy, M. J., Alves, K. D., & Romig, J. E. (2017). A Multimedia Tool for Teacher Education and Professional Development. In C. Martin & D. Polly (Eds.), *Handbook of Research on Teacher Education and Professional Development* (pp. 285–296). Hershey, PA: IGI Global. doi:10.4018/978-1-5225-1067-3.ch015

Romanowski, M. H. (2017). Qatar's Educational Reform: Critical Issues Facing Principals. In I. Management Association (Ed.), Educational Leadership and Administration: Concepts, Methodologies, Tools, and Applications (pp. 1758-1773). Hershey, PA: IGI Global. https://doi.org/ doi:10.4018/978-1-5225-1624-8.ch080

Ruffin, T. R., Hawkins, D. P., & Lee, D. I. (2018). Increasing Student Engagement and Participation Through Course Methodology. In M. Khosrow-Pour, D.B.A. (Ed.), Encyclopedia of Information Science and Technology, Fourth Edition (pp. 1463-1473). Hershey, PA: IGI Global. doi:10.4018/978-1-5225-2255-3.ch126

Sabina, L. L., Curry, K. A., Harris, E. L., Krumm, B. L., & Vencill, V. (2017). Assessing the Performance of a Cohort-Based Model Using Domestic and International Practices. In I. Management Association (Ed.), Educational Leadership and Administration: Concepts, Methodologies, Tools, and Applications(pp. 913-929). Hershey, PA: IGI Global. https://doi.org/ doi:10.4018/978-1-5225-1624-8.ch044

Samkian, A., Pascarella, J., & Slayton, J. (2022). Towards an Anti-Racist, Culturally Responsive, and LGBTQ+ Inclusive Education: Developing Critically-Conscious Educational Leaders. In E. Cain-Sanschagrin, R. Filback, & J. Crawford (Eds.), *Cases on Academic Program Redesign for Greater Racial and Social Justice* (pp. 150–175). IGI Global. https://doi.org/10.4018/978-1-7998-8463-7.ch007

Santamaría, A. P., Webber, M., & Santamaría, L. J. (2017). Effective School Leadership for Māori Achievement: Building Capacity through Indigenous, National, and International Cross-Cultural Collaboration. In I. Management Association (Ed.), Educational Leadership and Administration: Concepts, Methodologies, Tools, and Applications (pp. 1547-1567). Hershey, PA: IGI Global. https://doi.org/ doi:10.4018/978-1-5225-1624-8.ch071

Santamaría, L. J. (2017). Culturally Responsive Educational Leadership in Cross-Cultural International Contexts. In I. Management Association (Ed.), Educational Leadership and Administration: Concepts, Methodologies, Tools, and Applications (pp. 1380-1400). Hershey, PA: IGI Global. https://doi.org/ doi:10.4018/978-1-5225-1624-8.ch064

Segredo, M. R., Cistone, P. J., & Reio, T. G. (2017). Relationships Between Emotional Intelligence, Leadership Style, and School Culture. *International Journal of Adult Vocational Education and Technology*, 8(3), 25–43. doi:10.4018/IJAVET.2017070103

Shalev, N. (2017). Empathy and Leadership From the Organizational Perspective. In Z. Nedelko & M. Brzozowski (Eds.), *Exploring the Influence of Personal Values and Cultures in the Workplace* (pp. 348–363). Hershey, PA: IGI Global. doi:10.4018/978-1-5225-2480-9.ch018

Related References

Siamak, M., Fathi, S., & Isfandyari-Moghaddam, A. (2018). Assessment and Measurement of Education Programs of Information Literacy. In R. Bhardwaj (Ed.), *Digitizing the Modern Library and the Transition From Print to Electronic* (pp. 164–192). Hershey, PA: IGI Global. doi:10.4018/978-1-5225-2119-8.ch007

Siu, K. W., & García, G. J. (2017). Disruptive Technologies and Education: Is There Any Disruption After All? In I. Management Association (Ed.), *Educational Leadership and Administration: Concepts, Methodologies, Tools, and Applications* (pp. 757-778). Hershey, PA: IGI Global. https://doi.org/ doi:10.4018/978-1-5225-1624-8.ch037

Slagter van Tryon, P. J. (2017). The Nurse Educator's Role in Designing Instruction and Instructional Strategies for Academic and Clinical Settings. In J. Stefaniak (Ed.), *Advancing Medical Education Through Strategic Instructional Design* (pp. 133–149). Hershey, PA: IGI Global. doi:10.4018/978-1-5225-2098-6.ch006

Slattery, C. A. (2018). Literacy Intervention and the Differentiated Plan of Instruction. In *Developing Effective Literacy Intervention Strategies: Emerging Research and Opportunities* (pp. 41–62). Hershey, PA: IGI Global. doi:10.4018/978-1-5225-5007-5.ch003

Smith, A. R. (2017). Ensuring Quality: The Faculty Role in Online Higher Education. In K. Shelton & K. Pedersen (Eds.), *Handbook of Research on Building, Growing, and Sustaining Quality E-Learning Programs* (pp. 210–231). Hershey, PA: IGI Global. doi:10.4018/978-1-5225-0877-9.ch011

Souders, T. M. (2017). Understanding Your Learner: Conducting a Learner Analysis. In J. Stefaniak (Ed.), *Advancing Medical Education Through Strategic Instructional Design* (pp. 1–29). Hershey, PA: IGI Global. doi:10.4018/978-1-5225-2098-6.ch001

Spring, K. J., Graham, C. R., & Ikahihifo, T. B. (2018). Learner Engagement in Blended Learning. In M. Khosrow-Pour, D.B.A. (Ed.), Encyclopedia of Information Science and Technology, Fourth Edition (pp. 1487-1498). Hershey, PA: IGI Global. doi:10.4018/978-1-5225-2255-3.ch128

Storey, V. A., Anthony, A. K., & Wahid, P. (2017). Gender-Based Leadership Barriers: Advancement of Female Faculty to Leadership Positions in Higher Education. In V. Wang (Ed.), *Encyclopedia of Strategic Leadership and Management* (pp. 244–258). Hershey, PA: IGI Global. doi:10.4018/978-1-5225-1049-9.ch018

Stottlemyer, D. (2018). Develop a Teaching Model Plan for a Differentiated Learning Approach. In *Differentiated Instructional Design for Multicultural Environments: Emerging Research and Opportunities* (pp. 106–130). Hershey, PA: IGI Global. doi:10.4018/978-1-5225-5106-5.ch005

Stottlemyer, D. (2018). Developing a Multicultural Environment. In *Differentiated Instructional Design for Multicultural Environments: Emerging Research and Opportunities* (pp. 1–27). Hershey, PA: IGI Global. doi:10.4018/978-1-5225-5106-5.ch001

Swagerty, T. (2022). Digital Access to Culturally Relevant Curricula: The Impact on the Native and Indigenous Student. In E. Reeves & C. McIntyre (Eds.), *Multidisciplinary Perspectives on Diversity and Equity in a Virtual World* (pp. 99–113). IGI Global. https://doi.org/10.4018/978-1-7998-8028-8.ch006

Swami, B. N., Gobona, T., & Tsimako, J. J. (2017). Academic Leadership: A Case Study of the University of Botswana. In N. Baporikar (Ed.), *Innovation and Shifting Perspectives in Management Education* (pp. 1–32). Hershey, PA: IGI Global. doi:10.4018/978-1-5225-1019-2.ch001

Swanson, K. W., & Collins, G. (2018). Designing Engaging Instruction for the Adult Learners. In M. Khosrow-Pour, D.B.A. (Ed.), Encyclopedia of Information Science and Technology, Fourth Edition (pp. 1432-1440). Hershey, PA: IGI Global. doi:10.4018/978-1-5225-2255-3.ch123

Swartz, B. A., Lynch, J. M., & Lynch, S. D. (2018). Embedding Elementary Teacher Education Coursework in Local Classrooms: Examples in Mathematics and Special Education. In D. Polly, M. Putman, T. Petty, & A. Good (Eds.), *Innovative Practices in Teacher Preparation and Graduate-Level Teacher Education Programs* (pp. 262–292). Hershey, PA: IGI Global. doi:10.4018/978-1-5225-3068-8.ch015

Taliadorou, N., & Pashiardis, P. (2017). Emotional Intelligence and Political Skill Really Matter in Educational Leadership. In I. Management Association (Ed.), Educational Leadership and Administration: Concepts, Methodologies, Tools, and Applications (pp. 1274-1303). Hershey, PA: IGI Global. https://doi.org/doi:10.4018/978-1-5225-1624-8.ch060

Tandoh, K. A., & Ebe-Arthur, J. E. (2018). Effective Educational Leadership in the Digital Age: An Examination of Professional Qualities and Best Practices. In J. Keengwe (Ed.), *Handbook of Research on Digital Content, Mobile Learning, and Technology Integration Models in Teacher Education* (pp. 244–265). Hershey, PA: IGI Global. doi:10.4018/978-1-5225-2953-8.ch013

Tobin, M. T. (2018). Multimodal Literacy. In M. Khosrow-Pour, D.B.A. (Ed.), Encyclopedia of Information Science and Technology, Fourth Edition (pp. 1508-1516). Hershey, PA: IGI Global. doi:10.4018/978-1-5225-2255-3.ch130

Related References

Torres, K. M., Arrastia-Chisholm, M. C., & Tackett, S. (2019). A Phenomenological Study of Pre-Service Teachers' Perceptions of Completing ESOL Field Placements. *International Journal of Teacher Education and Professional Development*, 2(2), 85–101. https://doi.org/10.4018/IJTEPD.2019070106

Torres, M. C., Salamanca, Y. N., Cely, J. P., & Aguilar, J. L. (2020). All We Need is a Boost! Using Multimodal Tools and the Translanguaging Strategy: Strengthening Speaking in the EFL Classroom. *International Journal of Computer-Assisted Language Learning and Teaching*, 10(3), 28–47. doi:10.4018/IJCALLT.2020070103

Torres, M. L., & Ramos, V. J. (2018). Music Therapy: A Pedagogical Alternative for ASD and ID Students in Regular Classrooms. In P. Epler (Ed.), *Instructional Strategies in General Education and Putting the Individuals With Disabilities Act (IDEA) Into Practice* (pp. 222–244). Hershey, PA: IGI Global. doi:10.4018/978-1-5225-3111-1.ch008

Toulassi, B. (2017). Educational Administration and Leadership in Francophone Africa: 5 Dynamics to Change Education. In S. Mukerji & P. Tripathi (Eds.), *Handbook of Research on Administration, Policy, and Leadership in Higher Education* (pp. 20–45). Hershey, PA: IGI Global. doi:10.4018/978-1-5225-0672-0.ch002

Umair, S., & Sharif, M. M. (2018). Predicting Students Grades Using Artificial Neural Networks and Support Vector Machine. In M. Khosrow-Pour, D.B.A. (Ed.), *Encyclopedia of Information Science and Technology, Fourth Edition* (pp. 5169-5182). Hershey, PA: IGI Global. doi:10.4018/978-1-5225-2255-3.ch449

Vettraino, L., Castello, V., Guspini, M., & Guglielman, E. (2018). Self-Awareness and Motivation Contrasting ESL and NEET Using the SAVE System. In M. Khosrow-Pour, D.B.A. (Ed.), *Encyclopedia of Information Science and Technology, Fourth Edition* (pp. 1559-1568). Hershey, PA: IGI Global. doi:10.4018/978-1-5225-2255-3.ch135

Wiemelt, J. (2017). Critical Bilingual Leadership for Emergent Bilingual Students. In I. Management Association (Ed.), *Educational Leadership and Administration: Concepts, Methodologies, Tools, and Applications* (pp. 1606-1631). Hershey, PA: IGI Global. doi:10.4018/978-1-5225-1624-8.ch074

Wolf, F., Seyfarth, F. C., & Pflaum, E. (2018). Scalable Capacity-Building for Geographically Dispersed Learners: Designing the MOOC "Sustainable Energy in Small Island Developing States (SIDS)". In U. Pandey & V. Indrakanti (Eds.), *Open and Distance Learning Initiatives for Sustainable Development* (pp. 58–83). Hershey, PA: IGI Global. doi:10.4018/978-1-5225-2621-6.ch003

Woodley, X. M., Mucundanyi, G., & Lockard, M. (2017). Designing Counter-Narratives: Constructing Culturally Responsive Curriculum Online. *International Journal of Online Pedagogy and Course Design*, *7*(1), 43–56. doi:10.4018/IJOPCD.2017010104

Yell, M. L., & Christle, C. A. (2017). The Foundation of Inclusion in Federal Legislation and Litigation. In C. Curran & A. Petersen (Eds.), *Handbook of Research on Classroom Diversity and Inclusive Education Practice* (pp. 27–52). Hershey, PA: IGI Global. doi:10.4018/978-1-5225-2520-2.ch002

Zinner, L. (2019). Fostering Academic Citizenship With a Shared Leadership Approach. In C. Zhu & M. Zayim-Kurtay (Eds.), *University Governance and Academic Leadership in the EU and China* (pp. 99–117). IGI Global. https://doi.org/10.4018/978-1-5225-7441-5.ch007

About the Contributors

Fatimah Alhashem is an Assistant Professor at the Gulf University for Science and Technology (GUST), where she has also served as the Chair for the Center of Teaching, Learning, and Research (CTLR) from 2018 to 2021. With a doctoral degree in Curriculum and Instruction in Science Education from Arizona State University, she brings a strong academic background to her work. Previously, she held the position of General Manager for the Teacher Development Department at the National Center for Education Development (NCED) from 2015 to 2018. Dr. Alhashem is a dedicated advocate for teacher support, particularly for women in science education. Her involvement in various projects has centered around the development of teachers, and she has provided consulting services to organizations such as UNDP, UNESCO, and KFAS. Her professional interests lie in the areas of professional development for teachers, teacher practices and policies, and STEM education. Currently, her focus is on projects related to teacher effectiveness, teacher licensing, and promoting STEM education. In her research, Dr. Alhashem has explored topics such as the TPACK model and studies related to TIMSS (Trends in International Mathematics and Science Study). She was member of the National Science Teacher Association (NSTA) and Kuwait Soroptimist, further demonstrating her commitment to professional networks and the advancement of education.

Heather Pacheco-Guffrey is an Associate Professor of Education at Bridgewater State University's Elementary and Early Childhood Education program in Massachusetts, USA. Dr. Pacheco-Guffrey has been an educator for over 20 years, focused on inclusive, equitable and accessible teaching and learning. She is an alumna Einstein Fellow and NSF IGERT Fellow. Today, she is a STEM specialist, teaching tech-rich introductory and advanced methods courses in STEM for students at the undergraduate and graduate levels. Dr. Pacheco-Guffrey's research is focused on teacher technology-use for domain-specific instruction (TPACK). She loves learning about new technology applications for teaching and she authors the "Tech Talk" column for the National Science Teacher Association's practitioner journal, Science & Children. Heather is currently developing models of elementary teacher technology-use and working to identify areas of strength and growth in TPACK training within teacher preparation programs. She lives in eastern Massachusetts by the sea with her husband David and daughter Zola.

Jacquelynne Anne Boivin is an Assistant Professor of Elementary and Early Childhood Education at Bridgewater State University in Bridgewater, MA, USA, where she supervises student teachers, mentors honors thesis projects, and teaches math methods to elementary teacher candidates and seminars on deconstructing racism by integrating schools and decolonizing social studies curricula. She is co-chair of her department's Anti-Racism Matters committee and supports and facilitates student and faculty professional development focused on diversity, equity, and inclusion. She is also co-chair of the College of Education and Health Sciences' Diversity and Equity Steering Committee. She is a former elementary school teacher who uses her experience in the field to contextualize her instruction in teacher-preparation. She is the author of the book, *Exploring the Role of the School Principal in Predominantly White Middle Schools: School Leadership to Promote Multicultural Understanding* and co-editor of *Education as the Driving Force of Equity for the Marginalized* and *The Role of Educators as Agents and Conveyors for Positive Change in Global Education*. Her largest passion is authentically connecting academic disciplines with social justice skills and understandings. In her spare time, she enjoys outdoor adventures with her husband, Craig, a warm cup of tea with a good book and her cat, and cooking and baking with locally-sourced ingredients.

***

Tahir Albakaa, Research and Teaching Interests: - Modern Iraqi History - Middle East History and Politics - Modern Palestine/Israel history - Arabic language teaching and cultures and Arab – Israel Conflict. Academic Appointments: - Visiting Scholar, USA - Part-time Lecturer at Bridgewater State University January 2022- Present. - Professor, Middle East History, Suffolk University (2008- 2015). - Lecturer Arabic Language Bridgewater State University, Bridgewater MA, 2010-2017. - Visiting Scholar, Suffolk University (2006-2007) - Visiting Scholar, Harvard Graduate School of Education (2005-2006) - President, Al-Mustansiriya University, Iraq's second-largest university, with 37,000 students at that time, Baghdad (2003) - Chair, Academic Promotion Committee, Al-Mustansiriya University (1996 – 2003) - Chair, Department of History, College of Arts, Al-Mustansiriya University (1994) - Thesis Supervisor, M.A. & Ph.D. candidates Al-Mustansiriya University (1992- 2003) - Lecturer, Undergraduate courses, Ancient through Modern Middle East History, Al-Mustansiriya University (1983-2003. - Minister of Higher Education and Scientific Research under Iraqi Interim Government led by Dr. Ayad Alawi, Baghdad

About the Contributors

IRAQ (2004-2005) - Member of the Iraqi National Assembly (2005) - Member of the Iraqi Constitution Writing Committee (2005) Education - Certified Standard Arabic Teaching from Boston University - Ph.D., Modern Iranian History 1941-1951, Baghdad University College of Arts (1990) - Master of History, Modern Palestinian History. Baghdad University College of Arts (1983) - Bachelor of History. Baghdad University College of Education.

Sulaiman M. Al-Balushi is a professor of science education and the Director of Quality Assurance at Sultan Qaboos University (SQU) in Oman. He served as the Dean of the College of Education (SQU) for six years (2014-2020) and was a visiting scholar at the University of Exeter (2020-2021). He contributed mainly to leading the SQU College of Education to attain international academic accreditation by NCATE in the USA in 2016. He is also a member of the Board of the Oman Academic Accreditation Authority (OAAA) and a member of different journal advisory and editorial boards. He has also been awarded various national and international university teaching, research, and reviewing awards.

Jabbar Al-Obaidi received his Ph.D. in Communication from the University of Michigan, Ann Arbor, Michigan, a master's degree in art education from Hartford University, and bachelor's degree in drama and theater from Baghdad University. Currently, Professor Al-Obaidi serves as the Academic Director of Global Programs, the Minnock Institute for Global Engagement at Bridgewater State University (BSU). Previously, Al-Obaidi served as Acting Chair, Communication Studies Department in Spring 2022, and Fall 2017, and the Chair of the Communication Studies Department 2005-2011. He also served as the director of the Center for Middle East Studies (2011-2018) at BSU. In addition to his extensive teaching and administrative experiences in the US, he taught in Iraq, Jordan, Yemen, United Arab Emirates and China. Published books include Media Censorship in the Middle East, Broadcast, Internet, and TV Media in the Arab World and Small Nations, and Mass Communication: Mixing Views.

Summer Bateiha is Professor of Mathematics at Virginia Commonwealth University's School of the Arts in Qatar. She is the recipient of two university distinguished teaching awards. Her research is devoted to understanding an area of critical mathematics instruction that relates both in content and delivery to the transformative possibilities for society at large. She has successfully authored and co-authored peer-reviewed and invited journal articles, book chapters, proceedings papers, and other works, including the two-time international award-winning culturally situated children's book, Spring Bloom: A Math Adventure Story, co-authored with Sadia Mir and illustrated by Inna Ogando. She has also received and worked on

About the Contributors

several funded projects to improve mathematics instruction, most recently serving as principal investigator of the VCUarts-funded research lab Multimodal Mathematics: Interactivity and Cultural Relevance. The purpose of this lab is to provide an interdisciplinary and collaborative research environment that brings together scholars, practitioners, and educators in mathematics, creative writing, and art and design to create curriculum and to advance the potential of multimodal storytelling as an active element of STEM education.

Ahmet Baytak, after his undergraduate education in Mathematics and Computer in Turkey, completed his master's and doctorate education in the field of Instructional Systems at The Penn State University in the USA. In addition to his teaching experiences in the USA and Turkey, he worked as a faculty member at Erciyes University and Harran University until 2016. He has many academic articles and projects in areas such as the use of technology in education, game design-based learning, and web-based learning systems for teachers. Currently, he continues to provide private consultancy to businesses and institutions in the field of technology and education.

Carmen Echazarreta is Principal Investigator of the research team ARPA. She received her Ph.D. from the University of Barcelona. She is a professor in Audiovisual Communication and Publicity at the University of Girona. In addition, she has held the Coordinator of Studies for the Bachelor's Degree in Publicity and Public Relations.

Mohamed Ali El-Nagdi is an adjunct faculty at the Department of Educational Studies, Dr. El Nagdi has a diverse educational background and expertise especially in STEM Education. His publication focuses on STEM teacher identity, equity, assessment, curriculum development, and professional development

Heba EL-Deghaidy is a Professor of Curricula and Science Education. She is a tenured Faculty at the American University in Cairo where she teaches MA students at the Graduate School of Education. As a specialist in Science Education, she leads the STEAM education initiative as an internationally wide approach to an interdisciplinary learning model. She is the PI of the 'Bilingual STEAM education project' and Co-PI of the Erasmus + Project 'School and University Partnership for Peer Communities of Learners'. Dr. EL-Deghaidy was a member of the two-year joint project with University of Maryland and Baltimore City Council on 'Civic Education Curriculum Development: service learning; conflict resolution and leadership development'. Her doctoral degree comes from the University of Birmingham, UK. She is an active member at the National Association for Research in Science Teaching (NARST).

About the Contributors

Ghadeer O. Ghosheh is a Doctoral researcher at the University of Oxford finishing her PhD in AI for healthcare. Before joining Oxford, she received her Bachelor of Science in Computer Engineering from New York University Abu Dhabi. She works as an affiliated clinical informatics researcher at the Ghosheh Medical Surgical Complex (GMSC) in Ramallah, Palestine where she works on areas of Artificial Intelligence for healthcare. Before working with GMSC, she worked on developing a wide range of tech tools to inform decision-making in healthcare, by using large-scale datasets from the Middle East. Her current research interests include Artificial intelligence, health informatics and technology for low-resource settings.

Mohammad J. Ghosheh received his Bachelor of Medicine, Bachelor of Surgery (M.B.B.S) from Alfaisal University, Kingdom of Saudi Arabia. Dr Ghosheh currently holds a General Practitioner role with academic responsibilities at the Ghosheh Medical Surgical Complex (GMSC) in Ramallah, Palestine. At GMSC, Dr Ghosheh's academic role focuses on driving new research directions in medical training and digital health. Dr Ghosheh has a diverse experience in teaching, research, medical training and industry for various healthcare applications both on the Middle East and international levels. His current research interests include medical education, informatics, radiology and healthcare technology applications.

Hasan Gürkan is a Maria Zambrano Fellow at the University of Girona in Spain and Assoc. Prof. Dr. at Istinye University in Turkey. He holds his Ph.D. from Istanbul University Department of Radio, Television and Cinema. He did his post-doc research at the University of Vienna. He has also written the books Counter Cinema and Journalism Practices. His research articles have been published in the journals such as Feminist Media Studies, Studies in European Cinema, Online Journal of Communication and Media Technologies, Kome: An International Journal Of Pure Communication Inquiry, Medijske studije, Acta Universitatis Sapientiae: Film and Media Studies, CINEJ Cinema Journal. He focuses on counter cinema, Hollywood Cinema, alternative media, cinema and representations, cinema-migration-transnational films, and gender studies.

Sadia Mir is an associate professor of English at Virginia Commonwealth University School of the Arts in Qatar. Her interdisciplinary research interests include storytelling pedagogy, community writing and multi-modal documentary literary and media practices. She served as the lead Writing Specialist for the Young Writers Program, the first youth community writing program of its kind in Qatar. She is co-author of Spring Bloom: A Math Adventure Story (HBKU Press, 2019). Her scholarly and media work have been published and presented in both academic and creative arenas worldwide. Sadia holds an MFA in Creative Writing, (University of British Columbia) and an MFA in Documentary Media (Toronto Metropolitan University, Canada).

Ouelfatmi Meryem is a third-year doctoral candidate pertaining to CREDIF lab at Sidi Mohamed Ben Abdellah University. Her research interests explore the role of attitudes in the acceptance and use of technology by higher-education students. Her dissertation investigates the subset constructs that influence attitude and therefore, the intention to use technology for educational purposes.

Mohamed A. Shahat is an Assistant Professor of science education at Sultan Qaboos University (SQU), Oman, and an Associate Professor at Aswan University (AU), Egypt. He earned his Ph.D. in science education from the University of Duisburg-Essen, Germany. He attained a post-doctoral fellowship at the University of Duisburg-Essen. Currently, he is leading various national research projects, including STEM an entrepreneurial education at SQU. He participated in multiple national and international conferences. He published several articles in national and international journals. He published chapters in regional and global edited books. He is a member of different national and international journal editorial boards. He has also been awarded other teaching, research, and reviewing awards.

Index

21st Century Skills 37, 89, 127, 210, 215, 221

A

Active Learning 10, 12, 14-15, 17-18, 26, 126
Arab World 24, 92, 96, 116, 137, 190, 195
Artificial Intelligence (AI) 145, 166
Augmented Reality 50, 67, 141, 158, 165

B

Behavioral Intention 27

C

children's literature 241
Culturally Responsive Pedagogy 222, 231, 243

D

Decolonizing Curriculum 243
Didactics 8, 21, 25, 27
Digital Health 129-137, 139, 141-145, 147-148, 153, 155-156, 158-159, 162, 167

E

education 2-17, 19-47, 49-52, 54-85, 87-107, 109-113, 116-134, 137, 139, 141-144, 150-151, 154-166, 172-173, 176, 179-180, 183-191, 193, 195-196, 200, 203-207, 209-222, 225-226, 230-231, 233-235, 237-243
Educational technology 54, 122, 209, 220
E-Learning 1-2, 5-6, 9, 12, 14-22, 24-27, 122
Engineering 26-27, 36, 38, 44-45, 48, 50, 57-59, 66-68, 71-74, 77, 93, 95, 99, 101-102, 105-106, 108, 112, 116-118, 120-121, 123-127, 150, 157, 159, 164-165, 172, 175, 178-179, 183, 186-187, 190, 201, 210-212, 215, 218-220, 229
Eurocentrism 227, 238, 242-243
Experiential Learning 91, 94, 127, 216

G

GCC 89, 190, 206, 209, 220
Genomics 128, 132, 134, 150-154, 156, 159, 163, 167

H

Health Sciences 109, 128-134, 137, 142, 146, 148, 152, 154-156, 167
Hegemony 243
higher education 6, 8, 10-12, 14-17, 20-21, 23-24, 31, 36, 56-58, 72-73, 91, 94-96, 99, 101, 112, 117, 119-121, 124, 126-127, 130, 137, 160, 172, 183, 187, 190, 193, 195, 204, 206-207, 210, 242

I

Information Management 20, 91-92, 127, 146, 157
Innovation 7, 19, 23, 34, 36, 39-40, 54,

56-58, 60-63, 72-73, 77, 87, 89, 123, 139, 144, 155, 157, 172, 187, 210, 242
Interpretivism 236, 243
Iraqi Constitution 92, 96, 102

K

Kuwait 97, 137, 157, 190, 210-213, 215-216, 218, 220

L

Learning 1-6, 8-27, 34, 36-38, 40, 42, 48-49, 57, 65-72, 76-81, 85-89, 91, 93-96, 98, 101-102, 106, 109, 117-119, 121-122, 125-127, 129, 143-145, 148, 150, 156, 159-166, 183, 185, 189-197, 200-202, 204-208, 210-212, 214-216, 219-222, 225-228, 230, 233, 236, 239-243
learning process 13, 18, 26, 37, 195

M

mathematics 1-2, 9-10, 13-23, 25, 27-28, 33, 35, 40-41, 44, 46-47, 51, 54, 57-59, 67-69, 71-72, 74, 77-78, 85, 89, 93, 95, 98-99, 101-102, 105-110, 112-113, 116-118, 120-121, 124-127, 130, 146, 172, 175, 178-179, 182, 184, 187-188, 190, 205, 210-212, 215, 219-220, 222-231, 233-243
mathematics education 21, 23, 40, 44, 117, 225-226, 230-231, 234-235, 237-240, 242
Media Literacy 186
Medicine 20, 32-33, 109, 112, 120, 128-135, 137, 146, 148, 150, 153-154, 156, 158-159, 161-163, 165, 167, 169, 178, 220
MENA 1-3, 13-14, 16-19, 24, 26, 118, 126, 128-130, 137, 139-142, 148, 156, 167, 195, 209
Middle East North Africa (MENA) 167
Ministry of Education 4-5, 16, 57, 60-64, 69, 72-76, 78, 91, 105, 117, 120, 123, 131, 191, 205, 211, 218
Ministry of Higher Education 56-58, 72, 91, 117, 120
Model of Instructions 106, 127
Multimodal Mathematics 239, 243

O

Online learning 6, 11-13, 16, 20, 22-24, 191, 193-197, 204-205, 207

P

Palestine 128-133, 135, 137-145, 148-150, 152, 154-156, 159-161, 163-164, 166
Pedagogy 1-3, 7-15, 18-19, 23-25, 27, 67, 69, 71, 106, 160, 196, 225, 231, 235, 242-243
Popularization of Science 176, 184, 187
Professional Development 17, 42, 46, 53, 71, 75, 81-82, 87, 89, 106-109, 119, 154, 189-191, 196, 202, 205-206, 212, 214-216, 219, 225, 235, 237
Professional Learning Communities 81, 86, 206
Professional Qualifications 107, 127

Q

Qatar 119, 126, 222, 225, 227, 235, 237-238

R

Research 1-2, 5, 7, 11-13, 15-17, 19-21, 23-26, 35-36, 38, 40-41, 44, 52-54, 57-59, 65-68, 72-73, 82, 88-89, 91-93, 96, 101, 117, 120-124, 129-130, 132-134, 138, 144-146, 148-150, 155-160, 162-164, 166-167, 169, 171, 173-176, 178, 181-187, 189-190, 192, 195, 197-198, 200-201, 204-207, 209-216, 218-221, 225, 227, 229, 231, 233-243
Robotics 26, 70, 128, 132-133, 145, 147-148, 150, 156-157, 164-165, 167

S

Saudi Arabia Culture Mission 76
Science 8, 11, 15, 22-28, 30-33, 35-52,

Index

54, 56-69, 71-75, 77, 79-80, 82, 85, 88-89, 95, 98-102, 105-110, 112-113, 116-118, 120-121, 123-127, 130, 135, 140, 146, 148-149, 151, 166-188, 190, 205, 210-213, 215, 219-220, 226, 230, 240, 242-243

Science and Technology 24, 28, 33, 35-37, 40-41, 43, 46, 51, 63, 72, 89, 123, 126, 172-173, 176-178, 182, 187-188, 219

Science Centers 28, 40-43, 49, 173, 176

Science Journalism 168-171, 173-177, 180-183, 185-187

Semiotic Representation 18, 27

STEAM 28, 49-50, 52, 54, 67, 70-71, 77-78, 88, 100-101, 112, 124, 127, 189-192, 196-197, 200, 203-205, 208, 219-221

STEAM education 52, 88, 100, 112, 124, 189-191, 203, 219-221

STEM 1-2, 12, 27-29, 32-55, 57-58, 60-96, 99-103, 105, 109-110, 113-114, 116-118, 120-127, 156, 169-187, 191, 196, 200, 203-206, 209-221

STEM Activities 33, 38-39, 41-43, 68, 123, 187

STEM Education 1-2, 27-29, 33-41, 43-44, 46-47, 49, 51-52, 54-58, 62-63, 66-74, 76, 78-81, 83-85, 89-91, 93-96, 99, 101-103, 105, 113, 116-117, 120, 122-125, 172-173, 176, 179-180, 183-184, 186, 190, 196, 204-206, 209-221

STEM in Education 57, 75, 184, 187, 205

STEM Management 127

storytelling 222, 225, 227-228, 230-231, 235, 237-239, 241, 243

Students 2-3, 5-6, 8-24, 27-28, 30-33, 37-42, 45, 47-51, 56-60, 63-73, 75, 77-81, 83-88, 93, 95, 99-101, 103, 106-111, 113, 116-120, 123, 125, 127-128, 130-131, 135-136, 139-140, 142-151, 153-156, 158, 160-161, 163-164, 172-173, 176, 185, 187-190, 192-197, 199-203, 207, 209-212, 214-218, 220, 223, 225, 227-231, 233-234, 236-239, 243

Symbolic Annihilation 227, 242-243

T

teacher training 6, 46, 48-49, 69, 71, 212, 214-217

Teachers 3, 6-7, 10-11, 14-20, 22-23, 27, 31, 34-35, 38-42, 45-51, 56-58, 60-69, 71-73, 75-77, 81-91, 93, 95-97, 100-103, 105-109, 113-115, 117-124, 127, 132, 172-173, 184, 189-191, 193, 196-197, 199, 201-206, 209, 211-218, 220, 222, 225, 228, 231, 235-238, 240-242

Teaching 1-2, 6-22, 24-27, 35, 39-40, 42, 53-54, 57, 62, 64, 66-73, 75, 78-80, 86-87, 89, 91, 93-96, 100-102, 106, 108-109, 112-113, 117-122, 124, 127, 132, 142-144, 162, 173, 183, 185-186, 189-198, 200-202, 204-208, 211-217, 219-220, 222-223, 225, 228, 230, 235-239, 241-243

teaching in Higher Education 204

teaching presence 194, 201, 204

technology 1-5, 7, 9, 11, 13, 15-21, 23-27, 29, 31, 33, 35-41, 43-44, 46-48, 50-54, 57-59, 63-64, 67-68, 71-72, 74-75, 77-80, 84, 88-89, 93, 95, 99-102, 105-106, 109, 112, 116-118, 120-127, 129-130, 135, 137, 139, 141, 143, 145-146, 150-152, 154-156, 158, 160, 162-163, 167, 169, 172-173, 175-179, 182, 187-188, 190, 193-195, 201, 209-212, 214-215, 217, 219-220, 242

The Importance of Science Journalism 187

Training 5-6, 12, 16-18, 34-35, 38, 42, 47-49, 55-58, 60-64, 68-69, 71, 74-75, 78-79, 81-82, 86, 93-95, 100, 106-109, 118-119, 121, 123, 127-133, 135, 137-145, 149-150, 154-156, 158-159, 161, 163, 165-166, 173, 209, 212, 214-217, 219

Trust Fund Strategic Grants 56-58, 68

Turkey 28-48, 50-52, 54-55, 119, 122, 124, 168-173, 175-177, 179-180, 182, 185, 188

Turkish Education System 28, 30-31, 34

305

V

Virtual Reality 67, 70, 132-133, 135, 141, 158-159, 162

W

word problems 223, 228

Recommended Reference Books

IGI Global's reference books are available in three unique pricing formats:
Print Only, E-Book Only, or Print + E-Book.
Order direct through IGI Global's Online Bookstore at **www.igi-global.com** or through your preferred provider.

Online Distance Learning Course Design and Multimedia in E-Learning

ISBN: 9781799897064
EISBN: 9781799897088
© 2022; 302 pp.
List Price: US$ 215

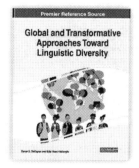

Global and Transformative Approaches Toward Linguistic Diversity

ISBN: 9781799889854
EISBN: 9781799889878
© 2022; 383 pp.
List Price: US$ 215

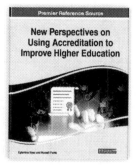

New Perspectives on Using Accreditation to Improve Higher Education

ISBN: 9781668451953
EISBN: 9781668451960
© 2022; 300 pp.
List Price: US$ 215

Impact of School Shootings on Classroom Culture, Curriculum, and Learning

ISBN: 9781799852001
EISBN: 9781799852018
© 2022; 355 pp.
List Price: US$ 215

Modern Reading Practices and Collaboration Between Schools, Family, and Community

ISBN: 9781799897507
EISBN: 9781799897521
© 2022; 304 pp.
List Price: US$ 215

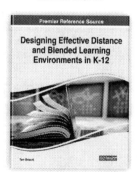

Designing Effective Distance and Blended Learning Environments in K-12

ISBN: 9781799868293
EISBN: 9781799868316
© 2022; 389 pp.
List Price: US$ 215

Do you want to stay current on the latest research trends, product announcements, news, and special offers?
Join IGI Global's mailing list to receive customized recommendations, exclusive discounts, and more.
Sign up at: **www.igi-global.com/newsletters**.

Publisher of Timely, Peer-Reviewed Inclusive Research Since 1988

IGI Global
PUBLISHER of TIMELY KNOWLEDGE

www.igi-global.com   Sign up at www.igi-global.com/newsletters   facebook.com/igiglobal   twitter.com/igiglobal

Ensure Quality Research is Introduced to the Academic Community

Become an Evaluator for IGI Global Authored Book Projects

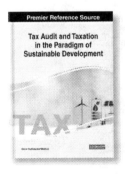  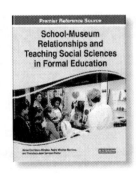 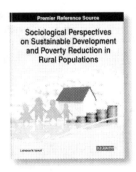

The overall success of an authored book project is dependent on quality and timely manuscript evaluations.

Applications and Inquiries may be sent to:
development@igi-global.com

Applicants must have a doctorate (or equivalent degree) as well as publishing, research, and reviewing experience. Authored Book Evaluators are appointed for one-year terms and are expected to complete at least three evaluations per term. Upon successful completion of this term, evaluators can be considered for an additional term.

If you have a colleague that may be interested in this opportunity, we encourage you to share this information with them.

Easily Identify, Acquire, and Utilize Published
Peer-Reviewed Findings in Support of Your Current Research

IGI Global OnDemand

Purchase Individual IGI Global OnDemand Book Chapters and Journal Articles

For More Information:
www.igi-global.com/e-resources/ondemand/

Browse through 150,000+ Articles and Chapters!

Find specific research related to your current studies and projects that have been contributed by international researchers from prestigious institutions, including:

- Accurate and Advanced Search
- Affordably Acquire Research
- Instantly Access Your Content
- Benefit from the InfoSci Platform Features

« *It really provides* an excellent entry into the research literature of the field. *It presents a manageable number of* highly relevant sources *on topics of interest to a wide range of researchers. The sources are* scholarly, but also accessible *to 'practitioners'.* »

- Ms. Lisa Stimatz, MLS, University of North Carolina at Chapel Hill, USA

Interested in Additional Savings?

Subscribe to
IGI Global OnDemand *Plus*

Learn More

Acquire content from over 128,000+ research-focused book chapters and 33,000+ scholarly journal articles for as low as US$ 5 per article/chapter (original retail price for an article/chapter: US$ 37.50).

7,300+ E-BOOKS.
ADVANCED RESEARCH.
INCLUSIVE & AFFORDABLE.

IGI Global e-Book Collection

- Flexible Purchasing Options (Perpetual, Subscription, EBA, etc.)
- Multi-Year Agreements with No Price Increases Guaranteed
- No Additional Charge for Multi-User Licensing
- No Maintenance, Hosting, or Archiving Fees
- Continually Enhanced & Innovated Accessibility Compliance Features (WCAG)

Handbook of Research on Digital Transformation, Industry Use Cases, and the Impact of Disruptive Technologies
ISBN: 9781799877127
EISBN: 9781799877141

Handbook of Research on New Investigations in Artificial Life, AI, and Machine Learning
ISBN: 9781799886860
EISBN: 9781799886877

Handbook of Research on Future of Work and Education
ISBN: 9781799882756
EISBN: 9781799882770

Research Anthology on Physical and Intellectual Disabilities in an Inclusive Society (4 Vols.)
ISBN: 9781668435427
EISBN: 9781668435434

Innovative Economic, Social, and Environmental Practices for Progressing Future Sustainability
ISBN: 9781799895909
EISBN: 9781799895923

Applied Guide for Event Study Research in Supply Chain Management
ISBN: 9781799889694
EISBN: 9781799889717

Mental Health and Wellness in Healthcare Workers
ISBN: 9781799888130
EISBN: 9781799888147

Clean Technologies and Sustainable Development in Civil Engineering
ISBN: 9781799898108
EISBN: 9781799898122

Request More Information, or Recommend the IGI Global e-Book Collection to Your Institution's Librarian

For More Information or to Request a Free Trial, Contact IGI Global's e-Collections Team: eresources@igi-global.com | 1-866-342-6657 ext. 100 | 717-533-8845 ext. 100

Are You Ready to Publish Your Research?

IGI Global
PUBLISHER of TIMELY KNOWLEDGE

IGI Global offers book authorship and editorship opportunities across 11 subject areas, including business, computer science, education, science and engineering, social sciences, and more!

Benefits of Publishing with IGI Global:

- Free one-on-one editorial and promotional support.
- Expedited publishing timelines that can take your book from start to finish in less than one (1) year.
- Choose from a variety of formats, including Edited and Authored References, Handbooks of Research, Encyclopedias, and Research Insights.
- Utilize IGI Global's eEditorial Discovery® submission system in support of conducting the submission and double-blind peer review process.
- IGI Global maintains a strict adherence to ethical practices due in part to our full membership with the Committee on Publication Ethics (COPE).
- Indexing potential in prestigious indices such as Scopus®, Web of Science™, PsycINFO®, and ERIC – Education Resources Information Center.
- Ability to connect your ORCID iD to your IGI Global publications.
- Earn honorariums and royalties on your full book publications as well as complimentary content and exclusive discounts.

Join Your Colleagues from Prestigious Institutions, Including:

Australian National University
Massachusetts Institute of Technology
JOHNS HOPKINS UNIVERSITY
HARVARD UNIVERSITY
COLUMBIA UNIVERSITY IN THE CITY OF NEW YORK

Learn More at: www.igi-global.com/publish
or by Contacting the Acquisitions Department at: acquisition@igi-global.com

Individual Article & Chapter Downloads
US$ 29.50/each

 Easily Identify, Acquire, and Utilize Published Peer-Reviewed Findings in Support of Your Current Research

- Browse Over **170,000+ Articles & Chapters**
- **Accurate & Advanced** Search
- Affordably Acquire **International Research**
- **Instantly Access** Your Content
- Benefit from the **InfoSci® Platform Features**

THE UNIVERSITY of NORTH CAROLINA at CHAPEL HILL

" It really provides *an excellent entry into the research literature of the field*. It presents a manageable number of *highly relevant sources* on topics of interest to a wide range of researchers. The sources are *scholarly, but also accessible* to 'practitioners'. "

- Ms. Lisa Stimatz, MLS, University of North Carolina at Chapel Hill, USA

Interested in Additional Savings?

Subscribe to **IGI Global OnDemand Plus**

Learn More

Acquire content from over 128,000+ research-focused book chapters and 33,000+ scholarly journal articles for as low as US$ 5 per article/chapter (original retail price for an article/chapter: US$ 37.50).